Curriculum Progress 5–16

School Subjects and
the National Curriculum Debate

Edited by
Patrick Wiegand
and
Michael Rayner

 The Falmer Press

(A member of the Taylor & Francis Group)
New York • Philadelphia • London

UK   The Falmer Press, Falmer House, Barcombe, Lewes, East Sussex, BN8 5DL

USA   The Falmer Press, Taylor & Francis Inc., 242 Cherry Street, Philadelphia, PA 19106-1906

First published 1989

British Library Cataloguing in Publication Data

Curriculum progress 5–16: school subjects and the national curriculum debate

1. England. Schools. Curriculum. Reform.
I. Wiegand, Patrick.   II. Rayner, Michael.
375′.006′0942
ISBN 1-85000-532-X
ISBN 1-85000-533-8 (pbk.)

Library of Congress Cataloging-in-Publication Data

Curriculum progress 5–16.

  Includes bibliographies and index.
  1. Education, Elementary—Great Britain—Curricula.
2. Education, Secondary—Great Britain—Curricula.
I. Wiegand, Patrick.   II. Rayner, Michael.   III. Title:
Curriculum progress five–sixteen.
LB1564.G7C885   373.19′0941   88-33622
ISBN 1-85000-532-X
ISBN 1-85000-533-8 (pbk.)

Typeset in 10½/12 Caledonia by
Imago Publishing Ltd, Thame, Oxon

Jacket design by Caroline Archer

Printed in Great Britain by Taylor & Francis (Printers) Ltd, Basingstoke

Contents

Contents

Introduction

Michael Rayner and Patrick Wiegand

It shall be the duty of the Secretary of State so to exercise the powers conferred by subsection (2) below as —

- a) to establish a complete National Curriculum as soon as reasonably practicable (taking first the core subjects and then the other foundation subjects); and
- b) to revise that curriculum whenever he considers it necessary or expedient to do so.

The Secretary of State may by order specify in relation to each of the foundation subjects —

- a) such attainment targets;
- b) such programmes of study; and
- c) such assessment arrangements,

as he considers appropriate for that subject.

(Education Reform Bill, 1987, p. 3)

The advent of the National Curriculum in 1987 should have come as no surprise since for more than a decade the Government had been showing an increasing interest in enhancing its influence over what was taught in schools. Before Callaghan made the Ruskin speech in 1976, which is now taken to be the initiation of the 'great debate', there were a number of persistent signs of unease with the educational status quo. The 'Black Papers' (Cox and Dyson, 1969a, 1969b, 1970), for instance, had criticized, with varying degrees of cogency, academic standards and teaching methods in progressive primary schools and in the increasing number of comprehensive schools. The Assessment of Performance Unit (APU) had been set up in 1974 to monitor standards nationally as a result of DES anxieties (Lawton, 1980). The William Tyndale Junior School case gave rise to wide concern about educational standards through eager reporting in the popular press in late 1975. The following year the press also seized

Michael Rayner and Patrick Wiegand

Figure 1:   *Chronology of the National Curriculum*

1976	Callaghan speech at Ruskin College, Oxford, 18 October.
1977	DES Education in Schools: A Consultative Document. Cmnd 6869.
1977	HMI Curriculum 11–16.
1977	DES Circular 14/77 LEA Arrangements for the School Curriculum
1979	DES Aspects of Secondary Education in England.
1979	DES Local Authority Arrangements for the School Curriculum: Report on the Circular 14/77 Review.
1980	HMI A View of the Curriculum.
1980	DES A Framework for the School Curriculum.
1980	Education Act
1981	DES The School Curriculum
1981	DES Circular 6/81 The School Curriculum.
1981	DES Curriculum 11–16: A Review of Progress.
1983	DES Circular 8/83 The School Curriculum.
1984	Keith Joseph's speech to the North of England Education Conference.
1984	DES The Organization and Content of the 5–16 Curriculum.
1985	DES Better Schools.
1985	HMI The Curriculum 5–16.
1986	Education Act
1987	Kenneth Baker's speech to the North of England Education Conference.
1987	The National Curriculum 5–16: Consultation Document.
1988	Education Act.

on Neville Bennett's *Teaching Styles and Pupil Progress* (1976) as indicating the superiority of traditional classroom methods over more progressive methods.

The agenda for the 'great debate' was officially set in the publication *Education in Schools* (DES, 1977a). There were four themes: the school curriculum 5–16, the assessment of standards, the education and training of teachers and school and working life. (Although our concern is only with the curriculum, it should be noted that parallel developments were occurring in the other agenda items.) The debate has been conducted both globally and locally. At the global level the DES, HMI and others have produced a string of publications which have formed the structure of the debate. Locally, individual subject communities have attempted to tackle the implications for their own subjects. The significant publications at the global level are shown in Figure 1.

A fuller analysis of many of these documents, together with an overview of the politics of curriculum control may be found in Lawton (1980) and Holt (1983). For our purposes we wish to highlight

i) dissatisfaction with people assembling their own curriculum, for example pupils exercising wide choice over their options at secondary level and teachers choosing topics freely at primary level

ii)   the repeated stress on the need for a curriculum which is broad, balanced and coherent

iii) the need for continuity between phases of education, that is across the whole 5 to 16 age range

iv)   a difference of sophistication and subtlety between HMI and DES documents.

The last point is worth elaboration. DES documents appear to be more naive and take many things for granted. Whilst one would expect HMI to demonstrate more awareness of the realities of teaching, it is nonetheless disconcerting to find paucity of argument in DES publications. Not only do the authors of the latter appear to find justification of their positions unnecessary, they also appear unaware of alternative conceptualizations. For instance, if one compares *The Organization and Content of the 5–16 Curriculum* (DES, 1984) with *The Curriculum from 5 to 16* (HMI, 1985) one finds the DES talking of a curriculum only in subject terms whereas HMI acknowledges that other modes of organization are possible (and indeed proposes a curriculum based on nine 'areas of experience' — even though the origin of these is wrapped in mystery). Pring has commented (referring to the National Curriculum Consultation document) that it is written 'as though the world began only a few seconds ago' (Pring, in Golby, 1987). It is certainly true that most of the documents listed in Figure 1 make no reference to the extensive literature available on the curriculum.

With the Conservative election victory in June 1987 the movement towards central control over the school curriculum, which as we have seen lasted over a decade, reached its destination. In the Education Reform Bill, set to rival in importance Butler's 1944 Act, the government brought forward proposals which ostensibly are to place education less under the control of its producers — LEAs, teachers, advisors and inspectors — and more in the power of its customers, taken without discussion to be the parents of schoolchildren. This, of course, is but one aspect of the market ideology embraced by the Thatcher governments. The 1980 Education Act had gone a little way on this path by requiring schools to provide parents with information about themselves, including sanitized figures on examination performance, and by requiring LEAs to consider parents' preference for a particular school. There were, however, ways in which parental choice of school could be contained by reluctant authorities.

The 1986 Education Act put more parents on governing bodies at the same time as it ensured that LEA representation on those bodies was reduced to a minority presence. It also required governors to issue an annual report and to hold an annual meeting of parents to discuss it. In many respects the Education Reform Bill goes further: schools are to have much more control over their finances; so-called 'open' enrolment is to increase the places LEAs must offer at their schools; and parents who want to take their school out of LEA control altogether have the opportunity to do so. Such measures are designed, it seems, to increase the system's responsiveness to the customer, though it has to be asked how much control DES will be able to exercise over the grant-maintained schools. Against this background model of the school as the corner shop, prospering only if it provides what parents want, stands the notion of a National Curriculum. Here the worries of the past decade or more, justified or otherwise, about what children are taught and to what standard, have borne fruit in the shape of a massive piece of anti-customer paternalism. The customers in this case are not to be trusted to exercise their choice, they do not, for some unexplained reason, know best. The successful attack on teachers' professionalization of curriculum policy, perhaps best symbolized by the demise of The Schools' Council in 1984, has not wrested whatever control actually lay with the producers (less than government statements might suggest) and presented it to the choosing parent, but given it instead to the producer-control of DES. This contradiction in policy stands out a mile and has been pointed out by the more consistent Institute of Economic Affairs, one of this government's influential supporters. There may be good reasons for a National Curriculum — the economic health of the country, continuity at the age of transfer or on moving from one part of the country to another, and so on — and the main political parties seem agreed in broad terms that there should be one, but this government cannot with consistency embrace them. Only independent schools will be able to escape this extension of the 'nanny' state: *their* customers are deemed to have a right to consumer sovereignty. The competition between schools, which is a mechanism said to raise standards, will, then, be a circumscribed one, limited, for example, to differing levels of performance on the National Curriculum (probably adjusted in some way to allow for out-of-school factors).

The National Curriculum

The proposals were published in July 1987 (DES, 1987a) for consultation. This consultation period was short and coincided largely with the schools' summer holidays, though the Secretary of State extended the time available by saying the process could continue after the Bill had started its progress through Parliament. The details of the document are well-known and have been added to by another publication: *Education Reform* (DES, 1987b). The National Curriculum was to consist of ten (now eleven) foundation subjects: — English, mathematics and science (and now Religious Education) form the 'core' subjects and a modern language, technology, history, geography, art, music and physical education make up the other foundation subjects. This scheme will be imposed in varying degrees on all schools outside the independent sector. (City Technology Colleges are to follow 'the substance' of the National Curriculum.) We say 'in varying degrees' because most of the curriculum time in primary schools will be devoted to the core subjects, whereas in the example of years four and five of the secondary phase which is given, (DES, 1987a) something between seventy-five per cent and eighty-five per cent of the timetable is filled with foundation subjects. '. . . the foundation subjects commonly take up eighty to ninety per cent of the curriculum in schools where there is good practice' (p. 8). (The phrase 'good practice' never ever explicated so that one might recognize good practice when one sees it, is beloved by DES and HMI. It rouses one's suspicion that it is identified in a circular fashion, so that 'good practice' schools do whatever it is that is being approved of, in this case they have a curriculum like the National Curriculum.) The consultative document gives little more to go on. Indeed, not only did the bill contain no time-allocations, the Secretary of State now says there is no maximum or minimum time to be devoted to the foundation subjects but that he could not envisage the work being covered in less than seventy per cent of the timetable. Jostling for whatever space remains will be, according to the *example* of fourth and fifth years in the document: a second modern language, classics, home economics and business studies; together with more of those which appeared in the compulsory list: science, history, geography, art, music and drama. 'Subjects or themes such as health education and use of information technology can be taught through other subjects. . . It is proposed that such subjects or themes should be taught through the foundation subjects' (DES, 1987a, p. 8). In *Education Reform* themes and skills are referred to as having a key place in the core and foundation subjects. 'Examples are personal and social education, careers education and guidance, economic awareness and information technology skills' (DES, 1987b, p. 2).

In summary we have

1   core and other foundation subjects
2   subjects opted for outside the foundation
3   subjects and themes taught through 1 and 2.

It has to be stressed that a good deal of vagueness hangs over the proposals — both regarding the time that will in fact be needed at the various stages of education and the definition of the individual subjects. Such clarification will presumably come when the attainment targets, programmes of study and the assessments which are to be set for both the foundation subjects and the 'permeation' themes are decided upon. Even then, it not clear how closely subject content will be specified. 'Within the programme of study, teachers will be free to determine the detail of what should be taught in order to ensure that pupils achieve appropriate levels of attainment . . .' (DES, 1987a, p. 11). It remains to be seen just how much elbow room is available to teachers for the exercise of the 'full scope for professional judgment'. When the Secretary of State says that the subject working groups, which will recommend to him attainment targets and programmes of study, will not be prescribing a total syllabus, what degree of specification does he envisage? Power lies in the ability to control such matters.

Four further items are worth noting here. First, the proposals include the provision of more information to customers, following in the direction set by the 1980 and 1986 Education Acts, so that their choice can be more informed. Information about a school's curriculum, an individual pupil's curriculum and most importantly the performance of pupils in the assessments at 7, 11, 14 and 16 will be made available. (It now seems that a school's 7 year olds' results will not be made public.) Having digested this, parents can make their choice.

Second, a National Curriculum Council and a School Examination and Assessment Council will be set up, both memberships appointed by the Secretary of State. The former will replace the School Curriculum Development Council and will advise on the curriculum; in particular it will consult on the attainment targets and programmes of study produced by the subject working groups before the Secretary of State makes the relevant order to lay before Parliament. The latter will replace the Secondary Examinations Council and will advise on assessment and examinations but will not itself compile the tests.

Third, parents will have machinery for complaint if a school is not delivering the National Curriculum.

Finally, broadly speaking, no extra finance will be made available, save for that involved in setting up the two councils referred to above and for supporting assessment. However, there must be resource implications in increasing the range of subjects taken by all pupils. It is conceivable, for example, that the foreign language teaching load may increase by one quarter. Could enough teaching be provided from existing resources? The same sort of argument could be mounted in respect of technology, already a shortage subject.

Such an innovation necessitates a great deal of planning and it will take several years before the new scheme is operating. Subject working groups have to be set up — only mathematics and science are in existence at the time of writing — and it will take time to produce a final report which will then have to go out for consultation. It could be well into the 1990s before we see the effects. A start will be made on the core subjects, with mathematics and science being introduced at the primary level in 1989, though that prediction is conditional on there being no further fundamental disagreements in the subject group looking at mathematics. It will not only be subject working groups that will determine the rate of progress. Assessments, if they take the benign form recommended by the Task Group on Assessment and Testing, will take up to five years to develop.

Effects of the National Curriculum on School Subjects

The proposed foundation subjects will not simply endorse existing practice, as some have claimed. Agreed, mathematics, English and some sort of science were on all secondary schools' curricula right through to the leaving age, but half their pupils drop a modern language for the last two years of their school life, nearly half do not study technology for five years, nor does everyone take history, geography, art, drama, music and design. In those respects at least, the proposals are innovatory. Similarly, primary schools are now legally required to teach science. An advantage for those subjects given protected status will be that staffing will have to be provided to support them: curriculum-led staffing is official.

Conversely, as some subjects gain status, others have become déclassé or even threatened with elimination. A second modern language, classics, home economics and business studies all fight for option space. Some are likely to decline and classics may almost disappear. Again, the themes and skills supposedly teachable through other subjects (by whom?) — information technology, careers education, personal and social education, economic awareness and health education — will get some sort of consideration through being specified in the attainment targets, but where is there mention of moral education (increasingly in ministers' minds), environmental education, political education, multicultural education and sociology? Their existence cannot be unknown to the DES. Nor can the existence in some schools of peace education. Of course it may not be that omission was intended. It may simply be that these did not feature in the lists of examples provided in the best descriptions we have of what the National Curriculum will look like. Given the degree of public and professional concern that must have been predicted it is disappointing that at some critical points the consultation documents provide only *examples* and not a more definite model.

Finally, it is uncertain what the position of Technical and Vocational Education Initiative (TVEI) will be. This scheme, once looked at with hostility by many teachers, has now been incorporated more readily into schools (and is now extended to all authorities) both because one suspects it has been to some degree made to 'go native' and because the new approaches to teaching which it encourages have paid off. The reference to TVEI in the consultative document covers four lines. Teachers will have scope to 'allow curriculum development programmes such as the Technical and Vocational Education Initiative to build on the framework offered by the national curriculum and to take forward its objective' (DES 1987a, p. 11). Whether time will be available and whether tests will deter the teaching styles associated with TVEI must remain to be seen.

Michael Rayner and Patrick Wiegand

General Comments on the National Curriculum

The first major observation to be made here must be the almost total lack of argument for the National Curriculum, both in general terms and in detail. We can agree that the consultation document contains sentences which purport to provide a justification but at no point do they amount to more than speech-day vapour. The aims are so general and so vague as to be capable of wide interpretation. A sample will convey the flavour: 'the school curriculum ... will develop the potential of all pupils and equip them for the responsibilities of citizenship and for the challenges of employment in tomorrow's world' (DES, 1987a, p. 2). That can only be a parody of the banalities one finds in thought-free statements about education. Of course the persuasive quality of the rhetoric may engage consent and the vagueness disguise a much more specific programme based on more narrowly specified aims but we, the consulted, cannot know. The next few paragraphs add little. Is it any more enlightening to be referred to 'the knowledge, skills and understanding that (people) need for adult life and employment' (p. 1)? Here, if anywhere, when a major break with the past is to be introduced one might have expected more.

Once that absence is recognized, the apparent arbitrariness of all that follows stands out. Why are the foundation subjects the ones listed? How do the aims entail *that* list? Why not another list compatible with the aims? No effort at all is made to help us to see that a National Curriculum has to be translated into this particular programme. No attempt is made to show that the balance, coherence and width so often mentioned in official documents is actually present in what is proposed. More fundamentally, there is the assumption that these aims have to be translated into subjects at all as a way of organizing the 'knowledge, skills and understanding needed'. One would never know that, for better or worse, there are alternative ways of organizing a curriculum, one of which we mentioned earlier, namely a curriculum based on the 'areas of experience' referred to (we cannot say argued for) by HMI in several of their publications, most recently in *The Curriculum from 5–16* (HMI, 1985). On this view subjects are not taken as ends in themselves but are used to achieve aims beyond themselves and arranged accordingly. But as far as the current proposals go, modules, themes, interdisciplinary work, forms of knowledge, areas of experience all might never have existed. Rather we have a 'commonsense' reliance on one way of organizing the curriculum, possibly with the same sentiment which lay behind The Hillgate Group's criticism of school curriculum innovation where they refer to 'tried and lasting subjects' and to 'spurious alternatives' (Hillgate Group, 1986, p. 3), and to 'proven subjects' (p. 7) with no criteria provided to help us see how they have been tried and proved. The policy has all the marks of DES thinking (*cf.* DES, 1984) written on the back of an envelope.

If there is a certain vagueness about general aims, there is, too, likely to be dispute over what each subject's aims and contents should be. A subject is no single body of 'knowledge, skills and understanding'. Even if it were, time would necessitate selection and therefore the need for (disputable) priorities. As it is, a variety of ideologies about a subject is possible. (For example, is English an expressive art or an adjunct to social studies or a language skill? Is history about national history or not, is it about historiography? Is technology defined in craft terms or not?) Such disagreements are illustrated in many of the chapters which follow. Subject working groups will also have to deal with this, either by revealing disagreements or by defining the subject so as to suppress them. The mathematics interim report, as we have mentioned, illustrates the problem in that a dissenting minority statement was produced alongside the majority report. However, in the end, the powers given to the Secretary of State can override such considerations, as the quotation at the beginning of this chapter showed. Furthermore, any school which wishes to engage in curriculum innovation will now have to obtain the Secretary of State's permission if such a development entails deviating from the National Curriculum (section 9 of the Education Reform Bill).

This Book

Some of the great debate has been conducted within each subject community. Discussion about one part of the curriculum has not always been informed by discussions relating to other areas. The purpose of this book therefore is to make the whole debate accessible to all those with interests in the curriculum. The 'subject communities' chosen are a fairly traditional list — mathematics, English, foreign languages, geography, history, art and design, science, craft, design and technology, home economics, physical education and moral and religious education. We might have included computing science, personal and social education, environmental education etc. but these latter are often viewed as permeation issues across the curriculum. We had a hunch at the conception of this book that the National Curriculum would take a familiar, traditional form and we wanted to identify features of the debate within old-established subject communities. Much early criticism of the National Curriculum proposals has focused on the selection of traditional subjects as its base.

Each contributor was invited to identify the unique contribution of his or her subject to the school curriculum and, to a lesser extent, to show how the subject relates to other parts of the curriculum. The response of the subject community (consisting of subject teaching associations, HMI subject panels, LEA advisers, teacher trainers, etc.) to the developing debate was to be outlined. Frameworks for illustrating the objectives of each part of the 5–16 curriculum were to be quoted where such frameworks existed. If the nature of the subject in question posed particular problems for the specification of such 'objectives' or 'expectations' these were to be mentioned. Finally, any critical issues or growth points within each subject that had a bearing on the current debate were to be highlighted. It was suggested that specific attention be paid to information technology and prevocational preparation.

Authors were actually free to develop their response to this template reasonably loosely, depending on the subject under review. What emerges is a fascinating glimpse of large curricular issues being worked out at the individual subject level by colleagues responsible for curriculum delivery. Is it possible to pick some general themes out of the curriculum debate as it has been enacted within each community? Direct comparison between the chapters of this book is difficult. Each was written by a member of the subject community but each author has inevitably put his or her own gloss on what were perceived to be the essential tensions within that subject during the debate. Each chapter is, therefore, an individual response as well as an attempt to portray a shared view of issues by a wider community. The section below will attempt to trace some common threads through the contributions.

Firstly, although each chapter deals with a 'subject' it is clear that these subjects are not unified. Some of them are aggregates. Parry has demonstrated that PE is a 'rather loose collection of physical activities' (typically consisting of a 'Basic 6', comprising gymnastics, dance, competitive games and athletics, fitness and exercise programmes, outdoor activities and swimming). Similarly, Jepson has identified four separate components of home economics (child development, textiles and fashion, home economics and food and nutrition). Penfold shows how CDT is 'a label' applied to the range of learning that goes on in school workshops. 'Craft', 'design' and 'technology', like the traditional subject labels they replaced all mean something different. What ends up comprising each collection is determined by culture and history but the resulting assemblages can sit uncomfortably with notions such as 'areas of experience' or 'forms of knowledge'. In PE, home economics and CDT the need to present aims for teaching or to generate criteria for examining has highlighted the diversity within these subjects. It further appears that the absence of an academic or professional career structure in these fields may have stunted curriculum debate. 'Traditional', 'single honours' subjects have a wider range of expertise on which to draw in the formulation of aims and policy and in the pressure that can be brought to bear on those responsible for the pecking order of subjects in the National Curriculum.

Internal diversity is not limited to PE, home economics and CDT, however. Nellist shows that although there is 'considerable agreement within what might be thought of as the scientific educational establishment about the framework of the science curriculum' there are nevertheless territorial disputes within the scientific community. Many science teachers in the secondary phase see themselves principally as teachers of biology, physics or chemistry rather than 'science'. Although the case for broad, balanced science is well argued there remains a resistance to change among the three core science subjects. Specialists perceive their own distinctive ways of working. This specialist/generalist division is not the same in foreign languages although Page contrasts general 'language awareness courses' with specialist language teaching. Also, although there may be broad agreement between foreign language teachers about methods of teaching and examining and so forth, there is the overall diversity created by the presence of these 'untapped alternatives to French'.

In history, Foster reports a 'fundamental split' between those historians who see content as the key to selection for what goes into the history curriculum and those who see content as relatively unimportant provided that the skills and methodology of the historian are effectively taught. Among the 'content oriented' historians there remains the question of 'what content?'. Progress here is achieved by establishing agreed criteria for selection of content. The division in geography between physical and human is not of the same type. These branches of the subject are seen by Bailey as complementary rather than in opposition.

Within Religious Education there are those that see RE as an initiation into the dominant faith and those who favour a comparative study of different religions and cultures. A similar dichotomy is found in music between those who adopt the European classical tradition and those who see music as an opportunity for offering children the widest range of musical experiences from other cultures. This contrast between a former, narrow, interpretation of subject matter and a newer, broader approach is also seen in mathematics. Wain notes that an important development in, for example, the geometry syllabus, is the recognition of other forms of geometry (including that based on transformation of shapes, co-ordinates, vector methods, perspective, etc.) to the traditional Euclidean content.

Within the subject 'English' there exists controversy over the knowledge *about* language that should accompany the *use* of language. Protherough details these 'basic and irreconcilable conflicts of principle and practice' over the teaching of grammar.

However, although considerable diversity exists within subjects it is clear that subject communities (given the spirit of the time in which these chapters were written), are keen to present a firm front in the face of the rest of the secondary school curriculum. Only three writers make much reference to the permeable nature of their subject's boundaries — mathematics, English and science — not surprisingly those in the strongest position as core subjects of the National Curriculum.

Wain stresses the need to integrate mathematics into other parts of the school curriculum. One of the most powerful aspects of mathematics is its ability to model reality in order to predict, plan and control. The purpose of modelling is to solve real problems and these problems are most likely to occur in the context of other school subjects rather than in mathematics itself. The relationship between mathematics and other subjects is therefore complex. So too is the relationship between English and other subjects. 'Every teacher is a teacher of English.' There is, as Protherough says, no agreement where the subject's place lies in the formal faculty structure of schools. Informally, teachers of English can find themselves pushed into a wide range of curriculum areas (but rarely, according to Page, into links with foreign language departments). Science teachers are being encouraged to look for links with mathematics, craft, design and technology and home economics but Nellist recognizes that these exhortations often fall on stony ground. The potential merit of cross-disciplinary links between science and other subjects has been well-established but there appears to be organizational and terrritorial friction with technology. The issues of trespass is also raised briefly by Penfold.

At the time of writing, only the core subjects could afford to be expansive about their relationships with the rest of the curriculum, and even here there was caution. The other subjects appeared to be defensive about their potential role with those most under threat demonstrating most forcefully that they fulfilled the criteria for inclusion in the National Curriculum. Jepson, for example, writing about home economics, a subject not included in the National Curriculum's list of Foundation Subjects is at pains to demonstrate the unique contribution it can make to organizational skills, intellectual development, understanding and decision making. Bailey provides a very strong justification for the inclusion of geography in the curriculum in terms of the principles of relevance, breadth, balance and differentiation. Considerable space is given to outlining the nature of the subject after thirty years of rapid and radical change. History too has changed and Foster justifies the nature of the educational value of modern history for children, stressing the uniqueness of its skills, concepts and ideas.

Most authors draw attention to the role of pressure groups in promoting their subjects. Bailey emphasizes the contribution made by the Geographical Association to the debate. This was a 'head on' approach to the Secretary of State, Sir Keith Joseph, in inviting him to address the membership of the Association at a critical period for the subject. Officers of the Association then responded promptly in publishing an answer to the challenges issued by the Secretary of State to justify the contribution that geography could make to the curriculum. The Historical Association also pursued the debate with vigour and Foster describes how a variety of history groups were mobilized to promote the cause of history at school and university level. It would perhaps be fair to say that at this stage history was able to capitalize on having more 'friends at court' than geography but nevertheless both Associations came to appreciate the value of media coverage in their campaigns and the power of effective lobbying. Both Associations established working groups which produced curriculum guidelines for the primary and secondary years illustrating how a National Curriculum in each subject might look in outline. The activities of these and other subject teaching associations reveal a great deal of organization in the setting up of regional conferences, dissemination of information and collating responses. Publications from subject teaching associations have played a major role in shaping the direction of the debate, sometimes appearing in parallel with 'official' publications and sometimes foreshadowing them.

In promoting their cause, subject associations and others make use of both intrinsic and instrumental justification for what they have to offer, with some subjects making strong claims on both counts. Wain, for example, stresses the importance of mathematics as a tool for the study of other subjects, as a powerful means of communication and its problem solving function. It is seen not only as necessary for survival but also an important cultural component with aesthetic attributes. Nellist similarly refers to the justification for science for both interest and use — a rewarding activity in its own right which enables individuals to cope more adequately with an everyday life permeated by technology. Home economics rejected a strictly utilitarian approach of preparing (especially) girls for a particular role in society. Although primarily a set of craft and organizational skills the subject also has 'close links' with aesthetics insofar as pupils are able to express themselves through, for example, the media of fabric, thread and dye. Dyson develops the theme of the separation of the useful and the useless at length, exploring a false dichotomy between soft and hard approaches to art and design. He draws attention to the prevailing political attitudes regarding the criteria for the inclusion of subjects in the National Curriculum and asks: 'Is industry the *most* important customer?'

All the chapters in the book point to the important part played by HMI in the debate leading up to the National Curriculum. In craft, design and technology, HMI are at the 'apex of the subject's hierarchical career structure', giving their pronouncements in this subject a special significance and authority. Indeed, it was HMI that gave the subject its 'new' name. Especially prominent in the discussions have been the books in the 5–16 series. History and geography appear to provide good models of a creative and constructive relationship between HMI and other subject specialists in formulating an approach to the 5–16 curriculum. 'History in the Primary and Secondary Years' is described by Foster as very influential in shaping the thinking of history teachers and seems to have been broadly endorsed by the Historical Association's series of regional conferences. HMI were well able to give a substantial lead in developing the potential of geography and putting a case for the subject forward at the highest political levels. Both these subject associations and the HMI subject panels have profited from their close relationships. Bailey and Foster also emphasize the key role of the HMI staff inspectors in clarifying thinking not only within their own teams but also across the whole subject community. Nellist reinforces this glimpse of HMI working closely with colleagues in the same field. He refers to the striking consensus between HMI, the Association for Science Education and the Secondary Science Curriculum Review, noting the tradition of cooperative working spread across organizational and constituency boundaries. The HMI subject oriented publications are not without their critics, however. Page refers to a restricted level of argument and justification in 'Modern Foreign Languages to 16' and a shortage of examples and specific advice. Protherough describes the widespread and vigorous rejection of the contentious 'English 5–16', and the opposition of subject teachers to its proposed statement of objectives and its view of grammar teaching. Parry is pessimistic about the non-appearance to date of the position paper from HMI on physical education, and raises concern about the initial absence of PE from serious discussion at national level.

With some notable exceptions the primary phase has been poorly served with respect to subjects in official documents. There is much work to be done on curriculum continuity. Nellist notes the great changes that have taken place in the primary science curriculum over the past decade and suggests some reasons for these. However, even in science there remain critical issues for further development, chiefly those of content and progression.

Most subject communities appear, as a result of the great debate of the last decade, to have a sharpened view of what they can offer and of how to structure it and a broader view of the possibilities available in teaching it. The criteria exercise to GCSE has clearly been of benefit to thinking about teaching objectives. Work on criterion referencing and differentiation has made significant advances in assessment but there remain problems in practical implementation.

This book is presented as a contribution to the debate. It makes its appearance, we hope, at a time when subject working groups are being set up. We hope that the following chapters will inform both their deliberations and the opinions of teachers and others during the process of consultation. The National Curriculum has been variously described as 'a Frankenstein', 'repressive' and 'stifling'. Intelligent responses during the consultation process are clearly vital, therefore. It now seems likely that the development period, as well as the opportunity for debate will be longer than might at first have been envisaged. We would like to encourage readers to participate as fully as possible.

References

BENNETT, N. (1976) *Teaching Styles and Pupil Progress*, London, Open Books.
Cox, C.B. and DYSON, A.E. (1969a) *Fight for Education: Black Paper*. London, Critical Quarterly Society.

Cox, C.B. and Dyson, A.E. (1969b) *The Crisis in Education: Black Paper Two.* London Critical Quarterly Society.

Cox, C.B. and Dyson, A.E. (1970) *Goodbye Mr. Short.* London, Critical Quarterly Society.

Department of Education and Science (1977a) *Education in Schools: A Consultative Document,* London, HMSO.

Department of Education and Science (1977b) *Circular 14/77: Local Authority Arrangements for the School Curriculum,* London, HMSO.

Department of Education and Science (1984) *Organization and Content of the 5–16 Curriculum,* London, HMSO.

Department of Education and Science (1987a) *The National Curriculum 5–16: A Consultation Document,* London, HMSO.

Department of Education and Science (1987b) *Education Reform,* London, HMSO.

Department of Education and Science (1987c) *Education Reform Bill,* London, HMSO.

Golby, M. (Ed.) (1987) *Perspectives on the National Curriculum: Perspectives 32,* University of Exeter, Exeter.

Her Majesty's Inspectorate (1985) *Curriculum 5–16,* London, HMSO.

Hillgate Group (1986) *Whose Schools?* London, The Hillgate Group.

Holt, M. (1983) *Curriculum Workshop,* London, Routledge.

Lawton, D. (1980) *The Politics of the School Curriculum,* London, Routledge.

1   *Mathematics*

G.T. Wain

'There can be no question that mathematics should be compulsory
for all pupils'. DES (1984)

Even though mathematics has not had the *legal* status of being a compulsory subject in our schools, the practical reality has been that almost all
pupils from age 5 to 16 have had to study it for the equivalent of about five
single periods per week. If it is true that there is no question that such
compulsory status is fully justified then it is clearly in the best interests of
children that they should continue to receive a large allocation of time, and
the new National Curriculum proposals have recommended that they
should. It certainly does not follow, however, that there are no questions
to ask about the nature of that curriculum or that all is well with the
subject. There are many questions to be asked and many questions that
are, at present, unanswerable. Indeed, the very reasons that are usually
put forward for making mathematics compulsory, raise many uncomfortable questions which will be considered later. What is particularly important is to ensure that, by being given the protection of compulsion, what is
now taught as mathematics in schools is not accepted complacently as
being wholly good, of unquestioned high status and not open to fundamental reappraisal. It could be argued that many of the problems facing
mathematical education at the moment are due to an unquestioned
acceptance of its importance over the years, although it is now possible to
detect in many publications some elements of scepticism about the intrinsic value of the subject.

The development of TVEI and Certificate of Pre-Vocational Education
(CPVE) courses in particular have encouraged new alignments of subject
disciplines and the placing of mathematics within these schemes has raised
again some of the oldest questions about mathematics in education, in
particular the question of what mathematics at school is for and what its
contribution to education in general really is. It is important to clarify this
contribution before considering in more detail the current debate about

the subject, its legitimate curriculum objectives and some of the particularly pressing contemporary issues in the subject.

The Contribution of Mathematics to the General Curriculum

Arguments put forward in support of mathematics as a compulsory subject for all centre around a number of quite specific and distinct qualities:

it is indispensable for survival in modern society;
it is an important tool in the study of other subjects;
it is an important part of our culture with aesthetic appeal;
it is a powerful means of communication;
it contributes important elements to our ability to think in general
and to solve a wide range of problems.

It is worth elaborating briefly on each of these since each raises some of the questions referred to above that need to be resolved.

Survival in modern society requires the ability to use mathematics with ease and confidence in many everyday situations. The usefulness of mathematics is undeniable. At the most elementary level we rely on the recognition and understanding of numbers in a variety of contexts. We need numbers in order to be aware of a speed limit, in order to dial a telephone number, in order to catch a train, in order to cook a meal and so on. At a different level we use much more complex mathematics in launching a spacecraft, in designing a complex delivery system for manufactured goods or in designing a bridge. The uses at the elementary level are obviously necessary for full participation in modern society and ideally one would hope that all school leavers would acquire something near to mastery of these fundamental basic skills. These skills would be the ability to recognize numbers, to tell the time, to handle common measures of length, weight and capacity as well as to cope with basic money matters, and would seem to be an absolutely irreducible minimum for survival as an adult. To this collection can be added other desirable skills such as the ability to manipulate numbers, to use and understand a variety of shapes in practical situations, to read timetables, to plan spending and to solve a range of everyday problems involving numbers and shapes. The fact that, even at this apparently low level, many school leavers and adults lack competence and confidence is very sad and a severe indictment of the success of mathematical education. Many adults approached in a recent survey by Sewell (1981) revealed a deep fear of simple arithmetic when faced with very elementary problems. And this after receiving something like 1300 hours of mathematics tuition at school between the ages of 5 and 16! Some that were approached ran away from the interviewer when they realized that the survey was about mathematics. Faced with evidence such as this, one is tempted to rewrite the quotation at the beginning of this chapter in the form 'there can be no question that mathematics as a compulsory subject for all pupils has been extremely harmful to the confidence and well-being of many adults'.

The real question here is not whether it is right for mathematics to be a compulsory subject but how it is possible to enable all children to acquire competence and confidence in survival skills while also enabling many of them to develop the subject beyond that basic level still with confidence. First it is vital to accept that the acquisition of such skills is a difficult task for many children. This difficulty was acknowledged fully in the Cockcroft Report (1982) which went on, in a now famous section, to recommend for all pupils a foundation list of topics which, for the weakest, would constitute the greater part, if not the whole of the syllabus. The foundation list proposed includes the topics listed above plus extremely simple work with fractions, decimals and percentages, the understanding and use of the types of graphs and pictorial representation commonly seen in the media, the use of the calculators and some understanding of popular statistics and ideas of chance. The implication throughout is that the contexts in which these ideas are met should be entirely realistic, that the work should be 'about something' rather than solely an arid practice of skills.

It is difficult, of course, to see how this can be achieved without a positive effort to integrate the work in mathematics into other parts of the curriculum. All the topics mentioned have applications in other subjects where they are necessary tools for understanding. Much could be achieved if the idea of mathematics as something to be taught across the whole school curriculum could be developed in a realistic and coherent way. One of the severest indictments of the teaching of mathematics is that many children perform calculations but cannot identify what calculation to use in a practical situation. Teachers requiring the use of mathematical ideas in other subjects know this well enough. The problem has been well described by Brown and Kuchemann (1976, 1977) in articles that all mathematics teachers should read. If mathematics is to be justified as being useful then its usefulness must be realizable in the classroom and in a wide variety of contexts.

The greatest danger for the teacher is in making mathematics appear to be an isolated collection of routine skills that have no application. Some of these routine skills have, in fact, been given a position of pseudo-educational validity and are very difficult to remove from the curriculum even though they now have no place in it. For example, long multiplication and long division no longer have a place in a society which uses the calculator. It is possible that the reader is shocked with that statement, being convinced that there is merit in knowing ancient skills. It would be unfair not to explain precisely what is meant. The need to calculate occurs for most people on many occasions in their everyday life. There is a difference, however, between recognizing the need to perform a particu-

---

lar calculation and knowing how to carry it out. If, for instance, in planning a journey it is known that the total fare for each of seventeen people is £37.91, it is one thing to be aware that the total fare for all seventeen is 17 × £37.91 and quite another to be able to get the answer. Knowing that multiplication is the method to use is a purely mathematical piece of knowledge. Knowing how to obtain the answer depends upon the availability in society of methods for carrying out the multiplication. Someone living in Japan before the advent of the electronic calculator would have reached for an abacus, an ancient Egyptian would have used a method based on doubling, an early twentieth century Englishman would have used long multiplication, logarithms or a slide rule, but the method of contemporary society is to use the electronic calculator. The calculator is a natural part of our environment, readily available at very low prices, and an essential support to all mathematical work throughout the entire 5 to 16 age range. The importance of the calculator will be referred to again later in this chapter.

Recommending the removal of such skills as long multiplication and long division from the mathematics curriculum is a step towards making mathematics more readily usable by substituting a modern process (the calculator) for an outdated one which was always ill-remembered. There is evidence now that the availability of the calculator enhances confidence in using arithmetical ideas involving much more awkward calculations than were ever attempted before.

It is important, however, not to give the impression that the curriculum should be designed only because mathematics is useful. There is a danger in the current debate for relevance and usefulness to be elevated to positions of exaggerated importance. A National Curriculum for the subject seems almost certain to stress utility. It may be that for the weaker children practical work and real applications are vitally important in providing the necessary contexts in which to learn and practise foundation list skills. But mathematics is not an arbitrary set of skills waiting to be applied only to real problems. It also has an internal consistency and structure which have a fascination for many pupils and give rise to a genuine aesthetic appreciation which is accessible to almost all pupils at least some of the time. It is, for instance, possible to practise skills using them *within* mathematics in order to explore patterns, to gain greater understanding and to solve puzzle problems.

For example, the reader might like to try the following:

1 $2^2 = 4$ $1 \times 3 = 3$
   $3^2 = 9$ $2 \times 4 = 8$
   $4^2 = 16$ $3 \times 5 = 15$

Continue these patterns of calculations and compare the answers in the two columns. What do you notice? If your algebra is still in working order can you prove a general result?

2

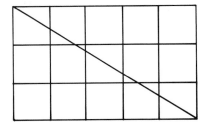

In this 3 × 5 rectangle of squares the diagonal marked goes through 7 squares. Investigate rectangles of other dimensions to find if there is a relationship between the size of the rectangle and the number of squares that the diagonal goes through.

In both of these it is necessary to use a variety of mathematical skills in order to investigate the problem. The level of skill needed to gain some insight is quite low but there are developments of both that require much higher levels. Problems such as this are now common in schools in providing a context for the practice of skills and to give opportunities to children to appreciate mathematics as something more than a means of dealing with everyday problems. In any mathematical curriculum it is vital that the subject is developed in its own right as an intellectual activity which has played a vital part in our culture. To see the subject only as a tool for solving problems outside mathematics is a gross distortion of its true value.

Mathematics is also seen as important in that it provides a powerful means of communication. On the one hand mathematics gives us a particular vocabulary which allows us to convey meaning in a concise and unambiguous way. Words like three, half, square, radius and angle have exact meanings which can enable communication to be precise and well-defined. On the other hand, however, mathematics provides relationships of a precise nature *between* elements in its vocabulary and a means of manipulating ideas and deducing one thing from another by a clear logical process. This aspect of the subject is unique and is not found elsewhere. Thus, in our usual system of counting, 6 × 8 not only has meaning in itself but it is also equal to 48. In addition the statement 6 × 8 = 48 not only provides a means of communicating a relationship between numbers but it also provides an abstract result which is applicable and has meaning in many different contexts. Thus 6 can be a number of apples and 8 the price per apple in pence. 6 × 8 = 48 provides the means of finding the total cost. But if a rectangular room is 6 metres by 8 metres then 6 × 8 = 48 can be interpreted as the number of square metres of carpet required to cover the floor. There are many other ways that 6 × 8 = 48 could be given meaning in this way. The subject is thus powerful as a communicator because it provides unambiguous statements each of which can arise from many apparently totally unrelated situations. Learning mathematics, then, is partly concerned with developing the ability to use a mathematical language appropriately in situations where it rightly carries important meaning. It is, however, also about learning the mathematical language in its own right so that future, often unexpected, valuable uses can be made of it. It is sad, therefore, to note that in many popular mathematics textbooks examples often require very contrived uses of mathematical language which do not carry worthwhile meaning and, consequently, children often feel that the subject is intrinsically meaningless as a language.

Perhaps the most powerful aspect of mathematics as a means of communication is its ability to provide models of reality which enable us to predict, plan and control. The accuracy of many mathematical models, particularly in the physical sciences, is so great that it is often tempting to confuse the model with reality. As an example consider the planning of a journey by train. If it is known at what time it is hoped to arrive, a train timetable will enable selection of a suitable train. Working from the arrival time the departure time can be found and then an estimate can be made of the latest time to set out for the station. Provided that all the assumptions (for instance, that the train runs to time) are valid the actual journey will happen as planned. In other words the journey itself can be planned and predicted in detail in advance of it happening. This ability to model and predict is an extremely important part of modern man's interaction with his environment and is a skill in contemporary society which was not available in earlier societies or in uneducated society today. It is a skill which enables aspects of the future to be forecast and hence planned with great precision. There are many things that could not occur unless such a modelling process can be carried out. It is very unlikely, for example, that a man would allow himself to be strapped to a huge rocket which was fired in the general direction of the moon in the hope of getting there unless the whole venture had been modelled and planned in the same way as for the train journey. The processes are the same. The level of complexity of the model is the only difference between these two examples.

The last twenty years has seen a great deal of writing about developing the process of modelling in mathematical education (see, for instance Hall (1978) and Ormell (1975)). It is clearly a powerful modern skill which is at the heart of technological development and rational planning. It is also a process that is not dependent on a high level of mathematical skill. The more mathematics that is known the more models that can be constructed at a high level of sophistication but only simple mathematics is required to model processes such as cooking, dressmaking, decorating, travelling, holiday-making and so on. Important questions arise, however, about the development of modelling in the school mathematics course. The whole purpose of modelling is to solve real problems and these problems are unlikely to arise in mathematics itself. They are most likely to arise in other subjects so that the relationship between mathematics and other subjects again becomes in important issue. The point is that it is not possible to make a worthwhile mathematical model about something which is not understood. Many mathematics textbooks have traditionally got around this problem by inventing situations (men digging ditches, taps filling baths) which have been called 'whimsical' problems. Their unreal nature cannot ever have been a good advertisement for the subject. Their purpose was often to simplify the arithmetic, something that need not be done in the calculator age.

The question as to how modelling can most effectively be taught is, as yet, unanswered. Many modern textbooks have tried to have much less whimsical examples than more traditional ones but attempts to embed mathematical models firmly in context, as for instance by Pollard *et al* (1983, 1984, 1985) have been criticized as not really being mathematical any more. The interrelation between mathematics and subjects into which it is applied is a complex one and has been analyzed elsewhere by Wain (1983). For many children and for modern society it may well be that a school curriculum based around traditional academic subject labelling may not be appropriate. The growth of TVEI, CPVE, technology courses and project work have all provided a considerable challenge to those who wish to preserve subject boundaries. No matter how the future national curriculum finally emerges mathematical modelling must feature as an important process skill within it.

A consideration of modelling leads us naturally to the last of the listed reasons for studying mathematics. Modelling is a process of problem solving. It is not a collection of particular mathematical techniques. As such it is representative of a range of process skills which mathematics may be considered to develop in the learner. It is often thought that mathematics teaches logical thinking, but, if so, it can hardly be unique in so doing. No specialist in another subject would claim that their subject taught illogical thinking! But mathematics in use either for its own sake or in its applications requires a particular way of working that is, in some ways, unique to the subject. Mathematics written up for the purposes of communication is almost always in tidy logical form but the process of creating the mathematics is anything but tidy. It is a process of hunch and guess, of hypothesis and trial leading to insight and understanding. Proof, the classic written style of mathematical recording, is often the last part of the process of invention. It is perhaps a pity that mathematical results are normally written in an arid, proof-form and that there are few accounts of the process of creating those results. Those that do exist throw interesting light on the contrast between the tidy record and the untidy activity. See, for instance, Hadamard (1945), and Wain and Wynne Willson (1987).

So what are the process skills that are involved? There have been many attempts recently to list them not only in mathematics but in other subjects as well. For mathematics the processes suggested seem to fall into two categories, broadly concerned with applications of the subject on the one hand and work internal to mathematics on the other. Those dealing with applications are really the skills of mathematical modelling. Included is the ability to abstract the mathematical ideas of relevance from real situations while being aware of assumptions that are being made in order to allow the abstraction to take place successfully. At the end of the modelling process it is always necessary to evaluate the model against reality and to do that requires an ability to judge the reasonableness and value of results, to reflect upon the assumptions made and the alternatives possible. Traditional text books usually provide applications in which these aspects of modelling are not required. The assumptions are clearly made, the abstractions are suggested and no evaluation of results is required. The examples are most often reduced to the use of mathematical techniques strongly hinted at in the context. Modelling for real leaves open the question of which mathematical techniques should be used — the techniques are often a consequence of the way the assumptions are made and the process of abstraction carried out.

Process skills concerned with internal aspects of mathematics are usually listed as those related to problem solving and investigatory work. They are the processes of the untidy activity of doing mathematics. It is rare, except in the practice of basic mathematical skills, for a solution to a problem to be obtained in a systematic and logical way. The process of reaching a solution requires complete understanding of the problem which often includes a period of trial and error, of trying special values or cases, of looking for analogues or simpler examples and also asking new questions about the data often in the form, 'What would happen if . . .?'. These processes themselves lead to the generation of various kinds of data and the need to order the data, represent it in various ways such as tables and graphs and to observe patterns and regularities. Then are needed the abilities to make and test hypotheses leading finally to the writing out of a solution in a coherent readable and logical form.

Most of these processes in themselves have not hitherto been considered explicitly in mathematics teaching in general. In fact, the presentation of mathematics as a series of particular skills to be learned has usually succeeded in removing the need to use these processes and examinations have encouraged arid teaching by not requiring the skills of modelling, problem solving and investigation. The new GCSE requirements, particularly in their full form from 1991 should encourage a much wider interpretation of the subject as a full contributor to general education by means of the process skills involved. Investigatory work, problem solving, practical work and projects have all been introduced into the examination regulations and will demand of teachers a considerable shift in their style of teaching. Two important questions that immediately arise are so far not resolved in a completely satisfactory way. One is how the new type of work required of children will be assessed by the teachers and the other is whether it is possible to teach the process skills discussed above. Both of these questions will be considered again later.

The processes of doing mathematics as outlined here are not completely unique to mathematics. They have a more general applicability to problems that are not necessarily mathematical in content although the expectation within mathematics is always that symbolization will be an important part of all the processes. It could be argued, however, that focusing on process aspects of the subject has the potential to make it much more important as a part of general education and as a contribution to the development of general intellectual skills.

The Current Debate

There are clearly, then, good reasons for making mathematics a compulsory part of the school curriculum and the discussion in the previous section has attempted a brief analysis of them. The actual form and content of mathematics courses is far less easy to determine and it would be a mistake to believe that it was an easy matter to construct a mathematics curriculum. Apart from a reasonably well agreed common core, approximating to the Cockcroft foundation list, there are no obvious agreements about what constitutes the content that extends that core. In fact, the content debate has been a fierce one for about thirty years during which there have been some quite dramatic attempts at change, perhaps the best known being the School Mathematics Project, one of the projects involved in the 'Modern Mathematics' movement of the 1960s. A detailed account of the evolution of that project and of the Midland Mathematical Experiment, recently provided by Cooper (1985), has given an interesting analysis of the conflicting forces at work in bringing about curriculum change in the subject. A particularly potent force in many countries involved in modern mathematics projects was that provided by the academic mathematical world represented by the universities. In Britain teachers have had a much greater say but have been, nevertheless, influenced by similar, if diluted, forces with the consequences that the modern mathematics movement was also dominated in Britain by the introduction of topics which were largely determined by the needs of higher education. The reasons for teaching mathematics discussed earlier have usually not been reflected equally in previous curriculum development. Curricula derived from the needs of the universities have not done justice to the usefulness of the subject for all children, nor the process aspects. There is a danger at present that the consensus of opinion is leading to the overstressing of usefulness and application.

During the 1970s considerable disquiet about the effectiveness of mathematics teaching was expressed by many including the Expenditure Committee of the House of Commons (1977) and James Callaghan, when Prime Minister, devoted a speech at Ruskin College, Oxford in 1976 to education in which, among other things, he criticized the mathematical attainments of the school leaver. His concern was that the needs of society at large apparently played too small a part in determining the curriculum.

G.T. Wain

He gave the needs of industry, in particular, explicit mention. One outcome of these concerns was the, so-called, Great Debate; another was the setting up of the Committee of Enquiry into the Teaching of Mathematics in Schools under the chairmanship of the then Dr. W.H. Cockcroft. The Cockcroft Report (1982) provided for mathematics a powerful statement about the subject in schools which has dominated the curriculum debate ever since. It would not be possible, in this chapter, to consider in detail the contents of this report but it is, nevertheless, important to relate some of the points that it makes to the developments in the curriculum that have taken place recently and which are proposed. As we shall see the report's recommendations are not always congruent to the proposals being suggested by the Department of Education and Science.

Perhaps the most significant message from the report is the unambiguous acceptance of the need to cater effectively for the full range of ability whilst, at the same time, catering for the needs of higher and further education, the world of work and the needs of adult life. To do this the report proposes that both the curriculum itself and the examining system should be constructed so as to allow for the subject to be meaningful to all abilities and to provide the chance for all pupils regularly to experience success. Consequently an important outcome of the report has been to provide legitimacy to the view that the curriculum should be designed 'from the bottom up', accepting the idea of a foundation list of content for all pupils and adding to it in an appropriate way for those who are capable of studying the subject to higher levels. The acceptance of this approach is much more revolutionary than may seem at first sight for it removes to a large extent the role of the academic mathematicians in curriculum construction. The usual approach to curriculum construction has been to devise an appropriate, academic, syllabus for the best and water it down to cater for the rest. It did not need the Cockcroft committee to tell mathematics educators how disastrous this approach has been in the past. In many CSE syllabuses and examinations, for instance, there has always been a shadow of O-level work often reduced to meaningless rote learning of skills that are inappropriate to the pupils involved. The Cockcroft Report summed up this situation by reporting that much of the mathematics teaching seen by members of the committee was 'not about anything' and recommending that, as a general principle, all topics should be taught in such a way as to allow pupils to apply them in ways which they can understand. This does not imply practical usefulness for all parts of mathematics. The explanation of internal features of the subject mentioned earlier can also provide motivation and a sense of accomplishment.

The report stressed that recommendations of this kind are not to be interpreted as lowering standards. Indeed it is clearly stated that, in a differentiated curriculum designed to meet the needs of all abilities, there should be opportunities for the ablest to take the subject far beyond what

26

has been achieved in the past; special new material should be provided designed to extend mathematical knowledge and understanding.

The arguments for differentiation of work are supported in the report by the clear acknowledgement that enormous differences in attainment appear very early and that, by the end of the primary phase, children are already spread across a wide ability spectrum; the weakest at eleven are no better than the average 7 year-olds and the best are better than the average 13 or 14 year-olds. This 'seven year difference' at age 11 has, of course, been known but not really appreciated for about a century. IQ testing, based as it is on a comparison of mental age with chronological age, has demonstrated clearly that these differences do exist. Applying the usual IQ approach shows that there is approximately a 'seven year difference' at age eleven, that the 'difference' is already about three years at age 5 and by the leaving age of 16 has grown to a 'difference' of nearly ten years. The need for differentiation of work has surely always been clear and necessary throughout the whole range of schooling from 5 to 16. The main message of the report is quite clear: 'We believe that if pupils follow a course where content is better matched to their level of attainment and rate of learning, they will achieve not only greater confidence in their approach to mathematics but also greater mastery of the mathematics which they study. This should contribute to improvements in attainment, attitudes and confidence and so to a raising of standards overall'. (Cockcroft Report, 1982, p. 145).

It is difficult, of course, to see how these recommendations match with more recent proposals from the Department of Education and Science which seem to be stressing the need for competence in the subject based on set targets of achievement at various ages beginning at seven. It is now clear that the Secretary of State is to introduce such attainment targets albeit devised apparently in such a way as to take account of different abilities. Many parts of the mathematical education community have expressed the fear that the setting up of such targets will undermine the progress made so far in responding to the carefully expressed recommendations in the Cockcroft Report. The idea that the curriculum should be fully differentiated to cater for individual children's needs does not live easily alongside a policy of attainment targets tied to specific ages. A possible compromise is to introduce assessment procedures which can be made available whenever a child showed readiness. The project GAIN (Graded Assessment in Mathematics) is exploring just this approach at the secondary level. It is by no means a consequence of such an approach that standards would be lowered.

At secondary level, however, attainment targets are now linked inextricably with the new examination requirements of the General Certificate of Secondary Education (GCSE). The form of the GCSE as far as mathematics is concerned is close to that recommended in the Cockcroft

Report and accepts fully the need for differentiation by ability. In fact the original draft national criteria for GCSE mathematics were amended in the light of the Cockcroft Report's section on examinations. The report suggested certain principles to be taken into account in any mathematics examination. The first was that assessment should enable pupils to demonstrate what they know rather than what they do not know and another was that examinations should not be such as to undermine the confidence of those taking them. It was also strongly recommended that the form of assessment should be consistent with the form of the curriculum, reflect the various ways of learning and teaching the subject, and hence involve other methods of examination than the traditional written paper. The importance of ensuring that the examination system itself does not encourage a sterile form of teaching was forcibly stressed.

These proposals are radical. They demand a considerable change in attitudes and teaching styles. They also make new demands on teachers because several of the new forms of examination proposed require teacher assessment of practical work, investigations and project work, all new to most teachers and examiners in the subject. There is also the new demand to assess process skills, an important issue raised above and discussed again later. Working out the consequences of the proposals is a hard task and will take a long time. The GCSE, examined for the first time in 1988, takes into account in its forms of assessment many of the Cockcroft Report's suggestions. The full implementation, to include teacher assessment of practical work and projects will not occur until 1991, nine years after the publication of the report.

One of the problems faced by mathematics assessment has always been that of finding ways of measuring pupil performance by the outcome of their work rather than by the level of the questions set. Traditional examinations have always contained questions which, in their construction, define a level of difficulty and so can only be answered by pupils who are at a particular attainment stage. A change to assessment partly by project work and investigations makes it possible that pupils of a wide range of ability can be set the same task to which they respond at different levels. The two examples given earlier are of this type. Such a form of assessment would make differentiation easier to achieve in practice.

The most recent proposals about assessment that have been made by the Secretary of State accept the new GCSE arrangements. The addition of proposals for monitoring performance at earlier ages is, however, extremely controversial. There is a fear that too hasty an implementation of attainment targets and procedures for monitoring could well go counter to the developments that have followed Cockcroft and tend to push the curriculum back into a more rigid framework. The fear of rigidity in the curriculum is deeply felt in English and Welsh education where the tradition has always been for decentralization of syllabus construction and content choice. That more centralized control should be exerted at precisely the time when the curriculum is subject to great change creates the fear that it might inevitably become impossible to respond appropriately to necessary development. The Secretary of State, Mr. Baker, has attempted to allay these fears in saying (1987) '... the national criteria must be capable of change and development. They must give teachers flexibility in the choice of content and permit them to adapt what they teach to the needs of each individual pupil and to try out and develop new methods and approaches. We must retain the professional enterprise which so many of our teachers display'. The criteria referred to here are those intended for the curriculum rather than for the GCSE. The curriculum is inevitably driven by the forms of assessment and examination laid down and it would really seem premature to seek to establish criteria for the curriculum before the effects on the curriculum of the new examination criteria have been felt. The more criteria there are the more one would expect that the flexibility that teachers are expected to have will be reduced.

The impact of the new system of examining that GCSE has introduced to mathematics must not be underestimated. Most O-level and CSE assessments have been made using Mode 1 and have consequently relied on traditional examinations based on a well-defined syllabus. The questions set have often been fairly predictable requiring candidates to show that they have acquired certain skills and techniques and can apply them to a quite small range of applications. Marking schemes have been very tight with almost all marks allocated to steps in the carrying out of techniques. The methods of assessment used have made it easy to order candidates and to define pass levels based on the average work for a year and the spread of marks about the average. The details of achievement are summarized in the statistics that apply to a particular cohort of examinees who are thus norm-referenced for assessment purposes.

Current discussion has challenged this traditional approach. Several new issues need to be faced. The idea of a foundation list, for instance, of topics for all pupils suggests that the testing of it should depend on the mastery of certain skills, in other words should be criterion-referenced. Mastery is an important idea. It reflects the Cockcroft Report's call for pupils to experience success in mathematics. It implies a drastic limitation of the syllabus for many children in order that success is realizable. Perhaps the most important development, however, is the requirement to assess not only by examination papers but also by course work based on investigations, projects, practical and oral work. These new forms of assessment will require from teachers and examiners a totally new attitude to both curriculum and examination.

The proposals in the Cockcroft Report, though not really new in themselves, have, because they are in the report, achieved considerable status and will be widely accepted under the new proposals. The report was welcomed as 'first class' by the then Secretary of State and considerable efforts have been made since its publication to implement the type of curriculum it proposed and financial help has been forthcoming to do so.

The report inevitably, however, dealt almost entirely with mathematics itself although it did include some references to the place of the subject across the curriculum. As has been mentioned earlier it may well be that for many children, particularly at primary level, much more subject integration is necessary. The proposals in the DES 'consultation document' appear to be aimed to maintain the separateness of mathematics in the curriculum at precisely the time when greater efforts at integration would seem appropriate. Separate subject working groups have already been established in mathematics and science with no apparent concern for a coherent relationship between the two. One of the clear lessons of the curriculum changes of the 1960s was the realization of the way new problems can so easily be created when closely related subjects such as mathematics and science independently change both content and teaching approach without regard to the other. The outcome at that time was a series of publications designed to reconcile conflicting developments. Will we see a repetition of this in the next few years?

The consultation document does hint that working groups may need to consider the integration of work in expressive subjects, between history and geography and also between science and technology but only in the primary phase. For the secondary phase it would appear that, for the Secretary of State, an academic subject-orientated curriculum is considered suitable and best for all pupils of all abilities.

There are, however, some important dangers inherent in such an approach linked to the new forms of assessment. With the increase in investigations, project work and practicals in many subjects there is the danger that pupils will be submerged in course work requirements from all subjects, each of which could well include a multi-subject dimension. The result could well be a great deal of overlap in the intellectual demands placed on pupils with the danger of repetition and redundancy. Surely the challenge of the developments going on at present towards resource-based, pupil-centred, project-type work is to provide a coherent integrated framework as a whole so that education in total has a meaning. The National Curriculum proposals seem to have completely failed to meet that challenge. Indeed the proposals may well lead to greater subject-boundary definition than hitherto unless specific steps are taken to avoid it.

Curriculum Objectives 5–16

The current debate about national criteria and the proposals in the Cockcroft Report came at the end of a long period of experimentation in the mathematics curriculum. There is now in existence a large body of recent research on what and how children learn the subject, on the mathematical needs of people in society generally and in the world of work. (See, for instance, Hart (1981) and Fitzgerald (1981), (1985).) From all of this there is emerging a clearer idea of what the mathematics curriculum ought to try to achieve and, even more important in a way, a clearer statement of the problems still to be resolved. The crucial task is to match the curriculum to the realities of the world in the last years of the twentieth century and beyond. Let us look now at some of the implications in constructing such a curriculum.

There is now a reasonable consensus that mathematics syllabuses for most pupils have been overfull. Attempts to cover too much have led all too often to failure, despair and a lasting lack of confidence. What has been covered has also stressed too much the learning of isolated skills for their own sake. It is common now to consider limiting the syllabus while at the same time enriching the curriculum. In other words expecting less in the way of technical skill but much more in terms of application, understanding and exploration of ideas. This distinction between syllabus and curriculum has acquired a new and significant importance as far as mathematics is concerned.

Too often in the past the syllabus was the curriculum, what was stated as a list of skills to be learned became the whole of the activity in the classroom. A typical lesson would consist of the teacher explaining a new technique on the board and then giving the class sets of practice examples to consolidate their skills. Sadly it is certain that many mathematics lessons are still of this kind. The main aim of such teaching is to 'cover the syllabus'. In such a situation the syllabus achieves a status which it should never have in that it becomes a statement of what particular groups of children must know from the body of knowledge called mathematics. Mathematics for the learner is what is in the syllabus and anything not in the syllabus has no legitimacy. This has always been a travesty of a subject which is enormous in content and growing at a staggering rate.

One of the important lessons of the curriculum developments of the 1960s in particular was in realizing that there was no single syllabus that could be claimed to be the best. In the case of geometry, for instance, there are now acknowledged to be many forms that the subject can take in schools whereas only a few decades ago there was almost no doubt that the content should be based on the sequence and style of that produced by Euclid in the third century BC! Now it is common to acknowledge other forms of geometry including that based on transformations of shapes, on co-ordinates, on vector methods, on perspective, on projections and so on. Content then must be relatively open because of the vast range of choice although, as stated earlier, it is relatively easy to produce a foundation list of skills and techniques which should be known by everyone. For the weakest children that list will be the syllabus to 'cover' between the ages of 5 and 16. For them it is important *how* the syllabus is covered. Their

31

curriculum can be rich in activities based upon limited content knowledge. For the brightest pupils the foundation list will be covered and known during the primary stage. For them the secondary stage is where content can become more open but based upon a coherent, limited syllabus providing many opportunities through investigatory work and projects to extend the content in any direction. Many new GCSE syllabuses seem to have been constructed to reflect such an approach. The importance of openness is to allow the pupil to experience ways in which the subject extends into many different types of work reflecting the purposes listed earlier for learning the subject. The very ablest pupils, for instance, must be allowed the chance of extending the subject for its own sake as far as they can take it. The current debate about the subject seems to be obsessed with the idea that mathematics is useful. For the very able this may well not be an important criterion.

One of the key aims in teaching mathematics should be to enable the learners to feel confident in their acquisition of knowledge. The fact that the teaching of the subject has often promoted fear is an awful indictment. Confidence itself is dependent upon many things. It can certainly be undermined by a feeling of inadequacy when trying to remember a particular teacher-taught procedure and finding that what is remembered is only partly complete. There is now a lot of evidence from both school pupils and industry (see the writing of Hart and Fitzgerald referred to earlier), that very few people rely on accurate memory of these procedures. Faced with a situation that is understood and a motivation to solve a problem many people construct their own procedure, or algorithm, for finding answers. The algorithms they construct can often develop through interaction with a calculator, equipment, models and microcomputers. The classic teacher-taught algorithms of long division, long multiplication, dividing fractions and so on were not remembered well enough and were often not in the form that suits the problem under consideration. An example will illustrate the point. A carpenter cuts pieces of wood $10\frac{1}{2}$ cm. long from a 40 cm. length. How many can he obtain and what is left? The formal algorithmic approach would be to divide $10\frac{1}{2}$ into 40 because the process seems to be one of division. The result would be

$$40 \div 10\frac{1}{2} = 40 \div \frac{21}{2} = 40 \times \frac{2}{21} \text{ (turn upside down and multiply)}$$
$$= \frac{80}{21} = 3\frac{17}{21}$$

Is this the answer? In practice, faced with the wood and the task to perform, the approach is more likely to be as follows. By estimation no more than three pieces can be cut — four would certainly require more than 40 cm. The length of three pieces would be $3 \times 10\frac{1}{2}$ cm. $= 31\frac{1}{2}$ cm. altogether. The piece left over would be $8\frac{1}{2}$ cm. or a bit less allowing for the thickness of the cuts. So the answer is: 3 pieces with about $8\frac{1}{2}$ cm. left. How does that relate to the 'formal' answer $3\frac{17}{21}$ obtained above? The reader is left to explain!

The purpose of this example is to show that formally taught algorithms are not necessarily useful. They are clever encapsulations of old procedures abstracted from context. The more practical approach described may well be all that is needed for solving many real problems and provides confidence in successful achievement for the person involved. Proposals in both the Cockcroft Report and in GCSE regulations for change in the mathematics curriculum seem designed specifically to encourage more problem-solving approaches such as this. The content to be 'covered' by most children should be less than at present but the contexts and activities within which that content is explored can provide a richness of understanding, a confidence to try and a mastery of some of the skills. Let us be quite clear that developments of this kind are indeed radical. They imply a dramatic move from an imposed syllabus with all the trappings of authoritarianism to an approach which respects the individual learners and, to a large extent, requires them to structure their own working as never before in the subject. The idea of an algorithm appears in a new guise. One modern way of solving mathematical problems is by a process of interaction with a calculator or computer. The skill of programming the computer to do what is required is also known as algorithmic construction: this is the skill of instructing the computer to do what is wanted. This must be the modern equivalent of the algorithmic learning of old.

The presence of the calculator and computer requires a significant reappraisal of the way the curriculum is organized. It would be wrong to suggest that there is any real consensus or confidence among teachers about how best to use the potential contained within the new technology. Indeed there are many teachers of the subject who have still not mastered either the calculator or the microcomputer in a way that makes them capable of a balanced understanding of what is possible. Increasingly mathematics must be appreciated as something best done as a partnership between human beings and machines. It makes no sense whatever to deny to the pupil the modern accepted ways of doing arithmetic (the calculator) or for producing graphical display, solutions of equations and statistical analysis (the computer). There is no suggestion that the understanding of ideas should be reduced. In fact the opposite is possible with more human time devoted to conceptual understanding and more machine time to routine tasks. What is needed, above all, is intelligent use of the new technology and the curriculum must be such as to allow teachers to find ways of bringing that about in their pupils. At present, many pupils are extremely competent with computers and there is a danger that the teachers will prevent their development because their own competence lags behind that of the pupils.

Of particular importance where calculators and computers are used is the absence of a necessity to restrict the complexity of what is done. Providing there is understanding the assistance of new technology makes it possible to deal with complicated situations as easily as simple ones. One important consequence is to encourage the use of mathematics in a wide range of real situations which provide the motive to find solutions to problems that arise. The great advantage is that mathematics can be used in a natural way and be seen to be useful.

Important Current Issues

The Cockcroft Report has provided an extremely important forum for the debate about mathematics in schools. Coming at the time it did it enabled discussion about the development of GCSE and the associated curriculum change to take place against the background of a well-researched and wide-ranging statement about all aspects of mathematics. The report, however, pinpointed several crucial problems and it is important to realize that, since its publication, certain of these have become even more serious and others have arisen. In this final section it is proposed to deal with three issues that concern not only mathematics itself but which have wider implications for curriculum planning and school organization. They are the shortage of teachers in the subject, the differential performance of boys and girls in mathematics and some further points about the impact of the microcomputer on learning, teaching and the content of the curriculum.

Teacher Shortage

A shortage of teachers of mathematics has been acknowledged for more than twenty years but has only recently (DES, 1986) been officially accepted as a problem of crisis dimensions. Early optimism that the recent fall in pupil numbers and the consequent reduced need for teachers would solve the problem of a shortage in mathematics has very quickly been seen to be quite misplaced. The rate of entry of new mathematics teachers into the profession has been well below the level to replace losses (let alone build up numbers) for many years and the wastage rate from the profession is higher than the average for all subjects. And yet the importance of there being an adequate number of well-qualified, able teachers to respond to the new demands of the mathematics curriculum discussed earlier cannot be overemphasized.

Traditional views of mathematics as tightly prescribed by carefully structured text-books and with an emphasis on learning a series of discrete techniques, has given to many teachers the idea that mathematics is easy to teach. The development of process-oriented work, investigations and projects will demonstrate clearly that that idea is no longer tenable. The subject is just as difficult to teach as any other subject, if not more so, and requires a large number of excellent teachers if it is to be maintained as a compulsory subject in the curriculum.

In recent months there have been a number of attempts to counter the shortage. Higher education institutions have received large sums of money to mount new programmes designed to attract more people into teaching the subject and it remains to be seen how successful these initiatives will be. It would be wrong to be more than guardedly optimistic because all the signs are that the problem is both severe and deep-seated. A-level entries for mathematics, which had shown a steady increase for many years, have now begun to fall back, possibly at a greater rate than the decline in the number of pupils of the appropriate age. Even during the period of increasing entry numbers those following an A-level course in mathematics were also following an increasingly mixed A-level programme in general. The old dichotomy in the sixth form between arts pupils and science pupils has long since gone. The result has been that the larger number of passes at A-level has not resulted in equivalent increases in those following the subject in higher education. Numbers on mathematics degree courses have stayed reasonably steady for many years and there has been evidence recently that applications for such courses are now falling. At the end of a mathematics degree course a smaller percentage of students opt for teacher training than in previous years; the percentage has declined from over twenty to less than ten in the last twenty years; and all the signs are that alternative careers for mathematics graduates are becoming more numerous and tend to be more attractive financially. It has to be accepted, therefore, that the teaching of the subject in schools may have to be achieved in a situation of persistent teacher shortage and that has considerable implications for the organization of the subject and the deployment of staff. One move towards a solution would be a reduction in the amount of time given to the subject. The National Curriculum consultation document does suggest ten per cent of time should be spent on the subject compared to slightly more than that which is currently given. But the change is very small and can have no significant bearing on the shortage problem. Any radical reductions in time allocation would immediately raise questions about the place of mathematics within the whole curriculum and, in particular, its important role as a service to other subjects.

Another development which has implications for the number of qualified teachers has been the introduction of individualized learning schemes which enable pupils to learn on their own or possibly with a reduction in the need for well-qualified teachers. Such schemes certainly provide opportunities for rethinking how some teaching resources can best be used. One such scheme, the Kent Mathematics Project, was set up in the 1960s with the expressed intention of providing a mathematics course which was tailored to individual needs and could be monitored by non-specialists. In writing about this scheme Matthews (1970) wrote 'But the desperate shortage of mathematics teachers suggests the need also for what has been called "a disaster kit". This is a very much more advanced system which is virtually teacher-proof'. The originator of the scheme has written a detailed account of its inception (see Banks, 1971) in which he makes a number of points which remain extremely relevant over twenty years on. The learning, he states, must be self-checking. Each child inevitably follows 'a unique course specifically designed to strengthen weaknesses and cater for special interest. If a teacher cannot get the maximum benefit from the material, the children do better than if the teacher were teaching them in the traditional way'. Current interest in resource-based learning and open-learning is merely an extension of the work of schemes like the Kent Mathematics Project. The implications for the mathematics curriculum are considerable for, as has been mentioned above, 'openness' in learning implies that the contents of what is learnt are not confined to a defined list. Apart from the basic skills discussed earlier, there is no particular virtue in learning some parts of mathematics rather than others. The range of choice in the subject is so vast that, giving open access through resource-based systems to a larger content base, individual children will certainly follow uniquely different programmes and often learn material not known to teachers. The possibilities may well be exciting given the prospect of the availability of computer-controlled systems, interactive video-disc systems and so on. Developments of this type are currently being considered by Wakefield LEA and interesting work has already been carried out at Holyrood School and reported by Rainbow (1987). Open learning, by definition, seems to operate in defiance of subject boundaries and, once again, the question of how mathematics relates to other subjects and how it can be integrated into all the work of a school becomes an important one still to be resolved. Such prospects as these, which are now opening up, call once again into question the advisability of setting too precise attainment targets at various ages.

Differential Performance of Girls and Boys

A second problem issue which is receiving a lot of attention at present is the differential performance of girls and boys. The evidence that girls do less well in the subject is considerable and has been well summarized in the Cockcroft Report. What is not understood well enough yet is how to reduce the differential. In a world that is able to absorb mathematical talent with ease it is clear that girls are an under-used resource. There has been a considerable effort to reduce sex bias in books, teaching materials and examination questions and teachers are becoming more aware of the deep-seated attitudes that persist in classrooms in favour of boys. It is also true that attitudes in society have changed dramatically towards the education and employment of women but there is still some way to go in order to achieve equality in mathematical opportunity. One sad factor is that, in an age of equality a new subject, computing, has arisen which has turned out to be one of the most sexually divisive of all subjects. Computing has an important place in mathematics education and may therefore further contribute to the sexual division in the subject. Whatever decisions are made about the mathematical curriculum in the near future, the needs of girls will need very careful and very sensitive handling. Considerable efforts must be made throughout schooling to ensure true equality in the subject. Consequently careful guidelines need to be produced to ensure that the subject is as 'girl-friendly' as possible. It is also important to maintain careful evaluation of the situation as time goes by and to continue to identify new ways in which the subject can be made more attractive to girls.

The Impact of the Microcomputer

The third problem is related to the rapid increase in the use of microcomputers in schools which has been referred to earlier. The rate of increase is very great indeed and it is interesting to note that the Cockcroft Report, although it devoted a short section to the place of computers in mathematics teaching, gave no real indication of the enormous consequences of their use which are beginning to be realized. A much more detailed analysis of their potential was subsequently given by Fletcher (1983) but that report is also now out of date.

The use of computers in mathematics should not be confused with the subject known as computer studies. The two are quite distinct although the distinction has been blurred over the years by the fact that computer studies in schools has been taught for many years by mathematics teachers. Because of the ease of use of computers in some mathematical work it seemed obvious to many mathematics teachers that they should get involved in computer studies. The signs now are that computer studies in its own right is losing ground as the use of computers across the curriculum becomes more widespread.

In mathematics itself there are clearly many different uses ranging from drill and practice routines, where the computer plays the part of an extremely patient but unimaginative tutor generating endless simple exercises, to extremely imaginative simulations and adventure games where the mathematical activity is embedded in highly motivating contexts. One particular difference between these extremes of use is that the drill and practice programmes use material which is completely under the control of the teachers whilst in the simulations and games what is learnt by the pupil may not be known by the teacher and, even if it were, may not be learned in a way with which the teacher is familiar. This point relates back to similar remarks made earlier about the implications of open-learning in which the computer plays a vital role.

There is another problem that the presence of the computer poses.

On the one hand the computer has obvious value as an aid in teaching and learning the currently accepted content of the mathematics syllabus. On the other hand the very presence of the computer has an impact on that content that has not yet been fully appreciated and which could be quite revolutionary. In addition the new approach of learning mathematics in partnership with a computer, using it as an extension of the learners' intellectual power, typifies the subject as it exists in society at the present time. The consequences for mathematics education are extremely important and will need deep consideration in the years ahead.

The computer also enables many new things to be done in mathematics which were not possible before its advent. The ability of the computer to generate very large collections of numbers and to display results is one. Another is the ability to search systematically for answers. The graphical possibilities of the computer are also an important influence on geometry making the explanation of the properties of shapes potentially quite different from hitherto.

Current developments are very rapid indeed. So rapid that it is now frequently the case that pupils are more expert than those teachers who have studiously avoided involvement. The consequence, therefore, of the presence of the computer is to reinforce points made earlier about content openness. Computer interaction by pupils can easily lead them into areas of the subject not planned by the teachers and possibly not known by them. It may well be in consequence that it will be much easier in future for a few educationists to produce materials to be used directly by children rather than to attempt to retrain teachers to act as 'middle men or women'. What is clear is that the presence of the computer in the home, the school and society in general will have profound consequences for both mathematics itself and mathematics education, and the rate of change in the way computers are used must be absorbed as rapidly as possible into the work of the schools.

The three particular issues discussed here have very different implications for the curriculum. They each, in different ways, suggest that considerable curriculum development is both needed and inevitable in the near future. It is to be hoped that any new frameworks for mathematics arising from the setting up of a National Curriculum do not succeed in stifling the opportunities for worthwhile innovations.

References

BANKS, B. (1971) 'The Disaster Kit', *Mathematical Gazette*, Vol. LV, No. 391, pp. 17–22.

BROWN, M. and KUCHEMANN, D. (1976 and 1977) 'Is it an "Add", Miss?' *Mathematics in Schools*, Vol. 5, No. 5, pp. 15–17 and Vol. 6, No. 1, pp. 9–10.

COCKCROFT, W.H. (1982) *Mathematics Counts*, The Cockcroft Report, London, HMSO.

COOPER, B. (1985) *Renegotiating Secondary School Mathematics*, Lewes, Falmer Press.

DEPARTMENT OF EDUCATION AND SCIENCE (1984) *The Organization and Content of the 5–16 Curriculum*, London, HMSO.

DEPARTMENT OF EDUCATION AND SCIENCE (1986) *Action on Teacher Supply in Mathematics, Physics and Technology*, London, HMSO.

DEPARTMENT OF EDUCATION AND SCIENCE (1987) *The National Curriculum 5–16: A Consultation Document*, London, HMSO.

EXPENDITURE COMMITTEE OF THE HOUSE OF COMMONS (1977) *The Attainments of the School Leaver*, London, HMSO.

FITZGERALD, A. (1981) *Mathematics in Employment (16–18)*, University of Bath, Bath.

FITZGERALD, A. (1985) *New Technology and Mathematics in Employment*, University of Birmingham, Birmingham.

FLETCHER, T.J. (1983) *Microcomputers and Mathematics in Schools*, Department of Education and Science, London, HMSO.

HADAMARD, J. (1945) *The Psychology of Invention in the Mathematical Field*, Princeton, University Press, Princeton.

HALL, G.G. (1978) 'Applied Mathematics' in WAIN, G.T. (Ed.), *Mathematical Education*, Van Nostrand Reinhold.

HART, K.M. (1981) *Children's Understanding of Mathematics 11–16*, John Murray, London.

MATTHEWS, G. (1970) 'Cards, modules and kits', *Mathematical Gazette*, vol. LIV, No. 388, pp. 131–137.

ORMELL, C.P. (1975) *Mathematics Changes Gear*, Heinemann/Schools Council.

POLLARD, M. *et al* (1983–5) *Today's World Series: North Sea Oil; Coal in Britain; Energy Search; The Living Town; The Living Countryside; Patterns of Living*, Holt, Rinehart and Winston, Eastbourne.

RAINBOW, R. (1987) *Making Supported Self-Study Work: The Holyrood School Experience*, Council for Educational Technology, London.

SEWELL, B. (1981) *Use of Mathematics by Adults in Daily Life*, Advisory Council for Adult and Continuing Education, Leicester.

WAIN, G.T. (1983) 'Mathematics and other subjects,' *Educational Analysis*, Vol. 5, No. 3.

WAIN, G.T. and WYNNE WILLSON, W.S. (1987) '13, 14, 15: An investigation,' *Mathematical Gazette*, Vol. 71, No. 455, pp. 32–7.

2　*Moral and Religious Education*

Peter Mitchell

Moral Education

Its Traditional Status

British education has always had a strongly moral tone. Schools have been seen as places not only where knowledge was to be gained and under-standing increased, but also where characters were to be formed and values inculcated. Sometimes the motives were rather questionable, as was the opinion that a body of schoolmasters would be cheaper than a force of policemen. But not always. Often there was a genuine concern that the experience of schooling would influence for the good the be-haviour and attitudes of the pupils.

Thus in the new schools of the Victorian era values such as honesty, truth telling, obedience, hardwork, thrift, loyalty and the like received high praise. And these virtues found an advocacy over the whole range of English education.[1] Of course, important distinctions must be drawn between what received most emphasis for the poor and most for the rich.[2] And there were exceptions. Education has never been wholly monolithic and value conflicts have never been entirely absent from the educational scene. But on the whole a general picture can be drawn of moral unani-mity. The moral task of the school was unquestioned, and though they were often vague and ill-defined, the moral goals were largely agreed. Radical complaints such as Tolstoy's that English schools allowed no place for protest and choice were either unknown or unheeded by most English educators.[3]

Present Popular Expectations

The continuing influence for good or bad of this past story can be seen in many present day pronouncements on the place of moral education in English schools. Debates in parliament and reports in the mass media

Peter Mitchell

on educational topics all too frequently refer to the failure of schools to provide strong moral guidance in areas as diverse as soccer hooliganism, drug abuse, family breakdowns and workshop ill-discipline. Even teachers join in these complaints. So, for example, a resolution passed at the 1987 conference of the National Association of Schoolmasters/Union of Women Teachers (NAS/UTW) states, 'The education service should play a positive role in trying to reverse the rising tide of violence.'

Diverse Reports — HMI and DES Curriculum Guides

A more sophisticated approach is to be found in official documents originating from the DES or HMI during the 1970s and 1980s. Documents such as *Education in Schools*, (1977). *Curriculum 11–16*, (1977), *A Framework for the School Curriculum*, (1980), *The School Curriculum*, (1981) and *The Curriculum from 5–16, Curriculum Matters 2*, (1985), all agree that the moral dimension ought to be an essential component of the school curriculum. Thus *Education in Schools* includes amongst the educational aims of schools the need 'to instil respect for moral values'.[4] *Curriculum 11–16* goes further and states that pupils 'should be able to begin to formulate a personal code of conduct and to develop enough conviction to live by it.'[5] And in *A Basis for Choice* (1979) the Further Education Unit (FEU), concerned with development of post-16 pre-vocational courses, recommended a common core curriculum which amongst other things should 'provide a basis on which the young person acquires a set of moral values applicable to issues in contemporary society.'[6] Thus by 1985 *Curriculum 5–16* takes it as beyond argument that the curriculum of all schools should involve pupils in the moral area of learning and experience.[7]

However, whilst the importance of moral education is universally acknowledged, there are significant differences in the tone of the various documents. Two different strands of thought begin to emerge. On one side *Curriculum 11–16* in 1977 asserts, 'It is also safe to assume that the 1980s will not see a society based on a single set of values — indeed, the trend to pluralism is likely to continue and the next decade may well see an increasing polarization of views'. The virtues therefore to be fostered are 'tolerance and empathy' and the educational experiences to which pupils are to be exposed are 'not only of listening and talking to, but of living alongside, people of different persuasions and convictions.'[8]

From one point of view this reflects the optimism and confusions of the sixties and early seventies. The moral consensus has broken down. Value positions vary. So what is required is tolerance of those with whom you differ and courage to work out your own solutions and to live by them. Admittedly this poses problems. The document recognizes that this emphasis on the 'autonomous citizen' can lead to conflict with the role of

42

education in preparing pupils to take their place in society, but it is a conflict which is left largely unresolved.[9]

By 1985 the atmosphere has changed and the requirements of *Curriculum 5–16* are significantly different. The starting point is the school community itself. There are principles such as fairness and justice which are to be commended to pupils and this can only be done when teachers and other adults exemplify these same principles by their own lives and actions in the school community. Indeed, the school itself is a moral arena 'which provides experience which help to form and test moral convictions and to modify attitudes'. And there are moral facts with which pupils must come to terms. 'The views and feelings of others must be taken into account', and 'the interests of the institution must be weighed against those of the individual.' Even more important, where there are disputes 'the rational resolution of disagreement is possible and desirable'.[10] Far from emphasizing the breakdown of moral consensus, the document asserts that 'schools, homes and society at large are at pains to encourage values and qualities in pupils which will result in attitudes characteristic of a good citizen in a democratic, humane and free society'.[11] Whilst, therefore, 'no school can, or should seek to conceal from its pupils the fact that there are moral questions on which people of equal integrity and thoughtfulness may reach quite different conclusions', the emphasis is on what is shared. Schools 'have a clear duty to ground their pupils, by teaching and example, in those widely shared moral values like tolerance, honesty, fidelity, and openness to the truth which are essential for the conduct of individual and social life'.[12]

A similar emphasis can be found in the third report of the Education, Science and Arts Select Committee of the House of Commons, concerned with primary education (1986). It states, 'ultimately a society stands or falls by its social cohesion and by shared moral values. Education, perhaps particularly primary education, has a crucial role to play in promoting and safeguarding that cohesion and these values.'[13]

Moral Education and Moral Pluralism

These developments, however, do not merely represent a transient change of emphasis, two sides of the same coin. Rather they illustrate two very different approaches to moral education.[14] The first sees the subject as essentially concerned with controversial matters. This is not just because of the epistemological point that human knowledge is always open to future correction in the light of fresh information or more coherent theories. The problem is more fundamental than that. For in this view the value judgments which underlie moral actions are not open to any known knockdown proof. No authority, therefore, has any right to demand the acceptance of one set of values as opposed to any other. Each individual must make up his or her mind which set of values he or she is to follow. What is of supreme value is the pupil's autonomy as a free agent who must make his or her moral choices in a responsible and rational manner.

The educational tasks of the school follow from this. It must beware of imposing a set of values on the pupil. Any such attempt is labelled as indoctrination. Instead it must open the pupils' minds to the wide range of existing value positions and help them to become aware of the consequences of holding such positions. It must ensure that they learn how to engage in critical reflection at an appropriate level on their own and other people's value commitments. It must also help them to act consistently and courageously in accordance with their own values.

Of course, this approach to moral education itself reflects adherence to a complex set of values such as the worth of individual liberty, the importance of critical reflection and the necessity to show tolerance towards other people with differing values. It also presupposes the worth of courage and persistence in following one's own views in the face of opposition or derision. But all these things are seen more as procedural rather than as substantive values able to stand in their own right.

Not surprisingly this approach to moral education encapsulates the libertarian values of a free society with its emphasis on individual freedom and personal choice. It rests on an approach to education which stresses the need for pupils to learn how to subject all things to rational scrutiny and to develop into free autonomous agents. And it does at least represent an attempt to be sensitive to the presence in our society of large ethnic and religious minorities with their own distinctive value systems.

Such an attitude to moral education finds its classic expression in the 'value clarification' approach, popular though now also under attack in the United States, and used in a modified way in some English schools.[15] It can be found to a greater or lesser extent in the work of 'The Humanities Project', (1970),[16] the Schools Council Moral Education Projects, (1972 and 1978)[17] and the various influential writings of John Wilson (1967 onwards),[18] though in the later cases there is often also an appeal to some overriding principle expressed in non-authoritarian terms such as 'the need to get on with others, to love and be loved', or the desirability of maximizing happiness, and in Wilson's case there is a much greater emphasis on the use of rational procedures in establishing your own moral position.[19]

Moral Education and Shared Values

In contrast the alternative approach to moral education is concerned with the values we share. It begins not with the individual, but with the community and its shared basic moral values. To become a person able to contribute to and participate in a constructive way in the corporate life of the community the pupil has to be initiated into these shared values.

This form of moral education, however, has to be distinguished from a mere socialization into the conventions and mores of a given society. It aims to be more than this, else all it would produce would be unreflective and uncritical members of the social world, unable to act as agents of moral advance and improvement. Pupils have to be taught to stand back from their immediate concerns, to grasp something of the subject's complexities and to reflect critically upon it. But the starting point is the moral wisdom of humankind. There are moral principles to be learnt, such as justice and fairness, virtues to be emulated, such as honesty, loyalty, compassion and dependability, and fundamental human rights to be upheld, such as the right to life and liberty. Their application, relative balance, and embodiment are not easy matters. But they are the foundations of the moral life. The purpose of their practice is to enable human social life to flourish in a morally praiseworthy way. It is with these that schools ought to be concerned.

In moral education, therefore, the starting point for this approach is the school and the pupil's place in it. The school is viewed as an embryonic moral community, and the pupil, as a participating member, has to come to see the point of and share in the moral principles, virtues and rights embodied in its life and work. The hope is that he or she will thereby come to appreciate the place and hopefully participate in the practice and defence of these same values in the wider community.

Traditional defenders of this kind of moral education tend to emphasize the importance of those 'natural' linkages and relationships such as the family which bind society together. More radically inclined advocates of this point of view stress the necessity of becoming alert and reforming citizens keenly aware of the exploited and deprived sections of society. The focus of attention in both is not on learning to choose one's own values, but rather on the givenness of morality and the need for pupils to become responsible citizens who are able to direct their lives according to those shared values upon which the kind of social or community life we prize depends.

In the field of moral education the work of Peters and Hirst was in some respects a precursor of this position.[20] For, in spite of their emphasis on rational autonomy and the importance of the individual, their acceptance of a set of substantive moral principles to which all rational persons ought to adhere provides a strong educational argument for giving moral education a specific content. Even more significant is the direction taken by the work of Kohlberg, one of the dominant figures in the field of moral education. Beginning with the fundamental moral principle of justice, he sought to show how an understanding of this could be developed through a series of well defined stages in the intellectual life of the child. But he has now gone on to stress the importance of moral action and to investigate ways of building collective norms and ideas of community in the life of the school through what is sometimes called the 'Just Community Approach'.[21]

Agreement and Diversity

Where then does this leave moral education as an element in the school curriculum? It is unlikely that either of the views outlined above are adequate on their own. The first begins with moral controversy. But controversy is only possible where there is already a large measure of agreement. It also tends to emphasize the rights of the individual at the expense of society. But human beings are social creatures. Unless society is morally flourishing the individual stands little chance of preserving his or her independence and individuality. And as a member of society the individual has shared obligations and duties as well as personal rights and opportunities.

On the other hand the second approach lays great stress on moral unanimity. But the field of morality includes matters of dispute as well as areas of consensus. Indeed, an overemphasis upon agreement could easily turn moral education into a means of producing social conformity, an instrument by which the state could ensure that its citizens were obedient to the dominant ideology.

Moral education is, therefore, legitimately concerned with the initiation of pupils into the shared values of our society. But it has also to enable pupils to understand the nature and extent of moral controversy and provide them with the intellectual space in which they can learn to form their own moral judgments. If shared values alone are emphasized, controversial matters can receive too little attention. So the requirement of the 1986 Education Act that sex education be carried out in the context of family values seems to close down controversy too soon. And of course on the other side those who wish above all to introduce controversial topics to pupils can too easily ignore the social context and consensual values involved. The early attempt of the Humanities project to treat racism as a controversial area and some of the recent attempts to introduce teaching on homosexuality to younger pupils are examples of this. Recent legislation shows all too clearly the difficulty of achieving a proper balance in schools between what are accepted as shared values and what is legitimately controversial. So the same 1986 Education Act requires that when pupils are introduced to political issues 'they are offered a balanced presentation of opposing views', whilst the 1987 Local Government Bill outlaws the presentation of certain attitudes to homosexuality.

Moral Judgments and Moral Dispositions

Two further controversies have added to the complexity of the moral educator's task. Firstly, to what extent should moral education transcend the cognitive? No one would doubt that an important objective of moral education is to help pupils to think more clearly and with increasing sophistication about moral issues. Pupils need to be aided to become more mature in their moral judgments. Kohlberg's claim that the quality of a person's moral judgments improves as he or she progresses through a series of well defined and invariable stages of moral development is especially important here. And many classroom techniques have been devised to help this process on, such as the use of moral dilemmas, case studies, debates and structured discussions.

But is this enough? Morality is concerned not only with the capacity to make sound moral judgments, but also with the formation of appropriate moral dispositions, and especially with a willingness and capacity to feel concern and care for others. The development or mastery of emotions such as sympathy, affection, jealousy, envy, anger and the like form an important part of the moral life. It is, however, a matter of some dispute how far moral educators are justified in entering the emotional lives of their pupils. Some object on the grounds that it intrudes too much into what is personal and private and does not sufficiently guard the child's autonomy. Nevertheless, unless the pupil is able to feel concern for others and sympathetically appreciate their feelings and attitudes, it is unlikely that much moral progress will be made.

Moral Knowledge and Moral Action

Secondary, how far ought moral educators to be concerned with the behaviour of their pupils? This is not so straightforward as it seems. Of course moral judgments are intimately connected to behaviour. A central reason for helping children to become more expert in making moral judgments is so that their resulting actions will be morally praiseworthy. But correct thoughts do not always lead to correct actions. Moral educators have therefore become increasingly concerned to explore the connection between moral judgments and behaviour. But what of moral weakness, where behaviour does not match intellectual comprehension?[22] Ought the moral educator to become involved in programmes of behaviour modification or in the deliberate inculcation of 'good' habits? Again this would appear to undermine the development of the pupil's autonomy. Yet, especially with younger pupils, the formation of 'good' habits seems to be an essential part of their moral education.[23]

Moral Education in Practice

Partly because of these problems schools have found it difficult to respond adequately to demands to provide a satisfactory moral education for their pupils. Many schools across the whole age spectrum along with their LEAs include some reference to the moral dimension in the brochures or policy documents which they are now required to produce. Most find it much harder to translate such aims into a coherent curriculum provision.

A few schools continue to adhere to the tradition in English education that believes in an implicit approach to moral education. In this view values such as 'integrity, truthfulness and respect show themselves, or fail to show themselves, in the teaching and learning of the intellectual disciplines'.[24] It is claimed that if the school is true to its character as a learning institution, moral education can be left to look after itself. But whilst it is true that the moral dimension pervades the whole life and work of the school, this approach on its own leaves far too much to chance.

Many schools, therefore, now offer pupils opportunities to explore moral questions in a more direct and explicit way. Traditional school subjects often include a value component in their curriculum provisions. This is especially true in science education, but similar developments can be found in geography, history, English and religious studies. There has also been an explosion of courses, particularly at the secondary level, which are directly concerned with aspects of morality. Active tutorial work, personal and social education courses, world studies and peace education, multicultural education, health education and modular units on life skills in the vocationally-orientated programmes of TVEI, all to a greater or lesser extent include a moral education dimension in their work.

Almost all these areas of the curriculum have attracted study groups, professional associations, development and research literature and LEA curriculum guides. Perhaps the most notable of these has been the general field of pastoral care with its own national association, termly journal and numerous publications.[25] But similar things can be said about peace studies, world studies, multicultural education, health education and religious studies. And there has also been research into the provision made in specific localities, such as the Dudley Project (1982–4),[26] which have wider curriculum implications.

Some efforts have been made to produce materials suitable for use in the primary school, beginning with the Schools Council project, *Startline*, (1978) aimed at the middle school years, and including Olwen Goodall's work at Exeter with younger children.[27] The School Curriculum Development Committee have recently funded work by Dr. Brian Gates in the area of inservice training concerned with moral education for 5 to 8 year olds. And a few LEAs have prepared curriculum guides at the primary level, for example, Wiltshire's *Social and Personal Education: A Primary Curriculum Document*. In addition there has been some exploration of the role of school assemblies in moral education.

Outstanding Problems

What is largely missing are any agreed detailed objectives for moral education and any sustained attempt to work out the concepts, attitudes and skills necessary for advance in this area. John Wilson's early attempts to do this have not, for a variety of reasons, carried much weight and both official documents and school curricula remain very vague in this direction. Whilst more recent work by educationalists such Pring (1982; 1984; 1985)[28] are important steps in this direction, they remain at the level of personal endeavour and have not yet been translated on any large scale into curriculum action. There is also no agreement as to the proper balance which ought to be struck between the cognitive and academic on the one side and the social, emotional and practical on the other.

As a result schools' efforts in the field of moral education are too often fragmented and lacking in direction and coherence, leaving largely unanswered the central question as to how the link between moral understanding and behaviour is to be established in the day to day life of the school. There is also a danger of the New Vocationalism engaging in mere tokenism, offering an evaluative or moral element which it then fails to deliver. It is rare for schools to have a co-ordinated policy on moral education with a proper focus of responsibility. Yet this is something which becomes increasingly important as courses multiply and different areas of the curriculum acknowledge their values implications. Even those who wish to emphasize the importance of the moral atmosphere of the school and the necessity of participating in the shared values of our society rarely make clear exactly what this entails. And since this topic mainly lies outside the orbit of public examinations it has not yet benefited from the intense discussions on aims and objectives which has accompanied the development of the new GCSE.

Signs of Hope

Nevertheless, all is not gloom or darkness. A professional association for personal and social values in education is being formed[29] and a national network of centres for the study and promotion of the subject is coming into existence. There are, for example, The Moral Education Centre, St. Martin's College, Lancaster; the Centre for Social and Moral Education, University of Leicester; and the Centre for the Study of Personal, Social and Moral Education, University of Exeter. And the Social Morality Council has been active in this area for a number of years. Journals are being published, including *The Journal of Moral Education* and more recently *Values*, books for teachers and pupils are being produced, and a number of LEAs have appointed advisors for this curriculum area. The foundations have been laid and there is the possibility of large scale advance. As in many things much depends on adequate resources being made available. Whether they will be is another and more sombre question.

Religious Education

Agreed Syllabuses

Tradition and statute have combined to give religious education an entrenched position in the school curriculum. And in spite of complaints from such varied bodies as the National Union of Teachers (NUT)[30] and the Swann Committee,[31] there seems little likelihood of this situation changing to any large extent in the near future. The 1987 Education (Reform) Bill largely retains the status quo given legal form by the 1944 Education Act.

However, whilst the 1944 Education Act confirmed the long standing position of religious education in English schools and placed upon schools the legal obligation to provide religious instruction and daily acts of worship, it left undefined what that instruction should be. Instead this task was entrusted not to the schools, but to local standing conferences on which representatives of the churches and other religious groups, the teachers and the politicians were to serve, each group being given a right of veto. The decisive power in syllabus construction thereby passed to bodies outside the school, and it says much for the moderation and common sense of such organizations that this has rarely been felt to be an irksome restriction by teachers of religious education.[32]

Indeed, from such arrangements certain beneficial consequences have flowed, which may help to explain why opposition from schools has been so muted. Locally sanctioned agreed syllabuses can act as a convenient buffer between schools and any pressure groups wishing to object to what is being taught in an area which is potentially very divisive and controversial. And syllabus constructors and revisers have been obliged to keep in touch with the changing religious situation in their own localities. Agreed syllabuses have also often been the means of introducing innovations and reform into the subject area itself. Some agreed syllabuses have become relatively short documents supported by handbooks of suggestions. And as these have been produced largely by serving teachers, they have become a useful way of disseminating examples of good practice over a wider area.

Nevertheless, it still remains something of an anomaly that those who are part of the subject matter of religious education, that is the churches and other religious groups, should themselves have a power of veto over what is included in the syllabus. Only the system of careful checks and balances written into the 1944 Act has prevented this from becoming a straightforward contradiction.

DES and HMI Reports

Papers and reports emanating from the DES and HMI have accepted these statutory requirements as the framework for their suggestions about the nature and objectives of religious education. They agree that it is to be part of the core curriculum of all children except for those withdrawn on grounds of conscience. But once the attempt is made to go beyond this general requirement a certain vagueness almost inevitably surrounds what is recommended. Even in today's political climate central bodies can hardly be expected openly to arrogate to themselves what has been so firmly delegated in a statutory way to locally based decisions. It is significant that recent pronouncements about a nationally imposed curriculum have left the content of religious education to be settled by the present local arrangements.

However, some attempts have been made in various official documents to delineate what is involved in this area of the curriculum. Thus the spiritual is accepted by the relevant DES and HMI documents as one of the areas of experience with which the curriculum is to be concerned. But not until *Curriculum 5–16* (1985) are we provided with any detailed direct exposition of what is meant by this term.

According to this document the spiritual 'point at its most general to feelings and convictions about the significance of human life and the world as a whole which pupils may experience within themselves and meet at second hand in their study of the works and way of life of other people'. And it involves a recognition that 'there is a side of human nature and experience which can be only partially explained in rational or intellectual terms'. There is an 'element of mystery in human experience' borne witness to by dance, drama, music, art and literature, the sense of which can be evoked by a feeling of awe at the natural world or by aesthetic as well as explicitly religious experiences. It is necessary for pupils to acknowledge, reflect upon and value such experiences. 'Religious education ... is contained within this area but is not identical with it.' A central purpose of religious education, which it shares with other subjects, is, therefore, to help pupils to reflect 'upon those aspects of human life and the natural world which raise questions of ultimate meaning and purpose, and to recognize the spiritual dimension of experience'.[33]

Coupled to this subjective element in religious education, and providing an essential part of the raw material for this kind of investigation, is the more objective study of the world's major religious traditions and especially Christianity. Religions other than Christianity are to be studied partly because they are now significantly represented in our society and partly because they form an essential part of man's 'religious quest'. But the documents accept that Christianity should be given a central place in this study 'because of its pervasive influence on this country's religious life, history and culture',[34] and because for most pupils 'it is the most familiar form in which they encounter expressions of religion'.[35]

There remains a certain ambiguity in these documents about the relationship between religious and moral education. On the one hand the distinctive nature of morality is fully accepted. Yet on the other religious education is frequently closely connected to social practices and moral education. So in the 1978 HMI survey of primary education in England we read of 'social abilities, including religious education', and in the DES *A Framework for the School Curriculum* (1980) 'the Secretaries of State consider it right, as is commonly the case, for religious education to be linked with the wider consideration of personal and social values'.[36] This is echoed in *The School Curriculum* (1981). 'It forms part of the curriculum's concern with personal values.' *The Curriculum 11–16* (1977) went further. Whilst accepting that moral issues were not necessarily tied to religious settings, 'nevertheless, religious belief can have a powerful influence on conduct and any adequate religious education must provide not merely discussion of the ethical implications which arise from religion but also an opportunity for the practical expression of ethical concerns'.[37] A much less specific connection between religious and moral education is to be found in *The Curriculum from 5–16* (1985) perhaps reflecting the changing social situation and the desire to find common moral values which all can share.

The House of Commons Select Committee on Education

In contrast a rather different attitude to religious education can be discerned in the House of Commons Select Committee's report on achievement in primary schools (1986). 'England remains predominantly a Christian country and many who are not necessarily practising Christians nevertheless support Christian ideals.'[38] Schemes of work should therefore reflect the predominance of the Christian faith as well as an appreciation of the diversity of faiths now current in England.

The implication here seems to be that religious education is in some way an initiation into this dominant faith, an interpretation that is reinforced by the distinction which the committee draws between religious education and a comparative study of different religions and cultures. However, the report also recognizes that this approach is not entirely in harmony with the general educational tasks of county schools. There is, it accepts, a distinction between introducing and informing children about religious beliefs and engaging them in these beliefs and practices. The Committee acknowledges that the multi-faith nature of society is leading towards an acceptance of the former task as more appropriate to county schools, but it claims that the time for this move has not yet arrived.[39]

Progress since 1944

The 1944 Act was undoubtedly originally intended to make possible a similar confessional approach to the subject. Although the word 'Christian' does not appear in the Act, it was nevertheless hoped that most pupils would be initiated into the values and beliefs of Christianity very broadly understood. Specific denominational teaching was to be left to the denominational schools. The complex arrangements about agreed syllabuses and rights of withdrawal only make sense if placed in this confessional context.

By the late 1960s opinion had moved strongly against this approach, and in 1971 the Schools Council project on religious education in the secondary school came out decisively against confessional religious education.[40] It was inappropriate in schools serving a multi-belief society and was contrary to the modern open-ended critical approach to education. Instead, religious education was now to be concerned with the personal search for meaning by the individual pupil and the objective study of the phenomena of religion. Admittedly, it found it difficult to integrate these two aspects and so tended to stress the phenomenological study of religions, but both were necessary elements in religious education. And as *Discovering an Approach* (1977),[41] the primary school continuation of the Schools Council RE Project, stressed, this study of religion was to be plural, i.e. not limited to any one religious tradition, open, exploratory and above all aimed at developing the pupil's understanding.

The Ground Plan for the Study of Religion (1977)[42] went further and endeavoured to set out the intellectual framework required for the study of religion. As well as factual knowledge it involves understanding and evaluation. And this understanding is not only concerned with the central concepts of a religion but also with the emotions and feelings characteristic of that tradition along with its important rituals, actions and activities. The understanding with which religious education is concerned, therefore, is not to be limited to religious beliefs but must extend to the religion seen as a whole.

Most recent agreed syllabuses reflect this general approach,[43] some putting more stress on the pupil's search for meaning and others emphasizing the need to understand the nature of religion. So, for example, the Berkshire agreed syllabus (1982) is entitled 'Religious Heritage and Personal Quest', and the Bedfordshire agreed syllabus (1985) states, 'The aim of religious education in schools is to contribute educationally to the development of pupils as individuals and members of society by fostering a reflective approach to life in the context of a growing understanding of the experiences, attitudes, beliefs and religious practices of mankind.' The Cambridgeshire syllabus (1982) has a more stark aim. It is 'to enable pupils to understand the nature of religion, its beliefs and practices'.

The Scope of Religious Education

Thus in recent years the brief of religious education has undergone a transformation. Firstly, its scope has been considerably enlarged. Its field is now seen as the religious experiences of mankind with all the richness and diversity which that implies. The documents from the DES and HMI faithfully reflect this situation. Gone is the traditional approach that concentrated almost entirely on the study of biblical material. Instead the subject encompasses the religions of the world. And in place of nurture in a particular faith comes an exploration of the existential questions which arise from human life.

As a consequence of this development principles of selection have had to be devised to make such a vast store of material accessible in the classroom. Study has therefore tended to be concentrated upon five or six major world religions and especially upon their living contemporary manifestations. Material which is studied has, as far as possible, to be first hand and authentic. And religions are seen to involve certain discrete elements or dimensions, some of which are more intelligible and appropriate for younger pupils than others. Even more important has been the search for ideas or concepts which can be used in unifying the study of religion such as celebrations, pilgrimages, holy places, holy books and rites of passage.

The Importance of Understanding in Religious Education

Secondly, the aims or intentions of religious education are now hopefully seen in strictly educational terms. Success and failure is to be measured by the level of understanding achieved by the pupils, not by the beliefs they may come to espouse. And this understanding should be appropriate for the study of religion. Essentially, it should be both critical and open.[44]

By critical is generally meant two things. Firstly, it includes the ability to ask questions about the grounds for beliefs and behaviour in religion. Pupils need to learn how to assess evidence or at least understand why religious believers find certain kinds of evidence convincing. Secondly, it involves the capacity to hold the subject matter at arm's length, even when this relates to one's own beliefs, so that this critical scrutiny becomes in some senses of the word dispassionate though not depersonalized. For this reason an evaluative element has become an important part of religious education. Questions of truth cannot be avoided. But because of the diverse nature of religious beliefs and the neutrality of the county school towards different religious persuasions, this evaluation has in the last resort to be left to the individual pupils themselves. So, for example, the national criteria for the GCSE in religious studies allocates between fifteen per cent and twenty five per cent of the total marks for assessing the evaluative skills of the pupils themselves, but emphasizes that this is meant 'only to assess the extent to which they are able to express and support an opinion coherently'.

Understanding is said to be truly open when an individual is able and willing to see another person's religion from that person's point of view. This requires the development of the pupil's imaginative powers. It also involves qualities such as sympathy, tolerance and respect. An important additional aim of religious education, therefore, is to encourage in pupils attitudes of tolerance and respect towards other people's religious beliefs and practices and a willingness to enter imaginatively into other people's worlds, to see things from their point of view. Learning how to balance critical scrutiny with sympathetic and imaginative openness and to relate both to one's own beliefs and convictions thus becomes an essential but very difficult long term goal of religious education.

Developmental and Social Factors

A third strand in the curriculum development of religious education, and modifying to some extent the first two elements outlined above, has been the increasing recognition of the developmental and social factors which must be taken into account when constructing a religious education syllabus. The developmental factor was brought forcibly to public notice by the work of Goldman who, using Piagetian tools of analysis, claimed to show that the content of traditional biblically-based syllabuses was largely beyond the comprehension of younger children.[45] Their consequent misunderstandings were so deep as to cause irreparable damage to their future grasp of the subject. Whilst the ethnocentric restrictions of his work, the unsatisfactory nature of his solutions and methodological weaknesses in his research have become increasingly apparent,[46] nonetheless the general directions he set for religious education especially for younger pupils have continued to influence syllabus construction.

In order to remedy the deficiencies he uncovered, what is sometimes called implicit religious education has tended to dominate much of what is prescribed for younger primary pupils. This kind of religious education is concerned not with the investigation of the explicit phenomena of religions but with an exploration of the pupil's own experiences of themselves as individual selves and of their relationships with other persons and with the natural world. The hope is that by exploring and expressing their feelings about such experiences, pupils will become directly aware of some of the raw data from which the religious interpretation of life is said to spring. As they get older it is hoped that they will then be able to see connections between their own experiences and those questions and experiences which are claimed to lie at the heart of the religious quest. This will, it is claimed, in turn engender a reflective approach to life and provide a set of concepts which will allow the spiritual dimension of human life to be more fully investigated.

Even where, partly in reaction to this approach, explicitly religious topics are now introduced to younger pupils, it is recognized that care must be taken to relate them closely to the pupils' own experiences and stage of conceptual development. Similarly much more attention is now being given to the development of the general skills and capacities needed to understand the phenomena of religion, and especially the complexities of religious language and symbolism.

The social factors influencing syllabus construction in religious education are even more difficult to disentangle. On the one side there is the growing secularization of the structures and institutions of our society and the apparent decline in institutional religion. On the other side research findings indicate the widespread and largely unexpected occurrence of what seem to be religious experiences in the population as a whole.[47] Adding to the complexity of this situation, there are in some parts of the country sizeable ethnic communities with their own distinctive religious traditions.

Secularization perhaps represents the sharpest challenge to religious education. Many pupils bring to their understanding of religion a conceptual apparatus and a set of values cast in a secular mode. And often they have very little direct contact with religious institutions. They are therefore intellectually and socially very distant from the subject matter being explored. It is not surprising that Hargreaves reports that 'in the supportive research done for *Improving Secondary Schools* (an ILEA policy document produced under his guidance in 1984), RE was seen by pupils as the least useful and most boring subject'.[48] Much modern religious education can be seen as an attempt to overcome this customer resistance by building bridges between the pupils' secular interpretations of life and the data of religion.

The Distinctive Contribution of Religious Education

Religious education as at present conceived is therefore intended to do two things. It attempts to give the pupil access to that dimension of human experience which can be characterized as the spiritual. This task it shares with other subjects on the curriculum. Its own distinctive contribution is that it does this through the world of religions. Its defence is that this is the primary though not the only source of this aspect of human life.. Any exploration of the spiritual would thus be seriously distorted and attenuated if it ignored the world of religions.

Secondly, it helps pupils to explore at levels appropriate to their age and experience those existential questions which have troubled human beings over the centuries. Questions, that is, which are concerned with the nature of human beings, their destiny and purpose, the ideals for which they ought to strive, their response to suffering and death, and their relationship to the world and whatever might lie beyond. But it does not do this in a vacuum. The study of other subjects might and do raise such questions. The distinctive contribution of religious education is that it deals with them in a direct way, and that it does so in the context of the great religious traditions of humankind, where a variety of contrasting but well established methods of coming to terms with such problems can be found. Some of the most promising recent curriculum developments in religious education have involved attempts to integrate these two strands of study into a more coherent whole.[49]

The Status of Christianity

But is this not too large a task for schools to undertake, given the limited time available for the study of religion? Would it not be better to curtail pupils' horizons largely to the study of the Christian tradition? This, so it has been claimed, is much closer to the experience of the large majority of pupils in British schools and therefore is likely to be more intelligible and appropriate for them. And Britain's past history and cultural heritage only makes sense when the story of Christianity is known in some detail.[50]

Lying behind these arguments is the belief that a nation's cultural roots are essential to its contemporary life. Our present flourishing depends on our receiving nourishment from what has gone before. For what gives coherence and stability to a culture are those values and beliefs which have been shaped by and embedded in the national life over the preceding centuries. And Christianity's central role in this cannot be denied.

All this undoubtedly strengthens the view that the study of Christianity should have an important place in religious education in this country.[51] Education of any kind cannot ignore the cultural context in which it takes place. But, as has recently been pointed out, an important function of education is to help pupils transcend the present and the particular.[52] To concentrate attention on one tradition, no matter how noble and illuminating, would be to misrepresent to pupils the nature and complexity of man's religious quest and to limit their intellectual horizons in an unwarranted way. Not only do non-Christian ethnic minorities now live in this country, but even more important the world in which we all live is both multicultural and multi-faith and one in which no single religion is dominant.

Nor is it so obviously true that the study of what is nearest to hand is always the best way of proceeding. What is familiar and known may seem pedestrian and boring. The unusual and the unknown can sometimes stimulate more interest and attention. The danger in the wider study of religions is that this can deteriorate into a investigation of what seems to pupils to be exotic, weird and quaintly irrelevant. But this need not happen. By inculcating attitudes of respect and an appreciation of other people's beliefs and customs such distortions can be avoided. It is for this reason that our treatment of the distinctive religious traditions of our own ethnic minorities becomes an important benchmark on our journey to educational enlightenment. Indeed, Christianity itself is a world religion and its proper study requires more than a parochial attention to its influence on British life.[53]

The Controversial Nature of Religious Education

What all this also shows is that the place of religious education in the school curriculum remains irredeemably controversial. It cannot avoid resting upon a set of ideological presuppositions. It starts from the belief that religions are worthy of respect and that their study sensitively carried out can contribute to human development. But it is possible for societies, or at least their ruling élites, to be so alienated from religion that the subject is banished from the classroom as doing more harm than good, except in so far as it is portrayed as a consequence of human superstition. To allocate time on the curriculum to the serious and sympathetic study of religion shows we have rejected that point of view. But why? Is it just because we live in a world in which religions exist and where many people mould their lives and their actions according to their religious convictions? Do we study religions just because they are there?

Our curriculum decisions seem to go far beyond such a position. By accepting the spiritual as a component of education we are espousing the view that human life cannot be reduced to the technological, with its implicit assumptions that everything is manipulable and that human life can be successfully and safely depersonalized. There are many other subjects on the school timetable which also share this opposition to an invasive reductionism of human life. And one of the growth areas in the development of religious education is the attempt to produce genuine integrated humanities programmes in which the study of religion has a proper place.

But the study of religion goes further than this. John Hick claims that religions are fundamentally concerned in a multitudinous variety of ways with the transition of human existence from 'self-centredness to reality-centredness'.[54] If this is so, it brings religions into direct conflict with many other attitudes towards life. The subject matter of religious education is thus essentially controversial. To include the subject on the school timetable means we think it is worthwhile introducing pupils to this controversy. How to make it intelligible, interesting and relevant remains one of the most difficult tasks facing religious educators today.

Notes

1. See CHANCELLOR, V.E. (1970) *History for their Masters*, Somerset, Adams and Dart, p. 67.

2. See MacIntyre, A. (1967) *Secularization and Moral Change*, London, Oxford University Press, pp. 38ff.
3. See Pinch A. and Armstrong, M. (1982) *Tolstoy on Education*, London, The Athlone Press.
4. Department of Education and Science (1977) *Education in Schools*, London, HMSO, p. 6.
5. Her Majesty's Inspectorate (1977) *Curriculum 11–16*, London, HMSO, p. 12.
6. Further Education Unit (1979) *A Basis for Choice*, London, HMSO.
7. Her Majesty's Inspectorate (1985) *Curriculum 5–16, Curriculum Matters 2*, London, HMSO, para. 33.
8. HMI (1977) *op cit* p. 12.
9. *Ibid*, p. 9.
10. HMI (1985) *op cit* p. 26.
11. *Ibid*, p. 41.
12. *Ibid*, p. 27.
13. *Third Report from the House of Commons Education, Science and Arts* (1986) The House of Commons, Session 1985–86, London, HMSO, para. 2.2.
14. See Carr, D. (1983) 'Three approaches to Moral Education' *Educational Philosophy and Theory*, Vol. 15, No. 2, October, pp. 39ff.
15. See Simon, S., Howe, K., Kirschenbaum, H. (1978) *Values Clarification*, New York, Hart Publishing Co. See also *The Times Educational Supplement*, (1987) 24 April, p. 15.
16. The Schools Council/Nuffield *Humanities Project*, (1970) London, Heinemann Educational Books. See also Rudduck, J. (1986) 'A strategy for handling controversial issues in the secondary school', in Wellington, J.J. (Ed.) *Controversial Issues in the Curriculum*, Oxford, Blackwell.
17. McPhail, P. et al, (1972) Lifeline, *Moral Education in the Secondary School*, London, Longmans; (1978) Startline, *Moral Education in the Middle Years*, London, Longmans.
18. Wilson, J. et al, (1967) *An Introduction to Moral Education*, Harmondsworth, Penguin.
19. J. Wilson has modified his position over the years. See 'Method, content and motivation' *Journal of Moral Education*, Vol. 16, No. 1, Jan. 1987. 'There is a temptation, to which the present authors may well have yielded to give improper priority to method as against content. One detects here perhaps one's excessive fear of indoctrination' p. 32.
20. See Hirst, P.H. (1974) *Moral Education in a Secular Society*, London, University of London Press, and Peters, R. (1966) *Ethics and Education*, Allen and Unwin.
21. See Kohlberg, L. (1978) 'The moral atmosphere of the school' in Sharf, P. (Ed.) *Readings in the Moral Education*, Minneapolis, Winston Press, and (1980) 'Education for a just society' in *Moral Development, Moral Education and Kohlberg*, Birmingham Alabama, Religious Education Press.
22. Straughan, R. (1982) *I Ought To But ...*, Windsor, NFER-Nelson.
23. See Aristotle (1976) *The Nicomachean Ethics*, (Eng. trans.) Harmondsworth, Penguin, pp. 91f.
24. Phillips, D.Z. (1979) 'Is Moral Education really necessary?' *British Journal of Educational Studies*, Vol. 27, No. 1, Feb., p. 54.
25. *Pastoral Care in Education*, (termly) Oxford, Blackwells, 1983 onwards. Cp. Lang, P. and Marland, M. (1985) *New Directions in Pastoral Care*, Oxford, Blackwells.
26. See Brownjohn, P. (1985) 'The Dudley Project — Jan. 1982 to Dec. 1984,' *Pastoral Care in Education*, Vol. 3, No. 2, June, pp. 139ff.
27. Goodall, O., Beale, M., Beleschenko, A. and Muchison, P. (1983) *Develop-*

Peter Mitchell

ing *Social Awareness in Young Children*, University of Exeter School of Education, Workbook Series 4.

28. See PRING, R. (1982) 'Personal and Social Education' in WARD, L. (Ed.) *The Ethical Dimension of the School Curriculum*, Swansea, Pineridge Press; (1984) *Personal and Social Education in the Curriculum*, London, Hodder and Stoughton; and (1985) 'Personal development' in *New Directions in Pastoral Care*.
29. Association for Personal and Social Values in Education. See *Journal of Moral Education*, Jan. 1987.
30. NATIONAL UNION OF TEACHERS, (1984) *RE in a Multi-faith Society, a Discussion Paper*.
31. *Education for All*, (1984) HMSO, The Swann Report stresses the importance of RE for all pupils, but claims that the provisions of the 1944 Act are now obsolete and impractical.
32. There has been a change of attitude towards agreed syllabuses by religious educators in recent years. JOHN HULL, (1975) 'Agreed Syllabuses, past, present and future' in *New Movements in Religious Education*, London, Temple Smith, is one of a number of writers who doubted the efficacy of the agreed syllabus arrangements. A more positive approach is now evident. See NAYLOR, D. (1983) 'Agreed Syllabuses' in the *Dictionary of Religious Education*, London, S.C.M. Press, 1983, pp.
33. *The Curriculum 5–16*, pp. 32ff.
34. *Ibid*.
35. *The Curriculum 11–16*, p. 42.
36. DEPARTMENT OF EDUCATION AND SCIENCE (1980) *A Framework for the School Curriculum*, London, HMSO, p. 7.
37. *The Curriculum 11–16*, p. 43.
38. *Third Report from the House of Commons Select Committee on Education, Science and Arts*, para. 6.41.
39. *Op. cit.* para. 6.39.
40. Schools Council Working Paper 36 (1971) *Religious Education in the Secondary School*, London, Evans/Methuen Educational.
41. SCHOOLS COUNCIL, (1977) *Discovering an Approach*, London, Macmillan Education.
42. SCHOOLS COUNCIL, (1977) *A Ground Plan for the Study of Religion*, London.
43. See HAYWARD, M. (1987) 'The Agreed Syllabuses since 1980', in *The Shap Handbook on World Religions in Education*, London, Commission for Racial Equality, pp. 45ff.
44. There has been considerable controversy over the appropriateness of these two terms. They are not to be confused with scepticism and relativism in matters of religion. They also entail treating the pupils' own beliefs with respect and sensitivity. See *Critical Openness*, Oxford, The Farmington Institute, (1987), and *The Teaching of Islam in British Schools*, Cambridge, The Islamic Academy, (1985).
45. GOLDMAN, R. (1964) *Religious Thinking from Childhood to Adolescence*, London, Routledge and Kegan Paul.
46. See SLEE, N. (1986) 'Goldman yet again' *British Journal of Religious Education*, Vol. 8, No. 2. pp. 84ff., Spring; and (1986) 'A note on Goldman's methods of data analysis with special reference to scalogram analysis' *British Journal of Religious Education*, Vol. 8, No. 3, Summer, pp. 68ff.
47. See HAY, D. and HEALD, G. (1987) 'Religion is good for you' in *New Society*, Vol. 80, No. 1268, April 17, pp. 20ff.; and ROBINSON, E. and JACKSON, N. (1987) *Religion and Values at Sixteen Plus*, Oxford and London, Alister Hardy Research Centre and Christian Education Movement.
48. HARGREAVES, D. (1986) 'Curriculum for the future', in LEONARD, G. (Ed.) *Faith for the Future*, London, The National Society, p. 57.

49. See, for example, READ, G., RUDGE, J. and HOWARTH, R.B. (1986) *How Do I Teach RE*, (The Westhill Project R.E. 5–16), London, Mary Glasgow Publications, and GRIMMITT, M. (1987) *Religious Education and Human Development*, Great Wakering, McCrimmons. Grimmitt wishes to relate RE even more strongly to the pupils' own lives. 'RE's prime responsibility and function is not to produce phenomenologists of religion but to help students to come to terms with questions about their own identity, their own values and life styles, their own priorities and commitments, and their own frame of reference for viewing life and giving it meaning.' 'When is commitment a problem in Religious Education', *British Journal of Educational Studies*, Vol. 21, No. 1, Feb. (1981), p. 49. See also 'Religious Education and value assumptions', *British Journal of Religious Education*, Vol. 9, No. 3, Summer (1987), pp. 160*ff*.

50. See HALDANE, J. (1986) 'Religious Education in a pluralist society' *British Journal of Educational Studies*, Vol. 34, No. 2, June, pp. 161*ff*.; MITCHELL, B. (1980) 'Religious Education', *The Oxford Review of Education*, Vol. 6, No. 2, pp. 133*ff*. and 'Being religiously educated,' *Faith for the Future*, pp. 43*ff*.; and SCRUTON, R. (1986) 'The myth of cultural relativism' in PALMER, F. (Ed.) *Anti-Racism*, London, Sherwood.

51. Recent attempts to give this curriculum shape can be found in *The Chichester Project*, Cambridge, Lutterworth Press, 1982 onwards, *Christianity*, (Part of *The Westhill Project R.E. 5–16*) 1986 onwards and in the publications of the Farmington Institute for Christian Studies, Oxford.

52. See BAILEY, C. (1984) *Beyond the Present and Particular*, London, Routledge and Kegan Paul.

53. See ERRICKER, C. (Ed.) (1987) *Teaching Christianity, A World Religions Approach*, Cambridge, Lutterworth Press.

54. HICK, J. (1985) *Problems of Religious Pluralism*, London, Macmillan, p. 69.

3   Social Studies

Paul Armitage

This chapter seeks to describe in broad terms the nature of social studies in schools. It seeks to define the subject (perhaps more appropriately described as a 'field of study'), demonstrate the degree of diversity and uniformity within the subject and highlight some of the major issues confronting it.

Problems of Definition

What do we mean by the term social studies? A literal interpretation at GCSE level, for instance, would confine discussions in this paper only to those syllabuses entitled 'social studies'. A whole host of other syllabuses entitled, for example, social science, community studies, welfare and society, citizenship, as well as 'individual' subject syllabuses such as sociology, economics, politics and government, and law would therefore have to be ignored. Similarly, we would consider neither social education, nor social and life skills, nor indeed any of the courses now included under the title of PSE — 'personal and social education'.

The result would be a rather narrowly-focused chapter of only limited interest to the reader. More important, though, it would fail to paint a realistic picture of what is going on and the issues facing this area of the curriculum. Accordingly, therefore, we must seek a broader remit than a literal interpretation of social studies.

The problem then arises as to what the remit might be — and to do this, we must go beyond the superficiality of titles. A good place to start is GCSE. There are a number of reasons for this.

Firstly, it is only at this level and beyond that we have a reasonably well-documented picture of what is happening nationally. We have the benefit of clearly stated examination syllabuses as well as recorded examination entries.

Secondly, it is a level which has recently been the focus of much public interest and debate.

Thirdly, and perhaps most importantly, it is a level at which there has been a debate and an attempt to arrive at some form of consensus about the definition, aims, objectives, content, etc., of this area of the curriculum in the form of the National Criteria for social science.

The Characteristics of 'Social Science' at GCSE Level

At GCSE level, we have already noted a plethora of syllabuses which might be related to the social science area of the curriculum. We have noted such titles as social science, social studies, community studies, welfare and society, citizenship, and so on. In addition, there are other syllabuses which, some might argue, should also be added to the list such as integrated humanities, European studies, modern studies, local studies and other syllabuses with a regional focus where all or some of the constituent parts of the examination focus on the social sciences — for example, French or Welsh studies.

The interesting thing for the outsider looking at these syllabuses is that despite their different titles, varying approaches and diverse content, it may be argued that they do, in fact, share many similar characteristics, adopt common elements in methodology and have much in common in terms of content. Taken collectively, therefore, they could be taken as a basis for a definition of social studies — or, as it may be preferable to call it given the lead already established by the National Criteria — social science.

What are these common characteristics? A starting point for this discussion is the National Criteria for social science.[1]

In summary, these criteria provide a definition of GCSE social science. In GCSE, the subject is said to comprise the study, in an objective manner, of

> social systems, social structures, political and economic processes, and interactions between different groups or different individuals, with a view to establishing knowledge capable of being verified. (Paragraph 1.2)

In support of this, students are required to study a number of themes which broadly integrate aspects of economics, politics and sociology: —

4.1   The content of a course in social science for all candidates should be based on the following themes:

4.1.1   the social development of human beings and the changing contexts within which that development takes place;

4.1.2   the process of income and wealth generation and distribution, the problems of scarcity and choice, and alternative means of allocating resources;

4.1.3 the interrelationship and interdependence of social, cultural, economic and political factors at a range of levels: individual, group, institutional, national and international;

4.1.4 the sources, distribution and exercise of power in societies;

4.1.5 the processes of decision-making, formal and informal, at individual, group, local, national and international levels;

4.1.6 the patterns of social interaction and the implications of that interaction for individuals and for social groups;

4.1.7 the implications of gender for society and for the individual;

4.1.8 patterns of cultural and ethnic diversity and their social implications;

4.1.9 the ways in which ideas and values are generated in social life and the nature and role of these ideas and values in their changing social, economic and political contexts;

4.1.10 the interpretation and handling of data, simple descriptive statistics.

In the process of studying these content areas, candidates are required to develop an ability in a range of skills: —

All candidates will be expected to demonstrate:

3.1 skills of comprehension and communication of data presented in different forms including literary, numerical and graphical;

3.2 the ability to collect, analyze and interpret data;

3.3 the ability to acquire social scientific knowledge, both from personal experience and from the work of others;

3.4 the abilities to recall, organize, analyze, interpret and evaluate social scientific knowledge and to apply that knowledge;

3.5 the ability to distinguish between evidence and opinion. Evidence is material based on systematic observation which has been subjected to careful analysis. Candidates should be able to recognize deficiencies in material such as gaps, inconsistencies and bias, which reduce its value as evidence;

3.6 the ability to show how economic, social and political factors jointly affect social life.

As in all GCSE National Criteria, a large part of the examination takes the form of school-based assessment which will provide a good (though by no means exclusive) basis for developing practical skills especially in the collection, analysis or interpretation of data.

In addition, the criteria require that candidates are encouraged to reconcile personal with academic experience. This is a requirement of the social science criteria (paragraph 1.3) and the National General Criteria (paragraph 19 (k)) which state: —

> All syllabuses should be designed to help candidates to understand the subjects' relationship to other areas of study and the relevance to the candidates' own life.[2]

The social science criteria also require objectivity, and caution against the assessment of pupils' values (paragraph 1.3) while the General Criteria (paragraph 19 (h)) state that: —

> Every possible effort must be made to ensure that the syllabuses and examinations are free of political, ethnic, gender and other forms of bias.

Overall, therefore, what emerges is a picture of social science being an integrated subject drawing on the three key disciplines of economics, politics or sociology and the perspectives that these disciplines provide on a range of issues. It is firmly rooted in a range of skills encouraging an experiential approach to learning; it is student-centred in that personal and academic experience must be interrelated. Finally, it seeks to be objective, impartial and free from bias.

Social Sciences at GCSE Level — Some Examples

If we now consider a variety of syllabuses with a range of titles, the reader may begin to formulate a view as to the extent to which syllabuses do or do not relate to the social science criteria and the extent, therefore, to which diversity of titles hides an essential uniformity of content and approach. It should be noted that it is not the intention of the author to imply that the syllabuses should be retitled social science or that these syllabuses do or should wholly comply with the social science criteria. The intention is merely to provide the reader with an overview of developments in this broad field of study so that they may reach their own conclusions. What follows is deliberately based as far as possible on quotations from syllabuses so that the author distorts as little as possible the declared intentions of the syllabus designers. Readers should note that the quotations and summaries are based on syllabuses for examination in 1988. Syllabuses for 1989 and subsequent years may have been amended.

Example 1: Midland Examining Group (MEG) Social Science[3]

The aims and objectives of the syllabus mirror those in the National Criteria for social science. The subject content of the syllabus is divided into three core topics and seven option topics from which candidates must select two.

The three core topics are: —
1 The Family and Individual Development
2 People, Work and Economic Activity
3 Politics and Decision-making

The option topics are: —
1 Communities
2 International Relations
3 Resources, Environment and Development
4 Social Inequality
5 Conformity, Deviance and Social Control
6 Education
7 Communication and the Mass Media.

Example 2: Northern Examining Association Community Studies

Page 1 of the syllabus states: —

The subject matter which comprises community studies draws on a variety of disciplines in the social studies area of the curriculum. The common themes of the family, human development, inter-action with the community, communications and the media, inter-personal relationships and health and safety are all present in this field of study.

Hence, community studies implies the integration and inter-relationship of the methodologies and concepts of social studies disciplines using the focus of the community.[4]

Candidates undertake two compulsory modules and four out of eight optional modules.

The compulsory modules are 'You and Your Community' (dealing with the nature of a community, the family, roles within the community and community organizations); and 'Myself' (dealing with the stages of human development, the adolescent in the community and interpersonal skills and behaviour).

The optional modules are the Environment (local environment and the services which maintain it); Special Groups (definition of the term 'special' and the needs of, and provision for, special groups); the Pre-School Child (conception and birth, the needs of the young child, services for families, care of the young child); Healthy Living (personal and family health, community health issues, environmental health); Health and Safety (the home, at work, first aid and emergency services); Social Ser-vice provision (health services, personal social services, voluntary services); Leisure and Recreation (the development of leisure provision, leisure in the community).

To these, candidates are asked to apply the methodology and concepts of social studies and to demonstrate positive achievement in a range of objectives: —

recognition and recall of knowledge
investigation
problem solving/application of
knowledge
analysis/evaluation
communication/preparation.

Example 3: Southern Examining Group (SEG) European Studies[5]

This has a number of content areas. There is an introductory background topic dealing with the basic economic, political, social and geographical 'map' of Europe; then sections, on European political systems, the European economy, aspects of European society (the family, social division, education, leisure, pollution and conservation, the urban environment) and Europe and the Third World (economic, political and social relationships).

The objectives closely parallel those for social science covering recall, understanding, analysis and evaluation, presentation and communication, though with added objectives of what may be summarily described as 'empathy' and the ability to 'demonstrate originality and independence in approach'.

Example 4: Welsh Joint Education Committee (WJEC)
Social Studies

Objectives and content for the syllabus may be said to demonstrate close harmony with the social science criteria.

The aims and objectives are reproduced below. The content covers four main themes — the individual and the family, the local community, the nation and its government, and the wider world.

1   AIMS
The general aims of this course of study are to:
1.1   provide opportunities for young people to understand themselves in relation to society by promoting a critical awareness of social phenomena;
1.2   promote the acquisition of information and the practice of skills which will permit insights into the internal structures

of society — including a broad understanding of its institutional framework — and which will allow valid comparisons
with other societies;

1.3 provide an appreciation of social development as a dynamic
process and a consideration of the mechanisms involved;

1.4 develop a capability for objective judgment of information
and values;

1.5 promote insights into processes of thought characteristic of
related disciplines which provide different perspectives of
social structure.

2   *ASSESSMENT OBJECTIVES*
Candidates will be expected to: —

2.1 show acquisition of relevant information by demonstrating
the abilities of recall, comprehension, description and interpretation;

2.2 demonstrate an understanding of principles and concepts,
and to communicate clearly by means of an adequate vocabulary;

2.3 demonstrate an understanding of the relationships between
various forms of social information by means of logical explanation;

2.4 show an ability to use and where necessary to discriminate
between and evaluate various forms of evidence;

2.5 apply verbal, numerical and graphical skills in interpretation
and illustration of the subject;

2.6 show application in the investigation and use of acquired
information together with the operational skills involved in
the presentation of this material.[6]

*Example 5: Northern Examining Association NEA
Integrated Humanities*

According to the Introduction of the 1988 syllabus:

The subject matter which comprises humanities is the multitude
of social relationships which exist between individuals and groups
of individuals set in a variety of social contexts. Humanities
approaches its study of subject matter from many different perspectives using a diversity of methodologies and concepts in an
attempt to understand the social and moral aspects of these social
relationships.[7]

The syllabus specifies a number of modules of which candidates must
study five. The themes will not be unfamiliar to social scientists — the

community, law and order, people and work, the mass media, consumer affairs, education, the family, persecution and prejudice, inequality, war, politics and government, pollution and conservation, beliefs, health, leisure.

The objectives, though spelt out differently, again suggest considerable symmetry with those for social science. They cover understanding, investigation, interpretation and evaluation. Where the syllabus perhaps departs from social science is, however, in its appeal to other subjects: —

> ... Integrated humanities implies the integration and inter-relationship of the methodologies and concepts of primarily such disciplines as history, geography, sociology, economics, politics, anthropology, religious studies and also the expressive arts, in the study and consideration of important aspects of the human condition. Rather than being confined to any one particular discipline and its traditional subject areas it should be stressed that this integrated humanities syllabus is issue-based and should promote amongst students intellectual and experiential enquiry which draws upon the wealth of contributions offered by each traditionally discrete discipline.

Diversity in GCSE Social Science

Readers should, for themselves, judge the extent to which the above syllabuses appear to conform to the social science criteria (though admittedly such a decision is difficult given the limited information reproduced here). Certainly, it would be possible to argue that there is a symmetry between the objectives of the syllabuses and those for social science and that the study of the content of the syllabuses reveals that they cover much if not all of the course content specified in Paragraph 4 of the social science criteria.

Equally, however, we need to note that a case could be made emphasizing genuine diversity amongst the syllabuses. It undoubtedly could be argued that the different syllabus and course titles actually represent substantive differences. The titles may, for instance, represent differences in emphasis and content and, maybe, philosophy and these differences can be significant because they represent attempts at responding to particular student needs. Certainly, the designers of syllabuses and courses have chosen their titles with care.

For example, in GCSE community studies, courses are generally slanted towards the study of the students' local communities with relatively 'abstract' social scientific themes and concepts presented, analyzed, and made 'relevant' in terms of a local content. Local studies courses may also be viewed in this way though the emphasis given to local history and geography may be greater in such courses. In GCSE welfare and society courses, the emphasis may be placed upon the study of the need for and availability of welfare and caring services though the relationship of their provision to social, economic and political factors is carefully established. Citizenship and related courses may have links with older style civics or liberal studies courses, though equally course designers may claim links with more modern notions of personal and social education (PSE) which is discussed below. Citizenship courses generally seek to equip students with important knowledge and skills which will help prepare them for the adult world. For example, the introduction to the Southern Examining Group's citizenship syllabus says: —

> The study of citizenship involves individuals in attempting to come to terms with their role and the responsibilities in contemporary society. It draws its knowledge, skills, and methodologies from across a broad spectrum of the traditional curriculum.
>
> The citizenship course aims to equip candidates with the basic knowledge and skills required to understand their personal role in the society in which they live. It is intended to be a practical course in the sense that it helps young people to learn the skills needed to manage their own lives in a successful and responsible way in a democratic society, and to become enquiring, problem-solving and participating citizens.[8]

Another example of diversity might be European studies. Such courses have often derived from modern language departments where the teachers generally may not, for obvious reasons, see themselves as social scientists. It is certainly possible for such courses to concentrate on literature and perhaps geography and history and thus be very different from social science. On the other hand, however, the economics, politics and sociology of Europe normally figure strongly so that their definition is, at least, a point for debate.

And yet more examples of syllabuses could be used here. For example, there are currently GCSEs in urban studies, community care, British industrial society, social economics, community politics, community and business studies, local studies, world studies, vocational studies and so on, all of which, in varying degrees, have overlap and may be said to demonstrate both elements of diversity and uniformity within the general field of social science.

Local Education Authority (LEA) Guidelines for Social Science

This emerging image of social science as a subject integrating economic, political and social perspectives into an experientially based, relevant course is also borne out when one considers some examples of LEA guidelines.

For example, the Inner London Education Authority (ILEA) guidelines 'History and Social Sciences at Secondary Level' say that the term 'social sciences': —

> refers to the group of disciplines which includes sociology, anthropology, economics, political science, social history and geography.

It goes on: —

> Together (these disciplines) form a basic intellectual resource on which social science courses in secondary schools can draw.

The need for objectivity is also there in the ILEA definition: —

> It is not only in the field of theory, however, that the social sciences have enriched our learning. Social scientists have developed ways of working which offer a framework for looking at, asking questions about, and thus gaining an understanding of, society. In the course of this, the methods themselves are constantly being analyzed and refined. It is the concern of the social science teacher, at school and college level, to introduce pupils to these ways of working — as well as to provide access to areas of social science knowledge. With this knowledge, young people are helped to make constructive interpretations of their social world and their role within it...[9]

The guidelines then argue for an experiential approach which is relevant to students' lives by affirming that: —

> The study of the social sciences builds on a pupils' knowledge of, and natural curiosity about, the social life they experience.
> The study of the social sciences helps pupils to explore, and gain deeper understanding of, issues and topics which are relevant to their lives.
> The study of the social sciences is concerned to develop pupils' critical awareness and understanding (by engaging them) in the process of enquiry ... It encourages in pupils the spirit of enquiry, providing them with the means to investigate and make sense of the world they encounter.[10]

A similar approach is also reflected in the work of teachers in first, middle and high schools in the London Borough of Merton which, in a Schools Council publication 'The New Approach to Social Studies', said:

> We have taken the social studies to be those disciplines concerned with the study of man — history, human geography, and the social sciences (economics, sociology, anthropology and politics)[11]

and later, in a section specifically devoted to social studies from seven to nine, there is a reference which nevertheless has universal validity in terms of pupil age: —

> The new social studies are in many ways like the new mathematics. The objective of the new maths is to give children real mathematical perspectives, so that instead of simply being able to compute accurately, each child may work and think at his own level like a mathematician. In social studies teachers no longer aim to teach merely information, but to teach ways of thinking. Content is simply a medium through which they teach these ways of understanding and interpreting. The stress should be on examining evidence and asking questions of it — as geographers, historians or social scientists do — and employing the concepts they use to enable the child to draw his own conclusions.[12]

This view is also repeated in specific reference to primary education in an article by Alistair Ross when he states that the case for social studies in the curriculum rests on strong grounds: —

> Children need to develop ways of learning about how people cooperate and conflict in social groups, and they need to make hypotheses and generalizations about human social behaviour. With younger primary aged children, this will often focus on the social experiences that are close at hand: the family, the local community, and the school itself.
>
> Such work can be used to extend children's understandings in two areas. Firstly, their ability to use basic concepts of social organization such as power and authority, interdependence, tradition, social change, social control, the division of labour, cooperation and conflict can be developed. These concepts can only be explored and built up by case studies — studies of their own social organizations, with which they may be familiar but they will also need to analyze in conceptual terms; and studies of other societies, in different cultures and in different times.
>
> Secondly, this sort of study does not just help children understand better how their own society operates. It also can give a pattern for finding, testing and ordering information about other social groups. This way of linking second-hand experience of other societies to the children's existing knowledge of their own social environment can be shown diagramatically as in Figure 1.
>
> The large area indicating the child's own social experience represents the time spent in social studies in exploring the operation of the class's shared social knowledge, and using concepts to organize this. Case studies of other societies in time and space are used to directly link with this experience-based and developed model of social organization.[13]

Figure 1:

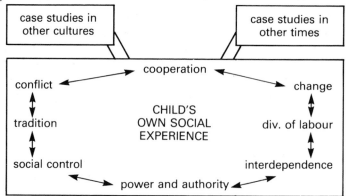

What emerges, therefore, is a broad range of variously titled courses all based upon a number of common characteristics — student centred, practically based, intent on linking personal to academic experience and variously integrating elements from at least economics, politics and sociology.

Social Science in Modular Syllabuses

Another contemporary development manifesting both uniformity and diversity are modular schemes incorporating social science modules. These are currently gaining in popularity throughout the country. They are largely seen as a way of responding to the problem of coping constructively with an overcrowded humanities curriculum, and as a means of creating a more responsive, relevant and manageable curriculum suited to a range of student needs.

For example, in character, a team led by the humanities adviser, Chris Warn, has developed the Manchester Modular Humanities (MMH) scheme. Thirty-nine centres have opted to take the scheme for entry to GCSE in June 1988 but it is now spreading rapidly to schools outside Manchester.

Five prescribed modules are combined to produce a GCSE in the single subject titles of either economics, geography, history, religious studies or social science. Alternatively, candidates may combine modules drawn from these different single subjects to produce GCSEs in local studies, world studies, political studies, modern studies, community studies, religion and society, industrial studies and humanities. Schools may also use modules for unit-accreditation leading to NPRA (Northern Partnership for Records of Achievement) certification.

Thus social science, conforming to the GCSE National Criteria is there, as is a social science contribution to the other GCSE subjects offered by MMH. The significance for social science, therefore, may be considerable if it means that it forms part of the curriculum diet of more students as a result of the introduction of modular programmes.

At the time of writing, this modular approach seems to be gaining momentum. It may thus be an example of things to come. It is interesting to note that advance publicity material from the DES on the City Technology Colleges might be taken to suggest that a modular (or perhaps integrated) programme is anticipated for the humanities.[14] Moreover, writing in an introductory paper to MMH, Chris Warn says: —

> We believe in Manchester that the MMH system is able to combine both flexibility and subject integrity for the humanities curriculum area. As such we consider this format to be a herald of the post-14 curriculum of the next decade. This provides a stimulating challenge for both teachers and examination boards.[15]

Seemingly, other local education authorities agree with him. For instance, Coventry and Sheffield are also developing their own modular schemes as are some examining groups. For instance, both SEG and WJEC are currently developing GCSE modular humanities packages. It remains to be seen whether the advent of the National Curriculum encourages or hinders this form of development.

Diversity in Social Science outside GCSE

Outside GCSE, there is diversity in the form of courses in personal and social education (PSE) and in social and life skills. In part, the former developed initially as a result of ROSLA, and all that that implies, as well as the genuine desire to help prepare children for the world of work. They also frequently had their roots in older style civics or liberal studies courses. Such courses have been extremely varied in aims, content and structure varying from, for example, the format proposed by the Schools Council social education project which aimed: —

> to provide an enabling process through which children will achieve a sense of identification with their community, become sensitive to the shortcomings and develop methods of participation in those activities needed for the solution of social problems[16]

to what ILEA calls the 'normative' model of social studies where courses

> adopt a factually-based approach rather than engaging pupils in a critical appraisal of social features.[17]

This amounts to a very broad definition — a definition which is further broadened when one considers the alternative titles sometimes proposed — for example, health and moral education, personal development, social and political education etc. The breadth of definition is also evident if one considers some further published views of the subject. For example, the Hargreaves Committee took the area of PSE to include, over the five years of compulsory secondary schooling: —

> careers education
> citizenship
> community studies
> comparative religious education (see 3.9.26)
> consumer education
> education for parenthood and family life (see Appendix 5)
> health education
> industrial education and work experience (see 3.16)
> mass media and leisure
> moral education
> political education
> social impact of science and technology
> economic education
> social and life skills
> information technology
> study skills.

> In many ILEA schools there has also been a considerable development in the use of tutorial time (eg 'the pastoral curriculum', 'active tutorial work'), largely under the inspiration and leadership of the ILEA Health Education inspectorate.[18]

However, other definitions are more narrow and perhaps demonstrate that while there is scope for considerable diversity and content, nevertheless, the aims and objectives of such courses show considerable uniformity and may be argued to be compatible to a greater or lesser extent with the definition of social science in the GCSE National Criteria. For instance, Kenneth David defines PSE as:

> Personal and social education includes the teaching and informal activities which are planned to enhance the development of knowledge, understanding, attitudes and behaviour, concerned with:
> > oneself and others;
> > social institutions, structures and organization; and
> > social and moral issues.[19]

Equally, life skills courses have also emerged from the desire to prepare children for adult life. While they had their roots in school-based social education and thus share much in common with PSE, they also frequently have the hallmark of MSC criteria and thus transcend the social science subject boundaries as they introduce students to, for example, technical and commercial skills as well as more traditional social skills. Modern counterparts to early courses lie, to some extent, in courses now being run under TVEI, BTEC and CPVE auspices.

In TVEI (The Technical and Vocational Education Initiative), for example, the emphasis in the early days on courses with a technological or overtly vocational thrust, is now giving way to a wider range of courses. This has been as a result of the MSC itself putting greater emphasis on the call from the Government White Paper *Better Schools* for breadth, balance, relevance and differentiation in the school curriculum, and as a result of a movement by teachers in the humanities generally, who have been concerned at their exclusion from 'vocationalism' and who had therefore looked critically at their subjects to see if they can be adjusted to take into account, in particular, the need for relevance.[20]

The result has been the development of new courses, sometimes crossing subject boundaries, sometimes within traditional subject boundaries, but with new content and an emphasis on the development of skills which are both appropriate to the discipline and transferable to other activities. Some examples of the new courses involving the social sciences include social and community care, industrial society and information technology, and caring studies for family and community.[21]

Similarly, in CPVE (The Certificate of Pre-Vocational Education), social science and related subjects have a role to play.

Students undertake a core involving the study and practice of basic skills, knowledge and aptitudes, including social skills, industrial, social and environmental studies, communications, science and technology, information technology, creative development, practical skills and problem solving. In addition, students undertake vocational studies which encourage the development of vocational skills and, in some instances, to obtain credit towards vocational qualifications. Vocational studies are organized into five categories each linked to a business sector: —

Business and Administrative Services
Technical Sciences
Production
Distribution
Services to People.

Finally, students undertake additional studies up to a maximum of 25 per cent of course time to allow for the development of further educational needs and to find the time for community activities, leisure, recreation and for reflection. Social science has a potentially important role to play in all three parts of the course.

Around this structure, schools build their own programme and it is, (and has been) possible to include, within the CPVE package, opportunities for students to follow courses leading to GCEs, CSEs, CEEs or GCSEs. In addition, it is of course possible to create entirely new courses for CPVE.

Paul Armitage

Social Science in the Primary School

In the primary sector, uniformity and diversity are again present. Diversity comes from the need to adjust the curriculum to the needs of individual children, classes and schools, an implication of the statement already quoted from Ross above. On the other hand, the basic subject matter will not differ greatly from the examples quoted previously and, methodologically, for it to be effective in the primary sector, teaching and learning has to be experiential or 'relevant'. Thus the familiar class project built around say a local community or family study is unlikely to be greatly at odds with the implied definition of social science in the National Criteria. Diversity at primary level is still comparable with the social science criteria. The definition of social studies in ILEA's curriculum guidelines for social studies in the primary school, published five years before the GCSE National Criteria, bears more than a passing resemblance to the criteria: —

> Children are rapidly acquiring knowledge of the social world in which they live; they have a natural curiosity and a general interest in the world about them. Social studies offers a structured approach through which children will be able to organize their experiences of the world and build upon them.
> Overall, social studies seeks to encourage children to
> a) recognize and value various sources of knowledge about society
> — their own experience
> — the experience of their contemporaries
> — the experience of others
> b) recognize and take into consideration the variety of social life and organization
> c) develop an enquiring attitude towards how society works
> d) come to an understanding of other people's views of society.
> Within these broad aims, social studies work provides opportunities to develop particular attitudes and skills, as well as contributing to aspects of children's general education.
> Among the attitudes which it seeks to develop are:
> a) an interest in events and their causes which leads children to questions such as Why? and How? as well as What? and When?
> b) a sense of empathy, that is, the capacity to imagine what it might be like to be in someone else's position
> c) a concern and respect for evidence, and for the experience of other people
> d) an awareness and appreciation of similarities and differences in social organizations.

There are certain skills which the study of society can foster and which teachers can help children to acquire and develop — such skills as the ability to:

a) search for information from a wide variety of different sources — pictures, graphs, reference books, other people
b) extract information with an awareness of the reliability of the evidence
c) organize the information they gather by using concepts and generalizations
d) organize this information to make hypotheses or tentative statements which they can test for themselves
e) explore their own personal attitudes, values and opinions and relate them to those of other people
f) work in small groups, discuss issues, listen to others and present arguments
g) learn and practise a range of general language skills: understanding and using appropriate oral and written language, using reference materials, organizing information and making records.

Social studies, concerned as it is with the study of people, makes an important contribution to children's general education, in that it helps them to

a) understand themselves better
b) develop the ability to understand and respond to other people
c) develop their understanding of the immediate community and the wider society of which they form a part.[22]

Uniformity and Diversity

Overall, therefore, the picture which is emerging is one of both diversity and uniformity. Neither is surprising. The diversity is there because of the attempts of syllabus designers to meet local needs. The uniformity is there because inevitably there will be commonality in some aims, objectives, content and methodology. Moreover, the possible universal validity of the GCSE National Criteria for social science may not be surprising since it could be argued that the criteria draw on this heritage of different syllabus types and approaches to arrive at its definition. The definition of social science embodied in the criteria may be said to encompass aims, objectives, content and themes which have made up, in the past, this plethora of syllabuses with their different titles. The definition of this area of study is therefore perhaps helped by the existence of the National Criteria. Whether they go far enough and whether they adequately encompass all potential courses or syllabuses remains a matter for debate.

Paul Armitage

How Much Social Science?

By now, the reader should at least have some feel for the variety in social science and some of the dilemmas of definition which surround it. Readers should also have some feel for the extent to which social science is taught in schools at this level. The number of syllabuses at GCSE level together with its introduction into vocational courses and its presence at primary level is very telling.

However, in practice it is very difficult to give a *precise* answer to this question because of the lack of any modern, authoritative overview based on evidence which has been systematically collected. And, of course, one reason for the lack of such an overview is the very complexity of social science's role in the curriculum. It is part and parcel of so many syllabuses and courses and at primary and secondary level and, in addition, stands in its own right in syllabuses and courses, with many different titles.

Some feel for the extent to which social science has found its way into the curriculum may be obtained from the DES Examination Entry Statistics though they, by no means, paint the whole picture.[23]

The latest published figures are for the 1985 summer examination. They relate, of course, to CSE and GCE and thus reflect the pre-GCSE situation. At present, we do not know the size of entry for the first GCSE examinations in 1988.

EXAMINATION ENTRIES: SUMMER 1985

	CSE	GCE 'O' LEVEL	GCE 'A' LEVEL
Religious studies	55,573	66,996	4,991
English	666,125	—	59,483
English language	—	519,684	—
English literature	—	236,343	—
History	163,058	126,609	35,075
French	163,326	147,657	22,140
German	31,855	42,616	7,949
Spanish	6,020	11,749	2,615
Music	11,206	18,155	4,432
Art and craft	173,468	158,727[3]	29,876[7]
Arithmetic	56,933	—	—
Mathematics	419,238	390,293[4]	87,682[8]
General science	87,146	5,819	—
Physics	149,849[1]	183,586	51,800
Chemistry	129,570	153,315	46,064
Biology	208,548	218,084	43,021
Geography	194,630	191,058	33,263
Domestic science	147,503	76,843[5]	4,777[9]
English economic history	1,631	38,453	3,356
Economics	11,924	39,306	41,916
Social studies	88,123	—	—
Sociology	—	53,195	17,781
British constitution	—	17,796	16,657

| Business subjects | $35,621^{(2)}$ | $19,456^{(6)}$ | $14,391^{(10)}$ |
| Other social science or vocational studies | 31,750 | 24,147 | 6,765 |

Source: Statistics of Education: School Leavers: CSE and GCE 1985, DES, 1987

(1) Includes physics with chemistry.
(2) Includes business and office practice, principles of accounts, other commercial subjects.
(3) Includes art (144,933) and craft (13,794).
(4) Includes maths, additional maths and commercial and statistical maths.
(5) Includes cookery, other domestic subjects and needlework.
(6) Principles of accounts.
(7) Includes art (27,139) and craft (2,737).
(8) Includes, pure, applied, pure and applied (66,306) and further maths.
(9) Domestic subjects.
(10) Includes principles of accounts and business studies.

The first thing to note is that at GCE 'O' and 'A' level, the single subject social sciences hold sway. Economics, sociology, British constitution, and economic history are all to be found in the list of subjects. Composite social science syllabuses such as those discussed earlier in this chapter do not appear except perhaps in the residual category of 'other social science or vocational subjects'. It is interesting to note how little penetration of 'O' and 'A' level there had been by social science as defined earlier in this chapter. Arguably therefore the advent of GCSE represents an important development for would-be former 'O' level candidates who, prior to GCSE, would only have taken single subject social sciences.

At CSE, economics and economic history still appear as single subjects but otherwise the emphasis is firmly placed upon social studies and, once again, the residual category. Social studies as used in the table is a general term applicable to a range of integrated courses with a diversity of titles.

Taken overall, these figures suggest that the social sciences form a substantial curriculum sector.

At CSE level, social studies alone ranks eleven out of thirty-nine subject categories listed in the original table from which this summary table has been prepared. At 'O' level, sociology ranks thirteen out of forty-nine subject categories, while the combined entries for sociology, economics or British constitution ranks eleven. At 'A' level, the predominance of the social sciences is even more striking. Sociology ranks eleven out of forty categories but when added together, the social sciences as a whole rank first, largely, it must be said, due to the high entry figures for economics 'A' level.

A second, recent source of information is a recent HMI report — 'A Survey of Sociology and Social Studies in Oldham', published in 1987.[24]

This report was based on the inspection of forty-two lessons in nine institutions. HMI attended classes in social studies for 13–14 year olds,

CSE social studies (modes 1 and 3), CSE sociology (mode 3), CSE community studies, 'O' level integrated humanities and sociology, 'A' level sociology, CEE sociology, CEE community studies and CFE (Certificate of Further Education) social studies. The CEE and in some instances 'O' level courses were available as part of CPVE (Certificate of Pre-Vocational Education) packages.

According to the report: —

1.3 Recruitment to the courses in schools was variable. In two schools all, or nearly all, pupils took social studies in the third, fourth and fifth years respectively. In two other schools recruitment to social studies options represented approximately half the year group. In only one school was the proportion small: no more than about one eighth of the year group. In total, some 1,550 pupils aged 13–16, and 372 students over the age of 16 (282 of whom were in adult or further education) were taking these courses.

A subjective response from the author to the HMI report is that such a picture is fairly typical of social science teaching in large parts of the country. A later section of the report also has a fairly familiar ring: —

4.2 In three schools CSE social studies (mode 3) was complemented by 'O' level integrated humanities to ensure that the course accommodated pupils from the full ability range. In one of these three schools the social studies/integrated humanities course formed part of the core curriculum for all the pupils in years 4 and 5. One other school had included social studies within the core curriculum of nearly all third years. This innovative course strongly emphasized political and economic understanding and covered such topics as the structure of government, political decision making, governmental expenditure and law and order.

4.3 In secondary schools the majority of the social science courses offered were options in years four and five. Five of the seven schools offered CSE social studies (mode 1 and/or mode 3), one other offered CSE sociology (mode 3) in addition to 'O' level sociology, and the seventh offered 'O' level sociology alone. In the sixth form, three schools offered 'A' level sociology; in one of these schools students entered for 'O' level sociology at the end of the first of the two years of study. Two other schools offered community studies and sociology (with either CEE or 'O' level certification) as elective studies within the CPVE.

4.4 Most social science courses in adult and further education prepared students for 'O' and 'A' level sociology but the college of technology offered social studies within its Certificate of Further Education. This is a full-time non-vocational course designed for students of average ability who have recently completed their secondary education; for some, the course may serve as a foundation for further studies. Social studies includes the study of population, the family, education, income and wealth, work, government, welfare provision and wider aspects of order and change in society.

Marrying together the evidence from these two sources with the evidence presented earlier, it is certainly reasonable to conclude that taken as a whole, social science is an important field of study which finds itself incorporated into the curriculum in a diverse pattern of ways. It may also be concluded that from the diversity of courses, from their frequency and from their inclusion in vocationally oriented curriculum packages, it is clearly felt that there is a need for courses which will enable students to organize their experiences of the social world in which they live. Social science — in all its forms, is therefore an important element in the contemporary school curriculum at all ages and ability levels.

The Future

At the time of writing this chapter, one important issue looms large — the National Curriculum. The Government's consultative document and Education Bill have now been published and, on first reading at least, it would appear that the social sciences will not be part of the National Curriculum for students up to the age of 16 unless they are included in whatever part of the curriculum is unregulated (or else find their way into core and foundation subjects as cross-curricular themes). If the development of history and geography is based on modular or integrated approaches, this may also provide scope for the inclusion of the social sciences.[25] The consequences of this for students, for the Curriculum and for social science will thus need very careful consideration.

The importance of this consideration is even more crucial given that this chapter has shown how significant is the place of social science in the school curriculum. This significance has, perhaps, not been realized because of the very diversity and fragmentation of titles which has been described in this chapter.

Social science courses have presumably developed because there has been a perceived need for them. Those needs now require careful reassessment and, maybe, recognition within the National Curriculum. These are weighty issues and the future of social science is bound up intimately with them.

Author's note: Any views expressed in this article are personal to the author and are not necessarily those of the author's employers — the Secondary Examinations Council.

Notes

1. DEPARTMENT OF EDUCATION AND SCIENCE (1985) *GCSE. The National Criteria: Social Science*. London, HMSO.
2. DEPARTMENT OF EDUCATION AND SCIENCE (1985) *GCSE: The National Criteria: General Criteria*. London, HMSO.
3. MEG *GCSE: Social Science Syllabus, 1988*. MEG, 1986.
4. NEA *GCSE: Community Studies (Modular) Syllabus, 1988*. NEA, 1986.
5. SEG *GCSE: European Studies Syllabus, 1988*. SEG, 1986.
6. WJEC *GCSE: Social Studies Syllabus 1988*. Cardiff, WJEC, 1986.
7. NEA *GCSE: Integrated Humanities Syllabus, 1988*. NEA, 1986.
8. SEG *GCSE: Citizenship Syllabus, 1988*. SEG, 1986.
9. INNER LONDON EDUCATION AUTHORITY, *History and The Social Sciences at Secondary Level: Part Three. Social Sciences*. London, ILEA, p. 12.
10. *Ibid*, pp. 12–13.
11. SCHOOLS COUNCIL (1981) *The New Approach to the Social Studies*. London, Schools Council, p. 7.
12. *Ibid*, p. 9.
13. ROSS, A. (1980) 'Why Social Studies should be part of the Primary School Curriculum'. *The Social Science Teacher*, 10, 2, pp. 54–7. Quote from page 56.
14. DEPARTMENT OF EDUCATION AND SCIENCE, *City Technology Colleges. A New Choice of School*. London, DES, no date. See, for instance, the charts and references to Humanities on pages 11 and 12.
15. WARN, C. (1987) *Manchester Modular Humanities, 1987*. Mimeoed leaflet, January.
16. RENNIE, J., LUNZER, E.A. and WILLIAMS, W.T. (1974) *Social Education: An Experiment in Four Secondary Schools*. Schools Council Working Paper 51. London, Evans/Methuen, p. 10.
17. ILEA, *op. cit*. p. 24.
18. ILEA (1984) *Improving Secondary Schools*. London, ILEA, p. 62.
19. DAVID, K. (1982) *Personal and Social Education in Secondary Schools*. Schools Council Programme 3. London, Longman for Schools Council, pp. 17–18.
20. DEPARTMENT OF EDUCATION AND SCIENCE (1985) *Better Schools*. London, HMSO, Cmnd. 9469.
21. Quoted in *TVEI: Technical & Vocational Education Initiative. Review 85*. London MSC, 1985, (pages 8–13), and in London Borough of Enfield. TVEI pamphlet, 1984.
22. INNER LONDON EDUCATION AUTHORITY (1980) *Social Studies in the Primary School*. London, ILEA, pp. 4–5.
23. DEPARTMENT OF EDUCATION AND SCIENCE (1987) *Statistics of Education: School Leavers: CSE and GCE 1985*. London, DES. (Reproduced with the permission of the controller of Her Majesty's Stationery Office.)
24. DEPARTMENT OF EDUCATION AND SCIENCE (1987) *Report by HM Inspectors on a Survey of Sociology and Social Studies in Oldham*. London, DES. (Excerpts reproduced with the permission of the controller of Her Majesty's Stationery Office.)
25. DEPARTMENT OF EDUCATION AND SCIENCE (1987) *The National Curriculum 5–16: A Consultation Document*. London, DES. (1987) *Education Reform. A Bill to Amend the Law Relating to Education*. 20 November 1987. London, HMSO.

4   Foreign Languages in Schools

Brian Page

Setting the Scene

In order to see what is happening in language teaching in the schools today it is necessary to have a clear idea of how we have got there. Modern language teaching in secondary schools in the United Kingdom has experienced two revolutions in the past twenty years. These have, as revolutions do, profoundly altered the generally accepted assumptions which had governed language teaching in the schools up till then and nothing can ever be quite the same again.

The first revolution occurred between the early sixties and the early seventies. At the beginning of that decade the typical situation was that a foreign language was offered to all pupils in grammar schools and to a very select few in some secondary modern schools. Precise figures are difficult to arrive at but that probably amounted to between a third and half of an age group depending on the area. By the early seventies, about 90 per cent of our secondary school population were being taught a foreign language for two or three years. The causes of change are always complex but undoubtedly, in this case, the introduction of CSE in 1964 and the spread of comprehensive reorganization through the late sixties were the major ones. This enormous expansion from languages for the few to languages for the great majority was accomplished by foreign language teachers with a great deal of hard work and anguish and not very much official recognition. The problems of teaching languages to ability ranges language teachers had not met before soon made themselves felt. Pamphlets, articles and courses on 'teaching languages across the ability range' proliferated and were always avidly received by teachers badly needing support and ideas. In the main, CSE courses were very similar in content and approach to 'O' level courses and they proved inappropriate for many. There then grew up the many European studies courses. These should have been genuine courses put on in their own right and some were. Most, however, were concocted to cope with the lower end of the ability

85

range who were seen as incapable of learning a foreign language but who had nevertheless appeared on the timetable of the foreign language department and had to be catered for. This mixture of inappropriate examination courses and uneasy compromise courses for the less able led to considerable malaise among both teachers and taught. Both suffered from a sense of aimlessness and consequent lack of motivation.

This was the major but not the only cause of the second revolution. This involved a complete shift of the basis on which language teaching had been operating till then. There are two ways in which to envisage the matter of learning a language. The first is to see the language as a mountain one is about to climb. The learner is led through the easy foothills of the genders and the articles and gradually approaches the steeper slopes and nastier traverses of the more complex structures of language. On the whole the mind of the learner is concentrated on the difficulties of the ascent and he does not have much time to look at the view. The idea is that finally the learner will arrive at the summit and be able to enjoy what has been so hardly won. The trouble is that most learners do not get there; many fall by the wayside and those have usually acquired little in the way of operational language. This results in the classic caricature, so often cited, of those who can conjugate the verb *être* but not order a beer in a café. The second way to view the matter is to turn one's back on the mountain and look at the learner, find out what she wants to know and teach her that. This has been the system over the centuries of the intrepid traveller who, since at least the Grand Tour, has gone abroad, phrase book in hand and triumphantly survived. The problem here is that if the native speaker does not respond with something that is in the phrase book then the learner has no theoretical knowledge of the language to enable her to work out what is being said. Some sort of compromise between the two approaches has to be made.

Up to the mid-seventies we were marching resolutely towards the mountain. Since that time we have increasingly been looking at the learner, trying to decide what her purposes in learning the language are and using those as the basis of the course. The implications are enormous and have involved an imaginative leap by teachers which should not be underestimated. As with all revolutions, there was first a rumbling of discontent, then attempts at piecemeal reform and finally a collapse of the citadel of the national examinations facilitated — again as so often is the case — by the conscious or unconscious complicity of the established power. The rumbling of discontent came, as I have mentioned, from the mismatch between the objectives of language teaching as they were with the much expanded language-learning population of the late sixties and early seventies. The courses provided, except for the European studies ones already mentioned, were usually the early years of the traditional five-year course to GCE 'O' level or CSE. Since two thirds of the starters were opting out at the end of year 3 it seemed singularly wasteful and indeed illogical to be starting them off on a course which most of them would never finish. But if they did not do that course, what were they to do? This prompted the question: 'If we are going to teach them French, what do we mean by that?' One of the immediate obvious answers was that we did not mean a five-year course. We must mean a much shorter one. From this simple principle grew the idea of the graded objectives scheme: we should work to a series of short-term objectives, each of which would represent a defined level of language attainment and each of which would build on its predecessor and point forward to the next one (Harding *et al.*, 1980; Page and Hewett, 1987). Moreover, pupils would be rewarded with a certificate on the successful completion of each objective.

The idea of defining an objective was relatively new. Objectives for GCE 'O' level had rarely been defined in any other terms than to say, for example: 'an essay of 120 words based on pictures'. CSE syllabuses tended to be more detailed and in some cases even listed the vocabulary that was to be known (Moys *et al.*, 1980). The objectives envisaged in graded objectives schemes were going to be much more specific. They responded to the question 'What do we mean by teaching French?' by saying that we teach it so that our pupils are able to use it for communicating in the real world. That meant, in the first instance, surviving in France. This basic principle then led to the definition of the behaviours expected and the language content of the courses. Reading, for example, would involve understanding signs and notices one would meet in public places and speaking would involving buying things, finding one's way in a strange town and acquiring the basic essentials of food and shelter. All these were considerably different from the objectives implied though not stated in national examinations of the time. It followed that, in assessing whether the French had been learnt, we would also be involved in applying another completely different principle. If the task given to the candidate was to buy a railway ticket to a given town and find out the times of departure and the platform number, then it was logical that if, in the view of the examiner, the candidate would have achieved that object, then she should be given full marks. The fact that her grammar might be defective was not necessarily a hindrance to communication. This was one of the imaginative leaps required by teachers who had been brought up to put red lines through grammatical errors of any type and take marks off for them. Many took readily to the idea and welcomed the fact that they were now allowed to teach their pupils to buy a coffee and a lemonade in a French cafe without having to teach or insist that one was masculine and the other feminine. Others felt uneasy that errors were not being penalized and that a defective performance could gain full marks. This point raises questions that we shall come back to and which, up to now, have not by any means been completely answered.

87

The Council of Europe

The work of the Council of Europe Modern Languages Project has had an important influence (Trim and Van Ek, 1984). It had a profound effect on the evolution of graded objectives schemes and has provided a new vocabulary for describing language. The Council of Europe was naturally concerned with the teaching of the Community's languages and, in 1971, set up a research project to look into the learning of foreign languages. In preliminary discussions it was decided to attempt to describe a series of modules (referred to as 'unit credits') which would add up to a competence in a foreign language. This obviously found an echo in the levels of graded objectives schemes. The competence was to be that required by an adult working in a foreign community to be able to live professionally and socially. This led to two questions. What are the needs of such a person and how can the language required to satisfy those communicative needs be categorized? The usual concepts of 'adjective' and 'irregular verb' do not tell us much about communicative competence. The answer to these questions led to the exploration of concepts like topic, role and setting and the description of the new language categories of function and notion, which now have at least as much influence in the language teaching world as the old ones of noun and verb. A function is what you do with language; you apologize, explain, ask for information, give permission, express whether you can do something or not, and enquire about all those things. Notions are what you talk about and these split into general notions — space, time, volume, temperature — and specific notions — table, chair, sun, run — which are the vocabulary of the job in hand. Functions can be realized in a number of ways often of different grammatical complexity and, to some extent, they give a reason in communicative terms for learning grammar. You no longer learn the past tense in French just because it is there, you learn it in order to report an event. The sort of past tense you use may then depend on the setting and the mode of communication (formal/informal, literary/non-literary, spoken/written, etc.). All these categories have proved extremely useful in describing the sort of communicative competence that is being asked for at a given level. It would have been difficult to construct the new GCSE syllabuses without them.

The Council of Europe went on to produce a basic level of competence which it called threshold level (for English). Similar descriptions for other languages — Niveau Seuil, Kontaktschwelle, Nivel Ombral, etc. (Council of Europe, 1975 onwards) and their inventories of topics, roles, settings, functions, notions (both general and specific), grammar and typical exponents in terms of actual words and phrases have proved invaluable for the construction of syllabuses.

GCSE and the National Criteria

The developments inspired by the graded objectives movement and the work of the Council of Europe led to growing dissatisfaction with the demands of the then current examinations at 16+. Many graded objectives schemes produced mode 3 CSE examinations to fit the method and philosophy of their systems and there were even some mode 3 'O' levels. When the great debate about the amalgamation of CSE/GCE 'O' level took place the modern language teaching community was then well placed to take advantage of the situation. Teachers had been discussing for several years new approaches to language teaching and the various ways in which syllabuses might be devised and assessments systems set up. It is hardly surprising, therefore, that the input from those experienced in graded objectives schemes was predominant and that the National Criteria eventually produced owe a great deal to that inspiration (Moys (Ed.), 1984). The GCSE criteria give official endorsement to the new view of language teaching and they have far-reaching implications.

Their function is to serve as the instrument with which the Secondary Examinations Council (SEC) judges the appropriateness of syllabuses submitted to it by the examination groups. These syllabuses must satisfy the criteria in order to qualify for awarding GCSE certificates.

The national criteria for French (which have been used as a basis for the other foreign languages also) contain aims, assessment objectives, principles governing syllabus content, and the relationship between assessment objectives and that content, recommended (and proscribed) techniques of assessment and, finally, brief grade descriptions. In the introduction it is made clear that 'these criteria deliberately refrain from laying down a single examination pattern to be followed by all syllabuses. Examining groups are free to explore and develop different examination models.' Nevertheless, the criteria are detailed enough to be definitely prescriptive in some areas and the working document derived from the criteria and used by the SEC to assess syllabuses contains a number of questions to be satisfactorily answered that are very detailed indeed. There have been complaints that there is not a great deal of room for manoeuvre. It should be remembered, however, that the framers of the criteria were aware that, for a great number of teachers (and, even, examination boards) their suggestions were going to imply a distinct change in direction and they were therefore very much concerned that it should not be possible to reinstitute the *status quo ante criteria*.

The aims are:

1 to develop the ability to use French effectively for the purposes of practical communication;
2 to form a sound basis of the skills, language and attitudes required for further study, work and leisure;

3 to offer insight into the culture and civilization of French-speaking countries;
4 to develop an awareness of the nature of language and language learning;
5 to provide enjoyment and intellectual stimulation;
6 to encourage positive attitudes to foreign language learning and to speakers of foreign languages and a sympathetic approach to other cultures and civilizations;
7 to promote learning skills of a more general application (for example, analysis, memorizing, drawing of inferences).

Of these seven aims, at least two are revolutionary. The first, which makes 'practical communication' the aim of language teaching, means considerable changes in the teaching styles of many teachers. The fifth, which makes 'enjoyment and intellectual stimulation' an essential part of the process implies almost a reversal of perspective in those classrooms which have hitherto not been particularly productive of either.

In order to assess appropriately all candidates in the wide range of ability of GCSE it is necessary for differentiated objectives to be offered. The criteria illustrate this by defining these in two levels, basic and higher. It is accepted that a three-level arrangement might also be possible. The objectives are described in terms of the four skills, listening, reading, speaking and writing, and illustrate the practicality of the communicative skills implied. In basic listening candidates are expected 'in the limited range of clearly defined topic areas' to cope with such things as announcements, instructions and requests and in reading, with public notices and signs, menus, advertisements, etc. They are also to acquire 'the ability to extract relevant specific information from such texts as simple brochures, guides, letters and forms of imaginative writing considered to be within the experience of, and reflecting the interests of, 16-year-olds of average ability'. Candidates will need to demonstrate only comprehension and not to produce precis or summaries. In speaking, candidates will be involved in simple role-playing tasks involving both taking the initiative and asking questions. The level of performance in speaking is that 'candidates should be expected to pronounce sounds in the foreign language well enough for a sympathetic native speaker to understand'. In other words, in order to get full marks, a candidate does not have to produce a grammatically flawless performance. Basic writing involves a simple letter or short message within the context of topics defined in the syllabus. The higher level objectives are described in a similar way and here again the situations are defined as being those 'which are within the scope and experience of a 16-year-old'. This ties the examination to an age range and has led to the production of separate syllabuses for mature students. All candidates must offer the common core assessment objectives (basic listening, reading and speaking) which give access to grades E, F and G. Thereafter, they may add whichever objectives they wish, though to achieve grade C basic writing must be attempted and to achieve grades A and B higher writing must be attempted.

The syllabus is required to be 'loosely defined' in terms of tasks, topic areas, vocabulary, structures, notions and functions and whether they are to be used productively (i.e. in speech or writing) or receptively (i.e. in listening and reading). Each of the skills is to be given equal weighting in the final mark.

The techniques of assessment section reflects the concern with practical communication. The statement of basic principle is probably one of the most important sentences in the document. 'The basic principle is that the tasks set in the examination should be, as far as possible, authentic and valuable outside the classrooms.' No longer can candidates be required to perform tasks designed to see if they can produce accurately formed sentences. The tasks must now be of the sort that the candidate would expect, as a user of the language in practical circumstances, to have to perform — reading and listening to authentic pieces of the language, involving themselves in role plays where they have to simulate potentially real situations, writing postcards and letters of the sort they really would write. The phrase 'practical communication' is, of course, susceptible of many interpretations but in effect has been taken to mean being able to communicate with native speakers for everyday purposes.

This has given rise to the concept of the 'sympathetic native speaker'. Since it is no longer appropriate to add up the number of grammatical errors to see what a final mark might be, there has to be some way of defining whether a message has been conveyed, whether communication has in fact been established. The concept of the sympathetic native speaker has been invaluable in this respect. If, in the judgment of the examiners, a sympathetic native speaker would have understood then communication has been effected. If the sympathetic native speaker would have had to seek clarification or repetition then, to that extent, the communication will have been less acceptable even if, in the end and with some difficulty, it had been established. Some gradation in the quality of a communication can then be defined.

Authentic is another word the interpretation of which leads to a great deal of discussion. Its use in the National Criteria, however, must be seen in the context of the times in which the criteria were produced. It is surprising to discover, for example, that, until the early 1980s (and then under the influence of graded objectives schemes) there had never been a genuine test of reading or listening in the public examinations in foreign languages at age 16+. The pieces of foreign language used for reading comprehension were either totally contrived or heavily edited to make them accessible to candidates. Listening comprehension pieces consisted of material written first, usually by non-native speakers, and then acted afterwards, sometimes rather indifferently. An authentic listening test must mean, however, that the material is intended to be heard, like news items or public announcements, and is at least in part spontaneous and unscripted like genuine conversation. In a similar way reading tests should be taken from magazines, newspapers and the like. The criteria allow for a minimum of editing or glossing at basic level.

It must be admitted that these requirements present considerable difficulties for examiners, who have to find genuine pieces which do not stray far outside the limits imposed by the vocabulary defined in the syllabus, for textbook writers and for teachers, who have now acquired an almost insatiable need for authentic material.

'Authentic' is applied to tasks as well as materials and this too creates similar difficulties. In the case of the criteria the principle is almost immediately broken by the recommendation for the listening and reading tests. Multiple choice questions are acceptable as long as they are not the only device used. But it is rare for anyone to find themselves in a situation in real life which resembles seeking the answer to a multiple choice question. The criteria go on to say that otherwise questions in English requiring answers in English are to be set. This has raised a considerable controversy since it implies a great deal of English in the examination paper and a great deal of English written by the candidate. The system can be defended in the sense that candidates might well find themselves in the position of interpreters for their family or friends and have to render in English at least approximately a message read or heard. Nevertheless, many teachers feel uneasy that a more acceptable way of showing understanding of the foreign language with less emphasis on the mother tongue has not yet been found. This is echoed in the HMI document, *Modern Foreign Languages to 16* (1987).

It must be remembered that during the discussion of the draft the National Criteria were overwhelmingly supported in the many meetings held up and down the country and therefore they must be seen as a reasonably accurate description of the philosophy of the modern language teaching community in the early 1980s.

Official Views on Foreign Languages in the School Curriculum

Current official thinking which, in many ways, has caught up with the general ideas of the profession as now represented in the GCSE, has been most recently publicized in two documents. *Modern Foreign Languages to 16*, published in March 1987, is No. 8 in the HMI series 'Curriculum Matters'. It expresses the view of Her Majesty's Inspectors, the observers, guides and mentors of language teachers in the secondary schools. *Foreign Languages in the School Curriculum* is a government document produced by civil servants but with, undoubtedly, considerable input from HMI; it expresses the government's view. It has in fact had a protracted history. It first appeared as a consultative document in 1983 to which all interested parties were asked to respond. A second consultative version eventually emerged in June 1986. The final version, at the time of writing is still awaited.

The HMI document has the following chapters: the contribution of modern foreign languages to the curriculum, aims and objectives, teaching and learning: general principles, teaching and learning: activities, assessment, the provision of foreign languages within the curriculum, implementation and a bibliography. Any summary is bound to be misleading but nevertheless it is with justice possible to pick out the main points in the HMI views and they serve as a useful framework within which to discuss several important issues.

The Contribution of Modern Foreign Languages to the Curriculum

The document concerns itself with 'modern foreign languages during the period of compulsory education'. It states that 'it takes as a guiding principle that learning a foreign language should be primarily a matter of using it for communication'. It does not define communication and therefore does not enter into the debate about what the word means. The learning of a foreign language 'makes a unique contribution to the curriculum' because it allows pupils to explore a culture different from their own and, hopefully, to acquire a sympathetic attitude towards foreign people. The HMI add that it also enables people to become aware of the nature and resources of language as a medium of communication and it provides a skill that can be useful in employment.

Aims and Objectives

The HMI see the aims of language study as two-fold and it is worth quoting them in full so that they can be compared with those of the GCSE National Criteria.

(a) Linguistic and literary

to provide successful and enjoyable learning experiences which may encourage learners to continue their study of a foreign language or to embark on the study of a new one;

to give learners the confidence and competence to communicate at levels appropriate to their ability with native speakers of the language;

to develop efficient listening and reading skills;

to foster sensitivity to language, its forms, sounds and rhythms; to promote pleasure in the use of words and an awareness of the expressive power of language;

to develop and reinforce the skills of analysis, classification, synthesis, analogy and inference;

to provide a satisfactory linguistic basis for the study of a foreign language beyond the age of 16;

(b)   Human and social

to increase social competence by promoting an awareness of and sensitivity to differences in social customs and behaviour;

to foster positive attitudes towards other countries and those who live in them and to counter prejudice;

to enable learners to meet foreigners in this country and to travel abroad with confidence, enjoyment, interest and advantage;

to awaken an interest in foreign cultures and life-styles and to foster a willingness to see one's culture in a broader context;

to develop a capacity for understanding and accepting the unfamiliar;

to encourage tolerance and a willingness to work together.

The objectives for 16-year-olds are then listed. These are substantially the same as the GCSE objectives already quoted. Like them, they are largely concerned with the practical use of language in everyday communication including listening to radio, TV, reading newspapers and magazines and writing simple letters. More able 16-year-olds would be expected to cope with more sophisticated material. The HMI do here briefly re-express the now generally held opinion that writing as a practical communication objective would seem not to be relevant to most learners — 'The majority of learners are unlikely in the long run to have much or any need to write foreign languages' — but underline its usefulness in the learning process. The HMI then add objectives for 14-year-olds because many, at present, opt out at that stage and should have a coherent course with recognized objectives. When the learning of a foreign language becomes compulsory up to the age of 16, which appears to be the ambition of both government and HMI, as it has long been of language teachers, these objectives as terminal ones lose their force but as interim ones would still have considerable value. In this case a list of thirteen topic areas (for example: exchanging personal information, simple shopping, staying with a family abroad) and practical objectives in the four skills (for example, reading: 'the ability to read common street signs and simple menus, timetables, advertisements and letters') are given.

Teaching and Learning: General Principles

The section on the general principles of teaching and learning deals with: the scheme of work, the use of the foreign language in the classroom, differentiation, confidence and correction, participation, variety and pace, relevance and breadth, authenticity, authentic material, the foreign background, the classroom, the treatment of grammar, translation, vocabulary and idiom, progression. In many cases it consists of necessary but obvious observations, the very statement of which suggests some possibly bitter experiences on the part of HMI. They rightly insist that the foreign language be used by teacher and pupils as much as possible in the classrooms. The old habit of explaining things in English and keeping the foreign language almost uniquely for practice of the grammar is still remarkably widespread. It was never satisfactory but, in the current situation, when the aim of the teaching is communication in the language, it is a contradiction to make all the genuine communications in the mother tongue and to reserve the foreign one only for the pseudo-communications of language practice. About schemes of work they say that 'as it is a working document, the policies which it contains should be reflected in classroom practice'. We are all aware of statements of policy which bear little relation to actual behaviour. In other sections they say, 'Encouragement, tolerance and the avoidance of destructive criticism on the part of the teacher are essential if language learning is to be effective.' One would say that was true for all learning. Similarly, 'Pupils learn better when they are actively involved. Practice in the use of the language is therefore more important than receiving information about it.' And further on: 'The most effective way of developing pupils' ability to understand the spoken language is for the teacher to use it at an appropriate level to deal with matters which are of interest and importance to the class. Similarly, encouragement for pupils to speak the foreign language is more likely to evoke a positive response if pupils are given opportunities to make statements and to ask and answer questions on matters important to themselves.' The pupil involvement mentioned by the HMI is limited to the teacher making sure that the material is of potential interest to the learners and to getting them to talk in the language rather than lecturing at them. However, other more genuine forms of pupil involvement have been explored in schools and are not mentioned. For example, at all levels, some decision-making by pupils is possible. At the elementary level it may be negotiation between teacher and class about which topic should be tackled next or allowing pupils a choice from a set of parallel exercises or activities. At later levels it might be the pupil will have a free choice of reading book or listening materials. At other levels again, where projects are possible, it is obviously best for pupils to choose their own within the limits of the availability of material. In all these ways pupils can be given some autonomy and so made responsible for their own learning. Tradition-al language teaching was always very teacher-directed and even where names have changed and more relevant goals been established the old practice of the teacher directing the pupils like a puppet master pulling strings remains very much the fashion. It can and should be broken down. Unfortunately, the HMI document does not mention either the necessity or the possibility.

In this section several other topics are raised which are in fact matters of considerable discussion. The HMI deal briskly and effectively with the problem of authenticity, the word very heavily used in the context of current modern language teaching, and point out the difficulty of just how far it is in fact possible to reproduce natural language behaviour in the language-learning classrooms. The problem is that in the classroom we involve ourselves in various activities in order to learn the language; in the real world we use language in order to involve ourselves in activities. It is extraordinarily difficult to get over this fundamental difference. The 'real thing' being difficult to encounter in the classroom, we should recognize that most of the time we can only rehearse for the 'real thing'. As the HMI say, 'Authentic circumstances requiring use of the foreign language are rarely immediately to hand in school,' and therefore the aim must be 'to achieve as much authenticity as possible ... by giving preference to authentic materials from the foreign country and to activities involving real communication in the classroom.' Unfortunately, once again, they do not define 'communication', which is another of the centres of debate. Considering how much the word is used in talking about foreign lan-guage teaching it is remarkable how difficult it is to define. If a pupil is required to recite the present tense of the verb *être*, is that communication considering that she is presumably conveying her knowledge of the verb? If the pupil takes part in a role play which involves finding out whether there is room at the campsite for her and her family, is that communication when there is no campsite in the classroom and the pupil and her family never go camping? Again, if a teacher asks a pupil arriving after the begin-ning of the lesson why she is late, the response would appear to be 'real communication' to use the HMI's phrase. The essential difference is obvious. In the last case, the teacher is concerned with the meaning of the response and not with its form — it is the message that matters precisely because the teacher does not know what the message is going to be. There is an information gap. Moreover, the teacher wants to know in order to decide what action has to be taken — the exchange has a purpose beyond the use of the language. In most foreign language exchanges in the classroom the teacher is asking questions she already knows the answer to and the purpose is not something outside the language — it is indeed the language itself; she wants to know whether the pupil knows how to say what is being asked. Even when an 'information gap' is engineered — the famous interrogation: 'What did you do at the weekend?' — the purpose is often lacking because the teacher is not really interested in what the pupil did at the weekend; she wants to know if the pupil has the language to express it. A game, which many consider to be the acme of communicative classroom activity because it includes both information gaps and purpose (for the participants) is being played not for its own sake, as games usually are, but in order to practise the language involved. It is therefore true that learning a language in a classroom is essentially an artificial business and opportunities for 'real communication' are few. Nevertheless, that essential artificiality must be kept to a minimum by making sure that classroom activities simulate normal language activities as closely as possible and are interesting in themselves to the learners. At the same time teachers should make the most of whatever opportunities for real communication arise.

Grammar and progression are the other words which become slippery of interpretation when used in the context of courses leading to communicative competence. The section on grammar is slanted towards the teacher who still teaches grammatical rules or verb paradigms as the main object of the process. 'Grammatical analysis can easily be over-emphasized,' the HMI say, and '[it] is then liable, with pupils of all abilities, to result in loss of interest in the foreign language and excessive exposure to English.' Several useful pieces of advice then follow on how to deal with grammar. There is, however, more to it than the HMI hint at. It has been said above how communication can be effected by formally incorrect utterances and the concept of the 'sympathetic native speaker' is used to help in judging these. But that does not altogether dispel the confusion many teachers feel about the place of grammar in the new courses. What is one to do with utterances which communicate effectively but which are grammatically inaccurate? Following the National Criteria, the mark schemes of many GCSE syllabuses insist that successful completion of the task is to be rewarded irrespective of grammatical accuracy. If one is not to count a grammatical error as a mistake to be penalized, what is the purpose of insisting on grammatical accuracy at all? If communication is being effected, what is correct grammar for? This is a question which is only beginning to be addressed by language teachers and it could be some time before we find solutions which can be applied to the classroom. In the meantime, we shall go on, as the HMI suggest, to teach correct grammar not just for communicative purposes but because, like Mount Everest, it is there.

The same problem arises with progression, the next topic dealt with in the document. The HMI define progression thus: 'Progression in language learning implies in an increasing range of vocabulary and complexity of structure and a developing confidence in the use of the language.' But this is to imply the 'grammatical' approach. In a grammatically based syllabus it is easy to define progression as moving through to structures that are more and more complex in form or concept or which are rarer —

the past anterior is about the last thing one learns in French because it is highly unlikely one will need to use or interpret it. A communicative approach would say that progression means the capacity to deal with more complex communicative situations. It is true that these need more vocabulary and increasing confidence in the use of the language but it is unclear to what extent more complex structures are required. Once again, the relationship between communication and grammar remains vague. The HMI's final statement in this section: 'The essential principle governing the selection and ordering of the structures to be learned is the increasing contribution which they can make to the ability of pupils to communicate,' while saying something which seems obvious common sense, in fact begs several important questions which make it exceedingly difficult to interpret.

Teaching and Learning: Activities

The section on teaching and learning activities is a useful compendium of practical classroom suggestions. They also raise, usually by implication, some interesting issues. As was seen in the analysis of GCSE criteria, language is still most conveniently divided into four skills. Increasingly, however, these are being seen as interdependent certainly from a learning point of view. The HMI say that '. . . it is normally best to plan classroom activities so as to integrate these skills, as happens in real life.' The old tradition of having separate lessons for each of the GCSE requirements — translation into the foreign language one day, out of it another — has to be rejected. The HMI repeat the primacy of oral activity using the same phrase, 'Oral activities need to be central at all stages,' twice in different paragraphs. They add a particular endorsement for group and pair work. '. . . Activities such as role play, cooperative work and interaction in small groups should be a normal part of pupils' learning.' Later, a separate section is given to the subject, giving two reasons for its use: it enables more individual oral practice to take place and frees the teacher from whole class direction so that she can 'work more closely to the abilities of pupils, supporting and encouraging the less confident and extending the more able.' Another major reason, which the HMI do not mention but which helps to fulfil some of their declared aims, is that pair/group work encourages pupils to realize the benefits of cooperation and allows them to help each other through difficulties. It is important to be aware that pupils can learn as much from each other as they can from the teacher if given the right materials and opportunities.

The responsibility of the teacher to provide her own activities is recognized: 'The teacher will need to be imaginative in devising situations and tasks in which pupils feel a genuine wish to communicate and are able to with the linguistic means at their disposal.' What is not recognized, however, is the burden this places on the teacher. Now, as at no other time, the foreign language teacher is required by the demands of the new curricula to provide a constant flow of 'situations and tasks' using up-to-date, imaginative, authentic material. Time and resources have, however, never been more scant. It should be remembered in this context that British teachers are required to teach more lessons than their counterparts in any other European country and in many countries outside Europe.

The HMI go on to say, 'At times this will lead to pupils experimenting with language. Although the teacher will naturally seek by careful planning and monitoring to minimize the risk of such experiments, it should be recognized that, especially for the more able linguists, they can be a source of fruitful learning and contribute to growing mastery of the language.' What is meant here is that, given situations in which pupils 'feel a genuine wish to communicate', they will make mistakes. These are not to be seized upon as totally negative but to be seen as inevitable stages through which learners go when they are striving to express their own personal meanings. This positive view of error is one of the fresh aspects of the new situation. Indeed, a new definition of error is crucial to the teaching of communicative competence. As was mentioned in the discussion of grammar above, we need to know more clearly when we are to correct a pupil's production and why. At the moment we do not. The HMI could have given the matter a good deal more space and recognized it as an issue to be faced.

It is interesting that, of the four skills, the section on reading occupies the most space (nearly a page and a half as opposed to a page for the others). This is a welcome emphasis as one of the possible lacunae in the new approach is a proper concern for extensive reading. In the early stages signs, public notices and short messages are the reading matter. Later, magazine articles and newspaper items tend to predominate. The nature of the end of course examination means that the final test is based on examination-size gobbets of two to three hundred words. None of this encourages the practice or helps teachers to teach the skills of fast, silent reading of longer stretches — stories and even whole books. A different assessment system which incorporated continuous assessment would help. In the meantime it is useful to have official concern expressed for extensive reading, a skill which is the easiest to continue to use even after leaving school and which is relatively neglected by current examinations. There is equally a recognition that both listening and reading require particular skills that are separate from those required in speaking and writing and that these skills should be taught. This is only just beginning to be realized. It has been too easily assumed that if learners were taught to speak and write they would automatically be able to listen and read. This is only partially true. Both these latter skills have peculiar difficulties which learners should be taught specifically to overcome if they are to become fluent readers and listeners.

A vital paragraph in this section concerns the classroom. Schools and LEAs on the whole have taken a long time to realize the necessity for foreign language teachers to have their own classrooms in which to work. The new approach renders this even more important as audiovisual aids and equipment, flash cards, posters, realia of all sorts as well as a great variety of books, brochures, newspapers, magazines, etc. need to be at the teacher's disposal. None of this is possible if the foreign language teacher is a nomad wandering from classroom to anonymous classroom to find her pupils. The HMI are right to point out, therefore, that a suite of foreign language classrooms and storerooms becomes a necessity. So does light adaptable furniture and, if at all possible, carpet on the floor. As they say, this serves 'not only to improve acoustics but also to reduce noise levels, for active language learning encourages talk, drama, singing and move-ment'. The different activities required of the foreign language teacher of today need a different sort of classroom.

Assessment

It is a truism that assessment should come after curriculum design — that is that tests should assess what you have previously decided to teach and they should not in themselves determine what one teaches. It is in fact the case that at least in foreign language teaching in schools this has never been so for the great majority of learners. The public examinations, GCE and CSE, always dictated the contents of textbooks and thereafter the content of lessons, even for the least able. In order to effect any real change in language teaching aims, it was therefore necessary to change the public examinations. This was the view of the pioneers who set up graded objectives (which were first, very significantly, called 'graded tests') and it has been shown to be the effect of GCSE. It is the national criteria of GCSE and the syllabuses and tests derived from them which now con-stitute the goal and therefore dictate the curriculum content of foreign language teaching in the schools. There is nothing wrong with this. Provided the aims are right and the testing techniques are appropriate for assessing them, they can perfectly properly constitute curriculum aims also.

   This aspect of examinations does not seem to be apprehended by the HMI. It is this which leads them apparently to misunderstand graded objectives systems, which they, significantly, still refer to as 'graded tests' though that phrase has been abandoned for some years. They say, 'The defined objectives of graded tests, especially at the lower level, generally deal in a narrow range of language and content and are not intended to represent complete teaching syllabuses. Used well, these schemes lead to pupils assessing their own progress and may improve their motivation without dominating classroom activity or restricting work in the subject.'

Graded objectives systems should, however, be intended to represent complete teaching syllabuses, otherwise they are not a graded objectives system. If one organizes a set of graded objectives to be reached in one's teaching why should they not embrace the whole syllabus? What is the point of leaving part of the syllabus outside the objectives to be assessed? Seen in this way, which is the way most enlightened and worthwhile systems operate, there is no danger of their 'restricting work in the subject', though, since they constitute the teaching aim, they do inevitably 'dominate classroom activities'. It seems the HMI may continue to be influenced, as so many teachers are, by an outdated view of what constitutes an examination. The old examinations did not pose altogether worthwhile goals and it was therefore proper that teachers should not allow them completely to dictate the syllabus and dominate the classroom even though in practice that is precisely what they usually did. Where, however, examinations do pose worthwhile goals then they should quite properly dominate the teaching.

The HMI outline the purposes of informal testing throughout teaching and of formal end-of-year testing in schools and have some very useful suggestions to make in both areas. Most particularly they point out that oral testing is not to be forgotten. Because it is more difficult to mark than a written examination, it is typically neglected. Teachers' mark-books rarely contain a mark for the oral proficiency of their pupils. The HMI also point out that 'the fact that whole classes are being examined simultaneously does not remove the need to match assessment to the different objectives set for pupils of differing abilities'. It is unfortunate that they do not give some practical examples of how this can best be done.

The HMI observe that many tests of listening and reading comprehension set questions in English to be answered in English (the GCSE national criteria actually require this) and suggest: 'It is best to avoid assessment procedures which lead to excessive use of English ....' Unfortunately they do not explain how to do this. They only hint at the interesting paradox that the more communicative the task set as assessment, the more necessary it becomes to explain in the mother tongue what has to be done. For example, if the candidate were required to translate a French passage into English, it would be safe to give the instruction in French: *traduisez en anglais*. If, however, the candidate is given something more interesting and 'authentic' to do, then the instructions might well be: 'You are staying in Paris with your French correspondent. His name and address is Jean Lenoir, 12 rue La Fayette, Paris 13. You have left your rucksack on a train, it was the 10.15 from Paris to Versailles. You have gone to the lost property office; be ready to answer any questions the person in the office will ask you. These will include enquiries about what the rucksack contains.' It would be difficult to put all that in the foreign language without risking the situation where the candidate fails to perform adequately because she misunderstands the instructions. There are many examples of tests in English as a foreign language which illustrate that circumstance. There is a genuine problem here which is not easily dealt with. The HMI suggestion that teachers should '. . . encourage imaginative approaches in which different language skills are combined' is praiseworthy but does not cope with the difficulty. The problem of how to test performance in the foreign language without resort to mother-tongue instructions has not yet been solved.

The Provision of Foreign Languages within the Curriculum

This is possibly the most interesting section for LEA curriculum planners, head teachers and others responsible for organization rather than methodology. While recognizing that there is 'no correct age at which to begin to learn a foreign language', the HMI accept that most pupils begin about the age of eleven. They make no attempt to argue that an earlier start would be preferable or express regret that circumstances make it impossible. And yet that argument exists. The great primary school French experiment of several years ago that concluded that an earlier start than age eleven was not worthwhile was very much criticized in its design, its execution and its evaluation. Current circumstances may hardly make an earlier start feasible but the situation should be left open and experiments encouraged. The HMI also reject mixed ability grouping except in the first year of language teaching. This again is a subject on which there is much debate and strongly held opposing views though none of this emerges from the document. Again, experiment should be encouraged and where teachers wish to and can show that they can operate mixed ability systems successfully they should be encouraged to do so.

The United Kingdom is one of the very few countries in Europe where it is possible (though not common) for even our most educated class, the future engineers, doctors, academics, to give up learning a foreign language at the age of 14. In fact, over half the school population at the crucial option period at the end of the third year choose not to continue learning a foreign language. The situation is improving — until recently two thirds dropped out — but remains completely unsatisfactory. It is evidence of the way in which society, its institutions and its business community have not considered a knowledge of a foreign language as important either for personal culture or for professional use. This attitude is gradually changing and the business community in particular has shown in recent years that it is becoming increasingly aware of the necessity of foreign language skills in trade. The language associations have long considered that a foreign language should be a compulsory element in all pupils' curriculum up to age 16. The HMI considers it both 'logical and desirable'. They maintain that courses which concentrate on 'background' and contain little language — often the only option offered to the less able

— are 'not to be seen as a substitute for the learning of a foreign language'. The current government, in observations made about the core curriculum, seem to be of the same view although the consultation document, *Foreign Languages in the School Curriculum,* mentions only that 'the great majority' should continue with one.

As any teacher knows time allocation can be crucial. Two sets of double periods on Thursday and Friday afternoons are not going to lead to effective learning. The HMI recommend that the absolute minimum is four periods of thirty-five minutes each ('It is hard to imagine satisfactory progress given less than this') and this should occur in 'at least three evenly spaced contacts' during the week.

For several historical reasons French has long been the dominant foreign language taught in the United Kingdom. The problem of 'the hegemony of French' has been widely discussed but, without official direction, no great changes will be effected. It is obviously desirable that there should be more diversification so that others achieve the status of first foreign language. The HMI's statement, 'Languages other than French could be introduced more frequently as first foreign languages either on their own or as alternative to French,' would therefore be supported by most of the professionals in the language teaching community. The HMI make suggestions how this can be done and point out that there are many teachers who at present are not teaching the languages they are qualified to teach. The one operational problem not dealt with is that caused by the mobility of the population. Currently a child moving from one area to another has a reasonable chance of continuing to learn the French she has started. Increasing diversity of first foreign languages in schools could cause distinct problems for this quite large minority of the school population.

The Second Foreign Language

This section of the document is likely to produce the most hostility among the language teaching community. Traditionally the second foreign language has been offered only to those who have shown proficiency in learning the first one. Those pupils have also had a shorter course, even, sometimes, only two years, to reach the same examination level as those following a five-year course. Second foreign languages have therefore tended to be confined to an elite. Over the past decade or so many schools have made determined efforts to spread the second foreign language to a larger group and over a wider spread of time. The HMI consider that all these arrangements involve distortion of the balance of the common curriculum which is offered in the first three years. Moreover, they say, a large proportion do not choose to continue their second foreign language beyond the age of 14 and, therefore, they think that the cost of provision is high for a sometimes small result. They consider that 'the most desirable solution seems therefore to offer the second foreign language from the beginning of the fourth year when option choices are made'. In order to reduce the problems caused by condensing the course into two years they suggest that more periods could be given to it by manipulation of the option blocks or the examination could be postponed until the first year of the sixth form. The HMI consider this forms part of a package of three elements: the diversification of first foreign languages, the teaching of a language to all up to the age of 16 and the provision of a second foreign language starting only in year 4. The unfortunate thing is that some head teachers and LEAs will see the last suggestion on its own as a way of rationalizing the awkward demands of foreign language departments and be able to justify themselves by reference to an official pronouncement. The implementation of this suggestion to delay the offering of a second foreign language till year 4 without the other two elements of the package would be massively retrograde. It would exacerbate the domination of French and reduce the possibilities of ever diminishing it. It would thereby deliver a death blow to many a fledgling course in Italian, Russian, etc., not to mention more solidly based courses in German and Spanish. It is a highly dangerous suggestion. Moreover, it dismisses too lightly those many schools who feel they are quite satisfactorily teaching a foreign language before the fourth year. In particular it ignores the imaginative possibilities for end-on courses, those where pupils may do three years French followed by two/three years German and get low-level qualifications in both. In the Lancashire/Cumbria graded objectives scheme there is a Certificate in European Languages which requires levels 1 or 2 in three European languages. This has been particularly popular with less able pupils. The same scheme is being implemented in North Yorkshire. The idea that only the most able should be permitted to attempt a second foreign language is a mistaken one which is unfortunately reinforced by the HMI's suggestions.

Implementation

This section is worth quoting in full:

> All schools are doing at least some of the things which have been recommended in this paper. Implementation of these recommendations depends on LEAs and governing bodies as well as on the senior management teams of schools and their modern language departments. The following is a list of requirements against which schools and departments should set their practices:
>
> o a clear statement of the aims and objectives of foreign language teaching and of the way in which these are related to those of the school;

- an understanding of the contribution which foreign languages can make to pupils' education;
- precise linguistic objectives which match the abilities and needs of pupils of all ages;
- clear human and social aims;
- a scheme of work which deals in detail with aims, objectives, teaching methods (including use of the foreign language in the classroom), resources and assessment, and which is revised and updated regularly;
- teaching which has appropriate variety and pace, with the foreign language as the normal means of communication in the classroom and with pupils encouraged to participate and use their initiative;
- substantial use of authentic materials and exploitation of every opportunity to make language learning authentic;
- appropriate use of books, and audio-visual and other resources;
- courses characterized by differentiation and progression;
- the fulfilment by pupils of all abilities of their potential for language learning;
- assessment closely related to objectives;
- provision of foreign languages within the curriculum which matches the needs and aspirations of all pupils;
- accommodation and resources which meet the needs of the department and of the pupils.

The document as a whole, then, is interesting as a statement of those elements of best practice which should be more widely followed. In this way it confines itself almost completely to what is already being done and gives little indication of where one might go from here. In that sense it is a document on which it is difficult to build since it makes no suggestions or projections for the future. It is tantalizing to think what might have been if the document had, as well as describing the best of the present, hinted at some vision of what the future might reasonably be and if it had deliberately raised specific issues for debate instead of leaving them to be drawn from descriptions of present practice. It is a discussion document on which comment is invited. A revised edition may appear subsequently.

The final document which will have an effect on the place of foreign languages in the curriculum and on the nature of foreign language teaching is *Foreign Languages in the School Curriculum*, which is still available only in its consultative form. At present it consists of five sections: (1) Towards a National Capability; (2) Availability and Take-up of Provision; (3) Which Languages?; (4) The Nature and Quality of Provision; (5) Action.

Each of sections 2 to 4 has a final paragraph entitled 'The Way Forward' and the final section sets out what has to be done and who should be responsible for it. Unlike the HMI document it has the specific intention of outlining the need for change and the ways in which it should develop.

The first section points out how important are 'worthwhile skills in foreign languages' (what that means is defined later). 'It is not only the individuals concerned who benefit from being able to communicate with foreigners in their own language. The country too can benefit economically and socially ...' These two ideas are expanded. The educational value to the individual is explained and it is pointed out that 'compared with many major trading nations, ours has a damagingly small proportion of people who understand and speak foreign languages.' The document goes on to say that reliance on English 'narrows opportunities in business and other respects'. The causes of our relatively poor performance in foreign language learning are complex but 'whatever the root cause, negative attitudes to learning languages are self-perpetuating'. It is up to the schools then to create 'both a firm foundation of skills and a sense of achievement in foreign languages which can be built on later in life as fresh motivations arise'. In the light of that, the statement 'argues that:

— more pupils should study foreign languages throughout compulsory secondary education and beyond;
— more pupils should have opportunities to study foreign languages other than French; and
— standards of communication in foreign languages should be improved among pupils of all abilities.'

To achieve this LEAs should 'prepare clear and positive policies for foreign language provision in schools in their areas' and schools 'should draw up their own aims for the teaching of foreign languages.'

It can be seen, then, that the thrust of this document is the same as that of the graded objectives movement and the National Criteria, both of which preceded it, and the HMI statement which postdates it.

In the second section the important principles are stated that 'the great majority of pupils 11–16 should receive a foreign language course designed to be of lasting value' (this is later restated as 'virtually all pupils') and that 'this should involve three years of study'; that 'most pupils' should continue with the foreign language 'throughout secondary education' and that a second foreign language 'should be offered from the second and third year to those who can benefit from it'. The first principle is generally agreed and is already in operation. The second is possibly less definite than the HMI suggestion which is supported by the language teaching community and the current ideas on the core curriculum, that virtually all should continue up to 16. The third is in disagreement with the HMI over the time of introduction of the second foreign language though it still contains the words '... those who can benefit from it ...' which leaves the matter wide open to excessive restriction. In a later paragraph it is stated that, in order to maintain curriculum balance, 'the curriculum time needed should come from the time given to all language studies including the first foreign language'. It is not at all clear what is meant. If for most pupils in years 1 to 3 four periods a week are allotted to French, does this mean that those starting German in the second year have only two periods a week each of German and French? This would not represent a serious course of study. Or do they mean that time should be taken out of the English allotment? This would scarcely meet the approval of English departments. The document does not here seem to have provided a reasonable solution to the problem of breadth and balance. It goes on to make the point that 'the option arrangements should not hinder those who have started a second foreign language from continuing to do it'. This would seem almost unnecessary to say except that one knows how many schools make the continuation, not only of the second foreign language but also of the first, difficult in years 4 and 5 by setting important options against them. This often has a particular effect on the take-up of foreign languages by boys — a circumstance which the document deplores.

The position of foreign languages post-16+ is partially dealt with. It is pointed out that many more than at present 'could profitably continue with a foreign language'. For some, A-level will be appropriate and new A-level syllabuses are welcomed as broadening the usefulness of foreign language study at this level. For other pupils, AS-level is seen as providing 'valuable new opportunities for sixth-form pupils who might not otherwise have done so to continue studying a language'. What the document does not say, however, is that the success of AS-level will depend almost uniquely on the extent to which university admissions tutors not only recognize it as a qualification but actively discriminate in favour of it. Moreover, if the intentions of the system are to be realized, the discrimination must be in favour of AS-levels in subject areas outside those of the admitting department. There will be no wide spread of AS-levels in languages among science students, for example, unless admissions tutors in science departments actively encourage them by making entry more likely for applicants with those qualifications.

Another notable omission in this statement is any serious recognition of post-16+ language qualifications except 'A' and AS levels. Courses provided by the Royal Society of Arts (RSA), or under the Foreign Languages at Work (FLAW) scheme, but no others, are briefly mentioned in four lines only. Yet the 16 to 19 area is one where foreign language courses are burgeoning. TVEI schemes which span the 16+ divide include some interesting language courses. So do some CPVE schemes. BTEC and the Institute of Linguists both provide new language courses relevant to this sector of the school population. There are many interesting opportunities available to the non-academic sixth-former in foreign language learning which this document ignores. This is a pity since that age and ability range could provide one of the biggest increases in language learning.

'The Way Forward' section makes it quite clear where the responsibility for change lies: '. . . the main agents for change will be the head and senior staff of each school, supported by the LEA's advisory service'. One wonders why the DES and the inspectorate is considered not to have any influence in this area.

Which Languages?

While allowing that it is difficult to predict which languages might be needed in commercial and industrial life, the document makes it quite clear that the fact that 'for the vast majority of pupils, an experience of foreign language at school is confined to French' is a situation which 'is clearly inappropriate to the needs of a modern trading nation'. Schools should make particular efforts to diversify their first foreign languages by offering ones in alternate years or, in large schools, splitting the intake year into two sections doing different languages. The document states that 'there is evidence within the existing teaching force that there is expertise in German, Spanish, Italian and Russian upon which schools are not drawing.' It is this hidden reserve which can provide the teaching staff for reorganized first-language schemes. It is recognized that there are difficulties; in-service training for teachers in languages they have not used for some time, the need to convince parents, the need for more initial training in less-taught languages. Nevertheless 'the need for diversification is pressing'. The final paragraphs of this section state that this will have to be done by 'redirection of existing resources' and the resolution of 'difficult decisions about priorities'. This is not the first or the last time that this document will imply that wonders are to be performed without any additional funds from central government. This raises a doubt about the government's attitude. If they really regard these proposals seriously they must be aware that extra funds are essential. Otherwise they are merely making pious noises.

Nature and Quality of Provision

The statement relates how the aims of language teaching have changed and how performance has generally been disappointingly low. It does quote findings from the APU surveys and from HMI reports that higher standards can be achieved. 'The foreign language provision in schools where high standards are regularly reached is characterized by successful expression of the curricular principles of breadth, balance, relevance and differentiation in terms of the content of foreign language provision and teaching methods.' Balance means 'the opportunity to develop the interrelated skills of listening, speaking, reading and writing' with a special place for the spoken word, the use of activities aimed at promoting communication and the realization that extended writing may be beyond the reach of some pupils. Breadth means making pupils aware of the people and country as well as the language, particularly through wide reading. Relevance refers to the fact that 'schools should make it clear that they may need to use a foreign language in a wide range of occupations and situations in their adult lives' and that therefore teachers should make use of authentic materials. The document shows a lack of sensitivity here. It is not at all clear to schools, teachers or pupils how exactly their pupils are going to need a foreign language in their adult lives. For any one of them it may turn out to be a necessity and even tip the balance between being offered a job or not but it is foolish to assume that the majority of our population will actually need a foreign language in order to earn their living. Pupils can see that that is not true as clearly as the writers of the document have failed to. The relevance we need to strive after is of another sort. The language should be relevant to the pupils *now* in the classroom, because it provides, in the words of the National Criteria, 'enjoyment and intellectual stimulation'. It should be relevant in the educational sense that, by using authentic materials, the teacher can show another culture at work and pupils can have an insight into another way of life with all its apparent similarities and real differences. Only in this way can pupils have balanced views about their own culture. Lastly, because the language learnt deals with practical communication, it does provide a usable skill that may be helpful in later life either in leisure or work. The document goes on in this section to say that 'the sensitive use of native speakers at all levels in schools and of visits abroad . . . is of considerable value'. No-one can quarrel with that. What the document fails to say is where the money is coming from. Foreign language assistants, the commonest form of 'native speaker' in our schools, are no longer provided by almost a third of our LEAs. Visits abroad, even school visits, are relatively expensive and therefore accessible only to a minority of pupils. The document says nothing about how these problems are to be overcome.

The teaching approaches favoured are those one would by now expect — 'communication', 'emphasis on speech', 'authentic' are the words used. The foreign language should be used rather than English in the classroom, topics should be of interest to the pupils and 'their efforts should be judged by the extent to which they get their message across as well as by its correctness'. Pair work is to be encouraged. Once again, however, the nature of the relationship of effective communication and formal accuracy and the weighting that should be given to each is not expressed. The need to differentiate objectives so as to provide appropriate goals for a wide ability range is underlined in a succeeding section. Progression and continuity are there dealt with. 'Progression should be planned and assessed to ensure that foreign language courses, whatever their length, represent a coherent and increasingly challenging experience for pupils.' To help this 'an even spread of single lessons over a week is likely to be more effective . . .' Continuity should be ensured on the one hand between the three-year course for all and the succeeding two-year course for the majority, and on the other between schools where different tiers may be teaching a foreign language.

It is one of the curiosities of British schools that subject departments frequently do not consult each other or exchange ideas. Consequently it is rare for teachers of foreign languages and teachers of English within the same school to have any formal professional links. This situation was typified in the Bullock Report *A Language for Life* (1975) which managed in its 600 pages not to mention foreign languages at all. Matters have marginally improved since then and this document states quite firmly that 'English departments and foreign language departments should share information about pupils and work together to improve linguistic skills'. In this context mention is made of 'language awareness' courses and while saying somewhat grudgingly that these 'can contribute to linguistic de-velopment' the document goes on to restate the view, often made by HMI, that schools should be careful that language awareness courses do not encroach on the time available for learning specific foreign languages. There is, however, much experience in schools that language awareness courses, of which there are many and for which some interesting textbooks now exist, do provide a positive start which makes pupils that much more effective in their subsequent foreign language learning (Donmall, 1985; Hawkins, 1987).

Assessment, an enormous subject, is dealt with very briefly in two paragraphs. The first says that assessment should be systematic though not necessarily formal, 'consistent with the school's detailed objectives for foreign language teaching', 'designed to motivate pupils' by assessing what they can do. The remaining two thirds of the paragraph are about graded assessments which meet with lukewarm approval. While acknowledging that such schemes 'have a valuable potential for stimulating pupils' enthu-siasm and even evaluating progress', they go on to say that they have 'relatively modest short-term objectives', risk 'inflexibility and fragmenta-tion' and that careful planning is needed so that 'the syllabus for the tests is not allowed to dominate classroom work'. This reflects the DES's usual narrow and out-of-date view of graded objectives schemes. It is true that there is always the potentiality in any approach to teaching that it should become inflexible, fragmentary and narrowing, and some graded objec-tives schemes undoubtedly suffer in this way. The statement fails, how-ever, to appreciate what has been done, what is happening and the continuous evolution of the schemes. If the writers of the document had looked even briefly at schemes like those in Lothian, Cambridge, East Midlands, Durham, Berkshire, Buckinghamshire, London, to name only a few, it would have been very difficult to talk of them in these terms. Graded objectives schemes now usually embrace quite advanced aims in their higher levels, have always used authentic materials and concerned themselves with communication, particularly oral communication, are coherent in their approach and objectives, and in fact aim to respect all the principles this document favours. It is true, as this document says, that 'there is much evaluation development skill to be done' because that is always true of anything in education but that does not excuse the document's failure to give a proper picture of graded objectives schemes or to recognize how they have evolved over the ten years since their tentative beginnings (Page, 1987).

The second paragraph of this section welcomes the arrival of GCSE, the development of new 'A' level courses and hopes that AS level courses will have a similar nature.

The final two sections after assessment deal with the difference in take-up of foreign languages between boys and girls and the needs of teacher training. The imbalance between the sexes in examination classes in particular has been remarked upon for many years (Powell, 1986). There is not time to go into the matter here but it should be said that schools should take positive steps to rectify it and the document points out that HMI have reported on schools that have been successful (DES, 1985).

It cannot be repeated often enough that learning a foreign language is just as important to males as to females. Its general educational value and 'relevance' in the sense discussed earlier are not gender specific. It should also perhaps be pointed out, and none of the official documents do, that a usable skill in foreign languages is likely to be at least as useful to both men and women in later life as a knowledge of any other subject. The salesman or woman is likely to need a language at least as much as a knowledge of physics and a hairdresser or motor mechanic may just as easily come across a French-speaking customer as have a need for secondary school mathematics. While society has been led to believe that an understanding of science and mathematics is essential for survival in the modern world, it has not yet accepted, in the United Kingdom at least, that a foreign language is as important. Both these official documents could have made a much stronger case.

Foreign language teachers possibly more than others are possessors of skills which can deteriorate if they are not constantly refurbished. PGCE courses, the document says, must maintain the linguistic skill of the students so that it 'is not allowed to erode during training'. Similarly 'the maintenance of teachers' own linguistic competence through foreign visits and exchanges should have a priority'. The help that can be given by the Central Bureau for Educational Visits and Exchanges is mentioned. What is not mentioned is that virtually all official visits and exchange involve personal expense by the teacher concerned and that most teachers maintain their skills at their own expense by spending their family holidays abroad. The DES should recognize that if it wishes to be seen as serious about the maintaining of teachers' foreign language skills then it must provide more money than it does at the moment to achieve it. The way forward, in this section, is again for LEAs, schools and teachers to profit by the example of 'more successful schools' and to use the principles outlined as the basis of detailed policies.

The final section entitled Action starts by saying 'the time is right for a reappraisal of foreign languages provision in schools' and goes on to claim, 'We have taken and are taking steps to create a climate within which the necessary changes can take place.' These include the setting up of new examinations, the confirmation of the role of the Centre for Information on Language Teaching and Research (CILT), further help for the Central Bureau and the planned short reports from the Assessment of Performance Unit on its surveys (DES, 1986). This also includes the promise that 'we are also providing funding for work to exploit to the full the findings of those surveys'.

The final two paragraphs deserve quotation in full:

70. Concerted and vigorous action is needed from LEAs, schools, teachers and their trainers to bring about the necessary changes.

LEAs should

— prepare and implement clear and positive policies for foreign language teaching in schools, addressing the availability and take-up of first and second languages throughout schools; the range of languages on offer; and the nature and quality of provision (including continuity between institutions);
— determine the amount and range of foreign language teaching expertise present in their teaching force and ensure that its deployment and the recruitment of new foreign language teachers is in line with their policies;
— consider the adequacy of the support they provide — in terms of in-service training, advisory services, curriculum development, foreign language assistants and arrangements for pupil visits and exchanges — to sustain these policies; and
— make arrangements for monitoring the success of their foreign language policies.

Governing bodies and the heads of schools should

— draw up their own aims for foreign language teaching, and make arrangements for the organization and delivery of the foreign languages curriculum within the school, in the light of their authority's policy, and monitor the effectiveness of this action;

— take the lead in promoting a positive attitude to foreign languages in the school; and

— ensure that parents are kept informed of changes, particularly where different languages are to be offered.

Teachers of foreign languages should

— review practice in the light of their school's policy and of best practice locally and nationally;

— ensure that they are up-to-date with professional developments; and

— maintain links with teachers of English and other relevant subjects.

Teacher training institutions should

— consider the scope to direct their PGCE courses more closely to practical language learning and to capitalize on the skills of students qualified in more than one language; and

— ensure that in-service training schemes are responsive to teachers' needs in terms both of linguistic competence and teaching methodology.

71. We recognize that some — but by no means all — of the necessary developments will require extra resources, and that the pace of change will depend on the rate at which those resources can be made available. We believe, however, that much can be done in present circumstances through a recognition of the importance of foreign languages and a determination to make a start on reshaping provision.

Paragraph 70, while saying clearly who should do what, significantly assigns no specific responsibility to the DES or the inspectorate. Paragraph 71 means in effect that extra resources are unlikely to be made available. The reaction of the language teaching community to the document was generally favourable. Criticism was of detail rather than of basic principles. One point above all was picked out and that was indeed the question of resources. Foreign language teachers feel themselves more stretched than ever. They are called upon to create materials, use a multiplicity of resources, teach more classes, have fewer non-teaching periods, adapt to change on a massive scale and are promised no extra resources with which to cope. It is not surprising that they sometimes feel rather cynical about the government's seriousness of intention as expressed in *Foreign Languages in the School Curriculum*.

The picture of language teaching as it should be in the schools that emerges from all this would appear thus.

In the secondary school a modern language is taught to all beginners from the age of eleven. On entry into the school they have a choice of foreign languages and/or the LEA ensures that there is a range of first foreign languages in its schools. In those areas where pupils still have French in the primary school or where middle school systems operate, which means that French is taught before entry into high schools, the receiving schools make special provision to build on the knowledge their entrants already possess.

The language is given at least four periods a week of at least thirty-five minutes each spread over no fewer than three occasions. The practice of having two double periods either too closely or too widely spaced no longer operates. Classes are mixed ability in at least the first year but may well be setted thereafter. In any case, a defined policy of differentiation of objectives adapts the teaching and the content to pupils of different abilities. The three years up to the option year form a coherent course which has defined and useful outcomes even if pupils drop the subject at that point. The great majority, however, continue up to GCSE.

The aim of the course is for learners to acquire the skill to communicate in the foreign language — 'communicate' here meaning being able to understand the spoken and written word as well as to speak and, to some extent, write to certain defined levels within a defined range of topics and settings. Other aims like learning to cooperate, to work in groups, to help each other, affect the way the teaching is carried out but are less susceptible of assessment than the content and skills. The LEA and the school have written curricular policy documents about foreign language teaching and the department has a scheme of work which expresses the department's philosophy and aims and sets out in detail how they are to be realized. A second foreign language is on offer, though when and to whom may differ widely from school to school. In larger schools other languages too will be available either before 16+ or as ab initio courses in the sixth form.

The modern language department has a suite of rooms and store rooms suitably equipped with tape recorders, overhead projectors, a video-recorder and appropriate tapes, modern text books and a collection of magazines, newspapers, etc. Most schools cannot afford regular subscriptions to foreign periodicals but these are purchased from time to time in order that an up-to-date view of the country is maintained. Computers are also used where they are available. In some schools computer links with French schools have been established.

In the classroom the walls are covered with posters, brochures, etc, and examples of pupils' work. All serve a teaching purpose and are regularly renewed. The head and the staff cooperate in making sure that public notices throughout the school also appear in the languages taught in the school as well as in those used by its pupils. The teacher expects to use the foreign language in the classroom for all purposes including announcements and classroom management though fanaticism is avoided and judgments made about when this can be counterproductive. The comparison of the foreign language and the mother tongue can be very fruitfully used in language awareness courses. As well as using and adapting text books, authentic written and spoken materials, audio and video tapes and possibly computer programs, teachers will also be producing their own materials often based on realia they have acquired from their visits abroad. To this end, the members of the department cooperate fully. In regular departmental meetings, suitable materials are discussed and members of the department undertake to produce teaching packages from them. These are kept, properly catalogued, in a departmental filing cabinet or other suitable store. The days when a teacher was an individual working out her salvation alone with her pupils and a text book are gone. If teachers are not to be grossly overworked in attempting to respond to new demands they must cooperate to produce teaching schemes and materials. Team teaching is sometimes used and pair and group work feature in virtually every lesson.

The work is regularly assessed both formally and informally. In particular, oral performance is as often assessed as the other skills. The pupils may well be involved in a graded objectives scheme which gives shape and purpose to the early years of learning and, in some cases, leads to a mode 3 GCSE. A TVEI scheme in the school also includes a foreign language module which can form part of the graded objectives scheme. In the sixth form, 'A' and AS levels are provided as well as more vocationally oriented BTEC (Business and Technician Education Council) and FLAW (Foreign Languages At Work) courses possibly within CPVE schemes. Ab initio courses are available sometimes leading to formal examinations and qualifications, sometimes not, depending on the size of the school.

The teachers experiment with forms of continuous assessment and techniques which allow pupils a greater degree of autonomy in their learning. Both for educational reasons as well as efficient foreign language learning, it is important that pupils learn to stand on their own intellectual feet and assume some responsibility for their own learning and the evaluation of their own performance. They can only do this if they have some powers of decision over what they do. Many teachers are working with considerable success towards systems which embody these ideas. The teacher's role then changes from director and 'feeder', to facilitator, provider of information on demand and collaborator in the learning process and its evaluation.

Some form of language awareness course is provided in collaboration with the English department either as a preliminary to the foreign language course or alongside it. Collaboration among all the language teaching departments, including the mother tongue, is close and regularly maintained.

The general principle covering all this activity is that as many languages as possible should be taught successfully to as many pupils as possible within the framework of the curriculum and the resources available.

Postscript

After this chapter was written, the consultation paper on the National Curriculum and the draft Education Act were published. These contain many proposals which will affect foreign language learning in schools but three have an obvious and immediate relevance.

i) A foreign language should be one of the foundation subjects studied by all pupils up to age 16+.

ii) The foundation subjects should occupy something between 70 per cent and 90 per cent of the available time.

iii) There should be tests administered at ages 7, 11, 14 and 16.

The first of these proposals, as has been mentioned above, will meet with the approval of many language teachers and their language associations. All, however, are apprehensive about the resource implications, on which the documents are silent or unhelpful, and few believe that sufficient staff will be found among those already qualified. Language teachers are in short supply. Entries to training courses have dropped dramatically over the past few years. Without immediate action from central government it is difficult to see how the new courses required by the National Curriculum can be adequately staffed. What is needed is a coherent development plan spread over several years. This does not seem to be implied in the legislation.

One of the answers to the problem would be to encourage the end-on courses in two foreign languages mentioned above. However, both central government and the inspectorate, for reasons which are not at all clear, seem to be opposed to this. A recent report by HMI[1] (DES, 1987) has been most opportunely published to reinforce the official point of view.

The second proposal, concerning the amount of time allocated for non-foundation subjects, could be crucial to the survival of second foreign languages. If these are squeezed not only into the final two years of the course but also into an inadequate time allowance within those two years, then the number of pupils courageous and/or able enough to take them up will be severely limited. There is a grave danger that fewer pupils than at present will have a realistic opportunity to learn two foreign languages. In the rest of Europe it is common practice for all pupils to learn two foreign languages for at least part of their secondary school career.

The question of tests at ages 7, 11, 14 and 16 is a thorny one. As far as foreign languages are concerned, virtually only the tests at age 14 are relevant; foreign language learning does not usually start until age 11 and the number of pupils not entering for GCSE at age 16 if the subject is compulsory up to that time will be minimal. However, at age 14, for foreign languages as for other subjects, the range of competence is enormous. At one end of the spectrum are those very able pupils who could already successfully embark on an 'A' level course. At the other, are those who will have difficulty coping even with the basic core of GCSE in two years' time. It is obvious that any suggestion of a norm would bear little relevance to the competence of the majority. If this could be officially recognized then the existing graded objectives schemes might well serve more appropriately to fulfil the intentions of the Act.

The provisions of the new Education Act and of the National Curriculum are in many ways superficially attractive, particularly for foreign language learners. They are, however, far-reaching and their implications do not seem to have been fully thought through by the government. Unless extreme care is taken in their implementation and unless appropriate resources are provided we may well end up with a situation even worse than that which already exists.

Notes

1   DEPARTMENT OF EDUCATION AND SCIENCE (1987) An inquiry into practice in twenty-two comprehensive schools where a foreign language forms part of the curriculum for all or almost all pupils up to age 16, London, HMSO.

Bibliography

ANON (1987) *German in the United Kingdom: Issues and Opportunities*. London, CILT.
BTEC 'Modern languages in BTEC courses.' Pamphlet periodically updated.
DEPARTMENT OF EDUCATION AND SCIENCE (1985) *Boys and Modern Languages*, London, HMSO.
DEPARTMENT OF EDUCATION AND SCIENCE (1986) *Foreign Languages Performance in Schools* (Assessment of Performance Unit survey), London, HMSO.
DEPARTMENT OF EDUCATION AND SCIENCE (1986) *Foreign Languages in the School Curriculum*, London, HMSO.
DONMALL, B.G. (Ed.) (1985) *Language Awareness*, London, CILT.
HARDING, A., PAGE B., ROWELL S. (1980) *Graded Objectives in Modern Language Learning*, London, CILT.
HAWKINS, E. (1987) *Language Awareness: An Introduction*, Cambridge University Press.
HER MAJESTY'S INSPECTORATE (1987) *Modern Foreign Languages to 16* (Curriculum Matters 8), London, HMSO.
LIMB, A. (Ed.) (1987) *Language and Languages 16–19*, London, CILT.
LONDON CHAMBER OF COMMERCE AND INDUSTRY (1985) *The Non-specialist Use of Foreign Languages — Industry and Commerce*.
LONDON CHAMBER OF COMMERCE AND INDUSTRY (1987) *Foreign Language at Work Scheme (FLAW) 1987–88*.

Moys, A. (Ed.) (1984) *Foreign Language Examinations: The 16+ Debate 1981–83*, London, CILT.

Moys, A., Harding, A., Page, B., Pointon, V. (1980) *Modern Languages Examinations at 16+: A Critical Analysis*, London, CILT.

Page, B., and Hewett, D. (1987) *Graded Objectives in Modern Language Learning*, London, CILT.

Pointon, V. (Ed.) (1987) *Facts and Figures: Languages in Education*, London, CILT.

Powell, B. (1986) *Boys, Girls and Languages in School*, London, CILT.

Trim, J. and Van Ek J.A. (Eds) (1984) *Across the Threshold: Readings from the Modern Languages Project of the Council of Europe*, Oxford, Pergamon.

Van Ek J.A. (1976) *The Threshold Level for Modern Language Teaching in Schools*, London, Longman.

5 *English*

Robert Protherough

English in Education

There is a profound ambiguity in the way that our society perceives English and its place in the education system. First, it is seen both as a subject at the heart of the curriculum, and as an assemblage of activities with no real discipline of its own. From the Newbolt Report of 1921, English has been presented as the central, unifying school subject: 'the one indispensable preliminary and foundation of all the rest'.[1] The Spens Report of 1939, saying that of all subjects 'English is most capable of giving a meaning and a unity to the whole course' up to the age of 16, suggested (using italics for emphasis) that

> for the majority of pupils *we think that the school itself should adopt a unifying principle in its curriculum, and we recommend that it be found in the teaching of English*.[2]

The Norwood Report of 1943 recorded similarly:

> the supreme importance of 'English' has been stressed ... an 'element' of education which is of vital importance to all subjects and should be the concern of all teachers.[3]

It would be easy to quote other heady comments to suggest that English is 'the central and dominating subject'.

However, the argument of George Sampson that English 'includes and transcends all subjects[4] can also be used to suggest that it is not a subject in its own right at all. If English is seen as the concern of all teachers, of importance to all subjects and synthesizing the whole course, then it becomes easy to question whether — in the conventional sense — it has a separate existence or is simply a servicing agent for the rest of the curriculum, and eventually for life itself. In many primary schools, 'English is not a subject at all but an activity permeating their lives'.[5] When the English Tripos eventually came into being at Cambridge in 1917, Sir

Arthur Quiller Couch lectured 'On a School of English' and immediately proclaimed that 'there is no such thing' as a subject called 'English Literature'; it cannot be 'treated as a subject all by itself, for teaching purposes'.[6] More recently Graham Hough has been only one of a number proclaiming that at university level English 'should never have grown into a separate and isolated "subject" as it has'.[7] At school level, reorganizers of the curriculum are particularly prone to subsume English in some form of 'integrated' course, and to announce the imminent 'death' of English as a separate subject.

At examination level, English has always been divided into two subjects, language and literature, and although GCSE introduces a unitary subject called English, with a literary element, it also maintains a separate, additional subject called English Literature. Significantly, at HSC or 'A' level, the title *English* has come to mean exclusively English *Literature*. Still more in Higher Education lecturers tend to assume that they have no direct responsibility for the written or spoken language use of their students, who learn to write by writing essays about what they read. Language is for many; literature is for the able few, the specialists. After twenty years of discussion, two boards have proposed a new subject at Advanced Level called English Language or English Language Studies, but their suggestions are concerned to give linguistic studies an equal status with literary ones, not to bridge the gaps between the two. We have no word to describe 'the joint study of English language and literature', with the possible exception of *Anglistics:* a late coinage (Oxford English Dictionary, 1930) of continental origin that is largely unknown and unused here.

A second aspect of ambiguity lurks in public love-hate perceptions of the subject's worth. There is plenty of evidence that in the opinion of pupils and their parents English is perceived as the most crucial element in the curriculum, 'universally valued by the 15-year-old ... of great use ... of great importance'.[8] In a recent attitude survey (1986) 87 per cent of respondents placed reading and writing at the top of those curricular subjects perceived as essential for 15-year-olds.[9]

Such general views have recently been given particular emphasis by the Secretary of State for Education, and there is no reason to doubt the genuineness of his concern, expressed in speeches over a period of six months shortly after coming to office. Following Sir Keith Joseph's description of English as a 'key subject in the curriculum',[10] he has stressed that 'the skills of literacy need to receive a very high priority' *throughout* the years of schooling.[11] He has proclaimed 'the importance of reading, both for its own sake and to build up the other language skills' and the power of literature to affect human lives.[12] He has said that he wishes to see 'a new emphasis on oracy', to help children 'to have confidence in using words in all circumstances'. One of the central purposes of any 'worthwhile system of education' is 'to make its pupils reflective users of our language'.[13] He has praised the ways in which the experience of creative writing can 'develop the sharpness of perception and the sensitivity to words that go hand in hand with a love of books and reading'. At the end of that speech he added, 'These things are close to my heart.'[14]

However, those subjects of which we expect most are also those which we criticize most strongly if they fail to match our expectations — and those expectations change as society changes. In English, our views of what 'functional literacy' means are constantly becoming more demanding. Even though there have been some improvements in national standards of reading and writing over recent years — which is more than can be said of some curricular areas — these are held by Mr. Baker to be 'less than satisfactory' to cope with 'the challenge of modern life' (defined by him explicitly as life in 'a fast changing technological society').[15] Improvement is not enough; it must be major improvement in specific respects that are to be defined from outside the profession by the 'consumers'.

A general belief in the crucial importance of English abilities goes hand-in-hand with quite differing views held by those consumers about which abilities are most important and about how they can best be developed. Parents, employers, engineering professors and — of course — politicians all express their ideas with a freedom they would not dream of adopting when speaking or writing of chemistry, say, or French. English teaching is like televised football: it provides a splendid opportunity for non-participants to feel that they know better than the professionals and to criticize what is going on. Saying that the standard of English teaching is 'patchy', Mr. Baker has remarked that 'many' schoolchildren are 'ill-equipped' in their ability to 'use written and oral skills flexibly', 'to employ languages as a vehicle for critical thinking' and 'to understand how language itself works'.[16] He is 'not at all happy' that the English language is receiving what, in horticultural terms, he referred to as 'cultivation . . . like a garden'. Employers complained 'frequently' that many school leavers 'cannot write simply, clearly and without obvious error'.[17] The Kingman committee has been set up to enquire into English teaching and 'make recommendations for its improvement', as part of wider moves 'to improve standards'.[18] English is simultaneously perceived as potentially vital and actually fallible: a dangerous conjunction.

A third aspect of these ambiguous perceptions of English is revealed in the way that its academic and political importance are defined. English is nowadays generally the largest subject department in a secondary school and is the one subject likely to be taken by all students up to the age of 16. Precisely *because* everybody takes it, however, the subject can be perceived as less 'serious' than those taken by an academically able minority. This is sometimes reflected in the allocation of staffing and resources. Although English has the greatest number of candidates for examination at 16+ (and English Literature the third greatest) and although for some years it has been second only to mathematics (inflated by double entries) at

'A' level, it is still an 'easy' option in some people's minds. There seem to be three main reasons for this. Some people feel that the 'softness' of English is indicated by the fact that it became established more rapidly in girls' schools than in boys', and that it was chiefly studied at university by women. After a period when the sexes were almost balanced at examination level, English is significantly returning to being a 'girls' subject': boys currently being outnumbered four to one at 'A' level. Others believe that English is more tolerant in its expectations and more sanguine about its benefits than other subjects. One study has shown that 'A' level English groups are twice as likely as mathematics groups to contain students who have failed at 'O' level.[19] For a few, the weakness is somehow there in the subject itself, too obvious to need argument. Graham Hough said of English at university: 'It becomes the bolt-hole of those who can't do mathematics and are too lazy to learn a language properly.'[20] Significantly, when parents were asked in a recent survey whether they would find it 'easy' to help their children with school homework at 'O' level, 60 per cent claimed that they could easily help with English, but only 15 per cent felt capable of assisting with mathematics or French.[21] The arguments used in the late nineteenth century to oppose the introduction of English to universities still live on: it is too pleasurable, it could be undertaken in leisure time, it is hard to assess rigorously (very much the arguments now being used to keep out media studies).

Because its importance is so general and not career-specific, and because of current governmental presures towards business and technology, English is not perceived as politically important. Although at any one time there are more unfilled English posts in schools than physics ones, and although more English than physics is taught by non-specialists, it is the situation in physics that causes the outcry. English has notoriously not received the injections of extra funds from government or industry afforded to science or mathematics, say. For decades, as HMI are well aware, English has been notorious as the great hidden 'shortage' subject. Not only has there been a deliberate attempt to play this down, but English has consistently been denied any of the injections of extra funds or training schemes, from government or industry, afforded to science, or mathematics or Craft Design and Technology (CDT). Nor has it even been the fashionable flavour of the month like computers, economic awareness or personal and moral development. A look at government and local authority priorities for INSET reveals vividly how little real will there is to spend money on improving the quality of English teaching. Any criticisms of 'unevenness' in English should be accompanied by a realization that the subject has been denied adequate resources to improve the quality of teacher education.

Why English is Different

It will be clear that this selectively illustrated ambiguity towards English results in part from pervasive uncertainty about just what that unstable term 'English' itself conveys and in part from the difficulty of applying to it criteria drawn from other curricular areas.

Teachers of all subjects naturally feel that their own is somehow 'special', but the unique position of English in the curriculum can easily be substantiated. Consider, for example, in brief, bold detail:

i)   The learning of most subjects begins with the teaching of that subject in school. However, children bring to schooling in English a wealth of existing experience in language: considerable development in talking and listening and — in some cases — also of reading and writing.

ii) Only a small part of the teaching of English is carried out by English teachers. 'Every teacher is a teacher of English' (and some of them rather poor ones), but so are parents, friends and figures in the media. Everything that is heard and read potentially influences 'English' attitudes and abilities.

iii) There is a notorious lack of agreement about the subject matter of the subject. Peter Wilby has quoted a senior HMI as saying, 'In maths ... there is very little disagreement over the content. In English nobody agrees about anything ...'[22] Just what is the special knowledge that an English teacher must have and transmit? If English is 'the process and practice of all those activities we engage in through language',[23] then it is virtually impossible to establish the priority of certain elements and activities over others. Nearly twenty years ago it was sardonically remarked that English content is 'whatever you can do in an English class just as long as you can get away with it'.[24] Even what once seemed clear-cut, the notion of 'English literature' is no longer a simple, agreed field of study.[25]

iv) The relationship between the student and what is studied is different in English from other academic subjects, which are essentially cognitive and analytic. In English, cognitive and affective are inseparable: the student's response to a text, attitudes towards the topic being discussed or feelings about the writing being undertaken are an essential element in what is being studied.

v)   The emphasis in English is on the developing individual: on personal experiences, responses to reading, expression of ideas. Other subjects tend to analyze and categorize experience by agreed common qualities. In English 'the experiences ... are those in which individuals *differ*'.[26]

vi) The boundaries of the subject are unclear. Formally, does what we call 'English' include Drama? Media studies? Communications? Or are these separate subjects in their own right? Informally, teachers of English discover that they are continually pushed into other curricular areas: history, other languages and literature, philosophy, sociology, art and music. Professor James Britton warned the International Conference on the Teaching of English at Sydney in 1980 of the dangers of any 'attempts to define subject English in isolation from the rest of a student's learning experiences, out of context in the curriculum as a whole'.[27] The multiplicity of links with other subjects is emphasized by the situation when secondary English has to be subsumed into a larger faculty. There is no agreement about where its place lies. English can be found in faculties of language, of humanities, of social studies and of expressive arts.

vii) Whereas most subjects fitted fairly snugly into one or two of the 'areas of learning and experience' as defined by the DES,[28] English teachers felt that they had a major contribution to make in at least five of these areas (aesthetic and creative, human and social, linguistic and literary, moral, spiritual) or six if drama is included. Many of them were also uneasy about the proposed separation ('in all areas') of knowledge, concepts, skills and attitudes as though these were discrete categories.[29]

viii) Whereas other subjects tend to have clearly defined goals, often with an explicit vocational emphasis (to prepare students to become scientists, technologists, linguists) English is expected to achieve objectives that are important for learning in *all* subjects and areas of life, as well as those more limited goals that are 'subject specific' to those who will become 'students of English'.[30] There is consequently much more pressure from non-specialists than in other areas of the curriculum to establish what *they* think from the outside English 'should' be achieving.

Professor Harold Rosen began his inaugural lecture at the London Institute by remarking on this curricular uniqueness. English, he said,

is the least subject-like of subjects, the least susceptible to definition by reference to the accumulation of wisdom within a single academic discipline. No single set of informing ideas dominates its heartland. No one can confidently map its frontiers ... the practices which cluster together uncomfortably under its banner ... appear so diverse, contradictory, arbitrary and random as to defy analysis and explanation.[31]

This, of course, is one of the attractions for many teachers (and students) since the situation offers an unparalleled freedom to bring curricular knowledge into existence through a series of classroom encounters. One fundamental result of this is that English teachers, while enjoying the sense of liberty to operate in ways they find most congenial and effective, also find it hard to be absolutely certain about what it is they *should* be doing or to convince others of the rightness of their diagnosis. A number of researchers have pointed to the different (and often irreconcilable) paradigms of English teaching that exist within the profession, and that even divide departments. By a historical study and by a cluster analysis of teacher opinions, Hodgson detected what he called five distinct 'models of the new consciousness' (personal-expression, sociological, negotiations, linguistics-based and synthesis-compromise).[32] More recently, Douglas and Dorothy Barnes detected five rather different but distinct models at work in examination groups (cultural tradition, personal growth, basic skills, belles lettres and public rationality).[33] Gerald Grace, in a study of sixteen comprehensive schools, found that there the 'English teachers represented a complete spectrum of ideological positions in education, from the Arnoldian stance to the Marxist'.[34]

> English as a school subject emerged from the research as a contested area of curriculum knowledge, inviting endless disputes about its proper definition. At any one time, one of the competing definitions may appear to be predominant but the disputation is never satisfactorily resolved for all concerned.[35]

The Coming of Subject English

It is hard for us in the eighties to imagine a previous age in which learning English was not important, and where English as a separate subject did not exist. We see it as central to the British school curriculum: English Language at 16+ attracts more candidates than any other subject; something like a million young people every year in England and Wales seek external qualifications in English Literature,[36] and English is studied world-wide by many of the 300 million or so who speak it as their first language, and the similar number who 'make substantial use of it'.[37] However, this assured placed has only recently been won. English did not even become established as a curriculum subject until long after classics, mathematics or theology, and later than history or modern languages or science.

The first recorded use of the word *English* meaning an academic subject for study is given in the Oxford English Dictionary as 1889, where it is defined as 'English language *or* literature as a school *or* university subject *or* examination'. The triple alternatives (and especially those between language *or* literature and subject *or* examination) are symbolic of the tensions within the concept, arising from its recent history. One important study has concluded:

> It is possibly fair to say that, before the turn of the century, English did not exist as a separately identifiable school subject at either elementary or secondary level. There were certainly very few teachers who could be called or would have called themselves teachers of English.[38]

For centuries the term English had simply signified the language itself, which was not seen as a subject for serious study. From the Middle Ages onward *grammar* meant exclusively Latin grammar and *Latinum* had come to mean language in general. Education in the vernacular was only for the very earliest stages or for those unfitted for the education of a gentleman. This situation remained substantially unchanged for many years. Until well into the nineteenth century a two-tier system existed. Basic instruction in reading and writing was given in dame schools, charity schools, elementary schools and mechanics' institutes by unqualified amateurs. At secondary and university level it was simply assumed that pupils should already have attained necessary competence in the vernacular.

> The ancient universities, public schools and grammar schools ignored English throughout the nineteenth century. This neglect was partly because of confidence in the superior humanism of the classics, and partly because of the vernacular's association with working-class education.[39]

Nowhere was there any concept of English as an organic field of study. As late as 1900, the Board of Education's Schedules for each age group show reading, writing and English as separate subjects, possibly taught by different teachers — and English exists simply in terms of formal grammatical knowledge. In the school curriculum, the activities were 'further fragmented into "recitation", "spelling", "handwriting" and so on', with separate periods for each. In 1900, Alice Zimmern wrote an article in *The Journal of Education*, putting forward what was clearly a pioneering claim that we should 'treat literature not as an isolated study, but as part of English'.[40] Indeed, she went further and proposed — as a novelty — that the half-a-dozen separate activities should be lumped together in the care of a single teacher:

> Give all the English in a class to one teacher; let him add together the hours now given to reading, grammar, composition, recitation, and literature, and redistribute them at his own discretion according as need may arise.[41]

The complex set of changes which resulted in the swift establishment of English as an academic subject at secondary level was given impetus by increasing dissatisfaction with the results obtained from the study of classics. Early nineteenth century attacks in leading journals like the *Edinburgh Review*, *Westminster Journal* and *Quarterly Journal* argued that other essential elements were being shouldered out of the curriculum by the exclusive concentration on the classics, and that work in classics had degenerated into grammatical drill and memorizing. The pleas for a modern humanism in such works of the 1860s as F.W. Farrar's volume *Essays on a Liberal Education* or Matthew Arnold's *Culture and Anarchy* argued the case for a significant experience of *English* literature. However, the subtext beneath these arguments has to be examined. The writers still assumed both the superiority of the classics over English literature, and the fact that the most able pupils would continue as classical scholars. English was seen as supplying the want of classics for the less able and those further down the social scale. It was not surprising, then, that prejudice against English continued in the public schools and the older universities. Thring's progressive regime at Uppingham in the 1880s offered a curriculum in which all boys studied classics and mathematics, history and geography, a modern language or science or drawing, and all 'learn singing who can' — but not English.[42] Margaret Mathieson has written of 'the reluctance of headmasters to include English literature in their curricula'.[43] Although the members of the Taunton Commission (1864–8) had suggested that English language and literature should be part of the curriculum in their proposed national system of secondary schools, they suspected that it would prove impossible to find staff who could teach such a subject adequately.

In 1904, the *Code of Regulations* of the Board of Education required all state secondary schools to include English language and literature in their courses. In one sense this could be seen as the first significant acknowledgement of English as a subject, to be followed by its appearance as a separate examination subject in the new Certificate (1917). On the other hand, it has to be remembered that these Regulations were introduced precisely because inspectors reported that English was commonly neglected, that many schools continued to teach other subjects under the guise of English, and that English was significantly divided into two separate subjects, frequently taught in isolation.

Despite the confident assertion in the Board of Education's 1910 circular that it was not 'necessary to dwell upon the importance of the subject' because 'The claim of English to a definite place in the curriculum of every secondary school is admitted',[44] there is also evidence of the 'failure ... in many schools' to establish the subject, and of the damaging effects of assuming that 'any master or mistress can teach English'.[45] The relationship between the existence of the subject and the qualifications of the teacher was even clearer in the public and grammar schools, where

English was by no means established at the time of the 1914–18 war.
S.P.B. Mais wrote from Sherborne School to say that in public schools 'it
cannot be pretended that English is taught at all' and that the crying need
was for 'specialist masters in English'.[46] At the time, those involved in
teaching it were either non-graduates of low esteem (later versions of the
'writing master') or graduates of other subjects, not formally 'qualified' in a
subject that had not previously existed at university level. These were
mostly classicists who brought with them into the new subject the
approaches developed in the study of the old. Writing in support of the
new English tripos at Cambridge, A.C. Benson based his case on a
supposed *future* (not present) need of qualified English teachers:

> I believe that English is very shortly going to become an integral
> part of every school curriculum ... and teachers for this purpose
> will have to be found and trained.[47]

Particularly in the public and grammar schools the impression remained for some time that English *should* be taught by specialists in other
subjects. Lord James has recorded that when he went to Manchester
Grammar School as late as 1945, only one of the masters in that large
school was qualified in English.[48] This may in part explain the ambiva-
lence of some of those who taught English when it came to recognizing it
as a subject in its own right. It may also help to explain the relatively late
appearance of organizations related to the subject and to its pedagogy. The
English Association did not come into being until 1906, thirty-five years
after the foundation of the Mathematical Association and considerably
later than the Modern Languages Association, the Geographical Association or the Classical Association. There were associations for those who
taught domestic science in 1896, physical education in 1899 and the
natural sciences in 1903. By contrast, the National Association for the
Teaching of English was not founded until 1963, lagging well behind
similar groups for teachers of mathematics (1952) and drama (1959), and
still further behind such minority subjects as Spanish and Portuguese
(1947). [NATE was also half a century behind its American equivalent, the
NCTE, founded 1911.] Awareness of the world-wide role of English
resulted in the eventual formation of the International Federation for the
Teaching of English — but not until 1983.

After such a late start, English established itself with extraordinary
speed as a central subject (perhaps *the* central subject) in the curriculum.
At school level, the crucial event was the publication in 1921 of the
Newbolt Report, *The Teaching of English in England*. Highly critical of
'inadequate' nineteenth century attitudes and methods, the authors put
forward a passionate and idealistic case for English in every child's timetable and for the notion that all teachers are (or should be) teachers of
English. In particular they stressed Arnold's argument for the power of
literature to strengthen men and women in times of cultural crisis. People

would lead 'starved existences' if they lacked 'that unifying influence, that purifying of the emotions which art and literature can alone bestow'.[49]

> We believe that in English literature we have a means of education not less valuable than the classics and decidedly more suited to the necessities of a general and national education.[50]

In other words, English was coming to be seen (in political and social terms as well as educational ones) as a unifying force. The Report criticized the differences in aims and curricula that separated the 'special treatment' of public schools from the severely practical emphasis in elementary schools, and which 'widened the mental distances between classes in English'.[51] The improved teaching of English in all schools was seen as an important way of bringing about necessary changes in society. Similarly the Report stressed that the university professor of literature 'has obligations not merely to the students who come to him to read for a degree, but still more towards the teeming population outside the university walls'. This quite new emphasis on the wider responsibility of the subject and on the special 'missionary' role of its teachers marked a significant difference from other disciplines. In the Newbolt Report and perhaps still more in George Sampson's influential book *English for the English*,[52] which shortly followed it, the centrality of English in the curriculum was a repeated theme.

Terry Eagleton has summed up: 'In the early 1920s it was desperately unclear why English was worth studying at all; by the early 1930s it had become a question of why it was worth wasting your time on anything else.' English at Cambridge had come to be seen as 'not just one discipline among many but the most central subject of all'.[53]

Towards Agreement?

The preceding sketch of the development of subject English and its place in the curriculum has pointed out some of the dissensions and disagreements about theory and practice that have marked its history. In 1910 and 1912 the Board of Education castigated common school practice for separating literature from writing ('they are organically interconnected'), for an obsession with grammar ('should not bulk largely') on a Latin model ('a mistake founded on a whole series of misconceptions'), for 'being dominated by the supposed requirements of external examinations', and for demanding an 'unnatural standard of quietness' (whereas, 'children should be encouraged to talk to one another').[54] An image was thus established from the earliest days of sometimes reluctant (and often unqualified) classroom teachers being urged towards more 'enlightened' practices. The Newbolt Report widened this in appealing beyond teachers to politicians and the general public to redefine the true role of English and the methods that might accomplish it. Culture *or* anarchy was the theme. In the years following the 1944 Act the pace quickened. The publication of *The Use of English* in the fifties, and the spontaneous growth of local groups of teachers associated with the journal, were perceived as re-emphasizing the Cambridge literary-critical traditions at school level, and relating these to a new concern for children's own powers of expression ('Growth of the Poetic Spirit'). That international gathering, the Dartmouth Conference, mediated to a wider public through John Dixon's *Growth through English*, was another attempt at forward-looking re-formulation. Dixon saw older models of English, marked by a concern for linguistic studies or for the cultural heritage, as being replaced by what he termed the 'growth' model: pupil-centred, experience-based, development-oriented. This model tended to be associated with the National Association for the Teaching of English, founded in 1963, and there were occasional, artificial arguments which suggested that all English teachers were divided, like Roundheads and Cavaliers, between *Use of English* people and NATE people (whereas many of us were both). The growth of linguistics as a discipline, and particularly the publication of *Language in Use*[55] (influenced to some degree by the earlier Ministry of Education pamphlet 26 of 1954 on *Language*) marked another shift of emphasis. Again there were the either/or disagreements, symbolized in the title of one article: 'Is literature language? Or is language literature?'[56] In 1975, the Bullock Report *A Language for Life* attempted, by placing language at the centre both of children's development and of the curriculum, to give a new coherence to English as a subject. In the long term, however,

> the result was further to undermine cherished illusions of common principle, to deepen the cracks in the consensus ... and to widen into a chasm the existing fissure between professional and public perceptions of the subject.[57]

The continuing failure to establish professional agreement about what precisely English *is* and how we should teach it has been accompanied by a wider failure to convince those outside the profession. The ground has thus been prepared for those who wish to *impose* 'agreement'. As I was completing work on this chapter, the lead story in *The Guardian* was headlined: BAKER SETS OUT NEW NATIONAL CURRICULUM. A newly-elected Conservative government 'would introduce a national core curriculum setting uniform standards in schools' and 'would lay down specific aspects which must be covered in English'. Legislation would ensure 'that every child studies the same nationally laid down curriculum' and 'all children would sit tests at the ages of 7, 11 and 14 to assess them against targets set nationally'.[58]

This effectively guillotined the continuing debate initiated by a whole series of DES publications throughout the eighties and perhaps most significantly by *Better Schools*, with its proposition that raising standards could only be achieved through 'broad agreement about the objectives and context of the school curriculum'.[59] Mr. Baker apparently abandoned that document's notion of 'broad agreement' and 'consultation' based on 'best practice' for one of 'laying down' by legislation, replaced 'the formulation of national *objectives*' with the creation of a 'new national *curriculum*', and interpreted a need to 'monitor progress' as meaning regular 'tests' and 'targets' for all. Nobody is likely to deny that there are serious weaknesses in our school system. HMI repeatedly draw attention to them, and the Secretary of State is right to look for improvement. However, he seems to *assume* that matters will automatically be better if we have more central control. It would be interesting to know what evidence he has that the weaknesses he proclaims are *caused* by a lack of curricular agreement.

Just what might be intended by that vague term 'a national curriculum' is still unclear. Politicians tend to use terms for their political impact rather than in the interests of academic precision, and English teachers — with their concern for language — have long been uneasy about the subtext lurking beneath the public statements of successive Secretaries of State for Education. I have analyzed in detail elsewhere the special rhetoric of Sir Keith Joseph with its limited notion of *quality* and *standards*, its emphasis on *securing returns* for *consumers*, its impersonal view of teachers as *manpower* to be *geared* or matched to certain needs, and its obsession with *appraisal of competence*.[60] Mr. Baker's preferred language has less of the monetarist terminology that sometimes made Sir Keith sound as though he was describing a supermarket and its balance sheet: UK Education plc. His imagery is of the production line: education is a *delivery system*, needing to *lever up* standards. Its job is to provide *grounding* in the *skills*, *training* in *basic elements* required by *industry* for *work* in a *modern, technological* society. Even the learning of different kinds of writing is described as giving children *hands-on experience*. To achieve this, he wishes to move in two — apparently contradictory — directions: on the one hand to establish a *national* curriculum with *national* objectives arrived at by a *national* process, and on the other to 'give the system's *customers* a bigger voice', 'devolution to the rim of the wheel'. The dual movement towards the centre and towards the rim is clearly intended to diminish the influence of the spokes: the teachers and the local authorities.

As far as one can tell from the context, Mr. Baker has at different times used the word *curriculum* in at least three senses. At first he seemed to intend what Jerome Bruner called 'a theory of instruction': a general consideration of how children's development is to be aided by particular principles and methodology.[61] Later, when he began to talk in subject terms (particularly of English and mathematics) he seemed to intend something closer to Bruner's 'curriculum': more specific discipline-centred goals. In the third formulation, however, with its stress on uniformity and 'aspects which *must* be covered in English' he seems to be moving into the area of syllabus design. This seems like a deliberate refutation of the conventional wisdom: 'No standard curriculum will do for all or even for most schools.'[62] Until now, DES advice has not been significantly different from that which the Board of Education offered in 1910:

> It does not profess to frame a syllabus of instruction or to pre-scribe in detail the methods by which teachers should proceed. Any such attempt would be useless, if not actively harmful, for several reasons. In the first place, English is the last subject in which a teacher should be bound by hard and fast rules ... [etc.][63]

In curricular terms, the Secretary of State's intentions can be seen in essence as an attempt to reduce the anarchy (or to restrict the freedom, according to your position) currently existing in schools. The implication is that this can be achieved in all subjects by establishing:

— greater agreement about what is the legitimate concern of the subject, what it is 'about' (which may or may not involve a degree of central direction)
— sets of specific goals which the subject is to achieve (by which 'customers' can 'judge')
— methods of assessing progress in that subject, to confirm what 'most' children of given ages 'should' be able to achieve.

Each of these three points can be discussed in terms of the applications to English, drawing here chiefly on *English from 5 to 16*: the only HMI subject paper to date that has drawn a massive and vigorous response, leading to a further paper *English from 5 to 16: The Responses to Curriculum Matters 1*.[64]

What is Subject-English?

First, then, how is subject English perceived? *English from 5 to 16* gives the clear impression that — to quote its opening words — 'achieving competence in the many and varied uses of our language' (not itself a particularly felicitous use of language) is the 'direct responsibility' of English teachers. Indeed *competence* is a frequently used word in the opening pages. Much of what follows in the booklet is structured by divisions between 'the four modes of language' (though we are assured that the four 'constantly interrelate'). The emphasis of the objectives (which are further discussed in the next section) seems to be on the acquisition of isolated language skills, so that it is with some sense of shock that we later read that 'good teaching of English ... is far more than the inculcation of skills'. The emphasis on progress as being 'continuously and methodically assessed' ('weaknesses must not be allowed to persist') is geared to the ill-defined 'requirements of living and working in society'.[65] This language meshes neatly with Mr. Baker's. He told the Conservative party conference that he wished to see 'basic elements of education, the three Rs, restored to their central place in the curriculum'. *Skills* is a word often on his lips, and his address to the World Congress on Reading seemed to *visualize* English as exclusively concerned with what he called 'the skills of literacy'.[66]

This emphasis is not one, however, that has been approved by those groups representing English teachers (NATE),[67] those concerned with English teacher education (ETUDE) or English advisers (NAAE). Indeed, the *Responses* paper describes the 'strong expressions of concern and fear' from those who were committed to views of English 'as a humane discipline'.[68] There are many reasons for feeling uneasy with a restricted definition of English as mother-tongue acquisition, with what many respondents saw as a highly functional emphasis and a comparative disregard for literary studies, for cultural diversity or for any interpenetration with media studies. Above all, however, there is a deadness of abstraction (in the objectives particularly) which seems to have forgotten that 'the *student*, not the *subject matter*, is at the heart of what we label "English" or "language arts".'[69] 'Achieving competence' in 'uses of language' is inadequate because it presents means as ends: the aims are skills-based. A mechanistic view of language as simple communication device gives an unbearably restricted view of what English is 'for'. The original document 'provides a way of evading central questions about how pupils learn'.[70] The word *literature* is mentioned only three times in the 150 objectives and it is 'viewed either as a form of entertainment, or as a series of linguistic hurdles'.[71]

The hottest controversy has raged over the knowledge *about* language that should accompany its use. This has been a recurrent debate throughout the century, and some teachers have always felt insecure that English seems to lack specific content. In a DES-led world seeking for uniformity, the fact that some subjects have agreed content and behavioural objectives seems a reason for insisting that *all* should. Consequently, the continuing debate was fanned to a blaze by the proposals in *English from 5 to 16*, which claimed that in addition to goals for speech, reading and writing,

> There is a fourth aim which applies over all the modes of language. This is to teach pupils *about* language, so that they achieve a working knowledge of its structure and of the variety of ways in which meaning is made, so that they have a vocabulary for discussing it, so that they can use it with greater awareness, and because it is interesting.[72]

There are several points of interest about this formulation. Unlike the other three aims which concentrate on what children should be able to do, this one concentrates on the *teaching*. It specifies knowledge *about* language rather than knowledge *of* language (rather like proposing that knowing about *Hamlet* is more important than knowing the play itself). It follows a suggestion earlier in the paragraph that the Bullock Report talked of the necessary interrelation of four modes ('interaction of writing, talking, reading and experience') but here quietly substitutes *knowledge* for *experience*. In talking about language studies achieving *knowledge of its structure* it seems to imply that there is general agreement about what that structure is and how it is to be described. There is little to support such a view. It is commonly suggested that there are something over two hundred definitions of *sentence*. In his massive historical study, Ian Michael has demonstrated that even by the year 1800 'grammarians gave their approval to fifty-six different systems of parts of speech', and concluded:

> If grammarians, few of whom are trying to make any change, disagree among themselves to this extent the categories they are using must be unstable.[73]

The triple justifications advanced for this knowledge in the HMI paper are all, at the best, dubious. First there is the idea that language knowledge improves language use ('learning about language is necessary as a means to increasing one's ability to use it').[74] Neither the classroom experience of teachers nor the weight of research evidence supports this claim. Indeed, the report itself admits that 'It has long been recognized that formal exercises in the analysis and classification of language contribute little or nothing to the ability to use it.'[75] However, despite the findings of the APU that when children are assessed they 'overwhelmingly use the grammatical forms typical of standard usage'[76] it is clear that a strong body of traditionalists believes — in the teeth of the evidence — that standards are falling, not rising, and that the remedy is instruction in formal grammatical categories. Engineering professors write to *The Times* sneering at creative writing and demanding a return to teaching what they called the 'rugged detailed structure of the language'.[77] The Queens English Society claims that 'the standard of English teaching has fallen badly' and points to newspapers and radio as proof. It proposes to petition Mr. Baker 'to introduce the compulsory study of formal grammar, including parsing and sentence analysis into the school curriculum'.[78] Members of the Inspectorate were not universally delighted to find themselves hailed as allies ('School inspectors want grammar at forefront in teaching English' said *The Times* headline; inspectors 'want children to receive more teaching of the rudiments of grammar' read *The Daily Telegraph*).[79]

Pam Czerniewska has argued interestingly about this persistent gut feeling that some people have that knowledge about language produces successful language users.

> The chain of causality is probably the reverse of this. It is not learning about language that makes you a better user but, instead,

it is becoming a versatile language user that makes you interested in its inner workings. It is hard to convince many successful language-users that knowledge of grammar and spelling rules is not the *cause* of their literacy ... [80]

Second, there is the assertion that knowledge of grammatical terminology is necessary for understanding and correcting mistakes ('Many pupils are taught nothing at all about how language works as a system, and consequently do not understand the nature of their mistakes or how to put them right').[81] It is a dubious pedagogic principle to advance the notion of teaching systems and terminology so that later some aspects of this may prove helpful in correcting errors, rather than starting from specific needs. Additionally, of course, it is precisely those pupils who 'do not understand the nature of their mistakes' who find it hard, if not impossible, to comprehend the grammatical concepts underlying the errors. The document itself admits that 'The least able at using language are the least likely to understand the terminology.'[82]

Third, there is the claim that knowledge about language is 'interesting'. Potentially this is true, but the *kinds* of knowledge specified in the lists of objectives do not seem likely to arouse interest in pupils. At eleven, they are expected to know 'the rules of spelling' (whatever they may be), terms like 'subject' and 'object' and the main parts of speech. *English from 5 to 16* showed a dangerous narrowing and over-simplification of that huge and complex area, knowledge about language, ignoring much work of the last twenty years to advance objectives more like those of fifty-year-old coursebooks.

It was hardly surprising that the sections on teaching *about* language 'prompted a good deal of disgreement and division', and that the case advanced there was felt by many to be 'unjustified' or 'justified on weak grounds'.[83] The tension running right through *English from 5 to 16*, between broad aims and specific objectives, was strongest here. The only 'clear trend' in the responses was 'a widespread and vigorous rejection of grammatical analysis and of teaching the terminology listed in the objectives'.[84]

Clearly this is a show that is going to run and run, because there are basic and irreconcilable conflicts of principle and practice. The Secretary of State has launched a national enquiry into 'what, in general terms, pupils need to know about how the English language works'.[85] He must be an optimist if he imagines that his oddly assorted 'high-level' committee, chaired by a mathematician, is going to produce an answer that will be more satisfactory and command more assent than the thinking and work of teachers, HMI, professional associations and university departments over half a century. As the *Responses* paper summed up: 'it will be a long time before the professional unity to implement a policy can be arrived at'.[86]

Objectives for English

The debate about what English teaching is meant to achieve has been given sharp focus by the publication of *English from 5 to 16*. In his accompanying statement, Sir Keith Joseph said firmly that 'the development of agreed national objectives for English teaching is ... a particularly important part of the Government's policies for raising standards in schools'. The core of the document, a proposed statement of objectives for English, we are told, 'evoked widespread disfavour especially from the profession', and the comments 'were strongly expressed and either critical or anxious'.[87] Why was this? Some respondents were opposed to the very concept of objectives or to the centralization implied by the document. Many, however, while not opposed to defining objectives had the strongest objection to the rigidity that a list of this kind might impose ('objectives cannot be agreed for all time')[88] and to the ways in which the 150 items had been formulated.

First, despite all the protestations that 'talking, listening, reading and writing should constantly and naturally relate'[89] the objectives were presented as self-contained lists under separate headings, without synthesizing or interrelation.

Second, there was the extraordinary assertion that 'Of the objectives defined none has primacy and none should be neglected in favour of any other'.[90] As I have argued elsewhere,[91] the worst feature of such lists of miscellaneous objectives is that they lump together a few essential aims ('have formed the habit of voluntary and sustained reading for pleasure and for information') with many desirable but comparatively minor skills ('use a dictionary ... time-table ... brochures'). Some of these objectives are major aims that will underlie the whole of a pupil's school career, others will only be introduced briefly at a particular moment; some are only slightly dependent on the teacher, others heavily so. The suggestion that, for example, 'To write clearly and perceptively about personal experiences and their response to them' is of no more importance than 'set out written material in tabulated form when appropriate' simply confuses broad universals with narrow behavioural objectives.

Third, the weird juxtaposition of major and minor goals is made even more bewildering by the language used, which is a strange mixture of the precise ('know the difference between vowels and consonants' or 'distinguish between sentence, clause and phrase') and the vague or undefined ('comprehend information conveyed orally', 'have some awareness of the relevance of imaginative literature to human experience'). We are told that 7-year-olds should be able to 'maintain their listening attention for a reasonable length of time when their interest is engaged'. Surely, if they are interested, then they are attending. And just what is 'a reasonable length of time'? They should 'set down directions and instructions when there is a clear purpose for doing so'. Who would propose activities of this kind that had *no* purpose? Some of these objectives for 7-year-olds have a chicken-and-egg circularity about them: 'Use a sufficiently wide vocabulary for the purposes of their writing'. And, of course, there is the crucial vagueness in the very way that these lists are introduced: at the age of 7, or 11, or 16 'most children should be able to . . .' What does *most* mean? 51 per cent? 75 per cent? 90 per cent? This stylistic confusion is caused, in part at least, by the attempt to turn a complex variety of goals into behavioural objectives. Such formulations may be possible for simple skills, but are inappropriate for those abilities that are not easily quantifiable (*comprehend, converse, sustain, show imagination, interpret* for 11-year-olds, qualified by question-begging terms like *accurately, responsively, with patience, confidently, pleasantly, succinctly, effectively, clearly*). This was the problem that bedevilled the formulation of criteria for English in the GCSE and that has involved the artificial 'grade descriptions' that accompany them (in spoken English, a grade 4 candidate will be capable of 'expressing intelligibly what is felt and what is imagined', whereas a grade 2 candidate will be capable of 'expressing effectively what is felt and what is imagined').

Fourth, many suspected that to formulate objectives in such terms would be more likely to lower standards than to raise them. Since all are lumped together as of equal importance, it will hardly be surprising if some teachers concentrate on achieving those objectives that can be directly 'taught' and neatly tested. This was, of course, precisely what happened when the Revised Code of 1862 laid down national curricular objectives: schools confined themselves to what was required and measurable, and ignored everything else. One can feel content at having 'achieved' such an objective as 'compose a curriculum vitae' or 'exercise control over . . . quotation marks', but one can never finally be satisfied about such objectives as 'write imaginatively in prose or poetry, with some awareness of structure and stylistic effects'. Some of these objectives are of the kind that can be simply marked off a check-list, others demand continued evaluation and mean little without highly complex discussion of what might be achieved by pupils of different levels of ability at different ages.

Fifth, the prescriptive, functional tone seemed to take us back, in a single leap, to the educational world of 1900. There was a clear similarity between the Board of Education's 'standards' at that time (Read a passage from some standard author . . . Write the substance of a short story . . . letter on an easy subject . . . parsing and analysis of simple sentences) and those proposed for the 1980s (Read aloud prose and verse . . . write stories . . . informal and formal letters . . . know the functions and names of all the main parts of speech). This is not to suggest that such objectives are in themselves worthless, but that most of us had assumed that such formulations had now been rejected as misleading, trivial and largely irrelevant. Indeed it is over sixty years since they were magisterially denounced in *The Teaching of English in England* (1921). The authors of that report were highly critical of what they called the earlier 'soulless' system, associated originally with payment by results, by which 'educational results, it was assumed, could be weighed with mechanical exactitude', (II, 47) and 'there is the danger that a true instinct for humanism may be smothered by the demand for definite measurable results...' (II, 56). Again and again, citing Kay-Shuttleworth and Matthew Arnold in support, the Report attacked the narrowing of curriculum that inevitably accompanied specific, assessable objectives, the separation of English activities from each other, and the emphasis on 'mean mechanical drudgery': grammar, spelling and rote learning. There is a world of difference between those objectives which suggest the kinds of language experience that should be offered to pupils and those which try to define expectations of what most children should be able to do or know at any age. It seems clear that it was this second kind that was uppermost in the mind of Sir Keith and that now animates Mr. Baker's talk of 'benchmarks' or 'attainment targets'.

Attainment Targets

The earlier section *Towards Agreement?* suggested that during the lifetime of the subject there have been continuing attempts to describe more precisely what 'reasonable expectations' of English might be. A similar process has been going on in other English-speaking countries, and teachers in general have welcomed these attempts at clearer definition (if only to dispel some of the *un*reasonable expectations of politicians and others whose experience is limited to particular educational backgrounds). However, most of them reject the idea that such a definition can be helpfully formulated in terms of what 'most children should be able to achieve' (and prove in tests) at given ages. Nothing has significantly affected the view expressed in the Bullock Report that 'it is certainly unrealistic to attempt to tie particular competences to given age-points'. At a high level HMI invitation conference at Birmingham early in 1987, a show of hands revealed virtually unanimous opposition. Geoffrey Thornton has written that experience and research 'cast doubt upon the value, indeed the very possibility, of setting age-related targets'.[92]

This does not mean, of course, that we are unable to *diagnose* the level of development of any individual. Considerable work has been done in recent years to illuminate the different ways in which development is manifested in language capacity (Wells, Perera), in writing (Wilkinson, Dixon and Stratta) and in response to fiction or poetry (Protherough, Atkinson). The more sophisticated our understanding becomes, however, the more distrustful we become of generalizations about what *most* children can do at any age.

Development in English is not (as it may be in some other subjects) a neatly linear process, in which one skill is 'acquired' and the next is then bolted on to it. Studies show, for example, that young children who have apparently 'learned' the 'correct' form of irregular past tenses revert for a while to 'incorrect' forms when acquiring more complex usages. Individuals can surprise their teachers by apparently making sudden leaps in some aspects of language while performing consistently much less well in others. Overall development is cumulative and incremental, certainly, and it is possible to point to general developmental sequences, but the individual variations in rate are huge. Gordon Wells has shown that even by the age of three there is a three-year span of difference in language development, whatever the measure used.[93] There does at last seem to be a fairly general recognition of the fact (officially proclaimed since 1910, and possibly earlier) that the mother tongue is not acquired like a second language, and that textbooks containing sequential exercises on subject and predicate, nouns, adjectives, verbs, simple sentences, compound sentences and complex sentences are based on a dangerous misapprehension. Unfortunately this does not mean that such books have disappeared from schools.

Despite the rejection of formal models drawn from classics or E2L, however, the rationale which underlays such models survives in the present debate over curriculum. It is manifested in the insistent concern for 'adult' language standards as the yardstick by which children are to be judged. Mr. Baker's has not been the only voice to define essential language skills as those necessary for 'adult life' in a 'fast-changing technological society'. The Secretary to the Kingman Committee (speaking for himself and not the committee) told a recent convention that the 'essential' task for English teachers is 'to raise levels of performance to enable pupils to make use of their linguistic skills, and to prepare them for the unpredictable demands of life after school'. Just how we are to prepare for the unpredictable is not immediately obvious. However, the argument is supported by the anecdotal complaints of employers and of some university teachers that school leavers are 'inadequate' for the language demands to be placed upon them. These are, of course, the same complaints that have been raised in every decade from the late nineteenth century onward, and probably earlier. In 1913–14 there was 'no foundation to build on' because 'the vast majority of English children cannot speak clearly ... and how many are there who can read with intelligence?' 'It has been abundantly proved that the average public schoolboy cannot write good English.'[95] To see the achievement of adult language standards as the ultimate goal inevitably involves what Stephen Judy has called a staircase model of the curriculum and consequent attempts to pin down what each step up the stairs involves (i.e. what 'most' or 'all' children should be able to do at 7, 11, 14, 16).

Such a process is beset by dangers. First, the notions of what 'skills' may be needed in an 'unpredictable' future may be gravely wrong. A recent report of the National Economic Development Office (1987) warns educators not to rely on industry's view of the future in designing the curriculum. It is not 'practical or desirable' for business and industry to define the kind of 'skill force' that can be 'translated into specific curricula', especially in a time of swift change. 'Teachers may be better judges than employers of what young people should be taught.'[96] Second, the notion of adult capability is a meaningless abstraction: it does not refer to the kinds of speech or the sorts of reading habits of *most* adults. What is meant is some notional ideal of what adults 'should' be able to do — and that, of course, varies according to the presuppositions of the speaker. Adult language behaviour is an unstable generalization which cannot be a satisfactory exemplar, since — apart from anything else — usage is continually changing. It is illogical to complain, on the one hand, that children are inadequately prepared for modern life and then, on the other, to complain about the language use of those adults employed on newspapers and on television. Third, an obsession with adult standards means seeing all young people as inadequate. In actual fact, virtually all of them use language competently in the different situations in which they are placed. To see them in the light of adult standards, however, involves looking for 'errors', treating them as perpetually remedial, rather than concentrating positively on what they *can* do.

In their comments on the responses HMI withdrew from the suggestion of their critics that the age-related objectives were intended as a central, DES-controlled attempt to dictate the curriculum. The spirit of the document, we are assured, is 'to invite teachers and others to establish their own hierarchies'.[97] The political reality, however, is that many groups will only be satisfied with checklists of skills that can be measured: less to assess the abilities of children than those of their teachers. The Director of Education for Croydon proposed to use pupils' scores on maths and English tests at 7, 9 and 11 as 'evidence to pinpoint poor schools and teachers'.[98] *The Sunday Times* records the Secretary of State as saying, 'The Croydon proposals are very interesting. I'm having a close look at them'; according to the newspaper with a view to introducing NFER tests, 'marked in town and county halls', 'to discover whether the targets have been reached'.[99] Such notions of skills-testing run against the principles expressed in *English from 5 to 16* and reaffirmed in the *Responses*. 'Assessment of work in English is not a matter of precise measurement', because only superficial features can be objectively marked. Confusion again arises because of using words like *skills*. It is simple enough to test whether or not a student has the *skill* of wiring a 13 amp plug correctly; it is quite another to assess *skills of literacy*. The editor of *The Use of English* has written more fully about this, and about the implications for English teachers:

Teachers have never had — and no innovative technique or method will ever give them — the ability to impart literacy with the directness that is possible when we teach or learn the skills we need for changing a washer or a wheel. The term 'basic skills' suggests otherwise. Teachers are, in such a reckoning, always seen to have failed. .[100]

Agreeing the English Curriculum

Who ultimately is to decide the nature of the English curriculum and by what criteria? Sir Keith Joseph said that the *Curriculum Matters* series was intended to 'initiate' a 'consultative process', and Mr. Baker has talked vaguely of his desire to establish a 'broad national consensus', but who shapes the agenda and who eventually writes the curriculum that embodies that consensus? There are already clear signs of a central desire to pre-empt key areas of debate. Any objections to age-related objectives for English are blandly countered by the assurance that this 'is a characteristic of the Curriculum Matters series as a whole',[101] not by any defence of the principle. Who *established* the characteristic? The terms of reference for the Kingman Committee are 'to recommend a model of the English language' and to consider what 'pupils need to know about how the English language works'[102] without apparently discussing *why* this should be done or whether it is a helpful activity. *English from 5 to 16* was intended to 'provide a framework for general agreement . . . or an incitement to others to provide a better framework'. *Which* others are to be trusted, and who decides which is the *better* framework? It was clear from the responses to the paper that members of the public (three quarters of whom were 'unreserved in their approval') and institutions 'not directly representative of teachers' differed markedly in their views from those actually involved in English teaching. Mr. Baker's wish to involve the 'consumers' would thus seem to make consensus even harder to achieve. The earlier sections of this chapter have shown that enormous efforts have been made in the past to bring about professional agreement. As Roger Knight has vigorously argued, it is 'simply insulting' to assume that the development of the English curriculum has proceeded throughout the years without continual professional debate. From Mr. Baker's speeches, 'you would think . . . that those responsible for teaching English had never before addressed themselves to the question of what children should know about English'.[103] It is perhaps time to frame some guidelines for any act of curriculum-making.

First, the curriculum needs to be grounded in an acceptable view of what English is and on the rationale for what it is to achieve (principles before applications). English surely needs to be defined as the subject pre-eminently concerned with what it means to be a human being in relationship with other individuals, growing within a culture. We come progressively to understand this through language. By language we create the world that we need to know about, we come to know ourselves and others, we discover how to learn and how to make choices, and at the heart of these processes is response to literature. What was crucially wrong with the objectives in *English from 5 to 16* was that they simply failed to grow out of the aims and principles there expressed. There was no real attempt to argue *why* particular objectives should be achieved, or how consistent they were with the expressed principles, with understanding of children's language development or with an expectation that they would bring about an improvement in performance. Means should not be presented as ends, and organic processes should not be broken down into separate, narrow 'skills' simply in order to provide a convenient list that will bear some resemblance to similar lists in other subjects.

Second, curricular thinking must be aware of what is really happening now in classrooms. Those who urge 'back to basics' seem unconscious of the fact that most teachers have never left them. Several enquiries have shown that something like 90 per cent of children have been led to believe that neatness, correct spelling and accuracy of grammar and punctuation are the chief marks of good writing.[104] A sample of teachers in one county showed that 84 per cent taught some grammar and that over half stressed the importance of grammar teaching in English.[105] Enquiries like those of Peter Medway[106], the School Curriculum Development Committee (SCDC) national writing project, and now the SCDC national oracy project all provide evidence that should prompt any view of English objectives. These observations are inseparable from what current research tells us about how children develop and learn. There is little point, for example, in proposing 'benchmarks of progress' in terms of lists of authors and titles, when it is clear from a wealth of recent studies that there is no significant relation between the quality of a book and the quality of an individual's response. If such benchmarks *are* to be established, then they must relate to experiences of texts, not simplistically to the pages that are turned.

Third, the different expressions of views about the English curriculum must surely chime with what currently seems to be informed thinking and practice within the profession. Mr. Baker's unworthy sneer at a system 'under which teachers decide what pupils should learn' and his assertion that 'the providers are not automatically right just because they are professionals'[107] does not alter the fact that professionals are, by definition, educated, trained and appointed to carry out the function. Teachers are not *automatically* right, any more than doctors or nuclear physicists, but it would be a dangerous world if professional opinion were to be generally overruled. As *Better Schools* expressed it, 'curriculum development is a professional activity'.[108] It is irrelevant to say, as he does, that 'many parents nowadays are at least as well educated as those who teach their children'. Apart from the fact that statistically 'many' means less than ten per cent, *general* education gives no automatic right to make judgments about subject-specific pedagogic decisions.

Fourth, priority should be given to those areas of principle where consensus already exists, building on the 'degrees of accord' which HMI detected in responses to their curriculum paper. They talk of the 'strong and wide endorsement for the aims with regard to the spoken word, reading and writing (Part I) and for the principles (Part III), adding that, 'It is plain that these should form the basis for the curriculum.'[109] The specific principles that were 'strongly and widely commended' included, in brief:

— 'the key principle of the inter-relatedness of the four language modes' and awareness that 'the promotion of [their] interaction should be a basic principle of the teaching of English'.
— the understanding that 'the most effective way of developing language competence is by applying it to an increasing range and variety of real needs and purposes, in which something of genuine interest is communicated'.
— the insistence that good English teaching is 'far more than the inculcation of skills', that 'formal exercises in the analysis and classification of language contribute little or nothing to the ability to use it', and the assertion that 'few aspects of English ... can be mechanically marked'.
— the endorsement of drama as 'an essential part of language teaching in primary and secondary schools'.
— 'strengthened emphasis upon the importance of the spoken word'.[110]

Finally, no curricular framework should attempt to impose such uniformity that teachers are tempted to take over ready-made planning rather than being themselves involved in course design and experiment. As long ago as 1911, the Dyke Acland Report stressed the dangers of an imposed, assessed curriculum, in which 'teachers must follow a syllabus which they have not worked out for themselves ... [and] are often not at liberty even to teach this syllabus in their own way'. In such a case, the teacher 'surrenders the role of an educator and becomes a "crammer"'.[111] This century's advances in English teaching have come from groups and from individuals (Caldwell Cook, say, or Denys Thompson, or David Holbrook) who have had the conviction to reject 'established' principles, and have thus helped to redefine 'English' for the future.

What might be the implications of accepting such guidelines? Perhaps the way forward for English lies in defining legitimate *expectations* (rather than objectives), oriented more towards what teachers, parents and employers really need to know. A coherent description of developmental markers does not need to be tied to arbitrary ages. It can be accompanied by some description of those principles and practices which seem in practice to aid that development. Indeed, professional opinion appears to be firmly in favour of defining what *schools* should be doing, what effective English *teaching* is like, the experiences which should be offered, rather than establishing behavioural objectives which *pupils* should achieve. The Inspectorate have already moved some way in this direction in the samples of recast objectives published as an appendix to *Responses*. It would be most helpful if they were now to accompany these by a fuller discussion or methodology, possibly in the form of checklists which schools and English teachers might use to evaluate what they are doing. Those of us who have been involved in groups carrying out such work believe that any statement about what English is to 'deliver' must depend on consensus about good practice. *What* is to be taught and *how* it is to be taught should go hand-in-hand.

Much depends on tone. Narrow, legalistic requirements result in narrow, legalistic teaching. Is it really too late to invoke the idealistic spirit of the Newbolt Report in its demands for 'a liberal education for all English children whatever their position or occupation in life'[112] —

> It is not the absence of a universal curriculum, an educational drill or uniform, that we are here regretting; it is the lack of a general appreciation of the true value of education and the best means of obtaining it ...
>
> English is not merely the medium of our thought, it is the very stuff and process of it ... In its full sense it connotes not merely acquaintance with a certain number of terms, or the power of spelling these terms correctly and arranging them without gross mistakes ... For the writing of English is essentially an art, and the effect of English literature in education is the effect of an art upon the development of human character.[113]

Notes

1. *The Teaching of English in England*, HMSO, 1921, para 6.
2. BOARD OF EDUCATION (1939) *Report of the Consultative Committee on Secondary Education*, HMSO, pp. 173, 218.
3. BOARD OF EDUCATION (1943) *Curriculum and Examinations in Secondary Schools*, HMSO, p. 91.
4. SAMPSON, G. (1921) *English for the English*, Cambridge University Press, Preface to new edition, 1925, p. xi.
5. SCHOOLS COUNCIL (1965) Working Paper 3, *English*, HMSO, para. 2.
6. COUCH, SIR A.Q., (1921) *On the Art of Reading*, Cambridge University Press, p. 95.
7. *Sunday Times*, 17 March 1983.
8. DEPARTMENT OF EDUCATION AND SCIENCE (1968), *Young School Leavers*, Schools Council Enquiry 1, HMSO, pp. 52, 61–2, 70.

9. *British Social Attitudes*, SCPR/Gower, 1986.
10. Statement accompanying *English from 5 to 16*, DES, 1984.
11. Address to the 11th World Congress on Reading, 31 July 1986.
12. ALAN PALMER lecture at Pangbourne College, 7 November 1986.
13. *Ibid.*
14. Speech to the Arvon Foundation, 29 January 1987.
15. Address to the 11th World Congress on Reading, 31 July 1986.
16. *Ibid.*
17. Pangbourne College lecture, 7 November 1986.
18. Announcement of 16 January 1987.
19. GOACHER, B. (1984) *Selection Post-16: The Role of Examination Results*, Methuen, pp. 47–8.
20. *Sunday Times*, 17 March 1963.
21. *The Guardian*, 6 April 1987.
22. *The Independent*, 13 November 1986.
23. KING, P. (1985) *Teaching English: A Teaching Skills Workbook*, Macmillan.
24. FRANZA, A. (1970) *English Journal*, September.
25. See PROTHEROUGH, R. (1986) *Teaching Literature for Examinations*, Open University Press, Chapter 1.
26. BRITTON, J. and NEWSOME, B., (1968) 'What is learnt in English lessons?' *Journal of Curriculum Studies*, Vol. 1, No. 1, November, pp. 68–78.
27. *English in Education*, Vol. 15, No. 2, Summer 1981, p. 7.
28. *Curriculum 11–16: A Review of Progress*, HMSO, 1981; *The Curriculum from 5 to 16*, HMSO, 1985.
29. *Ibid.*
30. This topic is being considered in detail in the *Students of English* research project. An interim report appears in *English in Education*, Vol. 21, No. 2, Summer 1987, and the full report is to be published by Methuen in 1988.
31. ROSEN, H. (1981) *Neither Bleak House nor Liberty Hall*, University of London Institute of Education, p. 5.
32. HODGSON, J.T. (1975) 'Changes in English teaching: Institutionalization, transmission and ideology', PhD thesis, London University.
33. BARNES, D. and D. with CLARKE, S. (1984) *Versions of English*, Heinemann.
34. GRACE, G. (1978) *Teachers, Ideology and Control*, Routledge and Kegan Paul, p. 70.
35. BALL, S.J. (1982) 'Competition and conflict in the teaching of English: A socio-historical analysis', *Journal of Curriculum Studies*, Vol. 14, No. 1, p. 1.
36. PROTHEROUGH, R. (1986) *Teaching Literature for Examinations*, Open University Press, p. 1.
37. BAILEY, R.W. (1985) 'The idea of world English', *English Today*, No. 1, January, pp. 3–6.
38. BALL, S.J. *op. cit.*, p. 2.
39. MATHIESON, M. (1975) *The Preachers of Culture*, Allen and Unwin, p. 17.
40. *The Journal of Education*, September 1900, p. 558.
41. *Ibid*, pp. 558–9.
42. LAWSON, J. and SILVER, H. (1973) *A Social History of Education in England*, Methuen, p. 345.
43. MATHIESON, M. *op. cit.*, p. 43.
44. *The Teaching of English in Secondary Schools*, circular 753, HMSO, 1910, para 1.
45. *Ibid*, para 7.
46. MAIS, S.P.B. (1914) 'Some results of English teaching at public schools', *Journal of English Studies*, Vol. 2, No. 3, Jan–May, pp. 187–8.

47. *The Cambridge Magazine*, 31 January 1914.
48. Introduction to MASON, W.H. (1964) *For Teachers of English*, Blackwell, Oxford.
49. *The Teaching of English in England*, HMSO, 1921, para 237.
50. *Ibid*, para 11.
51. *Ibid*, para 2.
52. SAMPSON, G. (1921) *English for the English*, Cambridge University Press.
53. EAGLETON, T. (1983) *Literary Theory: An Introduction*, Blackwell, Oxford, pp. 31–2.
54. *The Teaching of English in Secondary Schools*, HMSO, 1910, pars 10, 11, 12, 41 and *Suggestions*, circular 808, HMSO, 1912, p. 6.
55. DOUGHTY, P., PEARCE, J. and THORNTON, G. (1971) *Language in Use*, E. Arnold.
56. BURKE, S.J. and BRUMFIT, C.J. (1974) in *English in Education*, Vol. 8, No. 2, Summer, p. 33.
57. CLOUT, C. (1987) 'English from 5 to 16: The responses to Curriculum Matters 1', *Use of English* Vol. 38, No. 2, Spring, p. 8.
58. *The Guardian*, 8 April 1987.
59. DEPARTMENT OF EDUCATION AND SCIENCE (1985) *Better Schools*, HMSO, pp. 9–10.
60. PROTHEROUGH, R. (1986) 'The rhetoric of Sir Keith Joseph', *Journal of Arts Policy and Management*, Vol. 2, No. 3, May, pp. 4–8.
61. BRUNER, J. (1967) *Towards a Theory of Instruction*, Belknap, USA.
62. JUDY, S.N. (1981) *Explorations in the Teaching of English*, 2nd ed., Harper and Row, p. 63.
63. *The Teaching of English in Secondary Schools*, para 3. Compare DEPARTMENT OF EDUCATION AND SCIENCE (1985) *Better Schools*, HMSO, para 85.
64. DEPARTMENT OF EDUCATION AND SCIENCE (1986) *English from 5 to 16*, *Curriculum Matters 1*, HMSO, 1984 and *English from 5 to 16: The Responses to Curriculum Matters 1*, DES.
65. *English from 5 to 16*, pars 1.1, 1.2, 3.2, 4.4, 4.11, 1.6.
66. Address of July 1986 at London University.
67. See the pamphlet 'English from 5 to 16: A response from the National Association for the Teaching of English', NATE, 1985.
68. *Responses*, para 45.
69. JUDY, S.N. *op. cit.*, pp. 320–1.
70. NATE pamphlet, p. 1.
71. *Ibid*, p. 3.
72. *English from 5 to 16*, 1.6.
73. MICHAEL, I. (1970) *English Grammatical Categories*, Cambridge University Press, p. 507.
74. *English from 5 to 16*, 3.7.
75. *Ibid*, 3.8.
76. THORNTON, G., (1986) *APU Language Testing 1979–1983: An Independent Appraisal of the Findings*, DES, p. 27.
77. *Times Educational Supplement*, 28 February 1986.
78. *The Guardian*, 24 March 1987.
79. 3 October 1984.
80. CZERNIEWSKA, P. (1987) 'The English teacher's dilemma', *English Today*, No. 9, January, p. 14.
81. *English from 5 to 16*, 3.8.
82. *Ibid*.
83. *Responses*, paras 10 and 38.
84. *Ibid*, para 39.

85. Lecture at Pangbourne College, 7 November 1986, and announcements of 16 and 21 January 1987.
86. *Responses*, para 39.
87. *Ibid*, paras 7 and 18.
88. DEPARTMENT OF EDUCATION AND SCIENCE (1985) *Better Schools*, HMSO, para 32.
89. *English from 5 to 16*, 3.11.
90. *Ibid*, 2.2.
91. PROTHEROUGH, R. (1985) 'English in schools: An "objective" look', *The Gadfly*, Vol. 8, No. 1, May, pp. 3–13.
92. THORNTON, G. *op. cit.*
93. WELLS, G. (1982) *Language, Learning and Education,* Bristol University, pp. 4–5.
94. *Times Educational Supplement*, 10 April 1987.
95. ROUSE W.H.D. and PEERS E.A. (1914) in *Journal of English Studies*, Vol. 2, No. 1, 1913, p. 14 and Vol. 3, No. 1, p. 15.
96. 'Think tank pans move to industry-led curriculum', *Times Educational Supplement*, 16 April 1987.
97. *Responses*, para 25.
98. *Times Educational Supplement*, 2 December 1983.
99. *The Sunday Times*, 3 August 1986.
100. 'Versions of literacy', *The Use of English*, Vol. 38, No. 2, Spring 1987, p. 2. Compare FRANK PALMER, 'Skillsology versus culture', *Use of English*, Vol. 38, No. 1, Autumn 1986, pp. 37–44.
101. *Responses*, para 22.
102. Announcement of 16 January 1987.
103. *Times Educational Supplement*, 22 August 1986.
104. See for example the work of Graves, Kroll and Wells, Tamburrini and others, Diamond, Spencer and Protherough.
105. CHANDLER, R.J. (1986) MSc dissertation, Oxford University.
106. MEDWAY, P. (1986) 'What counts as English?', Leeds University PhD thesis.
107. Speech to North of England Education Conference, 9 January 1987.
108. DEPARTMENT OF EDUCATION AND SCIENCE (1985) *Better Schools*, HMSO, para 85.
109. *Responses*, para 45.
110. *Ibid*, paras 8, 12.i, 12.ii, 12.v, 14, 13, 31 and 45.
111. BOARD OF EDUCATION (1911) *Report of the Consultative Committee on Examinations in Secondary Schools*, HMSO, p. 75.
112. *The Teaching of English in England*, HMSO, 1921, para 10.
113. *Ibid*, paras 8, 14.

6   Craft, Design and Technology

John Penfold

Craft, design and technology presents a reviewer with more problems, contradictions and paradoxes than any other subject in the curriculum. Ten years ago, the new designation — recently minted by HM (handicraft) Inspectorate — was virtually unknown to parents, made little impact on the educational world at large and did not even enjoy a wide currency amongst its own practitioners. For most, practical subjects continued much as before — a male-dominated niche in which boys were taught woodwork, metalwork and technical drawing by men. The 1975 Sex Discrimination Act dented this bastion and helped bring CDT into the educational limelight but it was the events following James Callaghan's 1978 Ruskin College speech that gave it a starring role. Now no ministerial statement is complete without an obligatory reference to the subject accompanied by a deferential genuflection in the direction of 'designing and making' activities. They are held to be a vital element in the education of all children: girls as well as boys, primary, middle and secondary pupils alike, the academically able and those less so. As a consequence, in the last decade, CDT has become one of the most expensive and expansive subjects in the curriculum.

What has brought about this transformation in the subject's fortunes? A transformation all the more remarkable because CDT lacks even the semblance of a powerful professional association, like, for example, the Association for Science Education on whose territory some believe it is trespassing. It has few influential backers within the educational establishment. Nor can CDT's upgrading be attributed to substantive research findings. Indeed CDT stands out as the most under-researched of all curriculum areas. From outside the subject few have been attracted in to fill the void. From within, cynics complain that subject leaders have shown more expertise and interest in building the shelves on which the literature of the subject will eventually come to rest than getting down to write it! In the void created, even the most precious of CDT tenets remain untested and rest on seat of the pants hunches, educational folklore and hearsay.

For an explanation of CDT's changed status it is necessary to look elsewhere. It stems, almost entirely, from a transfusion of industrial life-enhancing blood pumped out by the DES and other government agencies intent upon regenerating the nation's industrial well-being. In this task the authorities have been helped and prodded by the subject's hyperactive proselytizers who have kept the pump working to full capacity. Yet, to visit a school with a humming CDT department bulging with highly motivated youngsters immersed in wide-ranging 'designing and making' problems leaves even the most disinterested of observers with the conviction that he is witnessing a stimulating, purposeful and utterly worthwhile educational activity capable of stretching the most able of pupils and, at the same time, bolstering the learning of those at the other end of the educational spectrum, fulfilling all emotionally in a way that few other subjects share.

Why then imply that all is not well in the CDT camp? Because for every school with a department in the above category, everyone knows others which continue in much the same mould as before. What will happen should the present favourable winds stop blowing? This occurred with chilling consequences when the subject was first introduced into the elementary curriculum a century ago. Then, similarly, it was expected that manual instruction would play an important role in restoring British industry so that the country could once again become the world's foremost industrial power. Today, the objectives may be more modest but the sentiments remain unchanged. As the 1987 Education Bill starts its journey through Parliament the words of Sir William Mather, the eminent Manchester industrialist, delivered in 1887 have a familiar ring. Addressing a meeting of the British Association for the Advancement of Science, he warned that employers of labour, like himself, believed that

> the present methods of teaching in our public elementary schools
> do not satisfy the wants of the nation, or do justice to the children
> who are compelled to attend them.[1]

Victorian school boards responded to demands to make the curriculum less 'literary', more 'practical' and more to do with 'things', with varying degrees of enthusiasm. Politicians, industrialists and educationists who observed working class lads hard at work in woodwork shops had fewer reservations, often marvelling at their skill and motivation. The parallel with what is happening today needs no underlining. Will present initiatives be any more successful than those of a century ago? No subject is more hostage to its origins.

Schools Council Initiatives

This has been most manifest in the traditional association of workshop subjects with the education of academically less able boys. Having failed at everything else, educational folklore deemed that their lack of academic prowess was compensated by their being 'good with their hands'. The same educational folklore was equally explicit for the more able. They were required to be removed from any taint of practical work at the earliest opportunity. Whilst today fewer publicly voice such opinions, underneath old prejudices persist. Nevertheless, attitudes are changing. The Crowther Report began the process.[2] It forcefully argued the case for an 'alternative road' approach to education and for the rehabilitation of the word 'practical' in the curriculum if the country was to benefit fully from the capabilities of all its young people. A report by Donald Porter, staff inspector for handicraft at the DES, and a firm supporter of the alternative road philosophy prepared the ground for the first major curriculum initiative to affect workshop subjects.[3] The Schools Council mounted Project Technology in 1966 at the then Loughborough College under the direction of Geoffrey Harrison (now Professor Harrison of Trent Polytechnic). It aimed

> to help all children to get to grips with technology as a major influence in their lives and, as a result, to help more of them to lead effective and satisfying lives.[4]

The project team distributed teaching material to over 500 schools participating in the scheme. However, the idea of teaching technology via a workshop route met with fierce opposition from many within the science establishment. One official of the Science Masters' Association declared

> It seems clear that his (Harrison's) project will not produce greater numbers of scientists. It is craft based; it uses the facilities and staff of the handicraft sections and is in many cases being handled entirely by the handicraft departments of LEAs without reference to science staffs.[5]

At the completion of the project, one researcher estimated that no more than five per cent of schools implemented curriculum change to incorporate technology teaching within their handicraft departments.[6] The reasons for this low take up are not difficult to understand. There was an almost total mismatch between Project Technology's objectives and those of the vast majority of handicraft teachers, who, at the time, were more influenced by the ideals of the arts and crafts movement than those of Harold (now Lord) Wilson's ideas to forge a new society using the white heat of technological revolution.

And, most importantly, it was obvious to most teachers that the Project Technology resource material, stimulating and professional-looking as it may have been, fell beyond the grasp of the low achievers who made up the bulk of their classes.

Handicraft teachers estranged from the objectives of Project Technology were more at home with the second of the Schools Council's projects initially labelled a 'Research and Development Project in Handicraft' under the direction of Professor John Eggleston then of Keele University.[7] Soon to become universally known as 'The Keele Project', many handicraft teachers warmed to its approach. Doubtless, guiding hands at the DES and the Schools Council saw Project Technology, the Keele Research and the Art and Craft 8–13 project based at Goldsmith's College[8] as three complementary development programmes that would soon coalesce to reinvigorate and give purpose to much lack-lustre workshop teaching. Few handicraft teachers at the time saw them in this light. Instead, most regarded them as tugging in opposite directions — contenders for the slowly disappearing handicraft empire.

Design Education

Outside the handicraft field, the design education movement which Peter Green and Ken Baynes fathered at Hornsey College of Art in the 1960s quickly had implications for the content and manner in which much workshop teaching was conducted.[9] The design educationists proved to be effective lobbyists and persuasive missionaries.

Mrs. Shirley Williams, the then Secretary of State for Education, a good catch, opened a conference on design education. In an enlightened address she told delegates:

> When it comes to the teaching of design itself, I hope very much that schools will not regard the teaching of design as being something that takes place in the woodwork class, or the craft class, or the home economics class or the art class ... the design approach is also just as badly needed in the engineering shop, in the metal shop, and in the woodwork shop. It is needed because the future technologist, or the future engineer, must be as conscious of the possibilities of design in what he is doing, as the future designer must be conscious of the limitations imposed by different methods of production.[10]

Sir Paul (now Lord) Reilly, Director of the Design Council and design mentor to the Prime Minister, endorsed these sentiments. He hoped that one day future generations would 'grow to speak the language of design as fluently as their mother tongue'. To promote this end the Association for Design Education was formed, soon becoming an active force for curriculum development in the ensuing years.

In particular the design education movement crucially influenced the future course of the Keele Project. Out went the production of artifacts from worksheets and well-thumbed textbooks. Instead, problem solving projects became the order of the day. Soon handicraft teachers became familiar with a new vocabulary — that of the design methodologist. Pupils were encouraged to employ analytical and synthetical criteria which moved from need identification to optimized solutions and their evaluation. Add to this a sometimes ill-understood reading of Bloom's taxonomy of educational objectives and one had a heady mixture for change. Within this new design-focused world technology teaching occupied only a minor place.

The 1975 Sex Discrimination Act

Post-Keele work in the schools received a boost from a totally unrelated source — the Sex Discrimination Act. Workshop facilities (and, conversely, home economics departments) had to be made available to both sexes. The admission of girls into the previously all-male domain received a mixed reception — enthusiastically by some, downright opposition by others, with most teachers somewhere in the middle. Even in 1987 the process of giving girls equal access with boys to CDT teaching is still not complete. The entrenched attitudes of a century-old tradition are not easily broken. Girls were most commonly accommodated into workshops by an organizational arrangement soon dubbed the circus system whereby boys and girls circulated from one area of activity to the next at termly, or half-termly, intervals. Girls and their parents often liked these 'taster' courses. At best, when conducted on a structured team teaching basis, these courses were outstandingly successful. Perceptive heads of department seized the opportunity afforded to give the emerging CDT philosophy a degree of coherence, often given a further dimension by the creation of a faculty system which usually embraced CDT, art and home economics, but only rarely science. It appeared to suggest pointers for the future. Youngsters of both sexes were provided with an enriching, rounded educational experience suited to their age and interests, and not simply a sterile preparation for examinations that the majority of them would never take.

This situation did not obtain for long. Critics rounded on it. They alleged that the circus system (weasel words to disparage the entry of girls into workshops) had trivialized workshop activities, forced down standards of craftsmanship, jeopardized examination results, and, above all else, proved an insuperable obstacle to the wider adoption of technology teaching. The allegations would have carried more weight if the situation in all boys' schools was demonstrably better. It was not. The arrival of girls into the workshops following the 1975 legislation could have provided that dynamic element the subject so urgently needed. Unfortunately, only a minority grasped the opportunity it presented. The Equal Opportunities Commission produced a useful document outlining examples of good practice and strategies to be pursued to make CDT more 'girl friendly'.[11] But the depressingly low number of girls who continue with the subject to examination level underlines the fact that there is still a long way to go before discrimination is ended: girls continue to have to overcome varying degrees of male prejudice, and its corollary — low teacher expectations — and, despite some improvement, suffer from a distinct lack of female role models; workshop environments and the work undertaken in them still, too often, reflect unsympathetic or hostile male values and the restricted currency value of CDT examinations remains a handicap. Finally, those girls who do show an interest in CDT frequently have their enthusiasm blunted by peer group and parental pressures — all factors which will have to be tackled if present trends are to be reversed.

CDT in the Primary School

If teaching girls sailed into uncharted waters for most CDT teachers, the same applied with equal force to a second new direction: the introduction of CDT into primary schools. The DES survey *Primary Education in England* published in 1978, expressed disappointment at the lack of provision then existing and recommended that more primary schools should afford 'opportunities to undertake some work with wood and other resistant materials and to learn to handle tools and techniques associated with them'.[12] The Equal Opportunities Commission endorsed this advice:

> Much of the work in primary schools can develop positive attitudes to designing and making activities of either an aesthetic or technological nature. Children are fascinated by things which work, but rarely are working models built as part of a topic or project.[13]

In 1985 the Minister of Education stiffened up proposals for the introduction of CDT into the primary sector when he decreed:

> The 5–16 curriculum needs to be constructed and delivered as a continuous and coherent whole, in which the primary phase prepares for the secondary phase, and the latter builds on the former ... In the government's view, older pupils in the primary phase should begin to be systematically introduced to teaching by a member of staff with expertise in an area of the curriculum other than that which the class teacher can offer.[14]

A Design Council working party on design activities in primary education came to the opposite conclusion. It advanced the opinion that primary schools should not be viewed

> as simply providing a grounding for secondary education. Primary education must also enable children to confront their world successfully. We echo firmly the words of the Cockcroft Committee,

in its report on the teaching of mathematics in schools: 'The primary years ought also to be seen as worthwhile in themselves — a time during which doors are opened on to a wide range of experience.'[15]

Who was right? By introducing practical work to develop the senses by manipulative exercises in resistant and plastic materials, Froebel, Pestalozzi and Montessori established the educational case for practical activities being an integral element in the education of all young children. Later educationists took their work a stage further. Practical work, they urged, brought colour to other curriculum subjects and acted as an aid to concept formation in literary, linguistic, scientific and mathematical studies. But this remains largely unproven. Nothing exists to correspond with Herbert Read's pioneering work in art education,[16] the voluminous research into reading readiness and the formation of number concepts or the teaching of science according to a child's conceptual development.[17] It could be so different. Peter Evans' brilliant teaching methods, described in his book published by the National Centre for School Technology, illustrates how technology, for example, can be a wonderful vehicle for education stretching right across the curriculum.[18] Unfortunately, much of the drive to introduce technology teaching into primary schools stems, as in the secondary sector, from political pressures rather than a desire to explore its educational potential. HM Inspectorate has resisted such short-term expedients and recommended the adoption of a balanced middle course in order that children might respond 'emotionally and intellectually to sensory experience, and to develop an appreciation of beauty and fitness for purpose'. Whilst aesthetic and creative development could be stimulated in any part of the curriculum, the inspectorate concluded that:

> Art, crafts, design, and some aspects of technology, music, dance, drama and the theatre arts, in particular, promote the development of the imagination and the creative use of media and materials.[19]

Teacher Supply

Whilst it is possible to warm to these objectives, it must be questioned how realistic they are given the present parlous state of supply of teachers with a CDT background. If CDT is to be taught effectively to primary school children, widen its appeal to girls, and, more generally, meet the increased demands being made upon it, the supply of teachers must be improved and greater provision made for in-service training.

This is not the occasion to discuss the chronic shortage of appropriately qualified and experienced CDT teachers which has plagued the subject since the mid-seventies — and before — suffice to say that teacher education programmes in CDT have been badly affected by matters of macro-educational planning. College mergers and closures have meant that, in a little over a decade, the number of institutions with a CDT department has fallen from over thirty to twenty. Despite this reduction, many places went unfilled.

In an attempt to increase the supply of teachers the DES has drifted from one short term expedient to the next. The chief of these — the one year retraining courses conducted in ten centres throughout the country — originally intended as a stop-gap measure, has, for the last eight years, been the main source of supply of CDT teachers. These courses may have provided a second wind for over-the-hill PE teachers (probably the largest single group) and opened doors for other subject teachers whose promotion or job prospects looked slim, but they are patently no substitute for graduate teachers entering the profession through the normal route, nor for recruits attracted from industry with good technological backgrounds. No more than a handful of teachers who have undergone retraining courses are capable of teaching technology with any degree of rigour. And all this has happened at a time when the subject has veered strongly in a technological direction! Nor are in-service courses for conventionally trained teachers more than a partial answer. Although there are undoubtedly some teachers with a traditional background who will have no difficulty in metamorphosing into competent teachers of technology, it is unrealistic to believe that they represent an inexhaustible pool of untapped ability. A long term solution to CDT teacher supply must be found if it is not to negate future curriculum progress.

Transition from Handicraft to CDT

Given the circumstances it is not surprising that the transition from woodwork and metalwork to CDT has been slow. Many in official circles who like to convey a shiny new image for the subject tend to gloss over the fact that, as late as 1985, the total number of entries for CSE and GCE woodwork and metalwork examinations (112,668), greatly exceeded those for design and technology (20,982).[20] Though the latter figure had crept up, the gap between the two examinations remained wide. Craft examinations, to the chagrin of some advocates of change, continued to be almost as popular as before. The denigrators of craft, for whom the word invariably carried pejorative overtones, regarded their craft origins as a source of embarrassment — a millstone round the subject's neck. The introduction of GCSE presented them with the opportunity to dispose of craft. Despite spirited resistance from some quarters, the Association for Advisers in CDT was able to report in summer 1987:

> The take up of GCSE courses in CDT as opposed to traditional craft based courses has been most encouraging with over 90 per

cent of candidates taking CDT rather than craft courses. The transformation of curricular practice in CDT may be seen as one of the major achievements of the new examination system.[21]

There are grounds for optimism but whether such a dramatic turnaround can be achieved by candidates in much the same ability range as in earlier years, taught by teachers who, by and large, are the same, with broadly the same resources as before remains to be seen.

When HMI Donald Porter first used the title CDT at the conference 'International Perspectives in Design Education' held at Keele University in 1973, he was keenly aware that the existing designation 'handicraft' had outlived its usefulness: its quaintness at odds with late twentieth century Britain. Nevertheless, his inclusion of design, and to a greater extent technology in the title, must be seen as more of an act of faith for the future than an accurate reflection of the strength of its constituent elements. Nor did the new designation initially imply a shift in curriculum direction. It was perceived to be more concerned with regularizing what was going on in the schools than proposing a change in philosophy.

This fuzziness of definition posed a major problem for practical subjects as its teachers moved tentatively towards graduate status. On what grounds could they justify the inclusion of their subject area within the emerging BEd structure? The University of London Institute of Education, for example, required its constituent colleges with handicraft departments to submit a body of knowledge. None existed. Avigdor Cannon, head of department at Shoreditch College, submitted the following definition:

> Handicraft is specifically concerned with all aspects of the artefact and its creative production. The complete productive sequence includes need identification, data collection, design proposal, workshop realization and ultimately evaluation of product against the need. The sequence can be entered into at any of the stages mentioned and each of them brings to bear upon the problem a variety of scientific, mathematical, aesthetic, social and communication disciplines.
>
> Artefacts of the past and their production direct attention to technological, social and aesthetic developments and their history; the nature and behaviour of materials within the production process involves their practical examination in numerically precise terms; technological developments, design opportunities and ecological balance reaffirm the social responsibility of the designer. The subject is therefore seen as the practical context of a liberal education.[22]

Handicraft, subsequently redesignated Design Technology, received the approval of the Board of Educational Studies. Crucially, Cannon attempted to give the developing subject a degree of holism and homogeneity it so urgently needed. He anticipated (correctly) that without this cohesiveness CDT would eventually be separated into its constituent elements. For Avigdor Cannon this was far from being simply a semantic issue. 'Design Technology' embodied a criticism of the popular idea of design. He envisaged

> design as comprising that amalgam of applied theory and practical knowhow that we call 'technology'. It is design as a technology. Such a view underlines the interdependence of theory and practice and, by eliminating the concept of design-on-its-own, removed the mystery that often attends this activity. Furthermore, the popular division (even antithesis) of design and technology results in design becoming solely an aesthetic activity and technology an engineering one, and this reserves the use of the imagination to strictly aesthetic matters as if the intuitive has no place in the engineering field.[23]

Subsequent events have led to both the definition and designation of Design Technology being discarded in favour of CDT. HM Inspectorate charged with communicating the evolving CDT philosophy in general terms explained:

> This label is applied to the range of learning that goes on in school workshops. Taken separately, each of the words 'craft', 'design' and 'technology' means something different. So do the traditional subject labels 'woodwork', 'metalwork', 'technical studies' and the many other terms that identify practical studies in the school curriculum. Yet they are all part of the family of practical activities which give pupils experience of designing and making. Unfortunately, the English language has no single word like 'literacy' or 'numeracy' which might be used to denote competence in working with materials. But even if there is not one word, there is an acceptance in British education, that boys and, to an increasing extent, girls in schools should discover the physical and aesthetic qualities of materials, acquire the skills to shape and perhaps, above all, learn to plan and to execute work of their own design.[24]

That HM Inspectorate should propose the new designation CDT exemplifies the special relationship that has always existed *vis-à-vis* the inspectorate and the subject. CDT, like its earlier manifestations manual training and handicraft, lies outside the recognized fields or forms of knowledge categorized by Professor Hirst. Beyond the school environs, it has no specific identity. Whereas in other fields the top positions are held by academics or leading professionals, in contrast no one aspires to be a craft, design and technologist. As a consequence, HM Inspectorate is at the apex of the subject's hierarchical career structure, standing above LEA advisers and teacher trainers. This gives their pronouncements an authority and significance which has always had a special bearing on the curriculum development of workshop-based subjects.

HMI Documents

The direct involvement of the DES in this respect has, in recent years, been reinforced by the work of the Assessment and Performance Unit. The Unit's report *Understanding Design and Technology* published in 1982 provided the framework for the GCSE in CDT. Earlier notions of embracing all the elements of CDT within a single examination were quietly abandoned. Instead the subject was divided into CDT: Design and Realization; CDT: Technology and CDT: Design and Communication. These sub-divisions are unfortunately guaranteed to cause future confusion among lay persons, parents and employers alike. True, the common core statements in the National Criteria are intended to reinforce the close relationship that is supposed to exist between the constituent elements. However, the small print of professional documents falls far short of establishing that degree of holism that it was once hoped to achieve.

Understanding Design and Technology argued the case for the subject to be equated intellectually with traditional subjects. At the same time it was quick to point out that in important respects it differed from them, especially to the extent that it cut across subject barriers. The committee, nevertheless, attempted to identify the unique features of Design and Technology ('Craft' had been dropped). The report stated:

> The dominant feature of activity in the area of design and technology is the bringing together of skills, experience, knowledge, understanding, imagination and judgment, whatever their limitations, in the execution of a specific task. In practice, it involves the integration of a complex of activities which are specific — because they relate to a particular need; inventive — because they call for a creative response; effective — because the end result should reflect a better fit or match between need and provision than existed formerly; and evaluative because the designer is called upon throughout the process, to exercise value judgments of many kinds when arriving at the proposed solution. Evaluating the efficacy of the final solution against the original need is perhaps the most demanding task of all.[25]

An additional two HMI papers helped set the parameters for CDT. The first *Craft, Design and Technology in Schools* published in 1980 might be said to accurately reflect the aspirations of the majority of CDT teachers at the time.[26] Schools in the survey mainly taught a mixture of craft and design based studies. Technology teaching did not feature strongly. The

John Penfold

efforts of a group of CDT HMIs committed to strengthening this aspect of the subject received a powerful boost as a result of the drive to improve education industry links. Notwithstanding, the second document *Technology in Schools* did not go overboard in its recommendations.[27] The inspectorate's carefully measured tones signalled that the wider extension of technology teaching presented problems.

Answering the question 'Why is technology in the curriculum?' decorum precluded any mention of opportunism or political pressure. This was mentioned indirectly. By far the most important influence affecting the introduction of technology teaching, according to the information provided by the teachers concerned, was that of the LEA adviser (incidentally, few of whom were — or are — technologists or engineers). Advisers and other protagonists, who had, over a period of years, espoused the teaching of technology, now found the national tide running strongly in their favour. In a few cases teachers complained of undue pressure on the grounds that advisers 'were encouraging a move towards technology too hastily and that technology was included because it was seen as a "bandwagon"'. Other factors that influenced the extension of technology teaching included the activities of the National Centre for School Technology and local Science and Technology Regional Organizations (SATROs).

HM Inspectorate described the work of some ninety schools in England and Wales — some 10 per cent of the schools then running technology courses within the context of CDT. Even within this small total the work must have been of a variable quality. Putting this to one side, the number of schools teaching technology in the early eighties amounted to no more than 500. Of the schools in the sample, HM Inspectorate noted that a high proportion restricted this kind of teaching to the higher ability ranges. This coded message has subsequently gone unheeded. Looking at the background of those teaching technology it was found that a significant number had an industrial background, usually in mechanical engineering. This doubtless accounts for the popularity of the structures and mechanisms components in CDT examinations. Pertinently, however, a number of teachers with this background expressed disturbing reservations concerning their ability to cope with the new technologies.

Education-Industry Links

Be this as it may, CDT is becoming increasingly enmeshed in current moves to strengthen education-industry links. It is a common misconception that workshop subjects, consisting mainly of woodwork and metalwork, were previously taught for vocational reasons. Only a minority of teachers pursued this approach, and they were regarded as a drag on the subject by the majority! Most justified their subject on educational grounds, just like other curriculum areas. Of course there was always a

160

vocational spin-off for some pupils but it was seldom considered of paramount importance. Now, a superficial similarity between CDT and the world of work has greatly heightened interest in the subject. The boundary lines between education and training are being deliberately blurred. CDT is now bound up in correcting what Correlli Barnett has described as the 'gruesomely adverse British balance' of technical training provision compared with that of our industrial rivals.[28]

Some apologists for the subject are very adept at larding the CDT vocabulary with the latest 'hurrah' words which find instant favour with politicians. Are expectations being unduly raised? There must be profound worries whether most schools are sufficiently flexible to cope with the ever changing vocational needs of future generations of students. Also, the question needs to be asked, 'is the technology being taught in many schools by teachers, often armed with no more than a sheaf of INSET handouts and the relevant pages of the modular technology textbook, really going to make that much difference to the economy in the year 2000'? Previous attempts at early specialization failed and already there are indications that some much vaunted schemes are proving less successful than was hoped.

The chief of these is TVEI which, after bitter resistance from Labour-controlled LEAs, has now been taken up by all of them. Much emphasis is placed on teaching transferable skills and helping students 'Learn to Learn'. But, as Sir Dennis Rooke, Chairman of British Gas, queried:

> Can we be sure that youngsters specializing in a technical and vocational course are those who might ultimately be the most suitable for craft and technical training? More importantly, will it provide a source of future innovators, as distinct from technicians? While the first industrial revolution was led by men of practical skill, the foundation of knowledge and experience required for innovation today is now both considerably higher and broader.[29]

Vocationalism may appear an appropriate response to an immediate crisis but it should not be embraced too wholeheartedly. Historically, the best example of vocational training at secondary level has been the provision of secretarial courses for girls. Taught in an enlightened manner, these studies afforded a great deal of educational, as well as vocational, validity. But how many academically able girls were encouraged to pursue those 'respectable' courses which led to an employment stratification from which few escaped? One might ask how many high flyers taking TVEI courses will find themselves in a similar position, especially as a route into higher education? This is not to deny that a vocational element can turn otherwise disenchanted youngsters into highly motivated model students. Yet, if vocational courses proliferate, disenchantment of a greater intensity will surface if job expectations fail to be realized. Will, for example, the success claimed for the Bedfordshire Technology bus experiment be repeated when the British School Technology trailers visit areas less propitiously blessed with high technology firms desperate for recruits? There is no doubt that TVEI, launched in a heady atmosphere which exploited public relations techniques to the full, has notched up some notable successes. Case histories from carefully selected successful students enhance the image. Industry, likewise, makes approving noises as it sees students enrolling for courses perceived to be appropriate to its needs. All this needs to be taken with caution. There is now abundant evidence to warn against the 'halo' complex. To expect the same results from schools without the same generous level of funding, resources, and staffing, as the first group, is unrealistic. Moreover, by offering enhanced salaries and promotion prospects, TVEI is sucking in some of the best qualified and most experienced CDT teachers. More often than not they leave unfilled vacancies and improverished CDT departments behind them. If the City Technology Colleges are eventually widely established they will exacerbate the situation. In the short term there is no prospect of change, the direction being set firmly towards more vocationalism. No one questions that a greater element of skill training in the secondary curriculum might ultimately inhibit the ability of a worker to retrain some years later when his initial skills become obsolete, as they undoubtedly will. As Professor Richard Pring observed:

> First, what constitutes a basic or generic skill, is very confused. But secondly, and more dangerously, the whole skills-based approach to the curriculum development represents a shift away from the curriculum as a set of transactions between teacher and taught, responding to the student needs as teachers sensitively identify them, towards a more mechanical and externally controlled conception of what the curriculum is about.[30]

Curriculum Justification

In the present fluid state of the subject, the precise reasons for the inclusion of CDT in the curriculum are seemingly endlessly changing. When Richard Stewart, at the time lecturing at the College of St. Mark and St. John, looked at the traditional justifications for the teaching of practical work, he found them wanting. He found systematic arguments advanced claiming that craft work developed logical thinking, contributed to the formation of moral values, encouraged children to become more self-reliant, persevering and moral and that it broadened and enriched the teaching of other subjects. Unfortunately, Stewart concluded

> they do not stand up well to the analysis of the philosopher or the doubts of the curriculum developer, at least when expressed in such terms. Statements relating to the development of desirable

intellectual or emotional qualities are too global to be meaningful, tending to indulge in outmoded faculty psychology. They do not relate specifically to the content of craft subjects.[31]

Notwithstanding Stewart's strictures and reservations, many current training programmes give a high profile to the development of such personal characteristics so close to the hearts of generations of workshop teachers. Qualities that are also valued highly by today's employers.

Dr. Bernard Down, who lectures in educational philosophy at Brunel University, has attempted, on a number of occasions, to give CDT that philosophical underpinning that it has lacked. After examining the scope of the work undertaken in a variety of school workshops, Bernard Down concluded that the practical nature of CDT provided it with that bed-rock on which the subject was built. Moves leading to the growing gentrification of CDT suggest that he was thinking in terms of limestone not granite. The very foundations of CDT are being eroded. Dr. Down warned of the dangers of intellectualizing practical work out of existence. Instead he urged:

> The theory has to go *within* the practical work: within the demonstration and instruction. It is sought as a means of assisting problem-solving. Obviously the amount of theory and the depth to which it is pursued, will depend on the capabilities of the children.[32]

Whilst such advice is still applicable to a wide range of workshop teaching, it does not necessarily provide the most appropriate framework if CDT continues to head in a more technological direction. It led Bernard Down to concede:

> There might be a place for a more theoretical course in technological analysis, involving studies in applied science and in the solving of theoretical problems related to, say, engineering, but such courses which would compete with subjects like physics at 'A' level, might only have a minority interest.[33]

The implications of Dr. Down's words for CDT went largely unheeded. Its face was set firmly towards more technology. Dr. Down believed that the educational and technological aims of teaching CDT should not be mutually exclusive. He maintained that the intention

> must be primarily that of preparing children, morally and politically for understanding and being critically aware of the social issues of technology. Secondly, it must involve learning how to employ technological devices, wherever appropriate. Thirdly, in relation to CDT, it must include some involvement in and understanding of the areas of technology that can be related to designing and making.[34]

The Association of Advisers in CDT, sensing that the time was opportune, felt sufficiently confident to produce a

> definitive policy statement which supports the government and industrial view that ALL PUPILS SHOULD HAVE AN EN-TITLEMENT TO CDT AS A CORE LEARNING EXPERIENCE THROUGHOUT COMPULSORY EDUCATION.[35]

In reality, there was nothing particularly new in the Association's paper. Essentially, using an earlier HMI matrix, it identified nine areas of learning and experience to which CDT could usefully contribute, namely: 'aesthetic and creative; human and social; linguistic and literacy; mathematical; moral; physical; scientific; spiritual, and technological'. Whilst doubtless CDT's involvement in the categories listed can be demonstrated, the assertions remain largely untested. Moreover, the subject is often purported to be interdisciplinary. But how often, in fact, do CDT departments liaise across subject boundaries? HM Inspectorate, for example, found scant evidence to support this in mathematics and science.

The 'confidence' that the Advisers' Association displayed could not have been more misplaced nor the timing of its document more unfortunate. Its publication coincided almost precisely with that of *The National Curriculum 5–16*. Craft, design and technology was not even mentioned. The document proposed that technology should be part of science, design taught under the heading of art and, as for craft, it had simply disappeared. Readers will be familiar with the author's scepticism of accepting some of the more extravagent claims advanced on behalf of the embryonic subject CDT. Nevertheless, this wariness has nothing in common with the gut-level prejudice against practical subjects displayed by the authors of *The National Curriculum*. Accepting the manifest weaknesses in the subject, CDT needed support and understanding, not demolition. Who will now do the work of reconstruction remains a moot point.

Notes

1. The British Association for the Advancement of Science, W Mather.
2. MINISTRY OF EDUCATION (1959) *15–18* (The Crowther Report).
3. PORTER D I.R. (1967) *A School Approach to Technology*, Schools Council.
4. SCHOOLS COUNCIL (1967) *Project Technology Pilot Study Report*, November 6.
5. McCULLOCH, G., JENKINS, E. and LAYTON, D. (1985) *Technological Revolution*, p. 171.
6. TAWNEY, D. (1973) 'Project Technology' *Evaluation in Curriculum Development: Twelve Case Studies*, Schools Council.
7. SCHOOLS COUNCIL (1969) Working Paper No. 26 *Education through the Use of Materials: The Possible Role of School Workshops in the Education of Secondary-school Pupils*.
8. SCHOOLS COUNCIL (1974) *Children's Growth through Creative Experience Art and Craft Education 8–13*.

9. Baynes, K. (Ed.) (1969) *Attitudes to Design Education;* Green, P. (1974) *Design Education.*
10. National Union of Teachers (1969) *Design in Education Conference Report*, 19 February, 5.
11. Equal Opportunities Commission (1983) *Equal Opportunities in Craft, Design and Technology.*
12. Department of Education and Science (1978) *Primary Education in England,* London, HMSO.
13. Equal Opportunities Commission (1983) *Equal Opportunities in Craft, Design and Technology.*
14. Department of Education and Science (1985) *Better Schools*, London, HMSO, p. 21.
15. Design Council (1987) *Design and Primary Education*, 1, 4.
16. Read, H. (1944) *Education through Art.*
17. Schools Council: (1972) *Science from Toys*
    (1973) *Metals*
    (1973) *Metals Background*
    (1972) *Working with Wood*
    (1972) *Working with Wood Background.*
18. Evans, P. (1984) *Primary School Technology*, National Centre for School Technology.
19. Department of Education and Science (1985) *The Curriculum from 5 to 16*, London, HMSO.
20. Department of Education and Science (1985) *Statistics of Education: Statistics of School Leavers GCE and CSE*, London, HMSO.
21. Association of Advisers in Craft, Design and Technology (1987) *Policy Paper Craft Design and Technology.*
22. University of London Institute of Education (1986) *Minutes* Board of Educational Studies, May.
23. Cannon, A. (1975) 'Design and realization as a form of knowledge' *Studies in Design Education and Craft*, Winter 1975–6, 40.
24. Department of Education and Science (1980) *Craft, Design and Technology in Schools: Some Successful Examples*, London, HMSO, 3.
25. Assessment of Performance Unit (1982) *Understanding Design and Technology*, London, HMSO.
26. Department of Education and Science (1980) *Craft, Design and Technology in Schools*, London, HMSO.
27. Department of Education and Science (1982) *Technology in Schools — Developments in Craft, Design and Technology Departments.*
28. Barnett, C. (1986) *The Audit of War*, London, Macmillan.
29. Rooke, D. (1984) 'Education investment in human assets' *The Standing Conference on School Science and Technology Annual Lecture for 1984*, British Gas.
30. Pring, R.A. (1986) 'The curriculum and the new vocationalism' *The Stanley Lecture*, October.
31. Stewart, R. (1977) 'Justifying craft in the curriculum' *Studies in Design Education and Craft* 9, Spring, p. 290.
32. Down, B.K. (1984) 'Craft as a liberal education? A response' *Studies in Design Education Craft and Technology* 16, Spring, p. 74.
33. *Ibid*, p. 74.
34. *Ibid*, p. 74.
35. Association of Advisers in Craft, Design and Technology (1987) *Policy Paper: Craft Design and Technology.*

7 Music

Marilynne J.R. Davies

A central concept of the essentials of education is the interdependence of skills and concepts and that the essentials include ... the ability of individuals to express themselves through the arts.[1]

Those of us involved in music education are constantly being required to justify the need to include music in the school curriculum. It is not an easy or straightforward task as the subject does not lend itself to modes and styles of measurement that would make secure its position within the curriculum and its status within the school. Maybe the lack of obvious usefulness and the abstract nature of the subject, which raises conceptual and experimental difficulties, lead to a reluctance on the part of music educators to produce 'a rationale that bears examination and stands up well against the views of different pressure groups'.[2]

The White Paper, *Better Schools*, stated 'The government believes that the curriculum offered to every pupil whether at an ordinary school or a special school should be: broad, balanced, relevant and differentiated'[3] so that it is matched to pupils' abilities and aptitudes and that all pupils 'should study elements drawn from the humanities and the arts'. If our expectations of schools go beyond the teaching of the skills of reading, writing and mathematics to the education of children for life as well as for making a living then the inclusion of music in a 'balanced curriculum' rather than a 'basics curriculum' is of vital importance. So often the curriculum overemphasizes the importance of knowledge and underemphasizes the importance of personal development. 'Music educators are among the few who realize that education conceived merely as a preparation for life diminishes the student for whom education is life itself. Teachers dedicated to the arts have the minds, the means and the mandate to transform reality for the full spectrum of people in our society. If we go beyond ourselves we may find ourselves.'[4]

Karl Heinrich Ehrenforth sees music as being important to the development of children for it:

(i) expands critical faculties and develops personality
(ii) penetrates the entire life, soul and spirit of the human being.[5]

Music is able to combine in ample and balanced measure the intellectual, the physical and the emotional — perception in music is a highly integrated and cognitive process. If it is accepted that music is able to make this contribution to the education of the whole child then it should be possible to ensure that music has a secured place in the balanced curriculum.

In the paper *Music 5–16*[6] HM Inspectorate suggest that music is intended for all pupils not just those who may show particular talent in the subject. If this is accepted then the implications for the organization and teaching of the subject need to be investigated. Currently the provision of music in our schools varies greatly depending so much on the attitude of the headteacher and the expertise and enthusiasm of the staff supported by the peripatetic and advisory service. While it may not be advisable to insist on a 'national curriculum' for music it would be advisable for primary schools to be working towards similar aims and objectives in music so that the suggestion that music is for all children could be realized. In order to achieve such a situation many schools would need to rethink their attitudes and approach to the subject.

'Music is too important to be left to the musician.'[7] This statement exemplifies the attitude that we need to adopt if we are to offer all children education in music. In the primary school the role of the teacher with special responsibility for music should be to act as a consultant to colleagues and a coordinator of the music curriculum. All primary teachers should enjoy making music with their own class whether they are trained musicians or not. If this aim is to be realized then there are implications for the initial and in-service training of teachers, for music is a subject in which the greatest problem for both students in training and teachers is lack of confidence. Therefore, perhaps it is for those involved in music education at the tertiary stage to ensure that there is sufficient in-service provision for teachers.

In the comprehensive school the provision of music consists of one, maybe two periods per week for the first three years, plus a range of extra curricular activities which, in the main, are geared towards those receiving instrumental tuition. Even though social surveys have indicated that music is one of the major spare-time interests of teenagers we, as music educators, have failed to make it a popular classroom subject. Is it to continue to be isolated in the 'leisure activity' bracket therefore allowing the subject to be 'de-schooled'? The GCSE examination syllabus is designed to 'admit those areas of musical experience in which pupils demonstrate keen interest and skill and to foster a greater understanding of music through more direct experience of the creative processes involved'.[8]

Perhaps this is the opportunity for extra curricular activities in music to be more broadly based and to become a logical extension of the music curriculum. As a consequence maybe some of the rather negative attitudes of pupils towards school music may become more positive. The new syllabus will involve changes of attitude and of organization. With the greater emphasis on practical music making will come the necessity to work in smaller groups and the closer involvement of peripatetic staff over a wide range of instruments including electronic instruments. This acknowledgement of a wider range of music may result in a greater enthusiasm for the subject at this level.

Music has always been an area which because of its abstract nature has attracted the interest of philosophers and psychologists and because of its impact on society has attracted sociologists but it has also, over the last twenty years, been an area in which there has been a proliferation of new ideas and suggestions on how the subject should be taught.

Primarily in music education we should be developing the inner ear and encouraging children to think musically in a sensitive, colourful and imaginative way. In order to help achieve this aim children need to be given a wide range of musical experiences from the beginning and these experiences need to be assembled in a systematic way if children are to gain confidence, awareness and skill in making music. Music education at primary, secondary and tertiary level has been uncompromisingly wedded to the European classical tradition. If we are convinced that we should (i) offer children the widest possible range of musical experiences and (ii) reflect the multi-ethnic composition of the school population then we need to alter our perspective to include not just music of the European tradition but also music from a wide variety of cultures and societies. The intercultural approach does not imply that the Eurocentric approach should be abandoned but that the common elements of music — rhythm, pitch, dynamics, timbre, texture should remain the basis for a music curriculum. It does, however, infer that these basic elements should be approached differently and from a broader perspective which will not only develop greater aural awareness but that will also develop in the children an open-mindedness to cultural diversity in music. Music is a universal means of communication; even though its language may not be universal it is the means whereby different cultures and societies are able to express differing emotions and aspirations and expect this expression to provoke a response.

It is, however, crucial that the rationale behind the use of music with an intercultural perspective must be essentially musical, otherwise we may find that we cause unnecessary embarrassment to pupils and 'devalue' a valid musical system. Therefore it is an approach to music education that needs to be treated with sensitivity, tolerance and understanding but an approach that we should be developing if music is to make a positive contribution to the education of our children.

Many early experiences of music have come through singing which must remain indispensable and one of the basic elements of a structured programme of music education. Children have the potential to sing from birth but it is a commonly held belief that children will not sing or that they will only sing when accompanied by the piano or amplified by the microphone. Through carefully selected songs children can be introduced to rhythm and melody, structure and form in music. Singing can also help develop inner hearing, vocal expertise and children can be made aware of the cultural heritage of a wide variety of societies. A large number of books of songs have been produced in the last decade, many of which have been received by schools with uncritical acclaim. If singing is to remain as one of the basic elements of a structured music programme then the selection of songs must be made bearing in mind criteria of which the following are indications:

  a) is the range of the melody suitable for the age of the children?
  b) is the rhythm interesting and complex enough for the age of the children?
  c) is the vocabulary suitable for the intended age range?
  d) will the song help the children develop particular musical skills?

Children should be encouraged to sing unaccompanied or with an accompaniment other than the piano so that they can develop a sense of rhythm, pitch and inner hearing. The piano is not the most suitable instrument for classroom singing as it forms a physical barrier between teacher and pupils, it masks the singing of the children and it can restrict the opportunities for spontaneous singing sessions as most schools only possess one piano and not all teachers are competent pianists. Singing should be a musical activity in which both teacher and children can participate frequently and with interest, increasing their repertoire of songs from a wide variety of cultures. A cautionary note must be sounded here. Resources of songs from some of the non-western cultures are a) difficult to locate b) so westernized in their transcription as to render them unrecognizable as folk music from the culture they represent c) so authentically accurate that they are alien to the child — for example — a child of Indian origin whose musical experience is derived only from Indian film and pop music and not from authentic Indian folk music.

The Hungarian composer and music educationist Zoltan Kodaly illustrates through his method of music education how music reading and literacy can be highly developed through the use of the voice. He combines singing with listening, movement and aural training using examples which are firmly rooted in Hungarian folk music to develop musically literate children. All work involving instruments and creativity is delayed until music literacy is achieved. It is this aspect of the method that raises an issue which is as yet resolved among those involved in music education. How early in the programme of music education should conventional western notation be introduced as the language of music — the only way to understand and appreciate music? There is the feeling among the non-musically literate that it was the stress on the importance of music literacy at an early stage that caused their disenchantment with the subject. The feeling among the musically literate is one bordering on disbelief that anyone could find the acquisition of notational skills difficult!

Obviously there must be a middle path that will encourage children's literacy in music while at the same time giving them enough skill to be able to pursue exploration in music. Carl Orff saw 'the development of the child's creative facility which manifests itself in the ability to improvise'[9] as being the most important element of any programme of music education. The development of creativity in music is an area that has been and still is a hotly debated issue arousing conflicting reactions. If we accept the aims of music education as expressed in *Curriculum Matters 4 Music 5–16*

The aims of music education are to:

— develop a sensitive response to sound in general and in particular to those organized patterns of sound called 'music';
— develop insight through music into areas of experience some of which cannot easily be verbalized;
— develop the capacity to express ideas and feelings symbolically through the medium of sound;
— develop the necessary skills and concepts whilst engaged in musical activity;
— develop social skills and awareness through making music together;
— offer pupils opportunities to experience the personal satisfaction and self-confidence derived from striving after the highest possible standards whilst engaged in musical activity;
— develop an awareness of musical traditions and developments in a variety of cultures and societies

then to approach music through creative music activities of performance, improvisation and composition is thoroughly justified. Those who abandon the idea of this approach dismissing it as 'trendy' or 'instant music' may have failed to accept that 'creativity is basic to all human mental processing'[10] and that we should nurture creative behaviour in children offering them the widest possible experience in music so that they can improvise, compose and perform. In this way children will develop the understanding and exhilaration that comes from making music for which they have been totally responsible, music in which they have been free to explore their own ideas and develop confidence in the expression of these ideas.

As the emphasis in music education is seen through its contribution to the personal growth of the child, creative activities and sound exploration in music have a place in the music curriculum. These activities must not, however, deceive the child into thinking that composition in music is an easy, indisciplined activity for 'to educate children with easy answers and painless solutions is to deceive them that they are composers when they are not'.[11] Activities involving sound exploration, improvisation and performance should be seen as a part of the total music curriculum. They cannot replace the need to acquire the fundamental skills and tools of the musician's craft. These exploratory and experimental activities in music should be seen as supporting and broadening the child's perception of sound and rhythm while developing the powers of sound discrimination. While there is no substitute for the acquisition of the language of music there is a responsibility to ensure that the interest in music is sustained.

'We cannot make children, or adults, love or enjoy anything. All we can do is provide opportunities. Love, enjoyment, pleasure are not realistic objectives. Of course we hope that these may, even will, occur but we cannot teach them. I propose interest as a more fundamental aim.'[12] Creative abilities in music can assist the achievement of such an aim.

The initial excitement of creating musical soundscapes using graphic symbols as a means of recording the progression of sounds and improvisation often identifies the need for children to acquire some knowledge of shape and form in music and also the need to be able to represent their ideas in a way that is recognizable to others. It is the recognition of these needs that brings together work on rhythm and pitch patterning, listening, singing and creative music making elements that form the music curriculum.

So often musical experiences in school have been confined to singing and/or music appreciation. Music appreciation can be passive sessions of listening without hearing, listening without understanding, listening without perception. If listening to music involves active participation in identifying the melody, rhythm, texture, harmony, form of the music then the listener is learning to grasp the organization of the music and become aware of what is happening. The recognition and appreciation of music for what it is and how it is constructed can be seen as a vital, dynamic part of the process of the development of auditory discrimination and lead to the broadening and deepening of the child's interest and understanding. All programmes of music education should encourage children to develop the concentration necessary to listen out for particular elements in music because only with 'listening markers' will the attention be directed and the concentration span increased. If we hope to develop aesthetic perception of music then it must be approached through active participation. This participation involves not only actively listening but also using practically the knowledge acquired through listening in improvisation, composition and performance.

The elements of music should be seen to be interdependent but all the aspects of music education are dependent on rhythm and pitch. The ability of the child to be able to recognize and respond to a steady beat, to rhythm patterns in various metres, to syncopation is fundamental to his understanding of all musics and the creation of his own music. Without the development of a sense of rhythm the limitations on the freedom to improvise, create, perform and understand music could lead to frustration and loss of interest in the subject. It therefore suggests that the child needs to be introduced to the concepts of rhythm as early as possible in any music programme. Coupled with rhythm children should be made aware of differences in pitch and pitch patterns as early as possible using the approach proposed by Zoltan Kodaly where the first interval to be introduced to the children is that of the falling third — the interval that is most frequently used by them therefore the most natural to them. Children's awareness of pitch and their ability to recognize intervals is reinforced in the songs they sing and melodies they compose on classroom instruments.

Music in the classroom today embraces a wide spectrum of activities and these activities need to be presented in a well structured and balanced music curriculum so that the foundations of musical knowledge are firmly laid. There is no short-cut, no speedy instant way in which the basic, essential tools necessary for music making can be acquired but they can and should be presented in an interesting and stimulating way. There are many resources available today which make it possible for music to be presented in a lively, dynamic fashion although some of these resources need to be approached with caution. Music as with so many other areas of the curriculum has not been immune to fashion and trends in education. In an effort to achieve and stimulate interest and enthusiasm in classroom music it is sometimes attractive to follow the latest fashion uncritically and find that long term aims are being sacrificed for short-term popularity and instant results. The justification of music in the curriculum does not and must not depend upon the contribution the subject can make to other subject areas or to topic work in the primary classroom. These associations may produce temporary benefits and instant acclaim but in the long term they will deny the inherent value of music and should therefore be avoided unless the rationale behind the association is essentially musical.

Although music is a difficult area of the curriculum to evaluate the current thinking is that all areas of the curriculum should be subject to regular assessment. Any mode of assessment in a subject that is concerned with individual feelings and emotions is bound to have limitations. While acknowledging these limitations *Music 5–16*[13] suggests that 'Effective systems of assessment may reveal shortcomings in certain pupils and developing abilities in others. Used with discrimination they can lead to remedial help for some and more advanced tuition for others.' Such assessment, it is suggested, could lead to 'improvement in progression and continuity of the music education being provided'. Whatever form assessment in music takes it needs to be based on the development of the individual and be non-competitive.

It is to be hoped that the progress made in so many areas of music education over the last twenty-five years will not be halted by government proposed new measures to limit expressive activities to ten per cent of the timetable, but that music education will be recognized as 'the epitome of holistic education: the simultaneous development of cognitive, affective and perceptual motor schemas'.[14]

Notes

1. LAST, L.M. (1982) *Music Art and Drama Experiences for the Elementary Curriculum*. Teachers College Press.
2. SWANWICK, K. (1979) *A Basis for Music Education*, NFER Nelson.
3. DEPARTMENT OF EDUCATION AND SCIENCE (1985) *Better Schools* London, HMSO.
4. HAUSMAN, J.J. (Ed) (1980) *Arts and the Schools* McGraw-Hill, New York p. 234.
5. BIERMANN, D. (1983) 'Future trends in music education — A European perspective,' *Music Teacher*, May.
6. HER MAJESTY'S INSPECTORATE (1985) *Music from 5–16 — Curriculum Matters 4* London HMSO.
7. SMALL, C. (1980) *Music, Society and Education* John Calder, p. 214.
8. DEPARTMENT OF EDUCATION AND SCIENCE (1985) *GCSE — The National Criteria — Music*, Introduction 1.2.2. HMSO, p. 1.
9. O'BRIAN, J.P. (1983) *Teaching Music* Holt, Rinehart Winston, p. 249.
10. OEHRLE, E. (1986) 'Creativity' *British Journal of Music Education*, Vol. 3, No. 2, July, p. 166.
11. JONES, T. (1986) *British Journal of Music Education* Vol. 3, No. 1, March.
12. BENTLEY, A. (1973) *Music in Education: A Point of View* NFER.
13. HER MAJESTY'S INSPECTORATE (1985) *op. cit.* p. 19.
14. HUTCHINS in ADLER. M. (1982) *The Paideia Proposal* New York, Macmillan.

8 Geography: New Subject, New Curricular Contributions

Patrick Bailey

> Geography is concerned to promote an understanding of the nature of the earth's surface and, more particularly, the character of places, the complex nature of people's relationships and interactions with their environments and the importance in human affairs of location and the spatial organization of human activities
>
> — General Certificate of Secondary Education.
> The National Criteria: Geography.[1]

Geography means literally the study of the earth; but what aspects of the earth do geographers study and how do they approach these studies?

After more than three decades of rapid and sometimes radical development, geography is now interpreted to mean the study of five related aspects of the earth. These are (1) the natural processes at work on land, in the atmosphere and in the oceans which together produce the earth's life-sustaining environments; (2) human interactions with these processes and environments; (3) the humanly generated environments, such as social, political and economic systems, which form the most immediate contexts of human life; (4) the interactions of individuals and groups with these human environments; and (5) the properties of space itself, such as distance and the various forms of cost incurred in overcoming it, which sometimes facilitate and sometimes constrain human activities.

Geography is therefore both a body of knowledge and a distinctive way of handling that knowledge. It is both content and process and the two cannot be considered separately.

Geographers derive their knowledge and ideas from observations of the conditions, events and processes of the earth's surface and of mankind's uses of that surface. The geographer's characteristic approach is first to try to explain location: why, that is, an activity is happening at one place rather than another. Geographers are therefore to be found analyzing the reasons for the locations of homes, farms, offices, shopping centres, finance houses, manufacturing industries, airports, towns and so on. Studies of location lead naturally to studies of distributions; of, for example, the distribution of coffee production or electronics manufacturing world-wide, the distribution of employment and unemployment in one country and the distribution of facilities within one town.

Such studies can be pursued to many different levels of explanation. For example, the distribution of world coffee production may be explained at the simplest level in terms of climatic and soil conditions, but at deeper levels its study leads one to consider the world political and economic frameworks of coffee production and marketing, with their undertones of international competition and possible exploitation of poor countries by richer ones.

Studies of location and distribution lead further into studies of movements and exchanges of various kinds and of barriers to movement. Thus people tend to move towards employment but variations in house prices act as barriers to movement. Capital resources move between countries, but their complete freedom of movement is limited by political barriers, such as the 'East-West' boundary. Knowledge or 'know-how', one of the most valuable forms of exchange, is only transferred within carefully defined limits set by considerations of political advantage and military security. The movement of people within towns is sometimes constrained by physical obstacles, but more often it is obstructed and channelled by barriers of ownership, land values and social status. Studies of movement and exchange, of people, materials, services, money and knowledge are central to geography; and again they may be pursued to any depth from the most immediate and obvious to the most widely-ranging and subtle.

In all that they study, geographers look for change in progress; and in trying to reveal the processes which produce change they hope to find ways of predicting future developments. Geography is thus an applied as well as a theoretical study. Through studies of wave and tidal processes geographers can suggest effective coastal protection measures; through studies of the spatial effects of social and economic policies they can identify problems which are likely to arise in different locations, such as pressure upon water supplies, and indicate ways of mitigating such problems. Geography is always a dynamic, not a static study. As the late Professor Fleure once remarked, 'Geography is the study of things becoming.'[2]

Decision Making and Decision-Makers

All locations, distributions, areal variations and movements associated with human activity result from people making decisions, the purpose of which is normally to make the most of opportunities and to solve problems. Studies of the ways in which decisions are arrived at and the consequences of decisions are therefore an important concern of geographers. Home location is a decision-making activity in which everybody in the world participates, though who exactly makes the significant decisions about where people should live is often hard to ascertain. The Peruvian peasant who brings his family to a Lima shanty town clearly has less decision-making freedom than the London stockbroker and his family who decide to live in a country village; but both are powerfully affected by the cumulative effects of decisions made by others, about how to price homes and services and how to set the conditions of work.

Moreover, decisions about where to live may be influenced as much by people's beliefs about what a new environment will be like as by a precise knowledge of the actual conditions. The Peruvian peasant may believe there is work to be had in Lima where in fact there is not; the London stockbroker and his family may be greatly disappointed when they find that their country village is mainly inhabited by other commuters and that it lacks much sense of community or life of its own.

It would appear that no such thing as a wholly objective environment exists for anybody. Individuals and groups, including governments, make important decisions on the basis of incomplete or even wrong information. To discover what people's perceived environments are like is therefore important, but it is also very difficult because of problems of access to information. Geographers have developed some techniques for approaching this problem in modest ways and such studies seem likely to grow in importance. They are of much more than academic interest. It is, for example, a matter of general concern that the world's political leaders should view the world as it actually is before they make decisions which, if mistaken, could lead to untold suffering, even the extinction of the human race itself.

Modern geography is concerned to discover and explain general principles and repeating patterns of human behaviour. This calls for the gathering of large amounts of information, much of it numerical. To handle this information, geographers make much use of the standard methods of data processing and have long been to the fore in exploiting the potentials of computers. They also try to extract order from large amounts of information by formulating theoretical models which attempt to express the gist of general relationships and trends. Widely used models include those which suggest how order may be drawn out of the visible complexities of town development, those which express general relationships between land-use and distance from markets and those which try to simplify economic, social and demographic processes. Where suitable data are forthcoming, dynamic computer modelling has been developed. Such developments strengthen geography's case for being considered a predictive science.

Perhaps the most important theoretical model used by geographers is the map, in many forms. Geographers are unique among subject specialists in their frequent and varied use of maps. Their interest in place, in locations, distributions, areal variations and movements causes them to record many of their observations and ideas in map form. In recent years, mapping has become increasingly sophisticated with the advent of satellite photography, remote sensing and computer mapping. Remote sensing is, for example, an essential tool for large-scale resource appraisal and it strengthens geographers' ability to study practical problems and contribute to their solution. As a result of the work of geographers, some neglected potentials of map technology have been increasingly recognized by workers in other fields as varied as civil engineering, history, medicine and archaeology.

Physical and Human Geography: Two Subjects or One?

All discussions of geography sooner or later reveal the obstinate problem of trying to relate the physical and human aspects of the subject. There is no relation, for instance, between a study of erosional processes at work along the edges of the Greenland ice-cap and a study of changing shopping patterns in Las Palmas, yet both are 'geographical' topics.

The ways in which human beings behave on the surface of the earth depend ultimately upon the natural conditions of that surface. To study people and the earth in association is therefore likely to yield insights into the human condition which we would otherwise lack. The problem is how to arrange these studies so that they demonstrate the unity rather than the duality of geography.

During the early 1980s the problem was somewhat reduced as physical geographers directed their studies more towards the elucidation of processes and systems rather than towards the explanation of landforms and the development of physical landscapes through time. In consequence it is now possible to define physical geography as the study, by geographers, of the natural life-support systems on which mankind depends. These systems include the atmosphere, the oceans, soils, the earth's mantle of living forms and the land itself which is subject to continual processing by mechanical, biological and chemical agencies. All natural systems are made up of combinations of processes; and the processes within each system, such as the soil, interact with those in other systems to produce earth's natural environments: forests, savanas, deserts, lands of Mediterranean climate and so on.

As soon as physical geographers began to concentrate upon process and system studies, it became clear that human interventions in these processes and systems had also to be studied. Physical and human aspects of geography are thus brought together. Such studies also enable physical geographers to offer practical advice about the management of natural environments and the mitigation of natural hazards.

Ethical Implications of Geographical Studies

All human actions have a moral dimension. Inevitably, therefore, many topics studied by geographers have moral, ethical, even religious connotations. For example, the layout of a town always expresses the distribution of wealth and poverty, status and power within that society. Topics such as the distribution of housing of different qualities, the location of industries and areal variations in access to resources are always likely to provoke questions about the justice of the whole social and economic system of which they form part.

Ethical questions are also raised by studies of the economics and politics of international trade, of the granting and witholding of aid to poor countries, of the exploitation of resources, of pollution, nuclear power generation and a host of other topics.

Geography and the Curricular 'Great Debate'

The nature of modern geography has been examined in some detail. Next, the ways in which geographers have developed the educational possibilities of their subject within the national debate about the purposes, content and methods of the school curriculum will be described and issues arising discussed. This 'Great Debate' (the phrase is attributed to Mrs. Shirley Williams) was officially launched in October 1976 by Prime Minister James Callaghan in an address at Ruskin College, Oxford. At first, developments were slow; but as the 1980s advanced, central government became clearer about what it thought needed to be done to bring the British education system into line with national requirements in the latter part of the century; and its educational intentions were made known through a succession of publications from the Department of Education and Science especially those written by Her Majesty's Inspectors of Schools, by frequent Ministerial statements and finally by a comprehensive Education Reform Bill. A convenient starting-point for the present discussion is *The Curriculum from 5 to 16*,[3] the second in the HMI *Curriculum Matters* series, published in March 1985.

In this document it is proposed that all schools should incorporate into their curricula the four cardinal principles of relevance, breadth, balance and differentiation. How does geography, when well taught, meet these requirements?

Geography is 'relevant' in many ways. The smallest child, equally with the managing director of some international company, lives in and has to take account of space as a dimension of life. A study which seeks to improve people's understanding of that dimension and their capacity to handle it effectively must therefore be relevant to everyone's life experience. Again, because geography helps us to understand the world as it is, the world of economics, politics and power, production and trade, poverty and wealth, it must be considered a 'relevant' study for the citizens of any country which lives by trade and by providing services which others wish to buy.

Geography certainly answers to the requirement for breadth and balance. By its very nature it is a relating and integrating subject. Geographers are concerned with the natural world and with human actions and their studies show the two to be inextricably related. Merely by existing, people affect their natural environments. By clearing forests, farming the land, fishing, opening up quarries and mines, manufacturing, generating power and travelling as tourists they affect it even more, sometimes in unexpected ways. Unexpected consequences are always the result of an inadequate understanding of the systems, natural and humanly generated, in which interventions are being made, or else of sheer irresponsibility. Geography helps us to understand these complex systems better and so to predict the effects of interventions. Unhappily neither geography nor any other academic study can provide a defence against irresponsibility, greed and other human failings.

Geography answers well to the requirement for differentiation, the capacity, that is, to be taught and learned at different levels of difficulty, even within one class. Most geographical topics can be handled in this way. Thus, very young children can be introduced to the elements of map understanding. Some will immediately realize that the locations and distributions of items in the home and neighbourhood can be represented pictorially or with the aid of models, while others will grasp the more sophisticated concepts of scale and the map's overhead view. The study of other places and peoples can begin simply with descriptive and perhaps anecdotal presentations; explanations can then be added step by step at levels appropriate to individuals and groups. For example, land-use in a given part of Europe can be described; it can also be described with some fairly superficial explanations; and it can be intensively explained in terms of land ownership, tax systems, competition from industrial wage-rates, population movements, international competition and so on. Even the truth about causes and relationships, when it can be unearthed at all, often turns out to be a matter of opinion.

Geography is thus well able to meet the specific requirements of *Curriculum 5 to 16*. Clearly, it can also contribute on a very broad front to the development of the whole school curriculum. The ways in which these broader contributions are being made will next be discussed.

Geographers have contributed to the national debate in many ways, the two most important of which have been through the committees, working parties, journals and other publications of the Geographical Association and through the team of geographers in Her Majesty's Inspectorate. The work of these two most influential groups will be discussed in detail later. Also important has been the work of the three Schools Council geography projects (*Avery Hill, Geography 14 to 18* and *Geography 16 to 19*) which, though disbanded, remain influential through regional follow-up groups and through their examination syllabuses at GCSE and 'A' level. In January 1986 the geographers on the Secondary Examinations Council produced the National Criteria for GCSE geography, together with training materials,[4] which are now shaping all work in secondary schools both below and also above the age of sixteen; they are now beginning to scrutinize and make recommendations about the various syllabuses at 'A' and AS levels, all of which have been substantially modernized recently to take account of developments in the pre- 'A' level years. Also notable has been the support of leading publishers who have provided teachers with a whole new generation of attractive and stimulating geography books, many written by teachers.

Certain local education authorities with geography advisers have carried out curriculum development work of the highest quality. Staffordshire, London, Kent, Avon, Sheffield, Hampshire and some others immediately spring to mind, but it is perhaps invidious to name particular authorities when space will not allow all to be mentioned. There have been some important local initiatives, such as the Birmingham Geography Teachers' Workshop; and some journals have appeared other than those of the Geographical Association which have put forward thought-provoking ideas. An example is the London teachers' publication *Contemporary Issues in Geography and Education.*

The enhanced interest in relating work in schools to the work of industry, something which has long interested geographers, has been given more precise shape in the form of the Geography, Schools and Industry Project, based in Oxford University and supported by the Geographical Association. Last but very important has been the work of very many geography teachers who have experimented with new ideas and materials in their classrooms and on their field courses and who together have provided the essential seed-bed for centrally directed curriculum reform. Many of these innovative teachers have reported upon their experiences in the pages of *Teaching Geography*, the Geographical Association's practical journal for teachers and in various local authority geography *Bulletins*. The excellent work of far more has gone unrecorded but all have contributed to the general forward movement of the subject in schools.

In many schools, geographers are to be found playing a leading part in the general curricular debate; and perhaps because of this a quite surprising number have been appointed to headships and deputy headships where their influence extends far beyond the bounds of their subject.

The Geographical Association: Sir Keith Joseph and After

The Geographical Association has about 6000 members and includes in its ranks most of the people who are active in the field of geographical education. Its membership spans the whole range of professional interests and includes teachers in primary and secondary schools, universities, polytechnics and colleges; local authority advisers and inspectors and members of HM Inspectorate; authors and publishers; and many interested private individuals.

The Geographical Association has contributed to the Great Debate on a very broad front, but its single most important achievement has been to invite the then Secretary of State for Education and Science, Sir Keith Joseph, to address its membership on the place of geography in the school curriculum. This memorable address was delivered at King's College, London, on June 19th, 1985 and published in *Geography* in October.[5] In it, Sir Keith assured geographers that their subject had a secure place within the curriculum provided that they took heed of developments in the wider national debate and that they formulated clear statements about the distinctive contributions which geography could make to the education of all young people. Sir Keith concluded by posing seven sets of questions about this special contribution and some related matters, to which he requested answers. In particular he asked for statements of the criteria which should be used to define the contribution of geography at successive age-levels, about the relevance of the subject to modern life and about the best ways of handling controversial issues.

As President of the Geographical Association for that year the writer of this chapter answered Sir Keith Joseph's questions in short form six weeks later in a paper which was later published in *Teaching Geography* (January 1986).[6] And, at the Association's Annual Conference in April he developed this response in the form of a presidential address entitled 'A geographer's view: contributions of geography to the school curriculum'. This was published in *Geography* (June 1986).[7]

At the time of this first response, the Association promised to send to the Secretary of State more substantial comments based upon a broad sampling of members' opinions. A series of regional conferences were therefore arranged by the Branches at Brighton, Bristol, Chorley, Leicester and Stevenage at which Sir Keith's seven questions were discussed and additional matters raised. During this period, Sir Keith Joseph was succeeded as Secretary of State by Mr. Kenneth Baker.

Following the various debates and consultations, a number of Geographical Association members drawn from different parts of the teaching profession were invited to write substantive answers to Sir Keith's seven questions. These answers were edited by Patrick Bailey and Tony Binns, Joint Honorary Secretary of the Geographical Association, and sent to Kenneth Baker in March 1987. Late that year they were published under the title *A Case for Geography*.[8] Also included in this publication was a report on the reasonable expectations for levels of attainment in geography at the ages of 7, 11, 14 and 16 prepared by a Geographical Association working party chaired by Patrick Wiegand. Both documents were used as the basis of a discussion between Kenneth Baker and Geographical Association representatives on June 30. At this meeting, the Secretary of State assured the Association that he regarded geography as an important part of all young people's education; and in the Education Reform Bill which he laid before Parliament in November, geography was listed as a Foundation Subject, to be included in the curriculum of all schools up to the age of 16.[9]

The following main points were made in the Geographical Association publications mentioned:

1   Geography is an essential part of everybody's general education because it deals with a fundamental aspect of human life, namely our place in space.

2   The approaches used by geographers to study the earth yield unique and important insights into the nature of that world and mankind's place within it.

3   All geography is based upon first-hand observation and enquiry. Therefore, all who learn it should have opportunities to make first-hand observations and enquiries themselves. Fieldwork is an integral part of geographical education.

4   Criteria for deciding upon the content and approaches for geographical education at successive age levels are to be derived (a) from our knowledge, admittedly imperfect, of what young people of various ages are likely to be able to learn; (b) from the overall aims of school-level education, as for example set out in *Better Schools*[10]; and (c) from the characteristics of geography itself. For example, controversial issues relating to the national economy and international relations are most suitably dealt with at the higher age levels.

5   In very general terms, geographical education in the primary school should emphasize activity and experience. It should seek to systematize the growing child's knowledge of the local environment and introduce the broad patterns of world geography; to arouse interest in peoples and places at home and abroad; encourage understanding of and identification with other people; and lay the foundations of map understanding.

6   Geography in the secondary school should build upon and extend the work done at the primary stage. It should aim to develop the individual's understanding of his or her place in the national and world community; examine Britain's place in a competitive world; and discuss some of the more pressing issues and

problems which now confront mankind, such, for example, as the nature, control and proper legitimate use of resources, the control of environmental damage, international inter-depend-ence and dominance and the causes of and remedies for areal variations in wealth and poverty.

7 Controversial issues arise naturally as part of geographical educa-tion. They are most effectively dealt with by pupils referring to factual evidence for themselves, whenever this can be arranged.

8 Continuity and progression can only be achieved when there is consultation between teachers at successive stages in the educa-tional process. In practice, neither time nor opportunity for this are built into school programmes. This needs to be corrected.

9 Progression is much more difficult to achieve than continuity because children learn at such different speeds and in so many different ways. In fact, a large reservoir of teachers' experience exists about what pupils of various ages and backgrounds are likely to be able to learn and this experience needs to be tapped and systematized. The Geographical Association has tried to do this, to some extent, through the pages of its journal *Teaching Geography*. Some of this experience has also been encapsulated in the Association's report on expectations in geography included in *A Case for Geography* and in other parts of that document.

10 There is no one right or wrong way to organize courses in secondary schools. However, the intense pressure upon limited curricular space at this stage would seem to point towards modu-lar forms of course construction. Such developments bring with them the danger of incoherence which needs to be guarded against.

11 Where attempts are made to integrate parts of the secondary curriculum, this should always be done on educational grounds, not grounds of expediency. Such courses should build upon earlier work and not ignore it; show the relations between differ-ent forms of knowledge; be foundational to later work; introduce pupils to the full range of learning experiences in geography, as in other subjects, so that informed choices can be made later; and be very well taught, so that they arouse the pupils' enthu-siasm for more advanced work.

The Geographical Association has published numerous books, reports and pamphlets in recent years which deal with aspects of geographical education. Most important have been its primary and secondary hand-books, entitled respectively *Geographical Work in Primary and Middle Schools* (Mills (ed), 1981 and 1988) and *Handbook for Geography Teachers* (Boardman (ed), 1986). Recent developments in examination and assessment techniques have received attention in *Profiling in Geography* (Graves and

Naish (ed), 1986) and *Evaluation and Assessment in Geography* (Orrell and Wiegand (eds), 1984). Other recent Geographical Association publications deal with links between schools and industry, teaching slow learners, the design of integrated courses, profiling, geography and TVEI, geography and careers, geography and the multicultural society and geographical applications of computers in schools. The Association's two quarterly journals, *Geography* and *Teaching Geography* respectively publish papers on geographical topics with the prime aim of keeping readers up-to-date with the subject and on practical aspects of geography teaching in classrooms and in the field. A third journal is shortly to be added to the Association's regular publications, dealing with geography in primary and lower middle schools. Through its journals the Geographical Association provides a comprehensive review service of books, software and other learning materials and facilities. It may be noted that the Geographical Association is an independent body and that all the work done for it by members is voluntary and unpaid. It works closely with the Royal Geographical Society, the senior geographical body in Britain, which has a general interest in education though its main concerns are with exploration and research. It also has links with the Institute of British Geographers which represents the interests of geography in higher education and with the Scottish Association of Geography Teachers.

Beginning in 1985, the Geographical Association took the lead in trying to bring into being a Council of British Geography, representing all geographical interests and able to speak authoritatively for the subject at the highest national levels. This Council is now established and held its first meeting in January 1988. Its first publication was a report on British geographical research and education, prepared for the 1988 meeting of the International Geographical Union in Australia.

The Work of Her Majesty's Inspectors

The role of Her Majesty's Inspectors of Schools has changed significantly in the past decade as a result of more direct governmental interventions in education, culminating in legislation for a national curriculum. This new role has shown itself in an increasing number of HMI publications which, while they may be styled as discussion documents, are in fact increasingly detailed and explicit statements of policy. Geographers have been fortunate in this period in that the team of geographers within the Inspectorate have shown themselves well able to give a substantial lead in developing the potentials of the subject in schools and to put the case for geography effectively at the highest political levels.

Two recent HMI publications merit particular notice. Both have attempted to deal with the obstinate problem of deciding what aspects ot geography ought to be taught at successive stages of the school curriculum.

First, immediately after Sir Keith Joseph's address to the Geographical Association in June 1985, Trevor Bennetts, the senior HMI for geography, presented a paper entitled 'Geography from 5 to 16. A view from the Inspectorate' which formulated concise objectives for geographical education at the primary and secondary stages, together with the components of an effective teaching syllabus which some schools still do not have. This paper did a great deal in a short time to clarify the thoughts of geography teachers about the way their subject would need to be developed within a school curriculum which was genuinely conceived of as a continuum from 5 to 16. Bennetts' paper was published in *Geography* in October 1985[11] with the text of the Secretary of State's address.

Eighteen months later, the Inspectorate published a more substantial and fully worked out sequel to Trevor Bennetts' paper in the form of *Curriculum Matters 7: Geography from 5 to 16* (HMSO, 1986).[12] This document was part of the *Curriculum Matters* series, to which it therefore conforms in style; but is in fact one of the most practical and clearly written of that series. In this booklet Her Majesty's Inspectors formulated concise aims for geographical education in general, then set out detailed objectives for the early primary, later primary and secondary stages. They made practical suggestions about how to plan courses at each stage and about appropriate teaching approaches and added suggestions for the effective organization of a school geography department. Suggestions for achieving progression and continuity were supported by a fully worked-out example. A final short section summarized recent thinking about assessment and pointed out that this has always to be viewed as an integral part of the educational process.

The HMI document has been criticized as being somewhat conservative in approach and for accepting too readily an 'objectives' model for curriculum development. This may be so; but it represents a major clarification of thinking for many and probably most schools. It brings together in a concise and lucid way the characteristics of sound practice which is widely applicable and it provided a basis for action, not mere discussion. The document has been widely welcomed in primary schools where it is regarded as the most closely reasoned and complete statement on geographical education yet to appear for this stage.

Some Current Issues and Problems

This final section attempts to draw together a list of the main issues which now confront geographers working in schools. It may be convenient to itemize them by way of a summary. All have been mentioned in the preceding discussion, at least by implication.

1 The nature of geography itself means that it is potentially a power-ful force for curriculum integration. It spans the arts and sciences divide and cannot be categorized solely as a 'humanity', though many of its concerns lie in this field. This integrative potential has yet to be properly harnessed; meanwhile, attempts are made at other forms of integration which are both narrower and concep-tually inferior to that which geography can provide.

It is to be hoped that schools, faced as they are by intense pressure upon their curricula, will work towards forms of integra-tion which are genuinely time-saving. This can be done by asking all their subject specialists to define, briefly, the essential ele-ments of their subjects; and then by putting together curricula, probably in modular form, which incorporate these essentials and build upon the links between them.

2 Related problems arise when schools attempt to 'integrate' geogra-phy, history and perhaps religious education under a 'humanities' umbrella, usually to save time. Such courses seem to be most effective educationally when the participating subject specialists focus their expertise upon agreed themes. Other kinds of course may be in no definable sense integrated; and in some of them important aspects of the curriculum may be omitted altogether. Such total omissions are unacceptable now that geography is listed as a Foundation Subject in the National Curriculum. Schools need to think out the criteria on which all their joint and combined courses, existing or proposed, are constructed. The proposals for such criteria made in *A Case for Geography* as part of the re-sponse to the Secretary of State's sixth question and summarized earlier in this chapter offer a possible way forward.

3 Progression continues to be a hard problem to solve because of the nature of geography. However, for many years, geography teachers have been tackling the problem with considerable though usually private success. In broad terms, progression in geography means advancing from the simple to the complex, from the known and directly observable towards the unknown and less-observable, from the concrete towards the abstract, from the small-scale to-wards the large-scale, from the particular towards the general.

Such very general principles have to be interpreted by skilled teachers in the light of their knowledge of how boys and girls learn. This, as every teacher knows, varies from pupil to pupil, morning to afternoon, week to week, year to year. The most useful single exemplar for developing topics at increasing levels of sophistication is to be found in *Geography from 5 to 16*, pp. 49–57, the topic being manufacturing industry.

4 It has been pointed out that all geography begins with somebody, somewhere, making observations. And that, if they are to learn as

geographers, boys and girls in schools must have opportunities to make observations for themselves. The *National Criteria for Geography* accept this point and require that all GCSE candidaties shall plan and carry out individual investigations of their own which will often include fieldwork. Sir Keith Joseph in his address to the Geographical Association affirmed that

> ... geography also has its special contribution to make to the acquisition of skills which will be of long-term value. In geography that means practical investigations, both inside and outside the classroom ... Fieldwork has, of course, the additional advantage of enabling pupils to investigate real problems and to learn from direct observation and experience. At their best, geographical enquiries involve the pupils in defining the questions to be tackled; in planning the methods to be used; in collecting, analyzing and interpreting information; and in presenting their findings in a suitable form.

It is therefore extremely worrying to find that a number of much-publicized accidents to school parties (not one of which was engaged in fieldwork), accidents to pupils in mountains and some recent court rulings and legal opinions have made local education authorities very nervous about allowing school pupils of any age to undertake fieldwork unless it is directly and continuously supervised. It has also been argued in the courts that the full costs of all work which a school prescribes must be met by the local authority. Such total subsidy has never been customary and the ruling, if upheld, could put an end to all but local fieldwork, except perhaps in more affluent areas where parents might waive their right to subsidy, and in the independent sector. These developments affect not only geographers but also all others who arrange out-of-school activities, such as the Duke of Edinburgh Award schemes, and at the time of writing the difficulties are unresolved. They pose the most serious threat which fieldwork has ever faced.

Conclusion

Modern geography is an exciting subject to teach. It deals with some of the most interesting and urgent matters which concern the well-being and future survival of humanity. Yet at the same time it is relevant to the experience of the youngest child.

Tolstoy once wrote that 'the highest wisdom has but one science, the science of the whole — the science explaining the whole creation and man's place in it' (*War and Peace*, 5,2). The nearest approach we have to that ideal science is modern geography.

Notes

1. DEPARTMENT OF EDUCATION AND SCIENCE (1985) *General Certificate of Secondary Education. The National Criteria: Geography*, London, HMSO.
2. FLEURE, H.J. (1953) Quoted by Professor S.W. Wooldridge in an address to the Geographical Association Summer School, Pulborough.
3. DEPARTMENT OF EDUCATION AND SCIENCE (1985) *The Curriculum, from 5 to 16. Curriculum Matters 2, An HMI Series*, London, HMSO.
4. ORRELL, K. and TOLLEY, H. (1986) *Geography. GCSE. A Guide for Teachers.* Secondary Examinations Council, Milton Keynes, Open University Press.
5. JOSEPH, SIR K. (1985) 'Geography in the school curriculum' *Geography*, 70, 4, pp. 290–7.
6. BAILEY, P. (1986) 'Geography in the school curriculum. A reply to Sir Keith Joseph's seven questions'. *Teaching Geography*, 11, 2, pp. 64–7.
7. BAILEY, P. (1986) 'A geographer's view: Contributions of geography to the school curriculum'. *Geography*, 71, 3, pp. 193–205.
8. BAILEY, P. and BINNS, A.J. (Eds) (1987) *A Case for Geography*. Sheffield, The Geographical Association.
9. DEPARTMENT OF EDUCATION AND SCIENCE (1987) *A Bill to Amend the Law Relating to Education*, London, HMSO.
10. DEPARTMENT OF EDUCATION AND SCIENCE (1985) *Better Schools*, London, HMSO.
11. BENNETTS, T.H. (1985) 'Geography from 5 to 16. A view from the Inspectorate' *Geography*, 70, 4, pp. 299–314.
12. DEPARTMENT OF EDUCATION AND SCIENCE (1986) *Geography from 5 to 16. Curriculum Matters 7. An HMI Series.* London, HMSO.

9   Home Economics

Margaret Jepson

> Home economics is concerned with using and managing human
> and material resources for the benefit of individuals, of families
> and, where appropriate, of communities. It draws from at least
> three different ways of knowing about the world — scientific,
> creative/aesthetic and social. The ways the subject is taught reflect
> the range of methods used by the contributory disciplines. It has
> social usefulness and relevance for pupils for it focuses on the
> home which lies within the current or future experience of all
> young people. It aims to provide pupils with a coherent map of
> knowledge, skills and values so that they can make informed
> decisions. (Cumming *et al*, 1985)

Home economics has grown out of those subjects on the timetable which
were variously known as needlework, cookery, laundrywork, housewifery,
housecraft, domestic subjects and domestic science. The progress of the
subject is the result of the interaction of many factors: changes in the
structure of education, social changes particularly the role of women in
society, and changes in educational theory and teaching methods. The
strictly utilitarian approach of the early days preparing girls for a particular
job/role in society has been replaced by the more liberal approach of an
interdisciplinary subject which aims to help both boys and girls to

> lead effective lives not only as individuals but also as members of a
> family and community, within the context of a culturally, socially
> and economically diverse society. (*National Criteria Home Econo-
> mics*, DES, 1985)

Home economics-has as its content four main components: food,
textiles, home and family studies, but all components are, in practice,
integrated since the context is the identification and fulfilment of human
needs. The provision to meet the needs of individuals in a household,
family or community setting is central to home economics and thus requires the components to be considered, not in isolation, but as resources

for the achievement and enhancement of a personal lifestyle in an increasingly complex society.

Home economics as an applied subject which synthesizes theory with practice uses a variety of practical approaches, design briefs, experimental work, creative use of food and textiles, which allow pupils to develop a wide range of skills. These do include the craft skills but also the skills of organization and management which cannot always be learned in a theoretical context. The practical workshop nature of home economics brings realism and understanding to learning opportunities and allows pupils to develop critical and analytical skills, the ability to transfer knowledge and understanding from one situation to another.

Pupils are encouraged to analyze and recognize the variety of human needs and propose solutions which can be tested by practical application. The decision-making process in home economics requires that pupils have the knowledge and skills to analyze, research, order priorities, plan, organize resources, both human and material, make judgments, implement a plan of action and evaluate solutions. This complex and challenging process is applied to real life situations, to which pupils can easily relate and use their own experience to build knowledge, understanding and skills. This relevance is a strength of home economics.

Although pupils still work with food and fabrics, home economics is a far cry from just 'cooking and sewing'. There has been a move away from the isolated production of a perfect end product which sometimes stifled interest and imagination by its concentration on a narrow range of traditional techniques and repetitive and circumscribed processes. Pupils still require standards of craft skills but these are firmly set in the framework of problem solving and designing to fulfil human needs. In order that pupils develop the skills of management of resources (both human and physical) equal to this task, a range of strategies, knowledge and concepts is required.

> The essential contribution and strength of home economics and its potentially unique position in the curriculum, is the opportunity it offers for the synthesis of a wide range of knowledge, skills, attitudes and values and its application to real life situations. (DES, 1987a, Llandudno Conference)

Home economics could therefore fit readily into a broad, balanced curriculum as a practical subject which has as its central tenet the application of knowledge and the development of a range of skills.

The proposed national curriculum does not appear to have been designed with such principles in mind. The very traditional list of core and foundation subjects which will take up 80–90 per cent of the curriculum time does not include home economics. Home economics is referred to as one of the other popular subjects which are taught by many schools and will continue to be a valuable part of the curriculum for many pupils in the secondary as well as the primary phase (DES, 1987b, para. 17).

The popularity of the subject with pupils in terms of numbers of examination entrants at GCSE level is apparent. The concern of the subject community is that the LEAs, governing bodies and headteachers would take a strict interpretation of the times suggested in the national curriculum consultation document (para 15) which would leave very little time, approximately two hours twenty minutes in the average secondary school, for all other popular subjects. The competing claims of other subjects such as a second foreign language, personal and social education, business studies, careers education, will all have to be satisfied within this remaining 10 per cent of curriculum time. Additionally, home economics requires a degree of specialist accommodation, specialist teachers and a level of resources which, when a school is in control of its own finances, may be regarded as expensive.

The response of the subject community was one of concern, even hostility. For example, the National Association of Teachers of Home Economics (NATHE) at their AGM in 1987 passed a resolution condemning the omission of home economics from the foundation curriculum. A delegation representing the subject community met with the Minister of State in September 1987 to present the case for home economics and were given a reassurance that it was not the intention of the government to remove home economics from the curriculum; there would be time for the subject outside the foundation subjects but also elements of home economics could be taught in a variety of foundation subjects such as science, technology and art. This dichotomy has left the subject community with a feeling that there is little understanding of the subject and its contribution to the curriculum. There are obviously very close links with other subjects but there is also a role for the subject in its own right.

The foundation subject 'Technology' is not defined in the consultation document and home economics can make a significant contribution to this area of the curriculum. As early as 1984, when the DES issued 'The Organization and Content of the 5–16 Curriculum', NATHE highlighted the rationale given for CDT as a rationale for home economics as it also requires pupils

> to study and solve problems involving the use of materials and which entails some element of designing and making things (DES, 1984b, para 25).

The materials used for making things are likely to be food and fabrics rather than wood and metal but the problem solving nature of the subject is shared.

In *Curriculum Matters 2; The Curriculum 5–16* the DES defined technology as 'the process of bringing about change or exercising control over the environment' (para 84). This process of problem solving in home economics is concerned with change and control over the domestic environment, with the provision of shelter, food, clothing, methods of maintaining health in order to satisfy human needs. Within this context, pupils will readily appreciate that technology is about 'people controlling things, not things controlling people' (*ibid*, para 84). The common use of the design process, design loop, as a method of teaching and learning is one of the reasons why home economics and CDT departments are often part of the same faculty in a school.

Indeed APU (1987) recognized the difficulty of defining technology, preferring to use the term 'design and technological activity'. The diversity of existing practice in the area of design and technology, notably in subjects such as CDT, home economics and art and design was noted. The research team, which included a home economist, stated:

> The basic premise of design and technological activity is that by using materials, tools and systems, human beings can intervene to modify and improve their environment. Underlying this intervention is the motive of responding to human need (para 2.1) ... From this premise, it follows that design and technological activity is not the preserve of any single subject, but rather refers to an activity that may be exercised in a range of subjects, albeit with some different emphases. (APU, 1987, para 2.3)

The working party for technology has yet to be appointed and a definition of the subject and the extent of the contribution of home economics remains unclear.

The science working party has been established and part of its remit is

> to take account of the possibilities for close cooperation between science and home economics so as to exploit fully the contribution that each subject can make to the other (correspondence from Minister of State, 1987).

There is a link with science particularly obvious in the range of curriculum materials produced by the Nuffield-Chelsea Curriculum Trust. The Nuffield Home Economics Course for years 1–3 and textbooks for GCSE examinations are in accordance with the Nuffield tradition, i.e. it aims to show how scientific concepts can be understood and applied. Pupils are stimulated into making their own investigations into materials and equipment, while guidance is provided to ensure that the research is on the right lines and that the significance of the findings is appreciated. The content of the lesson is related to the skills the pupils will develop; the Nuffield research group identified six groups of skills.

1. *Observing*
   Measuring
   Estimating

2. *Analyzing*
   Classifying
   Deciding criteria
   Identifying causes
   Interpreting graphs
   Using statistics

3. *Planning*
   Suggesting and designing tests
   Suggesting hypotheses
   Selecting equipment
   Practical skills (dexterity and manipulation)
   Reasoning logically

4. *Assessing*
   Validity
   Relevant factors
   Accuracy
   References

5. *Communicating*
   Graphs
   Writing
   Speech
   Diagrams
   Maths

6. *Applying knowledge*
   Assessing ideas
   Evaluating results

(Faulkner and Mansell (eds), 1982)

These skills could be developed through activities where scientific and mathematical concepts are applied in a realistic situation. The materials suggest practical work through which pupils are encouraged to consider a range of possibilities, there being no single right answer. The approach is particularly suited to home economics where links between scientific theory and everyday practice are frequently made. The use of scientific method as part of the investigative approach in home economics links the subject with science in the curriculum, although in home economics problem solving is complex.

> Scientific method can help in solving problems but it is rarely sufficient in itself since so many factors affect choice and influence decisions ... many factors such as personal choice, availability and acceptability must be considered when making the final decision. (Hadley and Hogarth, 1987)

Home economics also has close links with aesthetic subjects, particularly art and design. Pupils have the opportunity to express themselves through the media of textiles; a variety of creative experiences is provided by the diverse uses of fabric, thread and dye. Techniques such as weaving, batik, hand painting on fabrics, spraying, silk screen printing, quilting, machine embroidery, hand embroidery, textile sculptures or 'structures' are just as likely to be present in the textile curriculum as are the techniques of garment construction. Again, in home economics the emphasis is on practical work.

The subject community had been engaged in a detailed analysis of the knowledge, concepts, skills and attitudes which can be developed through a study of home economics since the early 1980s. This was in response to the need to produce national criteria for examinations at 16+. The traditional emphasis on craft skills and the recall of knowledge, particularly evident in 'O' level syllabuses, had a stifling effect on development:

> There is a growing number (of teachers) who are far from satisfied with the present system and who see the 'criteria exercise' as an excellent opportunity to break away from the dichotomy and diversity in the present system (Christian-Carter and Hillerton, 1984).

For many teachers it was no longer relevant to courses based on the 'design, make, test and evaluate model' in years 1–3.

The Joint Council Home Economics Working Party produced criteria for four separate subject areas, namely child development, textiles and fashion, home economics, food and nutrition. Whilst the majority of teachers who replied to the consultation questionnaires were in favour of the proposals there was considerable opposition from HMI, the National Association of Teachers of Home Economics (NATHE) and the National Association of Inspectors and Advisors (NAIEA) in Home Economics. HMI felt that with four separate sets of criteria there was a danger that each component would be taught in isolation with emphasis on manipulative skills which was at odds with the view that home economics was concerned with organizational and management skills in relation to resources and the needs of people in the home and community. NATHE urged a major reconsideration and suggested a single subject with a core focusing on home economics as

> the study of the needs of the individual in the socio-economic environment with reference to the home and family and with the emphasis on the practical evaluation of applications of knowledge employing a problem solving approach to the living situation (NATHE, 1982).

The working party produced and presented to the Secretary of State a single set of revised criteria around aims and objectives common to all aspects of home economics early in 1984. In August the Secretary of State rejected the criteria as one set of criteria covering four separate aspects of the subject. The Secretary of State was of the opinon that home economics syllabuses

> should have as a common core an integration between all four aspects although further, in-depth study of one or more aspects would be appropriate (DES, 1984a, 14 August).

The working party had to work quickly to present the criteria to ensure that an integrated course was achieved which did allow for integration and this 'in-depth study'. The National Criteria were accepted in February 1985.

This whole discussion had highlighted the tensions within the subject community. The separate subject areas of needlework and food had been enshrined in teacher training courses and in schools in different rooms or resource areas often not even physically close together. Traditional teachers either saw home economics only as an umbrella term encompassing their subject area or rejected the term outright. There were others who saw home economics as an integrated subject with the individual within the family in the community as the focus of study, particularly those who trained during the sixties and seventies on home economics courses to whom integration was familiar. The expansion of 16+ and Mode 3 courses during the 1970s allowed for more integrated courses in home economics to be planned and numbers, particularly of pupils on 16+ courses, had risen dramatically. The tensions between those who saw the criteria as the end of their subject specialism and those who saw home economics as an integrated subject have to a certain extent been reduced as the integration achieved through an emphasis on the process by which pupils learn, through the assessment objectives and common themes, does allow for specialist content to be used.

The National Criteria for home economics represented a shift of emphasis from syllabi that presented content and recall of knowledge to one primarily concerned with the process of education. The key to the influence of GCSE is apparent in the assessment objectives (see Table 1).

The assessment objectives embody the problem solving and decision making skills essential for active learning and the synthesis of knowledge and skills. Those teachers who had been trained in, and were content with, the traditional curriculum with its emphasis on craft skills and the production of perfect artefacts, with the recall of knowledge which was unquestioned fact, were less easily persuaded. The in-service training, when well presented, quelled many fears as teachers realized the possibilities open to them to plan a variety of learning opportunities. The assessment objectives embodied the problem solving approach and encouraged pupils to make decisions for themselves. The common themes were also a device which revealed especially to those who were trained in a traditional manner, the way in which the subject could be integrated. It was through the common themes that teachers who had been trained in a particular specialism, for example, food or textiles, could relate to the other major aspects. The common themes are: —

Human development including physical, social and emotional development according to age and sex.

Health including well-being, and satisfaction of physical and psychological needs.

Safety:protection as from accidents and ill-health, damage to materials and property and financial loss.

Table 1: Assessment Objectives	Allocation of marks (percentage)
3.1 To analyze situations in the field of home economics by identifying the various human needs and material factors involved, and to recognize the inter-relationships of these needs and factors.	40–40
3.2 To recall, seek out, select, record and apply knowledge relevant to the needs and factors identified.	
3.3 To use investigative procedures 3.3.1 to test and compare methods, materials and equipment; 3.3.2 to observe, measure and record observations accurately and systematically; 3.3.3 to interpret evidence in its various forms as a basis for making judgments and choices; 3.3.4 to justify judgments and choices in the light of evidence.	30–40
3.4 To decide upon and plan a course of action which takes into account the priorities identified.	
3.5 To carry out the planned course of action by applying the required skills.	Max 20
3.6 To assess and evaluate the effectiveness of the course of action.	

Source: DES (1985) p. 3.

Efficiency, as of methods of working, performance of materials, tools, equipment and artefacts and in the management of money, time, and value for money.

Values including personal and communal values, priorities for choice.

Aesthetic as related to the quality of life through the enhancement and enjoyment of food, textiles and the home.

Interaction with environment including consumer rights and responsibilities.

The presence of the common themes allows for a common element in all home economics courses which along with a common emphasis on the organization and management of resources presents an integrated course. The skills which are common to all main studies are investigational, measurement, communication, management, psycho-motor and technological. The national criteria did truly represent

good present practice and reflect the curriculum development taking place in the subject field (DES, 1985, para. 1.5).

HMI meanwhile produced *Home Economics from 5–16, Curriculum Matters 5* in September 1985, which set down aims and objectives for pupils of different ages. Home economics was presented as

> essentially concerned with planning, designing and working in ways which involve investigation and experiment, and the organization and management of time and materials. It has to do with important issues concerning the social and material welfare of people living, with a greater or lesser degree of independence, as members of families (HMI, 1985, p. 27).

The aim was to prepare boys and girls for some important aspect of everyday living and the adult responsibilites of family life. The document was well received in the main and the discussion presented was constructive. NATHE felt that the section on principles of teaching home economics made pertinent statements about the teaching of the subject. The emphasis on work in home economics as 'practical and investigative in nature' (*ibid*, para 8) and

> providing opportunities for pupils to think for themselves is essential if they are to consolidate learning and gain confidence in making the judgments and decisions which will be required of them in daily living (*ibid*, para 9)

was commended. This framework of the process by which pupils learn was widely acceptable to the subject community.

The objectives were presented in terms of content in three main areas of home and family, nutrition and food, and textiles. The document did stress that if such a framework were used the three areas should be interrelated to provide a balance of experience for the pupils and to reflect the reality of domestic life and the responsibilities of parenthood. The objectives appeared to some critics as separate and very traditional which could reinforce the tendency for teachers to separate into the narrow areas of experience rather than cooperating to develop more cohesive courses. The means by which the interrelationships could be achieved were not given enough consideration.

> An indication of the interrelationship of these areas should be emphasized and made more explicit throughout the document. (NATHE, 1986)

The School Curriculum Development Committee (SCDC) hoped that this 'apparent rigidity does not exclude a more flexible approach' (SCDC, 1985).

An area for concern was expressed in the framework of objectives for textiles. The objectives appeared to overemphasize the practical function of the subject rather than the creative and aesthetic. The broader interpretation of the design brief using a wide range of criteria including aesthetic, creative, as well as the utilitarian, was suggested.

A major area for concern was the home and family where again the practical aspects of running a home are given a greater priority than the personal and social development of the pupils and the complexities of roles and relationships in family life. There are references to these in the objectives but perhaps not detailed enough for those home economics teachers who see a role for child related studies in home economics. Through a study of the needs of children, pupils, particularly age 14+, can reflect on and increase their understanding of their own personal identity and role as well as their future roles as parents.

There was throughout *Home Economics 5–16* a stress on home economics as suitable for both sexes.

> Home economics is an appropriate area of study for all pupils, both boys and girls, at all stages of schooling (para 7). It is necessary to stress that homemaking is equally important for both boys and girls, and that in adult life the responsibilities of family life should be shared so that both men and women have sufficient opportunity to continue their own personal development (para 5).

However, the acknowledgement was made in the objectives for 16-year-olds that

> although it would be ideal for all pupils to study home economics until the age of 16 ... the poor attitude of some boys to the subject may sometimes make this difficult (para 44).

The gender imbalance amongst pupils taking home economics at examination level is very slowly being redressed. There were no recommendations on effective teaching strategies or activities to negate the influence of gender divisions. There was only one suggestion on reading schemes for the primary school which involved anti-sexist education. Strategies which teachers could use to allow pupils to explore and challenge preconceived sexist attitudes which come from the peer group, the home and the media do need to be developed.

Home economics is rarely taught as a discrete subject in primary schools but work with food, textiles and materials can offer a range of experiences. The integrated and cross-disciplinary approach which enhances the quality of work in primary schools can readily adapt to work in home economics. The Schools Council Project Home Economics in the Middle Years (1979) used 'key concepts' as a framework of reference for the selection of course content. This was an approach shared with Blyth *et al* (1976) *Schools Council Project History, Geography and Social Science 8–13*. The key concepts in home economics were identified by the consideration of the needs of individuals, the needs of society, the knowledge available which related to home and family education and the long term purpose of teaching home and family education. The key concepts of development, interdependence, management, nutrition and protection were those identified. The learning activities were based on ideas which consolidated knowledge and promoted progression in the acquisition of cognitive, social and physical skills.

This type of work in home economics in primary schools, where there is little specialist equipment and few specialist teachers of home economics, is in line with the best developments in primary education. Although NATHE criticized the activities listed in *Home Economics 5–16* as 'more concerned with the product than the process' (NATHE, 1986), the suggestions for the objectives in the primary school did include those which would develop understanding, skills and abilities. Work on homes and family membership will develop the child's understanding of their role in the family and the responsibilities of family members. Work with food should always be seen as part of nutrition education, the development of healthy attitudes and behaviour in relation to food consumption. This is an essential element in home economics. The choice of foods for practical work which depart from the present overdependence on flour, sugar and fat-based baking will enable nutrition education to take place as well as

> the development of manipulative skills, the experience of working cooperatively in groups, the opportunity to sharpen sensory perception, broadening experience by tasting different ingredients and foods, increasing accuracy in weighing and measuring, following pictures or very simple written instructions, and experiencing pleasure in making something to eat (HMI, 1985, para 33).

Experimental work with food and fabrics will allow pupils to develop a scientific mode of enquiry, to gain knowledge and experience of food, fabrics and materials and their reaction to certain conditions. Practical work with textiles could easily be closely linked to art and the development of aesthetic awareness of colour, line, shape, texture to shape, textiles to artefacts, either functional or decorative. Group projects or individual work where there is an element of pupil choice are more beneficial than classes where every child makes a similar item, predetermined by the teacher. Home economics has a cross curricular role in the primary school and as such does

> start to lay the foundations of knowledge, attitudes and skills which will be the basis for later, more formal work in home economics (HMI, 1985, para 30).

The proposals made in *Home Economics 5–16* regarding assessment were accepted by the subject community particularly since

> assessment is inseparable from the whole teaching process (para 68) and the primary use of assessment by teachers in the subject

should be as a diagnostic tool so that the discovery of gaps or discrepancies in the mastery of the work can be remedied and progess maintained at a rate appropriate to the individual (para 74).

This approach to assessment is particularly relevant to home economics because the subject is taught in many schools to mixed ability groups. Again the GCSE criteria had stimulated a great deal of debate on assessment with emphasis on positive achievement and strategies which would achieve differentiation. Traditionally home economics teachers have to a great extent concentrated on the assessment of products, whether the products were dishes, garments or pieces of written work. The assessment of the process of learning which the pupil has gone through in order to achieve the desired end requires a variety of assessment techniques. The assessment objectives of GCSE and the mark allocation gave an indication to teachers of the importance of the assessment of their skills. This has encouraged teachers to experiment with techniques such as pupil self assessment and skills checklists as well as assessment on successful completion of the product. Teachers often after GCSE, INSET, or within NATHE branches, have set up self help groups to assist one another by sharing ideas and experiences and to explore new ideas. This will provide an impetus for the development of courses in home economics in the future.

At the same time courses such as City and Guilds, TVEI, modular courses for Records of Achievement and school profiling schemes have heightened the awareness of teachers to the assessment of the skills and abilities of their pupils. The experience of GCSE has also provided teachers with the confidence and competence to develop home economics courses or contribute to other courses which emphasize the development of skills and abilities in pupils. This is, in fact, a growth point for the subject particularly in the area of pre-vocational education.

The TVEI and CPVE courses have a similar emphasis for assessment of skills such as the ability to analyze, to select relevant information, to plan and carry out a particular task and to evaluate the outcome of a course of action, i.e. problem solving skills. The recognition of strategies and activities that can help pupils to develop these skills has enabled home economics teachers to see a role for themselves and their subject beyond the specific craft skills. Home economics can contribute to 'life skills', 'personal development', 'preparation for life' courses as well as the specific vocational areas of food production, catering, fashion, textile production, child, family and community care; TVEI schemes with modules in home economics have been produced in catering, community care, personal services, textiles, and as part of technology courses dealing with food technology, textile technology and biotechnology.

This view of home economics as an essential contributor to the development of a wide range of skills must be realized if there is not to be a reversion to an emphasis on the craft skills involved in the production of food and clothing. Pre-vocational education should allow for curriculum development rather than curriculum regression. Home economics teachers should make sure that course planning teams are aware of the extent of the contribution of home economics beyond the traditional craft skills. Indeed the organizational and management skills of home economics teachers tend to be in demand by course planning teams!

The issue of courses available at 14+ is closely linked to option choice. In schools the concept is one of free choice by the pupil. In practice, research (Ball, 1981; Bardell, 1982; Jones, 1983), has shown that pupils' individual requirements have to be tailored into the existing situation. Pupils are constrained by prescribed columns of subjects, not all subjects are available to all pupils because of sections, or options made earlier; pupils are advised to take particular subjects in the interests of 'balance' or are refused entry into subjects. The result is a clear relationship between subject choice and ability.

> There is a clear relationship between pupils' ascribed ability and the type of subjects they choose. Higher ability pupils make their selections higher status, academic subjects, and lower ability pupils choose low status, practical subjects. (Jones, 1983, p. 2)

Bardell (1982) in his work for the Schools Council *Options for the Fourth* shows that ability and gender affect the choice of subjects (see Tables 2 and 3).

How Sex Shapes the Typical School Week (40 periods)

| | Average number of periods per week | |
Subject	Boys	Girls
Core Subjects		
Mathematics	6	6
English	6	6
Physical education/games	3	3
Options		
Modern language	3	2
Other humanities	8	9
Science	7	5
Aesthetic subject	1	1
Applied science or technology	0	2
Home or office related subjects	0	6

Source: Bardell (1982) *Options for the Fourth.*

Table 3: How Ability Shapes the Typical School Week (40 periods)

Subject	Average number of periods per week		
	Top ability band	Middle ability band	Bottom ability band
Core subjects			
Mathematics	6	6	6
English	6	6	6
Physical education/games	3	3	3
Options			
Modern language	5	2	0
Other humanities	7	8	10
Science	8	7	3
Aesthetic subject	1	1	1
Applied science or technology	2	3	7
Home or office related subjects	2	4	4

Source: Bardell (1982) Options for the Fourth.

Despite equal opportunities legislation and a policy of equal access in education the choice made by pupils is almost entirely on sex-associated lines. This continues to pose a problem for home economics, which is difficult to resolve when free choice is given:

> The assumption of gender differentiation was retained underneath the new ideology of free choice and pupils' needs ... the reproduction of gender divisions could be left to the now historically internalized attitudes and gender ideologies of parents, teachers, careers officers, employers and finally students themselves. In this sense the assumptions of male superiority and female domesticity (being unchallenged) were encouraged, albeit more implicitly, to prevail. (Arnot, 1983, p. 78)

NATHE is so concerned about the uptake of the subject at 14+ that it has initiated and, with the Equal Opportunities Commission, funded research on patterns of option choice and good practice which will help to eliminate this problem. The research findings due in late 1987 should stimulate further discussion, early reports highlighting the complex nature of the task.

The issue of sex-differentiation also has a direct effect on the careers choice of pupils. Home Economics 5–16 was criticised for its lack of emphasis on the career potential of a study of home economics. The only reference being to

> careers involving the care of children, the elderly or the handicapped; or catering in its various forms (para 6).

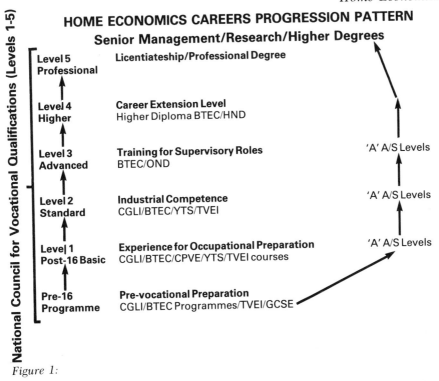

Figure 1:

This appeared to some to be a narrow interpretation of the careers available, no mention was made of further study in the subject and the wide variety of careers available to graduates of a study of home economics. Courses in home economics are provided at a range of levels and the courses in school should be seen as part of a career progression pattern as well as a preparation for

important aspects of everyday living and the adult responsibilities of family life.

A conference organized by DES to discuss issues raised by *Home Economics 5–16* was attended by local authority advisors, representatives of higher education institutions with home economics courses, NATHE and other interested parties who had responded to the discussion document. The conference reaffirmed the interrelated nature of home economics not in terms of content but in terms of philosophy and the skills pupils develop through the practical nature of the subject.

Home economics is concerned with the identification and fulfilment of human need in the context of the home and family. It assists pupils to understand the demands of everyday life and to recognize the diverse and changing nature of needs in modern society ... A wide range of skills is likely to be developed, ranging from skills in language, numeracy and communication to interpersonal skills and those of investigation, management, and decision-making. These are both applicable to everyday life and to the workplace (DES, 1987a, Llandudno Conference).

This implies, as was agreed at the conference, that the emphasis is on the development of skills within the problem solving context, where the teacher is the facilitator rather than the director of learning. This process of learning has been utilized successfully in the primary school and whilst the conference saw it as appropriate to the secondary school the implications for the whole school policy were raised.

The outcome of experimental learning is less predictable than prescriptive methods, requiring considerable confidence on the part of the teacher who, in turn, needs to create a stimulating atmosphere in which learning can take place. In-service training can help in the development of both confidence and expertise as can the contribution made by newly qualified teachers, who should be equipped with appropriate skills (DES, 1987a, Llandudno Conference).

The significant implications are for finance, accommodation, time allocation for both teaching and planning courses and ancillary support.

The financial resources required to fund investigative work in food and fabrics must be met by the school rather than the pupils and parents. The allocation of funds within schools may need to be amended to take account of this. Similarly the amount of preparation required by this work is greater and in most cases falls on an individual teacher. There are few home economics departments with ancillary support of any kind. Both NATHE and NAIEA are presently campaigning for support for teachers in this area. Some schools now find their accommodation inadequate to meet the needs of present courses and NAIEA is currently addressing this problem. The provision of microcomputers in home economics departments, rather than in a computer room occupied by another class, will greatly encourage their use. There are a wide range of uses, from the storage of information to the design of fabrics, which pupils can utilize in their problem solving exercises but access to microcomputers can be difficult in some schools.

Despite these difficulties, home economics departments are responding to the developments taking place within education. The subject has yet to conform to criteria referencing; the working party should report in late 1987 but curriculum development encouraged by GCSE should make the transfer to criteria referencing less problematic. The identification of objectives for the subject has been seen, to a great extent, in terms of the skills pupils develop through a study of the subject. The debate on subject content continues within this framework as home economics is a dynamic not static subject. This approach allows home economics to adapt readily to change, particularly to the present development of courses, TVEI, CPVE, YTS. It allows teachers to articulate the role of home economics within the course. In this way there is no loss of subject identity, rather a realization of the value of the subject to pupils and the contribution to be made to the curriculum as a whole.

Home economics contributes to the school curriculum by providing opportunities for pupils to gain experience in the important human and social area of learning and experience. By virtue of its context, and the rigour of the problem solving approach, pupils are able to relate to, and build on, their own experience to develop a wide range of knowledge, concepts, skills and abilities. A broad, balanced curriculum which includes home economics will ensure the remit given to subject working groups by the proposed national curriculum document, that

> programmes of work contribute to the development in young people of personal qualities and competence, such as self reliance, self discipline, an enterprising approach and the ability to solve real-world problems, which would stand them in good stead in later life. (DES, 1987b, para 68)

References

ASSESSMENT AND PERFORMANCE UNIT (1987) *Design and Technological Activity*, London, HMSO.

ARNOT, M. (1983) 'A cloud over co-education: An analysis of the forms of transmission of class and gender relations', in WALKER, S. and BARTON, L. (eds) *Gender, Class and Education*, Lewes, Falmer Press.

BALL, S.J. (1981) *Beachside Comprehensive*, Cambridge, Cambridge University Press.

BARDELL, G. (1982) *Options for the Fourth*, London, Schools Council.

BLYTH, A. *et al.* (1976) *Schools Council Project: History, Geography and Social Science*. Bristol, Collins ESL.

CHRISTIAN-CARTER, J. and HILLERTON, A. (1984) '16+ options for the future', *Modus*, Vol. 2, No. 2, pp. 42–4.

CUMMING, G. (*et al.*) (1985) *Where Does the Proof Lie? An Account of Assessment in the Home Economics Research Project*. Edinburgh, Moray House College of Education.

DEPARTMENT OF EDUCATION AND SCIENCE (1984a) 'GCSE — draft national criteria for home economics', DES circular, August.

DEPARTMENT OF EDUCATION AND SCIENCE (1984b) 'The Organization and Content of the 5–16 Curriculum', A note by DES and Welsh Office, September.

DEPARTMENT OF EDUCATION AND SCIENCE (1984) *GCSE The National Criteria Home Economics*, London, HMSO.

DEPARTMENT OF EDUCATION AND SCIENCE (1987a) *Proceedings of Home Economics Conference*, Llandudno organized by HMI.

DEPARTMENT OF EDUCATION AND SCIENCE (1987b) *The National Curriculum 5–16 — A Consultation Document*, London, HMSO.

EQUAL OPPORTUNITIES COMMISSION (1982) *Equal Opportunities in Home Economics*, Manchester, Equal Opportunities Commission.

Margaret Jepson

FAULKNER, H. and MANSELL, S.M. (eds) (1982), *Nuffield Home Economics: Teachers Guide*, London, Hutchinson.

HADLEY, F. and HOGARTH, F. (1987) 'Scientific method in home economics', *Modus*, Vol. 5, No. 5, pp. 188–90.

HER MAJESTY'S INSPECTORATE (1985) *Home Economics 5–16 (Curriculum Matters 5)* London, HMSO.

JONES, J. (1983) 'Option choice, a smokescreen for differentiation', *Link*, Vol. 4, No. 3, pp. 1–4.

NATIONAL ASSOCIATION OF TEACHERS OF HOME ECONOMICS (1982) 'Response of ATDS to draft proposals for 16+ national criteria', London, NATHE.

NATIONAL ASSOCIATION OF TEACHERS OF HOME ECONOMICS (1986) 'Response to *Curriculum Matters 5 Home Economics 5–16*', *Modus*, Vol. 4, No. 2, p. 72.

NATIONAL ASSOCIATION OF TEACHERS OF HOME ECONOMICS (1987) 'Careers progression in Home Economics' produced at NATHE conference, Devon.

SCHOOLS CURRICULUM DEVELOPMENT COMMITTEE (1985) '*Home Economics 5–16: Curriculum Matters 5* Response of SCDC', SCDC circular.

SCHOOLS COUNCIL PROJECT (1979) 'Home Economics in the Middle Years' in *Home and Family 8–13*, London, Forbes.

10   History

Elizabeth Foster

In an educational atmosphere increasingly dominated by utility, relevance
and a vocational and instrumental curriculum, history teachers have felt
their subject to be under threat for some considerable time. The growth of
social studies and integrated humanities encouraged by the Plowden Report (1967) and the Schools Council Humanities projects[1] brought a threat
in the 1960s and 1970s to both primary and secondary school history. In
the 1980s falling rolls and the loss of trained history staff (the number of
trainee teachers in history declined from 1000 in 1974 to 300 p.a. by 1985[2]
together with parent and pupil pressure for 'more vocationally relevant'
subjects at examination level have contributed to a situation where 50 per
cent of children do no history after the age of 14[3] and there are some
schools where no history as such is taught at all even to pupils in the 11 to
14 age range[4].

Recently, however[5], history gained a place in the core curriculum as
a foundation subject. In some respects this achievement should be no
surprise for the previous Secretary of State for Education, Sir Keith
Joseph, made strong representations for the place of history in the school
curriculum. In 1984 he argued that history is an essential component in
the curriculum of *all* pupils: 'it should be present throughout the primary
and secondary phases to age 16 and this should be made explicit in any
future statements of curriculum objectives for the primary as well as for
the secondary phase.' Furthermore 'within the humanities history's contribution is unique.'[6]

The uniqueness of history's contribution rests upon two major pillars:
it is the only subject concerned quintessentially with the study of people
and society over time — dinosaurs are not history; history is not 'the past',
it is not ultimately knowable and finite, but a credible reconstruction of the
past through critical appraisal of evidence and the interpretation, evaluation and judgment of it. It is then a form of knowledge centred on skills,
concepts and ideas; it is a rational investigation of the past according to
procedures and ideals which seek to establish the answers to such questions as 'how do I know this is true?', 'what was it like to be?', 'what
would I have done if?'. Its procedures depend upon discussion, the

examination of assumptions, challenging of interpretations and the setting forth of a case based upon evidence. Thus, as Lee stated 'Learning to use historical evidence, and perhaps above all acquiring the rational passions ... that are essential to the operation of historical procedures is both one of the major reasons for learning history, and a central part of what learning history actually entails.'[7] Taken together and informing each other, these two elements in the nature of history present a study concerned with examining and understanding real events and problems, a variety of human actions and behaviour in the past and change in human affairs over time. They can offer the pupil perspectives and insight into the present world and the pupil's place and experience in it unobtainable in any other discipline. Much has been written about the development in schools of 'the new history'. The fundamental emphasis in the 'new history' is on the process of enquiry with pupils working to reconstruct a picture of the past. It is an 'enquiry method' in which the selection of content is made by reference to the educational objectives to be achieved and the historical skills to be acquired.[8] This view of the purpose and nature of school history found most practical expression in the Schools Council History Project[9] which suggested five ways in which history could prove a useful and necessary subject for adolescent study: —

a) as a means of acquiring and developing such cognitive skills as those of analysis, synthesis and judgment
b) as a source of leisure interests
c) as a vehicle for analyzing the contemporary world and the adolescent's place in it
d) as a means for developing understanding of the forces underlying social change and evolution
e) as an avenue to self knowledge and awareness of what it means to be human.

By definition history studied in this way through evidence and problem solving with pupils reconstructing their own version of the past through analysis, interpretation and hypotheses establishes unequivocally that history is not a body of established and indisputable fact. Pupils are involved in a more reasoned and critical examination of the actions and decisions of people, develop a more penetrating and discerning use of evidence, establish bias, inconsistencies, lack of information and learn to build a case, argue a case and challenge a case. It establishes a way of looking at information which is of fundamental importance to pupils in training for adulthood and the challenges and persuasions of contemporary society, governments and the media. It is only, however, when these skills are allied with the study of the past, of events and developments valid in their own right, that history claims its uniqueness and its real justification.

Taught and learned in this way, history makes some far-reaching contributions to the school curriculum. It helps to explain the present, for it offers 'a sense of perspective for the present world which should be interpreted as merely part of a continuum extending both backwards and forwards.'[10] HMI in their case for history stated:

> Young people will be helped to cope with a bewildering world if they have some understanding of political and economic history, demonstrating the use and abuse of political power, the long term effects of policies and the complexity of cause and effect. But their effectiveness as citizens will depend above all on the crucial historical skill of assessing and evaluating the record of human behaviour. Without an understanding of history, young people will enter the world of work, citizenship and leisure blinkered and partly uncomprehending.[12]

History has a specific contribution to make through content and methodology to the personal development of individuals and the welfare of society at large. 'Thinking historically is not only one manifestation of an open society, it is also one of its guarantors.'[12] Thus those who are aware of societies other than their current one, of motives and actions of people of the past and of historical methods, concepts and ideas should not fall unquestioning victims to ideologies, assertions, statistics. It thus remains, as John Slater (Senior Staff Inspector for History) stated, 'a subject which is often uncomfortable and very rarely deferential'.[13] It is involved not only with controversial issues but often with politically sensitive ones and the history teacher must accept the responsibility this confers. Speaking of Irish history in the classroom David Harkness illustrates this forcefully:

> Gable-end graffiti thrusts history down the throat of child and adult alike, and the teacher must harness his or her talents to a broader view, challenge the crude and damaging stereotypes designed to foster hatred, assist the individual to a greater tolerance, a greater understanding of the perspectives of others. To refuse to do so is to allow tragedy to continue unopposed ... the teacher in the frontline classroom ... shoulders a weighty burden. It is an urgent burden, too, for the schoolroom will be the last open forum available: after the age of 16 the community will close round most of its children, confirming prejudices if they have never been shaken. But schools are as much part of the problem as part of the answer, laden as they are with their own assertions of tradition and unchallenged perspective. So schools too must look to their own circumstances, be continually self critical.[14]

A study of history offers a vicarious experience, a departure from egocentricity, a widening of experience beyond what can be achieved in the here and now. It encourages pupils to tolerance, flexibility, criticality and independence of mind, it depends on skills of reasoning, observation, interrogation, evaluation, judgment, communication. It develops an awareness of the nature of evidence, of bias, of change and continuity, similarity and difference, cause and effect, a sense of empathy, a sense of chronology and sequence and a wide range of oral, written, individual and group language skills. All of these skills and attitudes are fostered in other areas of the curriculum in some measure but some of them are rendered particularly accessible through a study of history. History has a role also within the total school curriculum. At a practical level it offers opportunities for exploration in all nine curriculum areas identified by HMI in *The Curriculum from 5 to 16.*[15] Art and craft, drama, role play are important areas within today's history classroom; graphicacy, numeracy, statistics, seriation, sequence, time and space must all feature within historical investigation and analysis and could be substantially and usefully extended. Questions of progress and change as exemplified through the history of mathematics is an aspect probably little touched upon in most history syllabuses but none the less worthy of attention for that. The human and social, moral, linguistic and literary and spiritual areas of learning and experience are probably the most intimately related to history as it is learned and taught but children have been known to recreate battles and expeditions of verifiable physical merit and skill; the scientific area is closely linked philosophically to history with its emphasis on abilities to 'solve problems in a systematic way to seek solutions and to synthesize valid conclusions' and fostering 'attributes such as open mindedness, flair and originality, co-operation and perseverance',[16] but history in school could well place greater emphasis upon the impact through time of science on society and notions of progress. In the technological area history has been identified as 'an excellent vehicle for the development of certain higher-order enquiry and data-analytic skills and may, indeed, be the optimum medium for such development'.[17] Technology itself offers a resource to historical study which allows data-retrieval work which would otherwise be prohibitively long-winded and which is of key importance in enabling pupils to ask historical questions, pose hypotheses and generate conclusions in a manner which significantly affects their quality of thinking and understanding in history across the entire age and ability range from 5–19.

Perhaps, too, history has a more general and more specifically historical role within the whole curriculum, for as other subjects inform the study of history, so it could be argued that history informs each other discipline in a critically conceptual way. No other discipline operates 'in limbo', in a time vacuum and it may be through the historical perspective that the curriculum can be most truly integrated.[18]

The curriculum debate initiated by Sir Keith Joseph has been pursued with vigour and considerable argument within the historical fraternity. The nature of the discipline does not encourage conformity and there must be almost as many history syllabuses taught in schools as there are history teachers. Perhaps, then, what is most surprising is the degree of broad consensus which has been reached about the value and place of history in the curriculum and the ways in which it should be taught, learned and assessed in schools.

It would be both misleading and unjust to assume that the measure of agreement reached and the very considerable progress made in meeting the challenges laid down by Joseph and HMI were a consequence solely of activity since 1984. Much of what has been achieved within the subject community rests very firmly upon work done over the last two decades, particularly by researchers into the nature of historical enquiry, of children's thinking in history and of assessment procedures. The introduction of the Schools Council History 13–16 project has probably done more than any other single agency to promote historical understanding and active learning in the classroom. For its part the Historical Association (HA) was already working as a 'power house' having been founded in 1906 for the very purpose of forming a pressure group. In 1980 the Association formulated plans to establish an advanced certificate in the teaching of history to be administered and validated by the Historical Association to encourage good practice in history and to remedy the lack of specialist historians to teach infant and junior children. The certificate came to fruition in 1984 and is now offered as a diploma. In 1983/84 the association set up three enquiries to ascertain more clearly the place and nature of history in schools[19]; within the universities the History at the Universities Defence Group (HUDG which works through and with the Historical Association) was in embryo in 1983 and held its first meeting on 4 February 1984; history lecturers in departments of education were urged by HMI at their conference in 1983 to have heed to the need for concerted action to promote history's cause; LEA history advisers in 1983 considered the time was ripe to form an association for themselves and thus the historical community was already mobilized, defending the place and promoting the role and nature of history in the curriculum.

Indeed it was through HUDG that the platform for history was presented so publicly and so supportively by Sir Keith Joseph, then Secretary of State and John Slater, Senior Staff Inspector for History at the group's second conference on 10 February 1984.[20] Since that time, however, the Historical Association with its Watchdog Committee, its meetings in the House of Lords[21] with members of both Houses, teachers and others in attendance has been the prime mover in publicizing history's contribution, obtaining audiences with Secretaries of State and pushing for a coherent and agreed response to the core and national curriculum issues. To this debate HMI have contributed immeasurably through their rapid response and publication in 1985 of *History in the Primary and Secondary Years, An HMI View*. Presenting a coherent and forceful argument for skills and concepts in identifiable history work from 5 to 16 and supported by practical examples and frameworks, this publication must have done more than any other to close the gap between primary and secondary history and bind each to the other.

Although the subject community in 1984 stood in a position of defence, raising public consciousness of the need for history in school, and speaking in May 1985 of 'widespread anxiety about the danger to social and national stability if future generations grew up in ignorance of the history of their country'[22] and reminding people in that Orwellian year of 1984 of the 'Party Slogan': 'who controls the past controls the future; who controls the present controls the past'[23], the community has moved to a more secure and established position. No-one underestimates the work to be done in schools and amongst parents, employers and, some would say, pupils,[24] to convince them of the value and importance of historical study but, it would seem, that particular ghost has been largely exorcised within the history community and the Historical Association. The debate has caused much rethinking, history's value has been reasserted and the belief of those who practise it has been confirmed by Secretaries of State and supported by HMI. Thus the tenor of the debate over the last two years has moved from defence to consolidation and practical support. The debate has moved from 'why history?' to 'what history?' and 'how history?'. The network of supportive organizations has been expanded: in 1986 PUSH (Public Sector History) was established to complement the work of HUDG; two ESRC projects have been established to investigate the training of history teachers[25] and the aims of history teachers in secondary schools.[26] Both of these are producing useful observations and comment on current training and how it might be improved and enhanced. In addition the Historical Association has established its Young Historian scheme[27], a remarkable project with a Leverhulme grant of £76,000 to provide support for the teaching and promotion of history through a national network of regional centres. Young Historian centres will be established in each LEA where teachers and pupils may meet and work together and enjoy resources of a kind unavailable to the individual teacher or class in school. The Young Historian Development Officer and his team of three Young Historian Project Developers are to create a framework to bridge the gap between school history and the world of work, building links with industry, commerce and public institutions and developing project and coursework schemes for GCSE, 'A' level and other examinations with particular emphasis on developing an interest in and understanding of local communities, firms and institutions. The Young Historian scheme with its emphasis on practical support for teachers and pupils and links with the world of work together with its national organization and physical centres will promote history in a way which has never been seen before and is a scheme of tremendous potential.

The shift in the debate towards 'what' history was illustrated clearly in the titles of the House of Lords debates: 'The importance and content of history teaching in Britain.' At these meetings the disagreement within the historical community was well evident[28] yet broad concerns are apparent. Thus few would dispute that local family or regional history, national history, some non-national history and a spread of periods are important to every child's historical study. But broad agreement is far from being a consensus when content is considered in any detail. It may, as Roberts suggested,[29] be accurate to suggest that those who place more emphasis on the history of Africa than on that of Asia or Japan take a very lop-sided view of the world as a whole, but such an assessment may not, for some, answer some of the issues raised in a multicultural society. Similarly while many would agree with him that those who thought they could understand other countries before they had acquired any knowledge of their own were mistaken, such a suggestion remains a generality in terms of actual subject matter and the extent of it within the history syllabus.

The Historical Association stands out in making firm proposals of content. They arose in the context of dialogue with and propositions put to the Secretaries of State for Education and reflect the commitment of the Historical Association to furthering the curriculum debate in the interests of historical study in school. Two papers were forwarded to the DES; the first, *History for Life* (May 1986) sparked off stringent controversy, but aroused interest and support too, and conversations are pending with the exam boards and Kenneth Baker, Secretary of State. It aroused sufficient interest for Baker to invite a further Historical Association deputation, which met him on 19 December 1986, to develop its ideas about history 7–14. This resulted in *Proposals for History in a Core Curriculum* being sent to him at the beginning of February 1987, as 'first, not last, thoughts'. A response is awaited and in the meantime the Historical Association has planned a series of consultative conferences for autumn 1987. In addition the Historical Association is exploring with the Politics, Geographical and Economics Associations the possibilities of reaching agreement over an interdisciplinary humanities programme of modules for GCSE.

For the 7–14 age group the Historical Association propose a curriculum calling for 30 per cent world history, 30 per cent national history and 10 per cent local history with 30 per cent content determined by teachers. 'The syllabus should have a proper balance between: political history, social and economic history; cultural history; scientific and technological history',[30] and should combine both outline and depth studies. Thus far the proposals reflect the general concern within the historical community for balance. It is on the proposed list of thirty topics in British history and thirty topics in world history that the disagreements will probably centre most strongly, although the notion of 'an outline of British, European and world chronology' and 'a sufficient outline of the sequence of ancient medieval and early modern past'[31] may rekindle rather than quench the skills/content and discontinuous syllabus[32] debates. The proposals for the 14–16 age groups provide for a compulsory modular course of British twentieth century history for all pupils. Centred upon seven key themes of: population trends national and international; Britain's changed position in the world; economic changes; trade unions; political and social democracy; welfare policy and social and cultural trends; it sets itself up to 'bridge the gulf' in children's knowledge of developments since 1945 and to promote 'a healthy democracy' through all citizens having been taught to share some knowledge of their national history.[33]

Notwithstanding the attempts of the Historical Association there remains a fundamental split between those who see content as the key to selection for what goes into the history curriculum, and those who see methodology, historiography, skills and concepts as being the fulcrum for selection; provided skills are correctly identified and effectively taught, the content does not matter. Yet there *is* much agreement on the necessity of skills and concepts within a history curriculum at all levels and phases of a pupil's schooling. There are few who would deny that they have a place, even for infant pupils, and it seems inconceivable that this will not continue. In broad terms, therefore, the 'how' and part of the 'what' of history teaching and learning is agreed. It remains for agreement to be reached as to the relationship between skills, concepts and fundamental content, or 'areas of knowledge' — the Romans, the industrial revolution, Rasputin, Florence Nightingale or the Modern World?

That balance must obtain in this matter seems reasonable and HMI in their pamphlet 'History in the Primary and Secondary Years' imply this in their identification of four criteria for selection of content: location, key issues in contemporary society, concepts and skills.[34] 'The periods a particular school chooses could more often be affected by the resources available outside the school and need not be wholly controlled, as they so often are, by the resources in the history stock cupboard and the school library.' The presence of a museum or county archive, a medieval church or a castle, or 'themes in our past that still inform the lives of the pupils within a particular school' could all play a part in determining what is taught, moreover 'the particular locality of the school not only provides opportunities for children to become familiar with a variety of evidence and to learn something about their own family roots but to relate the history of their village or town to great national events....'. So, local history linked to national history becomes one element, so does a degree of autonomy in syllabus construction. In offering 'issues in contemporary society' as a criterion for selection HMI acknowledge that 'any list is bound to be arbitrary, to reflect our values and current preoccupations, and thus to be open to challenge and debate', but they proffer six themes as suggestions: the growth of towns and cities and the consequent demographic changes; the effect of science and technology on our lives; the issues of an open society and choice in social, political and moral matters which require an understanding of the evolution of political institutions, of industrial relations, of religious freedom and the identification of ideals and values held in common; the issues of women in society; the concerns of a multicultural society and of an internationally interdependent society. In this latter theme they identify the historical experience of the USA and USSR as part of an explanation of their stances and attitudes in the world today, the issues of peace and war, historical perspectives on the movements of people and the distribution of wealth and other key issues in the modern world such as Irish history and the Middle East. For concepts and ideas HMI present a list of sixty concepts which includes 'many terms that young people should have met by the age of 16' and three concepts 'fundamental to all historical study and to which all others relate: cause, change and evidence. They must be present, implicitly at least, in the work of the whole age group'.[35] These concepts 'remain among the criteria that can help teachers to select periods or particular themes within periods' while 'General skills of study and specifically historical skills . . . offer a further group of criteria for the selection of content'.[36] Beyond this HMI make a further suggestion that whilst gaps in content must be considerable these should be explicit and planned rather than arbitrary and concealed and should ensure that coherence and a sense of chronology are not threatened. Thus pupils should build up, during their school career, a chronological framework to define the relationship of events and their relative distance from the present. This could form part of a 'map of the past' which could 'provide pupils with a shared framework of knowledge . . . serve as a reminder that people's lives and great occasions do not take place in isolation or out of context . . . act as a systematic reminder that shared recognitions and memories help give communities — national, cultural, class — a claim to identity'.[37]

HMI thus give much guidance on the range of criteria for selection of syllabus content, they go so far as to suggest explicitly certain themes, but in his speech to the Historical Association in February 1984 HMI Slater stated boldly what possibly the majority of history teachers, advisers, researchers and writers believe, namely that 'I do not believe that, no matter how long we sit, we shall ever get any national agreement about a core content'.[38] The national criteria for GCSE history also rejected any agreed content specification, choosing to express objectives in terms of understanding of concepts, skills and the perspective of people in the past. This is not to say that content does not matter, rather that we should seek agreement on the *criteria* for the *selection* of content.

This is a matter on which virtually all the LEA guidelines in primary and secondary history are explicitly in agreement. In common with the rest of the debate on the place and nature of history in the school curriculum, many of these guidelines were in hand or published before 1984. The majority concentrate on primary history and were largely a response to the critical assessment of history's contribution to the curriculum contained in the HMI Survey *Primary Education in England* 1978: 'In four out of five of all the classes which studied history, the work was superficial. . . It was rare to find classes where the work, even in a simple way, was leading the children towards an understanding of historical change and the causal factors involved, or where children were becoming aware of the value of historical evidence.'[39] Many of the LEA curriculum guidelines reject overt guidance on content: 'The most effective curriculum is likely to be one designed by each individual school aided by broad guidelines that draw on the wider experience of many teachers'[40] but most are in broad agreement about the place of skills and evidence based work alongside concepts and content determined by the pupils' stage of development. Thus ILEA states that 'content, therefore, must be important, just as the acquisition of historical skills and ideas is important'[41] and advises that history is concerned with roots and the relationship of roots to the present; 'with change rather than with a small factual account of a particular period'; with 'enquiry'[42]; that it is primarily about people, about learning about and understanding how they lived and behaved in a variety of situations in different times and places, and from its study emerges 'the child's attempts to reconstruct the past', to develop a concern for evidence, an awareness of continuity and change, an interest in cause and a sense of empathy.[43] ILEA list the skills to be developed through primary history: (a) the collection and analysis of evidence; (b) recognizing, understanding and using chronological conventions; (c) an understanding of sequence (and later duration) of time; (d) learning and practising a range of general language skills; (e) problem solving.[44] Thus during their primary years from 5–11 children should be learning, in addition to language skills, to: (a) think systematically, use information to arrive at conclusions, and solve problems based upon evidence; (b) use hypothetical modes of thinking; (c) look at visual sources to describe, explain, make suggestions, compare, explore and suggest inadequacies or incompetences of the source; (d) begin to assess the value of stories and simple written sources as evidence about the past; (e) empathize (with some anachronisms as yet) with people in other times and places; (f) make suggestions about causes; (g) begin to make and defend an argument.[45] Barnsley's draft guidelines contain a similarly detailed list including also the understanding and use of a historical vocabulary and expression of conclusions through speech, drama, writing, art, sketches, maps, plans, graphs, diagrams and models. Solihull's guidelines state that

> it is important to realize at the outset that history is a discipline — and as a discipline it makes a unique contribution to the educational process. This does not mean that it need always be taught as a separate subject in the primary school but it does mean that it should be an identifiable part of the curriculum and timetable in the young child's education. Unless the specific characteristics, skills and concepts of history are taught to children, and the historical component is considered separately, work in this area is likely to remain superficial. As a first step, whatever the teaching arrangement, schools should have schemes of work in history providing a framework of the content, skills and concepts being taught... The teacher will also have some specific objectives in mind which will inform the history curriculum: a concern for evidence, an understanding of time, a sense of empathy, an

interest in cause, an awareness of continuity/change, similarity/
differences, making judgments, using historical language, an
understanding of the world in which they live, an acquaintance
with national traditions, an appreciation of historic sites and
remains.[46]

Whether history should be a separate subject in the curriculum of the
5–11 child remains, often specifically, unresolved but there is general
agreement here and amongst notable writers/researchers in primary
history[47] that the historical dimension is distinct, the history element
should not be left to chance, and that it should be an identifiable part of
the curriculum. 'It is not argued that great stress must be placed upon the
division of knowledge into subjects at this stage. Children could, however,
profitably be made aware of the contribution of the various disciplines to
the tackling of specific problems'.[48]

When it comes to content in primary history the guidelines generally
fight shy of any degree of prescription other than in the most general
terms; however, particular examples of syllabuses and means of constructing them abound. Nevertheless amongst those writers prepared to commit
themselves there is evidence of unanimity over broad content areas. Thus
family history and/or local history are evident in LEA guidelines (Solihull,
Avon, Northern Ireland) and in the work of Blyth, Low-Beer, Noble and
West. There is also commitment to national history but with explicit
concern that this should be related to the locality and to the world. Thus
Avon suggest patches of mainly British history extended such that Roman
Britain would include Roman Bath and the Roman Empire;[49] Noble
recommends at least one non-national perspective;[50] Solihull LEA advises
national and world history;[51] Northern Ireland looks for balance between
local national and world history and Blyth values national history closely
related to local and world history where possible and suggests such
frameworks plus a multicultural syllabus in *History in Primary Schools*.[53]
There is a fairly general concern evident also for syllabuses in primary
history which assist the child's developing concept of sequence and chronology.

In the LEA guidelines for secondary history Batho found 'no vestige
of agreement on actual content'.[54] This may reflect a concern for greater
classroom autonomy amongst history-trained teachers with their very diverse history backgrounds encouraged by the growth of option systems
and research projects in undergraduate history courses, as too the strength
of influence of the skills/methods/concept approach to secondary history
evident over the last ten years and more.

A strength of all history frameworks primary and secondary is the
close identification of aims, objectives, skills, concepts with pupils' cognitive abilities and stages of development. HMI have clearly, and often,
identified their concern that history approached through skills, methodology and concepts is mistakenly identified by teachers and others as too

difficult for both young pupils and the less able.[55] 'A firm foundation can be built before a child is 9 . . . if it is firmly built on, older children can do much more advanced work than they are often considered capable of'. 'Before the age of 8, the foundations for historical understanding can be laid. Between the ages of 8 and 16 children may begin to move to more sophisticated stages of historical understanding'.[56] Speaking at the Historical Association conference 10 February 1984, John Slater said:

> I believe that history as a subject and as a discipline taught with integrity is accessible right throughout the primary age range and across the whole ability range in secondary schools. Very rarely is the problem in school that young people are being set tasks that are too difficult for them whether we are looking at sixth forms containing students, who without difficulty, will get into Oxford and Cambridge or whether we are looking at classes where there are a number of children with considerable learning difficulties. The problem almost invariably is that most of them are having tasks set that are too easy for them... If the language becomes more accessible, you can correspondingly increase the demand of the intellectual task. Some of the most exciting work that we have seen in schools is from lower achieving pupils using primary source material and thinking in a way that most of us would regard as genuinely historical.[57]

Work by Lee and Dickinson, Shemilt and others has indicated clearly that 'the inspectorate is quite correct in deploring the way children's ability is underestimated',[58] and that children's thinking in history can be profoundly affected and enhanced by the nature of the history teaching and learning they experience; where it is related to an evidential and problem solving approach their understanding and thinking can be significantly advanced. Thus 'different aims and approaches to the teaching of history may accelerate the development of thinking abilities amongst pupils so that the majority may reach the stage of formal operational thinking at an age somewhat earlier than 16'.[59] Work in the primary age range confirms that young children's awareness of the past is much more developed than some writers have previously assumed, that concept formation can be promoted through historical study, that history can give access to abstract ideas in a concrete form and that development away from an egocentric position can be achieved by empathy work and role play.[60] The grasp of historical concept has been identified by Blyth in 6-year-olds with whom, she found, concept formation even with regard to time was beginning to take shape in most of the children by the end of nine weeks' work and in whom there were also sporadic signs of the ability to reason logically and to classify materials into 'very, very old', 'very old', 'old' and 'not old'. These 6-year-olds grasped relationships between people in a family and between different objects, were able to make comparisons, and made progress with the concepts of time and evidence. Thus, she concluded, 'children of 6 are quite capable of beginning to understand some appropriate concepts and also practise skills needed for understanding the past if suitable teaching techniques and equipment are used and they are taught over a long period'.[61]

From this standpoint Blyth argues for a fairly structured framework for the teaching of history to 5 to 7 year olds: —[62]

Age	Term 1	Term 2	Term 3
5–6	Myth through stories.	Stories of the past grouped in topics — role play.	Study of artefacts brought first by teacher then by class.
6–7	Family history.	Local topics of own village, town area.	Local lists.

Blyth has produced further frameworks for the 7–11 age range which interrelate children's characteristics or capacities with key objectives or key concepts.[63] Progression in these aspects is crucial if the learning of 16 year olds is to be more advanced than that of 5, 6, 7, or 8 year olds rather than simply a matter of accumulating more 'facts' or information. Moreover the development of progression and the identification of objectives directly affect teaching and learning and it is only through a sound interrelationship of objectives with pupil interests, needs and capacities that pupils can be assisted to make maximum progression in their historical understanding and abilities and that teachers can be assisted to recognize the immense diversity of learning and teaching strategies and materials required to maximize their pupils' developments. HMI provide a matrix of much value in this respect provided that it is interpreted sensitively and in the awareness that the ages are best seen as intellectual rather than chronological and that in many classes, therefore, some pupils will be able to attempt more or less advanced tasks on the matrix than the majority.

With the assistance of a matrix such as in Figure 1, and the substantial body of writing available on children's thinking in history, on the use and abuse of evidence, skills and concepts and the many examples of frameworks available, history teachers are well placed to devise their own syllabuses. Whilst a national consensus upon content is at present both unlikely and on balance unpopular amongst historians it *is* possible with sensitive collaboration across schools not only for 'clutter' and 'repetition' to be avoided or minimized, but for the five basic principles identified within the curriculum — breadth, relevance, balance, differentiation and progression and continuity — to be achieved. Alongside these the calls made by Keith Joseph in his North of England speech for raising standards, developing the potential of every child, equipping *all* pupils with 'versatile

Figure 1: Some Objectives for Pupil Progression in Historical Skills.

	Reference and information-finding skills	*Skills in chronology*	*Language and historical ideas*
By the age of 8	Can scan pictures and simple books. Can read simple accounts. Can use page references.	Can use basic vocabulary (eg 'now', 'long ago', 'then', 'before', 'after'). Begins to understand the chronology of the year (eg seasons); and begins to record on a wall chart sequence of stories heard. Can put some historical pictures and objects in sequence.	Can 'use' terms commonly used in stories of past (eg hero, heroine, king, queen, nobleman, sheriff). Begins to use words such as 'the past', 'myth', 'true'.
By the age of 10	Knows which books supply information (eg topic, encyclopaedias). Can use contents, index and glossaries of books; and can read different passages to select information relevant to a topic. Can use visual sources (eg pictures, filmstrips, slides, artefacts); and oral sources (talk, tape, radio). Can list main points from one or more sources using teachers' questions.	Knows terms BC and AD. Understands 'generation' in a family context. Knows sequence of prehistoric, ancient times, middle ages and modern. Can put a wide range of historical pictures and objects in sequence. Can make a simple individual sequence chart.	Can use an increasing number of terms that arise from topics studied (eg knight, peasant, emperor, bishop). Knows words such as 'history', 'archaeology'.
By the age of 12	Can use a library catalogue (subject). Can read textbooks and topic books in conjunction. Can make more detailed notes under supplied headings using several sources. Can use abbreviations such as eg, ie.	Understands 'century' and how dating by centuries works. Can put dates in correct century. Knows sequence of Roman, Saxon, Viking, Norman, Tudor, Stuart, Victorian. Is aware of some historical period terms (eg Reformation). Can make a time chart using scale.	Can use an increasing number of terms that arise from topics studied (eg keep, lateen, sail). Can use common terms of a greater degree of abstraction (eg ruler, law, subject, parliament).
By the age of 14	Can use more complex cataloguing and retrieval. Can extract information independently from written and pictorial sources. Can make notes in a form that distinguishes main from sub-points.	Is able to put an extensive range of historical pictures and objects in sequence. Can make a time chart that compares developments in contemporary civilisations (eg Iron Age Britain and Ancient Athens, or 16th Century Europe and Aztec/Inca South America). Can make a time chart that records events in different aspects of history (eg war, politics, buildings, costume).	Can use an increasing number of terms that arise from topics studied (eg free trade, invention, protection, imperialist). Can use terms commonly used in historical explanation (eg motive, cause, change, reform, progress, economic, political, social).
By the age of 16	Can summarise. Can ask own questions of information to answer problems. Knows how to use and make footnotes and bibliographies (eg in project work).		Continues to extend knowledge of terms specific to topics studied (eg democracy, liberal, welfare state, fascist, marxist).

Source: Department of Education and Science (1985) *History in the Primary and Secondary Years: An HMI View* London, HMSO, pp. 15–19.

Use and analysis of evidence	Empathetic understanding	Asking historical questions	Synthesis and communication using basic ideas
Can describe the main features of concrete evidence of the past (eg pictures, artefacts, buildings) and hypothesise as to their use. Is familiar with the question 'How do we know?'.	Can say, write or draw what they think it felt like in response to some historical story that has been heard.	Begins to become aware of basic historical questions, eg. • What happened and when? • Why did it happen? • How do we know?	Using memory and recall, can describe orally and in writing some past events or story in narrative or dramatic form. Can make a pictorial representation.
Can define in simple terms 'source' and 'evidence'. Can understand and make deductions from documentary as well as concrete evidence (eg pictures, artefacts). Can describe the main features of simple maps, diagrams or graphs. Increasingly asks the questions 'How do we know?'	Can make a simple imaginative reconstruction of a situation in the past and how it appeared to some of the people in it, using the evidence available to draw, model, dramatise, write or tell the story.	Becomes used to asking of any historical period studied questions about the main features of everyday life, eg • When and how did people live and how did they clothe and feed themselves? • What was the available technology? • What were the life styles of different social and gender groups? • What are the differences between now and then?	Can describe orally and in writing some past events or situation recognising *similarities/differences* with today. Can state information in a graph, diagram or map. Can support an account or conclusion with some evidence.
Is aware of variety of historical evidence at different periods of time. Can distinguish between primary and secondary sources; and can understand and make inferences from primary and secondary accounts (text-books, fiction). Can recognise 'gaps' in evidence. Can interpret simple graphical sources.	Can make an imaginative reconstruction that is not anachronistic of a past situation based on several pieces of evidence, including historical fiction, and exploring some of the feelings participants might have had at the time.	Becomes used to asking of any historical period additional questions of increasing difficulty, eg • Who governed and how and with what results? • What did they worship and what values did they live by? • What was their art, music and literature?	Can put together orally and in writing a narrative of past events or situation showing evidence of *continuity* and *change* and indicating simple *causation*. Can make accurate diagrams or maps based on several pieces of evidence.
Can compare two accounts of the same events and note contrasts and similarities. Can recognise that evidence may not be impartial. Can distinguish between fact and opinion. Can begin to interpret simple statistical sources.	Can show understanding of a person's viewpoint within a given historical situation. Can consider the viewpoints of opposing sides and of people for whom they may not feel sympathy.	Begins to analyse historical events by asking questions, eg • What was the immediate cause? • Did any long-term cause operate? • Were there political, economic or religious causes, etc? • To what extent were personalities important?	Can write an account of some past events in terms of *cause* and *effects* supported by evidence.
Can distinguish relevant and irrelevant evidence. Compare various pieces of evidence and note contradictions and gaps. Can recognise bias and 'propaganda'.	Can identify the extent of choice available to a person in a given situation in the past. Can identify the values and attitudes on which human actions have been based in the past.	Can question different interpretations of past events.	Can write a structured account which, using evidence, argues clearly to a credible conclusion. Can write an analytical account of past events that takes into consideration different interpretations. Can write a longer account using footnotes and bibliographies properly (projects).

competence', developing records of attainment can also be met and it is indeed possible for 80 to 90 per cent of pupils to be enabled to 'possess some historical knowledge and perspective; understand the concept of cause and consequence ... compare and extract information from historical evidence and be aware of its limitations'.[64] The research, the writing, the experimentation, the consultations and discussion within the subject community have gone before; it remains for consciousness raising to be extended and for time and resources to be made available within each school curriculum.

If historians can appear to be, in some respects, smug, and deservedly so, for their achievements within the areas discussed in this chapter, it is nevertheless clear that there remain very many issues and problems to be considered within history in schools. Principal amongst these must be the resolution, by some means, of the issues of syllabus content and the avoidance of 'repetition' and 'clutter'. While a degree of autonomous decision making in this matter is seen to be desirable at LEA, school and teacher levels and whilst philosophical and practical objections can be levelled against any 'national' promulgation on subject content, it is nevertheless clear that repetition of subject content occurs all too frequently across the primary/secondary divide and sometimes within each sector. If skills are progressive it is possible to argue that repetition of content need not matter; it could be a benefit in terms of familiarity with content and context. At the same time it would be absurd for pupils to study local history, the Romans or World War Two every year of their school history programme. Content does matter; some have argued forcibly for the inclusion of specified areas of content be they British history, world history, medieval or modern history, but if agreement on precisely what subject matter should be learned and when is remarkably elusive, the principle of avoiding undue repetition and of achieving a balanced diet of historical study for every pupil must have merit and somehow must be carried into reality for each child. A broad measure of agreement can be seen emerging but in a practical day-to-day sense it may be insufficient to identify only broad areas — specificity of period, place, event, personality ultimately become a feature of any dialogue. Within the content issue there are key areas which probably require considerable clarification, most of them controversial such as issues of gender, race, peace, morality, bias, prejudice, indoctrination, shared values, culture, but others cross-curricular and concerned perhaps with technology, science, mathematics and creative arts which, in the reality of most traditional syllabuses, amount to insignificant elements. There is, too, the problem frequently visited upon historians by non-historians of teaching and realizing in or for their pupils 'objective truth'; issues like this will cause discomfort and probably unpopularity which historians and their subject must face up to. In the teaching and assessment of skills of historiography and methodology and of concept acquisition much has been achieved but the profession needs now to be wary of complacency and of creating new, immutable orthodoxies to replace others perceived now to be less valid, or less useful. It is important also that history remains a subject of enjoyment, probably of escapism, at least from time to time, and of lasting value and importance to those on the threshold of adulthood. At the same time history teachers must retain a place in the training and vocational sector of the curriculum, indicating not only that the subject can inform but that it can be informed by technology; that it provides an element and can be a coherent part of a CPVE, TVEI or City and Guilds course. History may be in the common core, but in what guise and quantity remains unclear; it may also be a less endangered subject at least at the moment, but its continuing place and value within the school curriculum will be determined by the nature and quality of its contribution. These are growth points which must be nurtured.

Assessment in history has made significant advances towards differentiation by outcome and the hierarchical ordering of levels of thinking and reasoning. The domain criteria proposed for GCSE history demonstrate the extent of the work already done in criterion referencing and differentiation by outcome but they present problems in practice and will undoubtedly require considerable modification and further research. Their effect nevertheless will reverberate throughout the entire curriculum 5 to 16 for the skills, concepts and understandings and the levels of thinking with which the criteria are concerned must be seen as part of a progression, and their development must underwrite the whole history curriculum in a manner appropriate to the different ages, needs, interests and abilities of pupils from 5 to 16.

The study and assessment of empathy remains an area of particular concern. Precisely what it is and how it can best be assessed are the subject of much heart-searching and writing but the approach adopted by the Cambridge 'A' level may well represent a significant advance in this area. Teachers and directors in this project have agreed that empathy can be best demonstrated as an aspect of historical explanation.

Non-written assessment in history also remains an important area where advance is merited. In a subject where diversity of source materials, of activities and methods are of the utmost benefit it is disappointing that GCSE has not taken the opportunity to build in a compulsory oral element. Again it has been left to the Cambridge 'A' level project to promote this aspect.

What has become essential within assessment for all pupils at all stages is a detailed and diverse teacher record to adequately reflect the changing nature of work being undertaken by pupils in history.[65]

'If pupils' understanding of the past is to be coherent and systematic it will depend on a greater degree of consultation and co-operation between the different phases of education'[66] wrote HMI; it may also depend upon and will certainly be assisted by a considerably increased teacher

Figure 2: *Draft Criteria for GCSE History within their Domains*

DOMAIN I — Historical Knowledge and Understanding

	a. Communicating narrative and description	b. Using concepts	c. Showing an ability to look at events and issues from the perspective of people in the past
Level 4. The candidate is able to:	present appropriate recalled or selected information in a connected and consistent manner;	demonstrate the use of concepts by selecting recalled or given items of information and presenting the items in a connected and sustained manner;	demonstrate knowledge and understanding of events and issues from the perspective of people in the past which is extensively supported, and to show a clear awareness of the complexity of perspectives;
Level 3. The candidate is able to:	present appropriate recalled or selected information in a connected manner;	demonstrate the use of concepts by selecting recalled or given items of information and presenting the items in a connected manner;	demonstrate knowledge and understanding of events and issues from the perspective of people in the past which is supported by specific examples, and to show awareness of the complexity of perspectives;
Level 2. The candidate is able to:	present recalled or selected items of information about a topic most of which are relevant to a given question in a manner that shows some connection;	demonstrate the use of concepts by selecting recalled or given items of information and presenting the items in a manner that shows some connection;	demonstrate knowledge and understanding of events and issues from the perspective of people in the past supported by general statements or specific examples;
Level 1. The candidate is able to:	present recalled or selected items of information about a topic, some of which items are relevant to a given question;	demonstrate the use of concepts by selecting recalled or given items of information and presenting the items separately;	demonstrate knowledge of the perspective of people in the past supported by general statements or disconnected specific examples;

DOMAIN II — Historical Enquiry

	a. *Preparing questions to acquire information*	b. *Locating evidence*	c. *Relating different types of evidence and recording findings*
Level 4. The candidate is able to:	construct an efficient framework for the investigation and pose questions most suitable for meeting the demands of the task;	locate all readily available sources and derive information suitable to satisfy the demands of the task;	select and relate information from at least two different types of source and record pre-connected findings according to a pattern well suited to satisfy the demands of the task;
Level 3. The candidate is able to:	construct a manageable framework for the investigation and pose relevant questions;	locate a range of sources and derive information suitable to satisfy the demands of the task;	select and relate information from at least two different types of source and record the connected findings in a coherent pattern;
Level 2. The candidate is able to:	pose relevant questions given an appropriate framework organised under suitable headings;	locate an appropriate source and derive specific information from it;	select information from at least two different types of source and record findings according to a given pattern;
Level 1. The candidate is able to:	pose relevant questions, given an appropriate framework organised under suitable headings and given specific guidance;	locate an appropriate source and derive specific information from it, given guidance;	select information from two different types of source and record findings according to a given pattern with guidance;

DOMAIN III — Historical Reasoning

	a. Assessing the utility of evidence	b. Interpreting evidence	c. Considering the reliability of evidence	d. Reaching a judgment
Level 4. The candidate is able to:	assess the utility of evidence by inferring its purpose and substantiating this with evidence;	offer a convincing interpretation supported by a process of cross-referencing;	undertake an evaluation of the evidence and explain this by a process of inference and cross-referencing;	reach an historically valid judgment supported by a process of cross-referencing;
Level 3. The candidate is able to:	assess the utility of evidence by illustrating the tone and impact of the presented evidence;	offer a convincing interpretation supported by information drawn from the source and from recalled knowledge;	undertake an evaluation of the evidence and explain this by reference to internal or external information;	reach an historically valid judgment supported by a range of internal or external information;
Level 2. The candidate is able to:	assess the utility of evidence by reference to the factual information it contains;	offer a plausible interpretation supported by internal or external information;	undertake a simple evaluation of the evidence supported by reference to the information it contains;	reach a straightforward, plausible judgment supported by internal or external information:
Level 1. The candidate is able to:	classify and identify evidence at face value;	offer a plausible interpretation;	undertake a simple evaluation of the evidence;	reach a straightforward plausible judgment;

Source: Teaching History (1986) No. 44. p. 4.

in-service training provision if the fairly radical developments of the last twenty years in history teaching and learning are to be taken on board smoothly, successfully and happily. Because of the influence of 13–16 history and of GCSE and because of the relative lack of identifiable history in primary schools in recent years, the developments could be construed to be top-downwards, pushing from secondary to primary but this may be erroneous. The work of many primary specialists testifies to the concurrence, in primary and secondary spheres, of research findings, suggested ways forward and the best classroom practices. More importantly it would be a construal which would be divisive and extremely damaging for the subject. The 5 to 16 curriculum debate provides the forum and the requirement for the secondary/primary divide to be broken-down and both sectors have much to learn from each other. It represents a tremendous opportunity for history to become a significant and progressive element throughout the school life of every child from infancy to the threshold of adulthood; thereby it fosters personal development and a questioning, thinking and responsible open society. The opportunity must not be lost.

In the last months of 1987 the Historical Association regional conferences of teachers and educationists have taken place and school history has held a high profile in the national press. Whilst it becomes apparent that history teachers may, in fact, nationally be covering much common ground in their syllabus content for 11–16 year olds it has become apparent, too, that when it comes to creating checklists of content the diversity of opinion is still very marked. The Leicester project discerned that although amongst seventy-five secondary schools spread across fifty-one LEAs syllabuses for 12–14 year olds ranged widely, yet broad patterns were evident. Most schools followed a chronological framework within which syllabuses were based on topics or patches. Accordingly, there was a predominance of ancient and early British history in years one and two followed by Tudors and Stuarts and exploration in years 2 or 3 and only one school offered a 4th/5th year examination course covering any period before 1750. The third year syllabuses were more varied than years one and two but the agricultural and industrial revolutions, American history, modern world history, democracy, World Wars I and II and revolutions were 'fairly well represented'. Over one third of schools included some local history in years 1 to 3; almost a quarter had some form of integrated studies and just under two-thirds included work on the nature of history and the use of evidence. In years 4 and 5 modern world history, Schools History Project and Modern British social and economic courses accounted for the provision in all but one school.[67] The findings are much like those reported by the Historical Association in 1985.[68] Yet, when it came to accepting the sixty themes proposed by the Historical Association there was little support from the delegates at the eight regional conferences. Some view the Historical Association proposals as abject appeasement to the Secretary of State and it may be that many who appear to disagree merely with the choice of subject theme or topic are, in fact, making a more fundamental rejection. Each individual can construct a different list of subject content for a 5 to 16 history syllabus but for each there quickly comes a point of crisis where content selection betrays fundamental political beliefs: should historical study be *allowed* to be Establishment, should it be *obliged* to be Establishment; should it be allowed or obliged to be subversive? Ultimately, history cannot be apolitical. This is as much at the heart of the Great Debate as other, no less important issues about what constitutes 'important' knowledge, facts, frames of reference[69] and how such knowledge relates to concepts and skills in the selection of syllabus content. This may explain why many history teachers feel a sense of utter dismay and betrayal in the face of governmental edict on curriculum content from whatsover party political persuasion that edict may come.

The data from the regional conferences is still being computer sorted yet it is already apparent that most delegates were prepared to accept broad guidelines with regard to content and syllabus construction 'but wished the central prescription to be minimal' and 'considered that the best judges of any guidelines were teachers of history'.[70] The conferences served to underline the unease felt by teachers in the specification of content and their conviction that criteria for syllabus content and skills and understanding provide a more suitable platform for debate and for agreement. Two striking products of recent years received endorsement: the HMI booklet *History in the Primary and Secondary Years* and the GCSE national criteria; so too did the discussion paper submitted to the conferences by Richard Brown. Laying emphasis on *criteria* for determining the curriculum — pupil understanding of change and continuity; cause and consequence; content and chronology; methodologies and interpretations; people in the past; the local dimension and the national dimension[71] — this document appears to be closer to the developments in history teaching and learning over the past fifteen or so years than does, at least at first glance, the Historical Association list.

Several months on, then, the picture does not look fundamentally different, but important developments have occurred. Noteable is the collection and collation of the views of some 600 teachers and educationists at the regional conferences; the calling of a further round of conferences before Easter 1988 to which parents, governors and business people will also be invited; the new schools' committee for the 5–16 age range, comprised of teachers and set up by the Historical Association to coordinate the 1988 conferences and formulate proposals about history as a foundation subject for the Historical Association Council; and perhaps, not least, the continuing liveliness in the debate. It is a debate in which diversity of opinion can be expected not only within the teaching profession but within society at large. In an age when 'heritage', be it myth, legend or reality, is seen to be sufficiently important and exciting to launch a new fortnightly magazine and be the mainstay of a seemingly endless stream of TV programmes and films, and when the launch of such a magazine can be heralded as 'unlike normal history books' because it is 'designed to bring history to life', the community of historians faces an enormous challenge.

Notes

1. Environmental Studies 5–8, Social Studies 8–13, History, Geography and Social Science 8–13 (Place, Time and Society).
2. BOOTH, M. (1985) *The Historian* No. 7 Summer. House of Lords meeting, 20 May 1985.
3. SYLVESTER, D., BATHO, E. (1985) House of Lords meeting, May 20.
4. HUGHES, S. (1985) House of Lords meeting, May 20.
5. Announcement by Secretary of State Kenneth Baker to House of Lords Select Committee 8 April 1987.
6. SIR KEITH JOSEPH (1984) Historical Association Conference, London 10 February. *The Historian*, No. 2, Spring, pp. 10–12.
7. DICKINSON, A.K., LEE, P.J. and ROGERS, P.J. (1984) *Learning History* Heinemann Educational, p. 5.
8. LAMONT, W. (1970) 'The uses and abuses of examinations' in BALLARD, M. (Ed.) *New Movements in the Study and Teaching of History*, Temple Smith. COLTHAM, J.B. and FINES, J. (1971) *Educational Objectives for the Study of History*, Historical Association TH35. JONES, R.B. (Ed.) (1973) *Practical Approaches to the New History*, Hutchinson Educational. ROGERS, P.J. (1979) *The New History — Theory into Practice*, Historical Association.
9. SCHOOLS COUNCIL (1976) *History 13–16 Project: A New Look at History*, Holmes McDougall.
10. BECK, P. (1986) 'Has History a future?' *Contemporary Review*, 249, November.
11. DEPARTMENT OF EDUCATION AND SCIENCE (1985) *History in the Primary and Secondary Years, An HMI View*, HMSO.
12. *Ibid.* p. 39.
13. SLATER, J. (1984) 'The case for history in school' *The Historian*, No. 2. Spring.
14. HARKNESS, D. (1986) at a conference on Irish History in the classroom, September.
15. This contribution is well presented in a paper produced by a group of historians from HMI (1977) in *Curriculum 11–16*.
16. DEPARTMENT OF EDUCATION AND SCIENCE (1985) *The Curriculum from 5 to 16 Curriculum Matters 2* London, HMSO, p. 32.
17. BLOW, F., and DICKINSON, A. (1986) *New History and New Technology: Present into Future* Historical Association.
18. For more extended argument see ROGERS, P.J. (1984) 'Why teach history' in DICKINSON, A.K., LEE, P.J. and ROGERS, P.J. *Learning History*, Heinemann Educational Books, pp. 35, 36 and cited references.
19. BOOTH, M. (1983) 'The Historical Association's 1983 survey on the teaching of history,' *Teaching History*, No. 40, pp. 20–1. BATHO, G. (1985) 'History: a most crucial element of the curriculum; LEA guidelines for the teaching of history 5–16,' *Teaching History*, No. 42, pp. 3–5. The third enquiry was that by VODDEN, D.F. into history in integrated studies.

20. *The Historian* (1984) No. 2, pp. 10–15.
21. 20 May 1985 and 13 January 1986. See *The Historian* (1985) No. 7, p. 23 and *The Historian* (1986) No. 10, p. 14.
22. LORD BLAKE (1985) House of Lords meeting 20 May *The Historian*, No. 7, p. 23.
23. COLLINS, I. (1984) 'President's page,' *The Historian* No. 2, p. 9.
24. An interesting contra indication is ALDRICH, R. (1987) 'Interesting and useful,' *Teaching History* No. 47, pp. 11–14.
25. BOOTH, M., SHAWYER. G., and BROWN, R. (1987) Cambridge University Department of Education. Research Report *Teaching History* No. 47, p. 29.
26. PATRICK, H., and PAUL, V. (1987) University of Leicester School of Education. Research Report *Teaching History* No. 47, p. 29.
27. PRONAY, N. (1986) The Young Historian Scheme anouncement, *The Historian* No. 11, p. 20; The Young Historians, *The Historian* No. 12, centre pull-out; HARDY, L. (1987) *The Historian* No. 13, p. 28.
28. *The Historian* (1985) No. 7, p. 23; No. 10, p. 14.
29. House of Lords debate, 13 January 1986.
30. HISTORICAL ASSOCIATION (1987) *Proposals for a Core Curriculum in History.*
31. HISTORICAL ASSOCIATION (1986) *History for Life*, p. 5.
32. SHEMILLT, D. (1980) *History 13–16 Evaluation Study* Holmes McDougall. History (S.C.) 1984 SUJB Examiners' Report.
33. HISTORICAL ASSOCIATION (1986) *History for Life*, p. 5.
34. DEPARTMENT OF EDUCATION AND SCIENCE (1985) *History in the Primary and Secondary Years, An HMI View*, London, HMSO, pp. 11–15.
35. *Ibid.* p. 14.
36. *Ibid.* p. 14.
37. *Ibid.* p. 15.
38. SLATER, J. (1984) 'The case for history in school' London conference 10 February, *The Historian* No. 2. p. 14.
39. HER MAJESTY'S INSPECTORATE (1978) *Primary Education in England* London, HMSO.
40. AVON (1982) *History and Geography in Primary Schools: A Framework for the Whole School* Avon, p. 1.
41. INNER LONDON EDUCATION AUTHORITY (1982) 'History in the primary school' *Curriculum Guidelines Series* ILEA, p. 9.
42. *Ibid.* pp. 2–3.
43. *Ibid.* p. 4.
44. *Ibid.* p. 5.
45. *Ibid.* p. 7.
46. SOLIHULL (1986) *Primary History Guidelines* Solihull, pp. 6–8.
47. WEST, J., NOBLE, P., BLYTH, J., LOW-BEER, A., GAULD, M.
48. NOBLE, P. (1985) *Curriculum Planning in Primary History* Historical Association Teaching History series No. 57.
49. AVON, *op cit.* p. 12.
50. P. NOBLE, *op cit.* p. 25.
51. SOLIHULL, *op cit.* p. 13.
52. NORTHERN IRELAND COUNCIL FOR EDUCATION DEVELOPMENT, (n.d.) *History Guidelines for Primary Schools* p. 42.
53. BLYTH, J.E. (1982) *History in Primary Schools* McGraw-Hill, pp. 14; 30–7. Also LOW-BEER A. and BLYTH J.E. (1983) *Teaching History to Younger Children*, Historical Association Teaching History series No. 52.
54. BATHO, G. (1985) 'History, a most crucial element of the curriculum; LEA guidelines for the teaching of History 5–16' *Teaching History*, No. 42, p. 4.
55. HER MAJESTY'S INSPECTORATE (1978) *Primary Education in England*

HMSO, Ch. 6, section 6.19; and DEPARTMENT OF EDUCATION AND SCIENCE (1980) *Report by HM Inspectors on Educational Provision by ILEA*, London, HMSO, *passim*.

56. DEPARTMENT OF EDUCATION AND SCIENCE (1985) *History in the Primary and Secondary Years* London, HMSO, pp. 8, 9.

57. *Ibid*. p. 15.

58. DICKINSON, A.K, LEE P.J. and ROGERS P.J. *op cit*. p. 146.

59. SHEMILT, D. (1976) *A New Look at History* Holmes McDougall, p. 10.

60. For example, WEST, J. (1978) 'Young children's awareness of the past', *Trends in Education* Spring, pp. 8–15, and 'Primary school children's perception of authenticity and time in historical narrative pictures', *Teaching History*, No. 29 pp. 8–10; GAULD M.B. (1982) 'History's contribution to environmental studies in the primary school' *Occasional Paper No. 1* Aberdeen College of Education Department of History, *passim*; and (1986) Seeking progression in the historical strand of environmental studies' *Occasional Paper No. 2 passim*; DONALDSON, M. (1987) *Children's Minds*, Fontana.

61. BLYTH, J.E. (1978) 'Young children and the past' *Teaching History* No. 21, pp. 15–19; and (1979) 'Teaching young children about the past' *Education 3–13*.

62. BLYTH, J.E. (1982) *History in Primary Schools*, McGraw Hill, p. 23.

63. *Ibid*. pp. 56–62.

64. SIR KEITH JOSEPH (1984) Speech at the North of England Education Conference, 6 January, para. 18.

65. Many LEA guidelines provide examples as do HMI in DEPARTMENT OF EDUCATION AND SCIENCE (1985) *History in the Primary and Secondary Years* London, HMSO, pp. 20–6.

66. *Ibid*. p. 39.

67. PATRICK, H. (1987) *The Aims of Teaching History in Secondary Schools*, ESRC report. PATRICK, H. (1987) 'Using the evidence', *Times Educational Supplement*, 11 December, p. 30.

68. HISTORICAL ASSOCIATION (1985) *History in Secondary Schools; A Profile of Current Provision*.

69. A useful discussion occurs in: ROGERS, P.J. (1987) *History: Why, What and How?* Historical Association Teaching History series, No. 60.

70. READ, D., and ROBERTS, M. (1987) 'Six of the best' *Times Educational Supplement*, 11 December.

71. HISTORICAL ASSOCIATION *National Debate on History in the Curriculum 5–16*, conference paper.

11   The Physical Education Curriculum from 5–16

Jim Parry

Introduction

This chapter was written, with the indulgence of the editors, in late 1987, some months after most other chapters were complete and at positively the last moment for inclusion in the collection. Had it not been included it would have been no major tragedy, since it would simply have been illustrative of a more general tendency. I am referring to the following instances of absence:

1   Physical Education (PE) was not one of the *twelve* subjects chosen by HMI for discussion in the Red Book of 1977.
2   Despite a *Curriculum 11–16. Supplementary Working Paper* on PE in 1979 of scarcely three pages in length, the long-awaited and long-promised 'position paper' has *still* not appeared. (Cyril Meek said in the Prince Philip Fellows Lecture in December 1985 that he understood that it was 'to be published quite soon'. Elizabeth Murdoch reported in May 1986 in the *British Journal of Physical Education* that it was 'due in the very near future'.) I was informed in May 1987 that although it was complete it was awaiting printing — but that, in any case, it would be available before the document on the national foundational curriculum appeared. Whilst the latter has just appeared the former still has not, so I can include no discussion of it here. (Postscript: there is still no sign of the position paper on going to press in January, 1988.)
3   Partly (but only partly) because of the above, there has been no organized response or initiative by the PE profession itself, either to chronic problems of self-definition and curriculum development or to the apparent unwillingness or inability of HMI or DES to show leadership. As Proctor warned:

> Arguably, no other subject *at a national level* has defaulted to such an extent in this vitally important area. (1974, p. 9)

The most alarming feature of the current situation, then, is the virtual absence of PE from serious, detailed, informed and open discussion of 'official' status at a national level. Despite disclaimers from HMI as to the significance of such absences, and despite the continued appearance of *something* called PE in specimen curriculum models, this sort of neglect might reasonably cause the concerned observer to question the commitment of HMI to the continued presence of PE in the school curriculum — or at least to wonder as to what *kind* and *amount* of PE is envisaged. An even more disturbing impression is generated if we consider the following circumstantial items:

4   Although many in the PE profession and elsewhere had long thought that PE and RE were the only two subjects which had a statutory place on the school curriculum, DES (1984) set the record straight by announcing that only RE enjoyed that status. It also floated the idea PE and Games should become a 'free option' in years 4 and 5 (see Meek, 1986, p. 76).

5   Over the past ten years or so there have been severe cutbacks in initial training places for PE students, followed by a readily predictable shortage of PE teachers. At one stage, PE was even quoted in the press in the top three shortage subjects with maths and physics.

6   These cutbacks have coincided with an expansion in the provision of places for the training of leisure and recreation professionals and in the privatization of fitness, health and leisure facilities whilst school playing-fields remain at risk.

7   In addition we are in the throes of a panic over school sport. A recent *Panorama* programme did an effective hatchet-job on the PE profession, and little was gained from a follow-up discussion programme. The ex-Minister for Sport, Dick Tracey, set up a forum to examine the place of sport in school, for which Elizabeth Murdoch has produced a 'desk study' for information purposes. The long-term consequences of this interest in the relation (or lack of it) between sport and education remain opaque, but it is surely a matter of the greatest concern.

I may be paranoid — but just because you're paranoid it doesn't mean they're not out to get you! In any case it is not necessary to believe in conspiracy theories to appreciate the thrust of the timetabling suggestion in Mr Baker's latest 'consultative document' (DES, 1987):

8   According to HMI (1981, p. 44) the average time allocation to PE in year 1 stood at 9.7 per cent. The new proposal is to *halve* that allocation to 5 per cent. A glum-looking headmaster, Mr. Pipes from Portsmouth, was pictured in the PE staff changing-room by *The Observer* (26.7.87, p. 6), fearing that this 'would toll the death knell for school games'.

Well, if this really is the case, then no wonder that HMI have been dragging their feet so heavily over their position paper. No wonder they have scarcely bothered to consider the future role of PE, beyond hinting at its marginality. No wonder training places have contracted. No wonder that no initiatives have been taken to preserve school playing-fields and to support school-based extra-curricular sport at this difficult time.

Of course, in the absence of more substantial documentation to consider, all of this may seem alarmist, nay, hysterical. Future events may render this introduction a rib-tickling relic. But I was not the first to issue dire warnings:

> The PE profession must decide if it is to be the guardian of this precious commodity of sport and, if not, should not attempt to negate the enthusiasm of those who assume it (Pickering, 1974, p. 10).

> It will become progressively more difficult to resist the proposals of those people who see no reason for avoiding the specific, cost-effective and administratively tidy calls for community based recreation leaders (Groves, 1981, p. 38).

I think that it is sensible to keep at the front of our minds the possible threat to the continued existence of (parts of) PE on the school curriculum whilst considering the implications of DES and HMI documents and the responses to them of individual PE professionals.

'Areas of Experience'

The 'Red Book' (HMI, 1977, p. 6) identified eight 'areas of experience' to which children should be introduced, including 'the physical', and these bear a close similarity to the eight 'modes of activity' suggested by the Munn Report on Scottish secondary schools issued some months earlier (SED, 1977). There are a number of problems with the whole notion of areas of experience. For a start the Red Book introduces them without any explanation or rationale, as opposed to the Munn Report, which offers a discussion of each suggested 'mode'. This is just one example of the irritating style of HMI documents, which are frequently assertive, rather than reasoned, and which frequently fail even to hint at the sources of ideas, let alone offer references. Where there are neither arguments nor authorities offered, where on earth is discussion or consultation supposed to begin? If we are not privy even to an elementary characterization of the notion of an area of experience, how on earth are we to begin a consideration of the adequacy of HMI suggestions? Did they plump for them? Or copy them from the Munn Report? Or is there a rationale behind them? How, for example, are we to begin to suggest alternatives or additions?

(HMI themselves are ambivalent about the political and the technological — and they don't even *consider* the philosophical, even though it is in philosophical terms that this debate must be conducted!) Perhaps the question should be turned around: on what grounds would (or did) HMI reject the possibility of an area of experience called 'the sportive' or 'the ludic' or 'the recreative'? Is not play an element of everyone's experience, and has it not been closely linked with education in the past? Is there nothing to experience or learn about in the area of leisure and recreation? Why are artistic cultural experiences acknowledged as valid and not sporting cultural experiences? Whose concealed value-judgments have dreamt up just this list? These are not idle theoretical questions, because hard practical consequences will flow from such value-laden constructions and omissions. Suffice it to say for the moment that there is, from the outset, not a shred of justification for this list, in terms of which the whole debate has been conducted.

But even if the notion of areas of experience were found persuasive (and the 'Red Book' list acceptable) their relationship to subjects, departments or faculties would still be problematic. Take language as an example. If a 'language across the curriculum' policy were taken seriously, what would this amount to? Either it would mean that the area (language) required greater attention across subjects or that a subject (say, English) would need to rethink its nature and role. Now, take the area of 'the physical'. Just what advantage is there supposed to be in considering this as an 'area of experience', as opposed to a subject? To be sure, there are physical elements to just about everything that we do: woodwork requires physical work, as do all crafts; dance, drama and music require physical movements, sometimes of great strength, dexterity, skill and challenge; science experiments often involve physical control of materials and instruments; in maths and English it is often useful to be able to hold a pencil correctly; and even in the library it is a body part upon which we sit. And what has all this to do with PE? I would dearly like to answer 'Not a sausage!' but this would disappoint those who believe that PE is to be defined simply in terms of its physicality. In the hey-day of human movement studies it was frequently argued that each school should have its 'movement specialist'. To be sure, this person would be responsible for the usual list of PE activities, but in addition would be able to advise other members of staff about the movement aspects of their subject work. In short, the PE teacher would become the movement consultant.

This strikes me not only as one more expression of the search for academic credibility through HMS, but also as a remarkably arrogant posture. The idea that one person, the PE teacher, is the one to advise specialists in music, craft, gardening and science about the 'physical' aspects of their pupils' activity strikes me as ludicrous. The movements made by the piano player are part of the music teacher's professional concern, not the PE teacher's. If we are to follow this approach, then it is 'the physical' which is to be seen across the curriculum, and not PE. All teachers are now to take special cognizance of the physical area of experience during their work — it is not an occasion for the occupational aggrandisement of the PE profession. I will return to this theme in a later section.

A further problem for the areas of experience, assuming that the curriculum remains subject-based, lies in the difficulty of collating across subjects just which subjects contribute (in practice, not only in paper claims) to which areas, in what way, when and to what degree. In what terms is all this to be recorded, and to what purpose? How is progress within each area to be evaluated, and through what means will the conclusions be expressed? If the areas are to be seen as a serious attempt to restructure our thinking about the processes of education in our schools then there will need to be corresponding changes in the structure and organization of staffing, teaching and evaluation.

If, however, the 'areas of experience' are viewed simply as suggestive 'checklist' ideas to which particular subjects might consider their relation, then no real structural changes will have to take place. And it will have been a useful exercise if it has encouraged each subject away from a concern only for its own internal values and interests and towards a concern also for the student's overall experience as she passes from subject to subject during the school week. But this is nothing new for PE. After all, we often hear claims that students learn about much more than physical activites during PE lessons. Indeed, at least in my view, there is already far too great a tendency to attempt to justify PE by claiming that it is really something else (such as aesthetic education or health education or human movement studies) or that it contributes to just about any value which current educational ideologies deem fashionable.

There is a real danger that each subject will feel itself constrained to make out a case for itself in terms of *each* of the 'areas', on pain of revealing itself as an inadequate candidate for inclusion on the curriculum. This seems a recipe for the proliferation of spurious justificatory claims as each subject strains to demonstrate its 'unique' contributions. It may also encourage a revival of the search for 'integration' for its own sake, as though it is self-evident that it is better to be able to apply two descriptions to an activity than one.

One way of assessing the degree to which HMI have considered the role of PE in the curriculum as a whole is to examine directly what they say about curriculum design. For ease of reference I shall look for this purpose only at the 1985 DES publication: *The Curriculum from 5–16*. Here we find (pp. 16–36, sections 33–89) an extended discussion of what have now become nine 'areas of learning and experience'. In the section dealing with the physical area, three strands are identified:

Firstly, traditional PE activities (in which, apparently, we should include drama and mime as well as dance — see section 68 *cp* section 65)

Secondly, general manipulative and motor skills applicable in many areas of the curriculum and life (in which PE activities are not mentioned — see section 69)

Thirdly, knowledge of how the body works and of what promotes its well-being (in which home economics, biology, PSE and even individual counselling are discussed, but not PE — see section 70).

This appears to be a model example of HMI thinking — an area of experience that might have been thought to be the preserve of physical educationists is neatly shown to be the concern of just about everyone. Would we not, by analogy, presume to discover, littered throughout the twenty pages of discussion, in what ways PE might have a legitimate concern in the other eight areas? If we did, we would be disappointed. The section on the 'aesthetic and creative' discusses dance, but no other PE activity is mentioned. (Compare this with the Scottish situation following the Munn Report, where Bob Carlisle has been pursuing his long-term concern to promote this and other areas as fundamental sources of justification for PE activities — see Carlisle, 1984, pp. 101–2.) Nor is PE mentioned in any of the other sections apart from the 'mathematical', which mentions 'the physical balance of the gymnast' (the final six words of this section), and the 'moral', which refers to games rules and to interpersonal relationships. In total, *three lines* are devoted to explaining the contribution of PE to the other eight areas, out of eighteen pages of discussion.

If this doesn't look too impressive, read on — it gets worse! HMI go on to suggest an alternative perspective for schools to consider (pp. 36–42, sections 90–105). Instead of looking at areas of experience planners might instead think in terms of 'elements of learning'. These elements are four: the knowledge, concepts, skills and attitudes which all schools should seek to develop in their pupils. PE is not mentioned in the the three sections on knowledge, concepts and attitudes. In the remaining section on skills there are listed thirty-one skills grouped under eight headings such as communication, observation, study, numerical, etc. Of course, PE could be seen to participate in the development of some of the skills under various headings — skills such as 'to express ideas' or 'to make informed choices' or 'to accept responsibility'. But consider the full list under the heading *Physical and Practical*:

to coordinate bodily movement and finer manual skills
to develop craft skills
to select appropriate tools and use them effectively
to write legibly
to use keyboards.

Even under what might be thought to be its 'home base' skills heading, PE only contributes to *one* of these skills, and PE skills are conspicuously omitted whilst other skills are thought worthy of specific mention.

I conclude that PE as a subject area has received nowhere near fair treatment from HMI either in their deliberations on 'areas' and 'elements' or in their failure to produce a detailed position paper within the last eight years.

'The Areas of Experience in PE'

There is a confusing ambiguity in the use of the term 'areas of experience' in HMI documents relating to PE. On the one hand it is used (as above) in the generally understood 'Red Book' sense. On the other hand (see HMI, 1979, p. 12) it is also used to refer to 'the areas of experience in PE' which means something quite different. In the section beginning with that title I expected to find some analysis of the contribution made by PE activities to the Red Book 'areas of experience'. Instead I found that 'areas of experience in PE' refers to *PE activities*. The motivation of the authors appears to be the reclassification of PE activities according to the 'main aim' of the activity. Five main aims are given:

— the development of skilful body management
— creating or being involved in an artistic experience
— competition between groups or individuals
— body-training for strength, stamina, endurance and a general feeling of well-being
— meeting challenges in varying environments.

Unfortunately, no *rationale* is provided for the selection of the above main aims, and so we are left in the dark as to answers to questions which we have been asking ourselves, such as *why* it is asserted that PE should develop (or retain) important connections with art, competitive games or the health movement. Why should not dance be a separate subject in school, or be seen as part of an arts faculty? Why should not sport be seen as the responsibility of Community Sports Leaders or Youth Sections of sports clubs? Why should not health be left to health professionals, parents or private health clubs? It is not much help simply to assert a preferred list of aims without some overall rationale which enables us to see how they are supposed to be understood. One way in which to do this, of course, would be to indicate some conception of PE which underlays the account being offered, but the only hint we are offered is that PE is concerned with 'physical experience', with 'psycho-motor competence', and that it 'focuses on the body' (p. 11).

Fortunately, however, these main aims do alert us to the real basis of the account. The concept of PE which is hidden here is quite simply exposed by examining the examples given to illustrate each aim. In effect, PE is seen as a loose collection of (mainly) sports and games, for each group of which a different 'aim' has to be thought out. Taking the above five aims in order, then, the shrewd eye might discern the following list of activities:

— gymnastics
— dance
— competitive games and athletics
— fitness and exercise programmes
— outdoor activities.

(Let us add swimming to this list, and stipulate that these 'Basic 6' activities cover nearly all of what goes on under the name of PE in schools. I don't think that the omission of 'movement' as a separate category is of relevance to the argument.)

It is as if the procedure has been as follows:

a) identify each categorically different activity which is 'normally' to be found in PE departments
b) thereby identify each group of the profession's constituents
c) ensure that no-one who might object has been left out
d) construct a 'main aim' for each activity (or group)
e) present these aims as defining the 'areas' of PE.

But surely this is an arcane device for rebottling old wine. What is gained by adding steps (d) and (e)? If the whole process is, in any case, determined by the existence of certain kinds of PE activity why cannot this be admitted at the outset? Why is it impossible to admit that PE is, indeed, a rather loose collection of physical activities, each of which will need to make its own separate case for inclusion or retention? The answers to these questions, it seems to me, are to be found in a closer examination of PE and 'the physical'.

Physical Education and 'The Physical'

HMI, 1979 (pp. 11–14 on PE) begins with the following assertion:

> PE is the part of the curriculum that can contribute most to the physical experience of the pupils. Its aims are concerned with the development of psychomotor competence in order to facilitate participation in worthwhile activities...

There is a problem here: there are those who would prefer to try to define PE in terms of the area of experience ('the physical') such that any activities coming under this umbrella become the business of PE (this would be the strong claim) or that PE activities provide the major source of such experience (the weak claim).

However, (as above) it really is difficult to be seen to be referring to what we all know as PE without reference to *some* range of physical activities, and we are driven back to the Basic 6 list. Once you start to give *any* list, it becomes as plain as the nose on your face that, whatever people claim, PE is *not* only about 'psychomotor competence' or some generalized 'movement capability' or any old 'physical experience'. It is about a certain *range* of physical activities which pre-exist the child's involvement, and into which she is to be initiated. This range of activities is historically and culturally conditioned. In Britain, at least, it presently includes *some* sports and games (but by no means all of them — only an approved few), *some* kinds of dance (where dance is included at all), sometimes outdoor activities, swimming if and when practicable, only certain forms of gymnastics, and so on. It does not include many other forms of physical activity, such as marching or other kinds of military drill (which used to be on the British curriculum); cheerleader routines (which are legitimate in the USA context); agricultural or industrial labour; massage; sex, etc. Neither does it pay much attention to such everyday 'psychomotor' concerns such as basic locomotion, posture, lifting and carrying, etc. The list of such skills offered in HMI, 1979 (p. 12) is quite clearly orientated (once again) to the Basic 6 activities.

This seems to me to be an unresolved contradiction at the heart of the subject's self-definition. Some would like to see PE as taking responsibility for the whole area of experience of 'the physical ', but they are constantly brought into contact with what PE has meant and does mean in schools. This contradiction is evidenced in the present circumstances by a tortured rhetoric of 'areas of experience in PE' or of 'psychomotor skills' (orientated towards seeing PE as encompassing and bearing a responsibility for 'the physical' as an area of experience) which is located within an HMI analysis which denies the premise. *No* subject, on the HMI account, bears sole and total responsibility for one area of experience, not even mathematics, which HMI identify as possibly the most plausible case.

Another way in which the contradiction emerges is as follows: the documents give the impression that HMI had adopted this procedure:

Firstly, think about children's movement needs
Secondly, deduce from this the experience they should be offered
Thirdly, select activities which best provide those experiences.

Indeed HMI John Parsons (1986, p. 197) makes explicit the claim that this is how we ought to be proceeding, arguing that, since games cannot provide all the experiences thus identified, PE should embrace activities other than games.

Well, no-one could argue with the conclusion that PE is more than games, but this is not because Parsons has produced a persuasive argument here. He has simply smuggled his conclusion into his premises. Since the list of experiences is in any case identified with reference to the Basic 6, and since games is only one of the Basic 6, it goes without saying that games alone cannot provide all the experiences identified. But we could have expressed the hope that PE should embrace other activities than games without importing all the accompanying jargon about needs and experiences. What does not follow is that anything other than the Basic 6 has been identified as the business of PE. Again, we have started with the language of psychomotor competencies and physical activities (the rhetoric of the 'area' approach) and we end up with the Basic 6 activities (the reality of the 'subject' approach). Is there any way out of this justificatory impasse?

On Justifying PE on the Curriculum

My basic position is simple: if the *content* of a subject is not seen as worthwhile, then it will be very difficult to persuade non-believers that the subject is justifiable on the curriculum at all.

Let us suppose that, on the HMI account, we are left with both subjects and areas. Let us further suppose (what I have already argued is false) that we have been provided with good reasons why 'the sportive' or 'the ludic' or 'the recreative' do not qualify as areas of experience. Now, there are two ways in which any subject, including PE, might attempt to justify itself on the curriculum.

1.   Firstly, it might try to show how it contributed to the nine areas. Mathematics as a subject has a strong case, given its obvious and direct relationship to one area. English has a strong case, given its plausible claim to make a major contribution to at least four areas and to have close connections with all of them. But neither of these routes is open to PE. Its claim to represent one area has been blown out of the water by DES (1985, pp. 28–9 and p. 40). The same document gives scant evidence that there is any major contribution to be expected from PE to any of the other areas, and this situation will not be alleviated by desperate calls for PE to seek integration (see Proctor, 1984, p. 9). This is because any subject *could* forge any number of forced links (but to what purpose, except as a last-ditch effort to invent relationships?). Most importantly, it is also because such links, even if they existed or could be invented, do little to advance the case — to show that PE might contribute to the 'human and social' area, for example, clinches nothing, for HMI identify government, law, literature, classics, foreign languages, drama, art, history and geography as interests which might contribute to this area. That is to say: PE is not even mentioned here, and even if a link *could* be shown it would avail little, since there are so many *other* ways of developing the human and social.

2. Secondly, it might try to show how it was of value in itself, as distinguished from the value it might have as a contributor to the areas. Indeed, it would be difficult to see why we should consider a subject for its areas-value unless we first had reason to believe it to be of some value in itself. Take English Literature, for example — presumably the literary achievements of our culture are believed to bear some value in themselves, independently of whether they are used in schools to promote experience in certain areas. Unfortunately, the same case is not often made for PE. Too often PE aims and justifications emphasize the quasi-incidental aesthetic, moral, and interpersonal elements, elevating these into the first-order values of the activities. I think this is because PE apologists have been persuaded that an activity has to be justified in terms of some 'higher' value, such as knowledge, morality, art, or health. As the HMI documents quite conclusively demonstrate, once it is accepted that PE activities have no value in and of themselves, but only as someone else's handservant, it becomes very hard to demonstrate what particular value there is in having PE on the curriculum at all. HMI keep it there, halved in stature, but on the evidence of their own documents they have no good reason even for doing that. On their 1985 account, I can't see any reason why it should not be scrapped.

Towards a Reactionary Concept of PE?

Against this, I would argue for the following account, which some may see as reactionary, in the senses both that it resists an existing tendency and also that it wishes to return to a previous orthodoxy. My excuses are firstly that the existing tendency is wrong-headed and dangerous, and secondly that the previous orthodoxy has been refined a little in battle.

1. PE is a Subject

In case anyone thinks that this scarcely needs arguing, consider this opening statement by the PE Committee of the Schools Council, introducing a 'basic framework for its later work':

> PE is an integral part of the process of education ... PE is an aspect of education rather than a subject.
>
> (Schools Council, 1971)

This kind of thinking is still with us, but there are two problems with it. Firstly, it identifies PE as an area of experience rather than as a subject, and we have already discussed the dangerous results of that. Secondly, it requires as a next step that a list of 'aims' be produced and, inevitably, we find a jargon-ridden list which is covertly determined by

245

the Basic 6. Even the 'process' jargon can't escape the conclusion that PE is a subject. Why on earth can't we bring ourselves to admit it?

2. *The Subject is Defined by its Activities*

PE is concerned with a range of physical activities which are valued as cultural forms. Now there are difficulties with that sentence:

i) What does 'valued' mean? I readily accept that it may be the case that competitive games, hazardous pursuits or strenuous exercise may not be everyone's cup of tea. But what I mean here is that the society as a whole must value these forms of activity for the human excellences which they promote and display if they are to be seen as worth spending time and money on in schools. If they are not generally so valued, then off with them (and so much the worse for a society which so decides, in my view). It is up to people who *are* committed to the cultural value of these activities to stand up for them and their *intrinsic* values (*if they have any!*)rather than relying on wonky-looking extrinsic arguments about rugby making chaps nice.

ii) What is a 'cultural form'? This is a difficult one, and I can only provide a few pointers for myself. I am referring, of course, to the Basic 6, which are specific, developed groups of activities, but the problem is how they are to be characterized. I want to avoid a 'unitary' account, since that would be to impose a false or spurious unity on disparate activities which have only contingently been collected under the heading of PE. However, with the exception of dance, which may be seen in part as belonging to artistic culture, the other PE activities are all forms of sport or games and/or require an element of physical exercise or exertion, and/or require the exercise of physical skill for the production of excellence. They are distinguishable from everyday *functional* activities, from *craft* activities and from *labour* or *military* activities, even though these may be seen as important elements of the 'physical' area.

iii) What 'range' is envisaged? There are many separate arguments on this issue, and any answer will be a response to wider considerations. At the level of basic groups of activities there may be disputes about whether dance, games or outdoor pursuits should remain. Within groups there may be disputes as to the relative merits of various forms of gymnastics or of various athletic disciplines or of particular games. In many ways, the actual choices made are not so important as the rationale behind the choices, and this will inevitably involve thinking about the role of PE in the curriculum as a whole given the constraints and opportunities of the particular school situation. There are scores of activities from which to choose, and there is no reason to be hidebound by tradition.

However, the *main* consideration seems to me to be the cultural value of the activity under consideration, because those qualities which make an activity culturally valuable are also those which are likely to contribute to areas of learning and experience. It is *because* Shakespeare's plays are recognized as possessing culturally valuable qualities that they are capable of being utilized to develop those attributes so fulsomely portrayed by HMI (1985) across four areas of experience (see sections 37, 41, 51, and 61). It is a pity that they did not achieve a similarly comprehensive and successful analysis of PE activities. Maybe this is because they didn't even try, or maybe it is because PE activities actually will not support such an analysis. What is a greater pity is that the PE profession itself has failed to shoulder the responsibility for this task. If HMI can't see a good case for certain forms of physical activity, this is because the PE profession has, in the last analysis, failed to get its act together.

3. The Subject should not be Confused with the Area of Experience

If we are tempted to do so there will be two inevitable consequences:

i) We will be distracted from the serious task of making a case for the subject (and its constitutive activities)
ii) We will be drawn into making territorial claims over the area of experience which will prove ultimately untenable.

The consequence of this, in turn, will be a crisis of self-definition and curricular justification — and this is precisely what has happened in the recent past and precisely where PE stands today.

The crucial task which now confronts the profession is the demonstration of the value of a range of its *activities*. Once this has been achieved it will be possible to address the secondary task of demonstrating the value of these activities in contributing to various areas of learning and experience (and this will include an attempt to alter or augment the areas suggested by HMI). These tasks must be addressed immediately if PE is to survive in anything like its present form in schools, never mind flourish.

PE Across the Age Range

A complicating factor in outlining the concept of PE and its justification lies in the broad age range of 5–16 which is under consideration, and which I have not yet discussed. In particular, this may be seen as a crucial factor by opponents of the view I have outlined. Surely, it may be urged, PE will be a different thing for disparate groups, and this will raise problems for any account which defines PE in terms of a given range of activities, as I have suggested. Moreover, there will be no such problem for a 'process' or 'area' account, since PE is here defined as the process for the development of the physical, and this process may draw on a different activity range for a different age range. In this way the apparent contradiction between subject and process is resolved, it may be argued, because the subject disappears into the process. The subject is not defined by the activities: rather an activity may or may not be incorporated into the process according to the age or stage of the student.

The reply to this kind of view should be now be apparent:

1   No matter how general seem to be the movement activities which are offered (especially in the earliest age or stage groups) the rationale for these activities will need to specify the *kind* of movement abilities which it seeks eventually to promote, and the *kind* of mature activities to which it hopes to lead. The subject of 'movement' does not, I take it, purport to promote the skills of craft, tool-selection, writing and keyboard use (all mentioned by HMI, 1985, p. 40). But any specification of what it *does* seek to promote *must* lead us to some such list as the Basic 6. PE is not *solely* reponsible for the physical area. Other subjects have a valid interest in it, too.

2   In any case, an activities-based account does not fall to the above objection. To begin with, I have not even begun to argue in favour of a *particular* set of groups of activities — I have not said, and nor do I think, that there is anything sacred about the Basic 6. It is just that, as a matter of fact, there appears to be some agreement over that. Neither have I argued over the place of particular activities within each group. All of this is up for discussion, and I would expect proposals for one situation to differ from proposals for another. PE for 7-year-olds in a rural village school in Chad will likely employ different activities from PE for 14-year olds in Detroit and from special school pupils in Leeds. What makes them all PE activities (and not occupational therapy, gardening or ringolevio) is explained in 2(ii) of the last section. An activities account can be as flexible across the age and stage range as a process account, either because different activities from within the same group become more appropriate, or because an activity may be modified to suit many levels.

I hope that I have given good reasons why the PE profession should abandon the attempt to lay sovereign claim to the physical area, and why the definition of PE as a process is not only unhelpful but positively dangerous. It is not a proveable assertion that the process or area account of PE is responsible for the mess we are in today, but I for one believe it to be true (well aware as I am of the fallacy of *post hoc ergo propter hoc*). The sooner it is abandoned, the better.

PE and the 5–16 Curriculum

The much-vaunted Great Debate of the last ten years has produced little of value for PE. Where PE gets mentioned at all there is scarcely a sentence throughout the official documents which suggests anything new or interesting specifically in relation to PE. The main recommendations (apart from the one which halves timetable time in a period when voluntary extra-curricular commitment is decreasing) are general ones to do with matters of emphasis, rather than substance.

1. For example, it is clear that HMI would like to see an overall framework which would support a broad, balanced, relevant and differentiated curriculum. Despite difficulties in the interpretation of these notoriously woolly adjectives (see Aspin in White, 1981, pp. 41–2) I think we can accept that too often PE teachers have unreflectively given over too much time to the routine and unimaginative teaching of team games. A more thoughtful selection of activities which more faithfully represents the legitimate range of PE activities would undoubtedly be an improvement.

2. HMI have suggested a number of ways in which planners might organize their thoughts: they might think in terms of subjects, areas, elements of learning, or topics/themes. In this latter category (which we have not so far mentioned) HMI provide a list of possibilities (see HMI, 1985, pp. 13–15):

— environmental education
— health education
— information technology
— political and economic education
— work preparation
— careers education
— equal opportunities
— ethnic minority interests.

Although PE is nowhere mentioned in these pages I think it is intended that each subject, as well as thinking about its own values and its own contribution to a student's education, should also consider the contribution it might make to areas, elements and topics. It must surely be a good thing for all subjects, including PE, to reassess their contribution to the whole life of the school and to enter fully into consultations regarding the general framework adopted. Such attempts to move away from a rigidly subject-centred approach are to be applauded.

However, each subject (and its professional associations) should have been interrogating these HMI suggestions (i) for their adequacy, so as to effect an input at an early stage if the suggestion failed to do justice to the subject, and (ii) to work out how the subject could best respond to them, or a revised version of them. I cannot see that PE has been at all successful in this regard. As I understand the situation from enquiries to professional asociations everyone is waiting for the position paper. By the time it eventually appears the battle will be all over bar the shouting.

3. Apart from these two general suggestions there are some specific points to be noted from the PEA booklet *PE in Schools* (1987). Each of the sections on primary and secondary schools concludes with a short summary (pp. 22–3 and 35–6) which incorporates conclusions from published reports of HMI school visits. We may learn something from this about HMI thinking, even if it has not found its way into official curriculum documents.

(i)   In primary schools the main areas of concern are:
       — the variation in length and quality of initial training
       — the possibility that students may receive no PE training
       — the gap between timetabling and actual PE practice
       — the inadequacy of in-service provision
       — that good practice often reflects only the interests of individual teachers or heads
       — that there is too great an emphasis on games and too little on dance
       — the lack of good schemes of work and means of evaluation.

It is emphasized that each primary teacher is responsible for the whole curriculum, including PE; that every teacher is capable of producing acceptable standards; and that teaching skill does not demand personal ability on the part of the teacher, but is rather a matter of methodology.

(ii)   In secondary schools the main areas of concern are:
       — that time allocation has reduced over the past twelve years
       — that teachers are over-committed with extra-curricular work
       — that curriculum plans and aims statements are not always available
       — repetitiveness, or minimally prepared sessions
       — supervision instead of planned teaching
       — poorly monitored progression
       — curriculum imbalance (too much team games).

Taking both sections, then, it seems that there is room for improvement in the training of teachers in practical work, planning and evaluation, and a case for more breadth and balance in the syllabus. However, the document does little to advance our thinking on the conceptual and justificatory questions which are of overwhelming importance if PE is to build a case for itself strong enough to resist the powerful forces which threaten its place on the curriculum. The final recommendations of the Commission recognize this. They begin as follows (p. 53):

> There is a need to prepare and disseminate widely a clearly articulated philosophy of physical education linked to a general strategy to guide educational practice and other commitments within our school systems .... We ... look to the PEA to initiate action.

Let us hope that it will not be too late.

Bibliography

CARLISLE, R. (1984) 'Government and UGC changes affecting the practice of PE, sport and recreation', *BUPEA Annual Conference Report*, Lancaster Univ DPE.

DEPARTMENT OF EDUCATION AND SCIENCE (1984) *The Organisation and Content of the 5–16 Curriculum* London, HMSO.

DEPARTMENT OF EDUCATION AND SCIENCE (1985) *The Curriculum from 5–16 — Curriculum Matters 2* London, HMSO.

GROVES, R. (1981) 'Stressing the education in PE', *PE Review*, 4, 1, pp. 38–43.

HER MAJESTY'S INSPECTORATE (1977) *Curriculum 11–16* (The Red Book), London, HMSO.

HER MAJESTY'S INSPECTORATE (1979) *Curriculum 11–16, Supplementary Working Papers: PE*, London DES.

MEEK, C. (1986) 'PE in the "New" Curriculum' *British Journal of Physical Education*, 17, 3, May/June, pp. 105–8.

MURDOCH, E. (1986) 'Future trends in the PE curriculum' *British Journal of Physical Education*, 17, 3, May/June, pp. 83–6.

PARSONS, J. (1986) 'PE — Recent Developments' (anonymous notes taken from a PEA/CCPR seminar presentation) *British Journal of Physical Education*, 17, 3, May/June, pp. 197–8.

PHYSICAL EDUCATION ASSOCIATION (1987) *PE in Schools: Report of a Commission of Enquiry*, Physical Education Association.

PICKERING, R. (1974) 'Sport and the young competitor: Virtues and vices', *Report of the CCPR National Conference on Sport and Youth*, London, 16 July.

PROCTOR, N. (1984) 'Problems facing PE after the Great Education Debate,' *PE Review*, 7, 1, pp. 4–11.

SCHOOLS COUNCIL (1971) 'Preliminary Statement of the Objectives of PE in the Secondary School' (used as a guide for seminar discussion at a conference at Christ Church College, Canterbury, 2–5, January on Teaching PE in the 1970s).

SCOTTISH EDUCATION DEPARTMENT (1977) *The Structure of the Curriculum in the Third and Fourth Years of the Scottish Secondary School*, (The Munn Report), HMSO.

WHITE, J. *et al* (Eds) (1981) *No Minister: A Critique of the DES Paper: The School Curriculum*, Bedford Way Paper 4, University of London Institute of Education.

12   Art and Design: A Parting of Ways?

Anthony Dyson

I will be dealing in this chapter with a field of study about which there exists considerable confusion and misunderstanding. It is a field usually referred to, simply, as art; but, for reasons which I hope will become clear, I shall call it 'art, craft, and design'. Even when, for the sake of brevity, I use only the word art, I shall wish it to imply a fusion of art, craft, and design; for it is my intention to argue a case for holism. I want to resist any suggestion that, because it is to do with the affective aspect of human experience, art is necessarily less technically or intellectually demanding than craft or design; and, conversely, I want to resist any suggestion that design relies solely upon that process that has come to be called 'problem-solving', or that a work of craftsmanship has function as its predominant criterion.

The tendency of government over the last ten years to divide the school curriculum into the 'useful' and (in the best sense of the word) the 'useless' is nothing new; nor is it hard to understand. This kind of categorization has a long history, and I will begin the chapter with a brief account of how art, craft, and design have been affected by it since the High Renaissance. I shall then deal, equally briefly, with the few years following the Ruskin College speech with which James Callaghan, then Prime Minister, launched the 'Great Debate' on education, in 1976. And finally, I shall look a little more closely at the relevant events since January 1984, when Keith Joseph announced to the North of England Education Conference at Sheffield his determination to raise standards in schools.

I

Art in Europe has had a bad press since the close of the Napoleonic Wars; for it was about then that the urge among many artists to express personal experience took on that peculiar intensity which became the chief characteristic of what we now call Romanticism. The Romantic spirit pervaded all the arts; but the abandonment by many eighteenth and early nineteenth century painters of the disciplines of academic training encouraged the enduring myth of the solitary, untutored, genius whose creative spark is sufficient justification for his apparent anarchism.[1] Rousseau's insistence that 'Emile should not have a drawing master who would only teach him to imitate imitations' was prophetic of a growing, more general disenchantment with traditional teaching methods, and was a resolution that was to find fuller expression in the words of Meyer, Goethe's pupil: 'Art must feel free ... if ruled and mastered it is bound to decline and vanish'. Such ideas have gathered force until, in popular belief, the subjective outpourings of the individual are thought to represent a sufficient definition of art. Vincent van Gogh is, for many, the archetypal artist, his passionate unconformity seeming to eclipse the disciplined study that, in his case to such an impressive degree, was at the root of his ultimate (and posthumous) success.

Art students, and those who teach them, are frequently suspected of an incompetence amounting almost to moral turpitude. Peter Fuller[2] has criticized the art schools for 'abandoning the teaching of traditional skills' and has claimed that in them 'every kind of silliness is condoned and encouraged'. Paul Johnston[3] has further castigated these establishments, having received unfavourable impressions of students' degree exhibitions in some of them. Liam Hudson, in *Contrary Imaginations*[4], has shown how deep-rooted in schools, too, can be the prejudice against art and those who teach and study it. 'Creativity', 'imagination', and 'self-expression' — those immeasurables — are thought to be the prerequisites for those engaged in art. And, unfortunately, many enthusiasts for the subject also believe to a damaging extent in the primacy of creativity. In his book *Ideals and Idols*[5], E.H. Gombrich reproduces an interesting exchange of correspondence between himself and Quentin Bell, then Professor of Fine Art at the University of Sussex. Expressing his view on this popular misapprehension, Gombrich remarked in one letter that a teacher he knew had argued that art is 'creativity' and that, this being so, it cannot be taught. If art cannot be taught, if a pupil or student must bear alone the burden of creative self-expression, what is the purpose of a syllabus? Would not a syllabus simply inhibit creativity? Elliot Eisner assures us that 'when [creativity] dominates a field ... [it is indeed] unlikely that curriculum content will be identified systematically'.[6]

Ten years ago, Alec Clegg commented sombrely on 'The Educational Pendulum'[7]:

The public education service has always been aware of the dichotomy between mind and spirit, between intellect and personality, between the cognitive and the affective ... It does not learn from experience, it makes the same mistakes over and over again — and occasionally it treats conventional recipes as if they were fresh inspirations. The pendulum swings, in fact, every quarter of a century or so.

After an account of the late nineteenth century predecessor of today's 'common core curriculum' campaign he went on to list the achievements, early in the present century, of those (like Susan Isaacs and the Macmillan sisters) who represented the return of the pendulum from what can be measured to what cannot. But now, he continued, prophetically:

> The pendulum is swinging back to what can be measured. Assessment and evaluation will be the criteria, and it will be done with calm and compelling wisdom and allegedly in the best interests of the nation's schools.

The swing to what can be measured has, in the field of art, craft, and design education, threatened a disastrous split. Until the late Renaissance what we now distinguish as art, craft, and design were closely integrated, but during the sixteenth century the proliferating academies stressed the social superiority of painters (particularly, though, also of sculptors and architects) over craftsmen by stressing the theoretical aspects of their work. By his day, Antonio Palomino (1655–1726) could say that 'Art is divided into liberal and ... mechanical art ... [and that] in liberal art we have more speculation than toil and in mechanical art more toil than speculation'. When the British Royal Academy was founded in 1768, engravers were written off as mere 'ingenious mechanics', and were thus refused admission.[8] 'The value and rank of every art is in proportion to the mental labour employed in it, or the mental pleasure produced by it', argued the founding President, Joshua Reynolds. 'As this principle is observed or neglected, our profession becomes either a liberal art, or a mechanical trade.' As the Industrial Revolution gathered pace, the division between the 'fine arts' and the crafts became more and more accentuated. In 1835 the Government, alarmed (as now) at industrial competition from abroad, set up a House of Commons Select Committee on Arts and Manufactures, with the aim of investigating ways of instilling into the labouring classes some degree of aesthetic appreciation — at least to the extent that such sensibility could contribute to the aesthetic enhancement of manufactured products. But, as the factory system led inexorably to an increased division of labour, these aspirations seemed ever more forlorn.

The arts and crafts movement (c. 1870–1914), inspired by William Morris and others, did much to encourage a reintegration of art and craft in education. By 1946, the Ministry of Education had established the National Diploma in Design as the standard qualification in what by then had come increasingly (and significantly) to be called the schools of art and craft. The National Diploma (and its preliminary, the Intermediate Certificate) required students both to undertake those disciplines associated with an academic training in fine art (life drawing, modelling, perspective, anatomy) and to engage in a craft (such as pottery, textile printing, embroidery, lettering, book illustration, or interior design).

The Coldsteam Committee, reporting in 1960, led to a system of higher education in art in which craftsmanship seemed once more to be of reduced importance, and in which it is still possible for a student of fine art to study for several years with little regard for traditional skills and disciplines. Hence the criticisms of Peter Fuller and others.[9]

What has all this to do with the schools? There are, naturally, courses of study in further and higher education for those wishing to engage in the 'useful arts' — say, furniture design, industrial design, or silversmithing. Such students frequently go into industry. But a significant opportunity for fine art graduates is in the teaching profession, and most of those who enter teaching do so at secondary school level. Thus, art in schools may be perceived to be heavily weighted in favour of fine art. It certainly seems to be so perceived by government planners; and for the last ten years at least, all the significant government papers dealing with the curriculum have exhibited a drift towards the separation of art (that nebulous field, which is thought to share with music, drama, and dance a responsibility for promoting 'aesthetic awareness') and design (a discipline which, together with science, mathematics, and technology, is believed to nurture a propensity for 'problem-solving'). John Steers has recently quoted a senior HMI as saying that:

> The government wants to bring about a shift of emphasis in further and higher education away from what have been described as the 'soft' subjects, that is the arts and social sciences, and towards the 'hard' disciplines of the natural sciences and the new technologies. There is, however, considerable interest in the education and training of designers ... who will create new markets and generate income.[10]

The attitude is reflected at school level; this is why the subject craft, design, and technology is receiving such enthusiastic official support. But the separation is false, and semantic confusion is signified by the presence of the word 'design' in the terms 'art, craft, and design' and 'craft, design, and technology'. Does the word have a different meaning in each context?

II

In his foreword to the Gulbenkian Report, *The Arts in Schools* (1982), Peter Brinson gave an account of a discussion held five years previously with Peter Newsam, then Education Officer of the Inner London Education Authority:

> [We] were discussing the public debate on education [initiated by James Callaghan at Ruskin College in 1976], particularly refer-

ences to a core curriculum and a recurrent emphasis on the three Rs. These seemed to exclude, not only the arts, but also some of the principles upon which the idea of a general education had been developed in Britain since the Education Act of 1944. If our assessment was correct, these public discussions would have profound implications for all education. Both of us saw the arts as a test case in this respect.

It was later in 1977 that Alec Clegg's 'Educational Pendulum' article warned of further progress towards government control of the curriculum; and in March the following year HMI published proposals for a common core curriculum comprising these 'areas of experience': the aesthetic and creative; the ethical; the linguistic; the mathematical; the physical; the scientific; the social and personal; and the spiritual. The DES had already set up (in 1975) the Assessment of Performance Unit (APU), which was given the task of providing a national picture of pupil performance in certain agreed aspects of the curriculum: the aesthetic; the linguistic; the mathematical; the physical; the scientific; and the social and personal. Not surprisingly, quicker progress was made in aspects such as mathematics and language than in the social/personal or the aesthetic field. The Exploratory Group on Aesthetic Development was formed in 1977, with the following terms of reference:

a) to consider to what extent it would be desirable to assess pupils' aesthetic development and at what age(s);

b) to consider whether, if such assessment were thought desirable, it would be feasible; and

c) to make recommendations to the Unit.

It took the Group six years to produce a discussion document.[11] Members saw themselves as 'engaged in largely pioneering work in an important aspect of education where guidelines were thought to be highly desirable and yet were found to be singularly lacking'. A major difficulty — and contradiction — is referred to on the very first page of the document: that of the relationship between 'the aesthetic' and 'the artistic'. By no means do these always coincide, though they frequently overlap; 'indeed', the compilers remind us, 'the power of a work may in some cases depend upon its being ugly and disturbing'.[12] The conflation of the aesthetic and the artistic into a general concept of aesthetic development appeared to the group to be unmanageable, and it was thus decided to concentrate in the document on artistic development[13] — although the title remained *Aesthetic Development*. Though the document is frequently puzzling and dotted with inconsistencies, it does provide some useful insights. For instance, it counteracts the government tendency to separate 'hard' and 'soft' subjects by pointing out that the fostering of aesthetic judgments is a responsibility shared by the arts *and* other areas of the curriculum such as craft, design, and technology[14]; and it insists, in spite of the reluctance of many arts educators to make explicit the implicit criteria for assessment on which they seem to depend, that:

a) artistic development certainly can be objectively assessed; and
b) this does not imply any restriction of [a pupil's] individuality and creativity.[15]

But, in March 1978, whilst the Exploratory Group on Aesthetic Development was beginning to prepare its argument for the assessability (and therefore the respectability) of the arts, there appeared in the *Times Educational Supplement* a sobering article by John Rae.[16] It was entitled 'Richelieu at our elbows', and in it Rae asked 'Can a curriculum ever escape fully from its country's history? ... we speak of broadening the curriculum or of giving proper status to applied as well as to theoretical studies ... [but] if we do not at least take note of the connection between school curriculum and national history we are always likely to underestimate the difficulty of releasing the former from the grip of the latter'. Reminding us of Richelieu's contention that a liberal arts education tends to produce people who raise too many questions, upset public order, and undermine the authority of the state, he went on to propose that Britain's survival must now be seen in relation to overseas competitors with more efficient manufacturing industry — a new imperative that will 'force the British to reform their educational system and in particular their school curriculum ... when [we] argue in favour of a liberal arts education and against central control of the curriculum [we] are not only living in the past; [we] are in danger of dying in it as well'.

In 1979, Professor Denis Lawton gave his inaugural lecture at the University of London Institute of Education. He called it 'The end of the Secret Garden'[17] — the secret garden of the curriculum, about to be exposed to the searchlight of critical scrutiny.

The following year, the DES produced its *Framework for the School Curriculum*; and on its heels, in March 1981, came *The School Curriculum*. The latter, 'the first explicit and definitive attempt by central government for half a century to steer curricula in a particular direction', provoked a quick response in the form of a collection of critical essays entitled *No, Minister*.[18] In his defence of the arts in the school curriculum, David Aspin, one of the contributors, argued that

> ... not only are there serious doubts about the basis for curriculum planning proposed by the Secretaries of State but that there is also at least one area in which their proposals exhibit serious deficiencies. This area forms a major part of what our education service and our community plainly consider to be absolutely indispensable elements in the civilized life towards which the young ought to be educated — the arts, in all their forms.

He continued:

> The principal demerit of *The School Curriculum* I regard as its
> apparently over-riding concern with instrumental considerations,
> its view that the school curriculum for all pupils must, at rock
> bottom, be dictated by starkly utilitarian concerns... Certainly it
> would be a brave man who would agree that we should 'take no
> thought for the morrow'; but this document seems to be almost
> entirely devoted to the cares of the morrow rather than the
> possibilities of the present.[20]

Teachers of the arts, he went on to say, are quite rightly suspicious of an
undue emphasis on intellectual attainments and are concerned to balance
such attainments by encouraging the development in their pupils of affective qualities, and

> Proof that [this is] among the reasons why artists and the arts are
> so distrusted and undervalued in our schools are the findings of
> HM Inspectors in their *Aspects of Secondary Education* that: 'The
> more able pupils tended to have narrow programmes heavily
> weighted towards science or languages and often omitting aesthe-
> tic, practical or humanities subjects...'. And this kind of spirit is,
> I suspect, to be observed in the grudging and concessionary tone
> adopted towards 'some aesthetic activity' in 'The Secondary Phase'
> section of *The School Curriculum*, in spite of the evidence of a
> regard for the importance of work in art and craft, music and
> drama in 'The Primary Phase'.[21]

During the late 1970s and early 1980s there were a number of
valuable initiatives by protagonists of art, craft, and design. Not least
among these was HM Inspectorate's *Art in Junior Education* (1978). It is
worth quoting at length from the introduction:

> What is art education, and what has art to offer to children? It can
> heighten their awareness of sensory experience and sharpen their
> powers of observation ... [of the] natural and man-made world.
> Form and order, pattern and design become clear to them [and
> the] ... practice of art — the stimulus of drawing, painting and
> making things — leads them also to a lifelong appreciation of
> works of art from different times and places and gives access to
> their meanings. The children come to realize that there are ex-
> periences for which words alone will not serve... Many teachers
> assert that language development is accelerated by association
> with drawing, painting and making things. They also value the
> contribution made by an understanding of pattern and form to the
> learning of mathematics and science ... [however,] it is worth
> remembering that the 11-year olds in primary schools may enjoy

only two or three more years of art education before having to make decisions which may severely reduce or even eliminate their formal education in the visual arts.

And in 1980, a remarkable art education centre was established by the Wigan local education authority. It was set up at the initiative of the authority's Art Adviser, A.R. Taylor, and it and its founder were to have a profound influence on the development of art, craft, and design education in Britain. The Drumcroon Education Art Centre, as it is known, encourages and complements the work of local primary and secondary schools and, by means of an enterprising series of workshops, exhibitions, and artists-in-schools schemes, it brings children into fruitful contact with professional artists and students in further and higher education. Rod Taylor was to go on to direct a highly successful national project, 'Critical Studies in Schools', sponsored by the Arts Council, the Crafts Council, and the then Schools Council.

In 1982, the *Journal of Art and Design Education* ('the first serious journal in the field for many years'[22]) was launched by the National Society for Education in Art and Design[23]; and in the same year the long deliberations of the Gulbenkian Foundation's Advisory Committee bore fruit with the publication of *The Arts in Schools*. The compilers insisted that 'the arts have an essential place in the balanced education of our children and young people ... whatever the social and economic circumstances of the day',[24] and identified vital contributions of the arts in six main areas:

a) in developing the full variety of human intelligence;
b) in developing the ability for creative thought and action;
c) in the education of feeling and sensibility;
d) in the exploration of values;
e) in understanding cultural change and differences; and
f) in developing physical and perceptual skills.[25]

The Gulbenkian Report was one of the most articulate justifications for the arts ever to emerge — a much-needed example of clarity and persuasiveness. And yet, a year after its appearance, John Steers was still able to observe morosely that:

In many schools there is no real art syllabus, or only one expressed in the vaguest terms. In a small survey which I conducted, only two out of the twenty-eight schools who replied offered more than a general statement of 300 words or so. It is my belief that this failure to articulate a fundamental philosophy of art education has led to the present imbalance between art and design in the minds of the government and the DES and the consequent enhancement of the provision afforded to craft design and technology and encroachment on the art allocation.[26]

The same year, however, and in much more sanguine vein, HM Inspectorate published the secondary counterpart of their account of good practice in primary schools. *Art in Secondary Education 11–16* contains a significant chapter entitled 'Craftsmanship and Design in Art Education' — a chapter describing departments in which all three elements are successfully fused.

III

When on 6 January 1984 Education Secretary Sir Keith Joseph spoke at the North of England Education Conference in Sheffield, he seemed to give a clear indication of his own view of the essential ingredients for a core curriculum. Stating his aspiration to bring '80–90 per cent of all pupils *at least* to the level [then] associated with the CSE grade 4 ... and to do so over a broad range of skills and competence in a number of subjects',[27] he chose as examples English, mathematics, science, history, and CDT (in which pupils would need to show that 'they can design and make something, using a limited range of materials and calling on a restricted range of concepts, and give an account of what they have done and the problems they encountered').[28] Neither art nor any of the other so-called 'creative' or 'aesthetic' subjects is represented in the list of examples, nor is there any mention of art anywhere in the speech. This seems a strange omission in view of Sir Keith's acknowledgement that the curriculum

> should be broad for all pupils both in the development of personal qualities and in the range of knowledge and skills to which pupils are introduced. That means, for example, that every primary pupil should be properly introduced to science; and that secondary pupils should not drop subjects in the 4th and 5th years in a way which leaves them insufficiently equipped for subsequent study or training.[29]

and that

> The various elements of the curriculum need to be balanced in such a way as to optimize the contribution that each can make to the total education of the pupil. Insofar as each main element does something for the pupil that no other element does, or does as well, no pupil should miss the chance of getting out of each such element the special competence and understanding which it helps him to acquire.[30]

One wonders if Sir Keith had room for the 'soft' subjects among the 'elements' he had in mind? Was the avoidance of any mention of art — of the arts — deliberate? Was the speech further evidence of governmental determination to stress the technical and vocational aspects of the school curriculum?

At any rate, late in 1984 the National Society for Education in Art and Design[31] published a discussion paper opposing what it saw as 'divisive policies for art and design education ... manifested ... by pronouncements that design can exist without art, that designers are not artists, and that the artistic merits of the work in progress and the finished product are not essential factors in the design process'. The Society's Standing Committee on Design in Education regarded such policies as 'harmful and retrograde inasmuch as they are a reversion to the separation of art from design and craft which guided thinking before the progressive and unified approach of [William] Morris, [Walter] Crane, [Charles Rennie] Mackintosh and [Walter] Gropius'. The Committee's paper, published in the *Journal of Art and Design Education*,[32] began as follows:

> Design does not exist as a separate entity in a vacuum. Art, craft and design are interrelated, interpenetrative, and interdependent in theory and practice, and should be so considered in education. While it is possible, and often useful, to divide art and design into various areas of activity for educational *practice*, their essential unity and interdependence should be stressed in each area.[33]

The compilers went on to maintain that

> Crafts still have an important part to play... The introduction into colleges of art and design, and into schools, of working in actual materials rather than merely drawing and theorizing, initiated a great rise in the *standard* of design education, and of industrial design itself, from the thirties onwards.[34]

And they conclude by deploring the fact that 'there are those trained as artists who encourage the narrow divisive view that art is an elitist, obscure subject, entirely centred upon self and free expression with no disciplines [*sic*] nor cognitive studies. A much broader attitude ... is necessary to retain and increase ... respect for [art, craft, and design] in public education'.

In September 1984, the DES and the Welsh Office published a note on *The Organization and Content of the 5–16 Curriculum*. Building on Keith Joseph's speech of that January, the paper concerned itself essentially with 'what all pupils should be offered during the compulsory period of schooling and what some pupils should be offered additionally'. In the paper, the 5–16 curriculum is discussed mainly in terms of subjects,[35] in spite of HMI's preference (expressed in the common core curriculum paper of 1978) for 'areas of experience'. Unlike Sir Keith's speech, this paper does contain various references to art — and, as always, one needs to read between the lines. As part of the preamble, there is an observation that 'the amount of time devoted to any subject relative to other subjects varies in accordance with the age and ability of the pupils and the pace of their progress (for example, infants spend relatively more time on language, number and art than older pupils; fourth and fifth year secondary pupils spend a large part of their time on subjects in which they are preparing for a 16+ examination)'.[36] What is thought to be the value of art experience for infants? Why is it apparently considered appropriate that children in this phase of schooling should spend such a high proportion of their time engaged in art? Does that engagement represent genuine learning? Or are young children loosely said to be 'doing art' simply because they happen to be using materials associated with art? And if art is thought to be so important for infants that it can vie for time with number and language, what good reasons are there for reducing so drastically the amount of time allocated to it during the secondary phase of schooling? In the examples of five secondary schools' curricular patterns appended to the paper, it seems clear that the time allocated to art *and* CDT together hardly occupies, on average, one tenth of the timetable.

The paper goes on to identify the ingredients of the primary school curriculum. As well as placing 'substantial emphasis' on language and mathematics, it should introduce pupils to science, provide 'worthwhile offerings' in history, geography and RE, offer physical and health education, introduce pupils to computers, give them some insight into the adult world, and *offer a range of aesthetic activities* (my emphasis). These 'aesthetic activities' are not specified, but they may be supposed to include music, dance, and drama as well as art. On the face of it, this hardly seems to suggest a generous allocation. The list is completed, significantly, by a *separate* item: 'opportunities throughout the curriculum for craft and practical work leading up to some experience of design and technology and of solving problems'.

Proceeding to consider the 11–16 curriculum, the paper states that:

> It is Government policy that the 11–16 curriculum for all pupils, in addition to RE, should contain English (including English literature); mathematics; science; a worthwhile offering of the humanities; aesthetic subjects; practical subjects; ... physical education; and a foreign language for most pupils ... there should be option choice for the 4th and 5th years [but not such that pupils can] undertake a programme that is insufficiently broad or balanced. These elements, together with the cross-curricular elements [such as personal qualities, desirable modes of behaviour, study skills, referred to earlier] ... would seem the minimum for a broad and balanced 11–16 curriculum.[37]

The paper then stresses the importance of sequential learning (paragraphs 13, 14); observes that aesthetic subjects, 'not being interchangeable, ought to be on offer in due variety, but need not be taken concurrently' (paragraph 23); urges that 'attention needs to be given to the application of knowledge and skills', notably to mathematics, the sciences, and the handling of computers (paragraph 24); and maintains that 'CDT is centrally the subject in which practical applications are fostered' (paragraph 25).

If sequential learning is so important — and it is — are not the arts and CDT 'circuses' (a term's painting, a term's 'wood and plastics', a term's home economics, a term's pottery — sometimes even with music and other arts in the roundabout) devised by some schools to be deplored? And whilst the paper quite rightly makes the point that 'aesthetic subjects' are not interchangeable, might not the observation that they need not be taken concurrently be seen as encouragement for the 'circus' solution? If the study of a subject 'should be sufficient to be of lasting value' (paragraph 13), should not the fragmented experiences, which are all that such a solution can offer, be replaced by a greater concentration — perhaps on a more limited range? Are knowledge and skills the prerogative of the 'hard' subjects? And *is* CDT *centrally* 'the subject in which practical applications are fostered'?

Although it was apparently not included in the circulation list, the National Society for Education in Art and Design reacted within two months to *The Organization and Content of the 5–16 Curriculum*, in a paper dated 1 November 1984. The Society welcomed the DES's call for greater continuity in the curriculum and between phases of education. It also welcomed the plea for better defined objectives in each subject, but found the term 'removal of clutter' (which seems to have originated in Sir Keith's January speech[38]) 'an unfortunate way of describing an aspect of curriculum development [when schools should aspire to] a careful, considered and on-going process which is radically different from [the implied] once and for all "attic clearance"'.[39] The Society fully accepted the view that 'the amount of time devoted to each subject during the compulsory period should be judged by the time needed to enable it to make its particular contribution to the total knowledge, understanding, skills and competence which the 5–16 curriculum is intended to foster[40] and, in doing so, emphasized that 'the growth of skills, knowledge and understanding in art, craft and design *demands regular study over a prolonged period of school life if the crucial contribution the subject should make to the total 5–16 curriculum is to be realized*'[41] (the Society's emphasis).

Where the 5–16 document's remarks on the primary phase are concerned, the Society considered it 'unhelpful to separate aesthetic activities and craft and practical work in the way implied'; and it rejected the offering of 'a range of aesthetic activities', believing it '*more important for children to have had access to aesthetic experiences of some quality, than for them to have had experience of a wide range . . .*' (again, the Society's emphasis).[42]

In connection with the document's observations on the secondary phase, the Society expressed its belief that *all* children should in years 4 and 5 continue to work in *one* of the so-called aesthetic areas, according to their abilities and aptitudes. And the Society went on to stress that art, craft and design is 'not simply an aesthetic subject but provides opportunity for the meaningful application of knowledge and skills in a number of curriculum areas including the practical area'. The suggestion that CDT is of central significance in fostering 'practical applications' ('of what?' the Society asks) is rejected; and, finally, the Society criticizes the curricular patterns of the five schools represented in the document's annex, particularly that of School 1, for which it is claimed that aesthetic and expressive subjects have a larger than normal presence. In view of the fact that in years 1 and 2 a rotational programme of only four periods (out of forty) per week contains CDT, art, pottery, and other 'traditional boys' and girls' crafts', the NSEAD's charge of 'gross exaggeration' seems well-founded.

In March, 1985, the Secretaries of State presented to Parliament their paper *Better Schools*. 'What is expected of schools', say the Secretaries, 'alters over time with changes in society and in national circumstances', and they go on to cite economic, social, demographic, and technological changes since the 1944 Education Act.[43] They proceed to refer to the qualities and skills pupils will need for work in a technological age, and to stress the need for education at school to promote enterprise and adaptability.

Of the primary and middle schools, they complain that whilst in a majority there exist guidelines for English and mathematics, such guidelines frequently do not extend to other important elements of the curriculum.[44] They challenge the belief, 'once widely held', that a concentration on the basic skills is sufficient for achievement in literacy and numeracy, and emphasize the important instrumental role of the aesthetic and other areas.[45] They criticize unduly close teacher direction, suggesting that this may inhibit opportunities for pupils to engage in solving practical problems; and they stress the need for teachers to be versatile if a 'broad curriculum pursued in depth' is to be offered. They single out science and craft as areas in which teachers may lack confidence and expertise, and find that, even when consultants have been appointed to offer colleagues guidance in such subjects, they rarely have the time, the status, or the encouragement to exert a real influence on the curriculum.

The ingredients of the primary curriculum, as set out in *Better Schools*, are closely similar to those listed in *The Organization and Content of the 5–16 Curriculum* issued six months earlier. Only one change need concern us here: the 'range of aesthetic activities' has become a 'range of activities in the arts'. Is the change of wording significant? Does it denote new thinking? Or is it simply further evidence of vagueness concerning the precise contribution of art — of the arts — to the curriculum? One thing is certain: though 'the aesthetic' and 'the arts' may overlap, they are not, as we have seen, interchangeable terms. Again, as in *The Organization and Content of the 5–16 Curriculum*, craft, practical work, design, technology, and problem-solving appear in a separate item;

and, again, one is puzzled by the implication that art does not involve all of these experiences.[46]

Once more, there is a welcome emphasis on the transition from the primary to the secondary phase: 'the 5–16 curriculum needs to be constructed and delivered as a continuous and coherent whole, in which the primary phase prepares for the secondary phase, and the latter builds on the former'.[47]

The 11–16 curriculum, like that for the primary phase, is largely a restatement of that set out in *The Organization and Content of the 5–16 Curriculum*. During the first three years of secondary schooling, say the Secretaries, the curriculum should be largely common to all pupils. 'Aesthetic subjects, where all pupils should study ... music, art and drama on a worthwhile scale; and ... practical subjects [which the foregoing presumably are not?], where all pupils should be introduced to design [which presumably has a meaning distinct from that brand of design which is necessarily entailed in art and in craft?] and work in a range of materials in the subject areas of CDT and home economics'.[48]

Going on to discuss the complexities of 4th and 5th year options, the Secretaries of State argue for a balance between catering for pupils' special interests and aptitudes and retaining breadth and balance. To achieve the latter, pupils should (among other specified fields) 'study elements drawn both from the humanities and the arts; and should take part in practical and technological work in a number of subjects, for example in CDT and not least in science'. As we have seen, the National Society for Education in Art and Design has pressed for concentration and continuity; 'elements drawn ... from the arts' seems to hint at a kind of breadth conducive to dilution.[49]

One passage on Teaching Quality deals with 'the practical dimension within the curriculum',[50] and this seems both to contradict and to be much more sensible than the earlier listing of curriculum ingredients (in, for example, para. 67), according to which 'aesthetic subjects' and 'practical subjects' are separable. The treatment of the practical as a *dimension*, the acknowledgement that this dimension is of significance *across* the curriculum, needs to be consistently argued if the false separations so often referred to in this chapter are to be discouraged.

Also in 1985 there appeared *The Curriculum from 5 to 16*, the second booklet in an HMI series called *Curriculum Matters*. The series was prompted by the Secretary of State's 1984 Sheffield speech and so far, in addition to the item in question, it includes publications on English, mathematics, music, home economics, health education, and geography. Sadly, there is as yet nothing on art, craft, and design.

The Curriculum from 5 to 16 is organized under three main headings: areas of learning and experience; elements of learning; and characteristics of the curriculum.

Under the first heading, the notion of curricular 'dimensions' is pursued. The 'aesthetic and creative' is given as one of these areas; and the idea that these areas are considered, rather, as dimensions is reinforced by the fact that they are 'not suggested as discrete elements to be taught separately and in isolation from one another ... nor are they equated with particular subjects (for example, pupils may gain scientific or mathematical experience from art, and aesthetic experience from mathematics)'.[51] Later it is pointed out, quite rightly, that 'aesthetic and creative experience may occur in any part of the curriculum, but [that] some subjects contribute particularly ... because they call for personal, imaginative, affective and often practical, responses to sensory experience'.[52] The only quibble one might have with this otherwise clear and helpful statement is that the opportunity to emphasize the role of the *cognitive* in such subjects has apparently been overlooked.[53] HMI go on to stress (as did the compilers of the Gulbenkian Report) that in arts education participation and appreciation are interrelated strands;[54] that there is an important 'relationship between aesthetics and fitness for purpose in design';[55] and that '[the arts] can [through discussion] enable pupils to develop an understanding of people and events in different historical and cultural contexts, and of people and places in different geographical circumstances'.[56] There has in the field of art, craft, and design education been a growing realization over the last few years that historical and critical studies are a vital component, hitherto neglected in general education. Such studies receive further mention in *The Curriculum from 5–16*, in a list of skills, one group of which is headed 'creative and imaginative' and which includes the capacity 'to envisage life at other times [and] as it may appear to other people'.[57]

The national project 'Critical Studies in Schools' has already been mentioned. In 1986 Rod Taylor, the project's director, published his report in the form of a book entitled *Educating for Art*.[58] This represents perhaps the most encouraging and convincing argument ever produced for the importance of historical and critical studies as an organic part of every child's art education. It is full of eloquent substantiation of the case for a fusion of participation and appreciation. It may also serve as an example of many other recent initiatives and developments in art, craft, and design education and in the arts in general.[59] For a detailed account of these, the reader can do no better than refer to John Steers' article, 'Current Issues in Art and Design Education: Resistance and the Freedom to Fly'. Steers concludes his article thus: 'In the United Kingdom we may or may not have the best art education system in the world, but it certainly appears to me that we are fortunate in that art, craft and design are more firmly established in the general curriculum than any other place of which I am aware';[60] and he writes from the vantage point of his General Secretaryship of the National Society for Education in Art and Design.

When on 9 January 1987 Kenneth Baker, Secretary of State for Education and Science, spoke at the North of England Conference in

Rotherham he urged a move towards a national curriculum based on national criteria for each subject area. He insisted that such criteria 'must be arrived at by a national process. They cannot just reflect what the government thinks best, or what the LEAs or the teachers think best, or what the customers — parents, and industry in particular — think best. They must be hammered out jointly....'.[61] Indeed, they must. But the voice of Richelieu has its persistent echo. A national curriculum seems to me sensible and inevitable — but it must provide a true education. *Is* industry the *most* important customer? Will we see in a national curriculum a still more pronounced shift towards the 'hard' disciplines? Is there a danger that, through the pressure of utilitarian concerns we will see what Peter Abbs has termed 'The poisoning of the Socratic ideal'[62] in education? Abbs has written:

> ... to entertain the Socratic notion of teaching is, in part, to free ourselves from the crippling assumption that the first task of teachers is to serve the economy, to turn out skilled robots and uncritical consumers for the 'hi-tech' age... The first principle of Socratic education is that it cannot be simply transferred. Education is not an object (a mass of knowledge or information or skills) which can be unambiguously handed from the teacher to the student. Education is ... an activity of mind, a particular emotional and critical orientation towards experience

And, lest it should be thought that Abbs falls into the elementary trap of simply defending 'soft' against 'hard' subjects:

> The principle of Socrates has, of course, in one way or another, informed the best innovations in the curriculum in our century: Nuffield science, investigative mathematics, contemporary drama.

He claims that:

> The 'debate on education' inaugurated by Mr Callaghan and developed so disastrously by Sir Keith Joseph was never an open debate, nor was it ever about education. It was about training, industry, skills, organization, management... The first priority of teachers should be to secure the necessary conditions for the autonomy of teaching and for the freedom to learn.

The Secretary of State tells us that the criteria for a national curriculum must be hammered out jointly. Let us hope that the voices of all interested parties are taken into impartial account — that, for instance, HMI as well as politicians, educationalists as well as industrialists, will collaborate on equal terms.

But is there a relentless parting of the ways in the field of art, craft, and design? The Secretary of State's further statement (of 7 April, 1987) on the national curriculum more than hints at this, when he says:

We want to ensure that pupils have a well-balanced foundation curriculum ... which during the compulsory period includes not only maths and English, but also science, foreign languages, history, geography and technology in its various aspects. *Time should be found for music, art and physical education* ... (my italics).[63]

An afterthought, Mr. Baker? (Surely, even the Secretary of State must fear the consquences of a curriculum impoverished by the banishment of art to its periphery?)

Acknowledgement

I should like to thank my colleague Roy Prentice for reading the draft of this chapter and making valuable observations which helped me improve it.

Notes

1. That the myth still endures is demonstrated by a caption in the *Times Educational Supplement*, 8 May 1987. It refers to the reproduction of a naive early nineteenth-century painting which is alleged to 'demonstrate in many delightful ways how freely the imagination can soar when unencumbered by an academic training'.
2. In the *Times Educational Supplement*, 26 February 1982.
3. In the *Times Educational Supplement*, 16 November 1984.
4. HUDSON, L. (1966) *Contrary Imaginations*, Methuen.
5. GOMBRICH, E.H. (1979) *Ideals and Idols*, Phaidon, pp. 167–83.
6. EISNER, E. (1972) *Educating Artistic Vision*, Macmillan, pp. 177–8.
7. In *The Spectator*, 31 December 1977.
8. Not until 1855 did the Royal Academy relent, for in that year Samuel Cousins became the first engraver to be admitted to full membership.
9. For material in this and the previous two paragraphs I am indebted to Dr. Clive Ashwin's excellent unpublished paper 'Art, Craft and Design: a Historical Perspective', March 1976.
10. STEERS, J. (1987) 'Current Issues in Art and Design Education: Resistance and the Freedom to Fly', *Journal of Art and Design Education*, Vol. 6, No. 1, p. 16.
11. ASSESSMENT OF PERFORMANCE UNIT (1983), *Aesthetic Development*, DES, September.
12. *Ibid.*, p. 1, 2.2
13. *Ibid.*, p. 1, 2.3
14. *Ibid.*, p. 2, 2.4
15. *Ibid.*, p. 3, 3.3
16. RAE, J. (1978) 'Richelieu at our elbows', *Times Educational Supplement*, 23 March.
17. Published by the Institute of Education.
18. WHITE, J. *et al.* (1981) *No Minister: A Critique of the DES Paper, 'The School Curriculum'*, Bedford Way Papers No. 4, University of London Institute of Education.
19. *Ibid.*, p. 40.
20. *Ibid.*, p. 44.

21. *Ibid.*, p. 48.
22. STEERS, J. (1987) *op. cit.*
23. Strictly speaking, the organization was still at this time the National Society for Art Education. Subsequently it amalgamated with the Society for Education Through Art, to become the National Society for Education in Art and Design (NSEAD).
24. GULBENKIAN FOUNDATION ADVISORY COMMITTEE (1982) *The Arts in Schools*, p. 3.
25. *Ibid.*, pp. 10–12.
26. STEERS, J. (1983) 'The Structure and Content of Art Teaching in the Secondary School', *Journal of Art and Design Education*, Vol. 2, No. 1, p. 62.
27. SIR KEITH JOSEPH (1984) North of England Conference Speech, para. 16.
28. *Ibid.*, para. 18.
29. *Ibid.*, para. 21.
30. *Ibid.*, para. 24.
31. Still, at that time, the National Society for Art Education (NSAE) (see note 23, above).
32. *Journal of Art and Design Education*, Vol. 3, No. 3, 1984, pp. 357–60.
33. NSAED Standing Committee Discussion Paper (1984) *Journal of Art and Design Education*, Vol. 3, No. 3, para. 1.
34. *Ibid.*, para 7.
35. Though it is also pointed out that 'pupils' timetables need not be structured . . . by reference to subjects'.
36. DEPARTMENT OF EDUCATION AND SCIENCE (1984) *Organisation and Content of the 5–16 Curriculum* DES/Welsh Office, HMSO, section 4.
37. *Ibid.*, para. 11.
38. SIR KEITH JOSEPH (1984) North of England Conference Speech, 6 January, para. 22.
39. *Ibid.*, para. 3(d).
40. DEPARTMENT OF EDUCATION AND SCIENCE, *5–16 Curriculum*, London, HMSO, para. 7.
41. NSAED (1984) *op. cit.* para. 7.
42. *Ibid.*, para. 8.
43. DEPARTMENT OF EDUCATION AND SCIENCE (1985) *Better Schools* London, HMSO para. 3.
44. *Ibid.*, para. 17.
45. *Ibid.*, para. 18.
46. *Ibid.*, para. 61.
47. *Ibid.*, para. 65.
48. *Ibid.*, para. 67.
49. *Ibid.*, para. 69.
50. *Ibid.*, para. 137.
51. HER MAJESTY'S INSPECTORATE (1985) *The Curriculum 5–16* London, HMSO para. 33.
52. *Ibid.*, para. 36.
53. Louis Arnaud Reid has devoted much of his life's work to exploring the relationship of the cognitive and the affective. See, eg., his *Ways of Understanding and Education*, University of London Institute of Education/Heinemann, 1986, pp. 38–49.
54. HER MAJESTY'S INSPECTORATE (1985) *op. cit.* para. 37.
55. *Ibid.*, para. 38.
56. *Ibid.*, para. 41.
57. *Ibid.*, para. 100.
58. TAYLOR, R. (1986) *Educating for Art* London, Longman.

59. For example, the Arts in Schools project, funded for three years by the School Curriculum Development Committee. At the time of writing, the Project is half way through its three-year course.
60. STEERS, J. (1987) *op. cit.* p. 25.
61. KENNETH BAKER (1987) North of England Conference Speech. 9 January, para. 31.
62. In *The Guardian* 13 January 1986.
63. KENNETH BAKER (1987) North of England Conference Speech. 9 January, para. 9.

13   Science

John Nellist

Rumour has it that on the day of his marriage to a famous actress, husband number four was heard to remark, 'I know what's expected of me but I'm not sure how to make it interesting'. Writing about the science component of the school curriculum presents a similar dilemma. Not that the learning and teaching of science or the philosophy underlying its curriculum presence are of themselves lacking in interest and intrigue but more because so much articulate and well argued writing has already been done.

Science is, to date, the only curriculum area supported by a Department of Education and Science Policy Statement. It has, again uniquely, been the subject of a major centrally funded investigation 'The Secondary Science Curriculum Review'. The publications of this enterprise alone are a rich source of science education lore and practice. It is no accident that the Association for Science Education — defined in its own terms as the major professional association in the United Kingdom for science teachers in schools and colleges and others concerned with science education — is the doyen of the subject teaching associations. ASE publishing output, through its official journals (*School Science Review*, *Primary Science Review* and *Education in Science*) and through a wide range of papers and books, is prodigious.

In short, there can be few, if any, of the conventional school subject areas so well researched, documented, defended and defined; the literature base is rich and extensive. What more can be written? Against this background any thoroughgoing run at the whole field risks superficiality and drift to catalogue and list. This chapter, then, will look particularly to trends and tensions within the science education context; 'best guesses' as to how science might contribute to, and shape, the emerging curriculum orthodoxy and the problems and challenges thereby raised. The business of education, like incidentally the practice of science, is a political and value laden activity. The views and stances taken here reflect therefore a personal sense of the important — my values and my politics. The coverage is partial, in both senses of that word.

A further challenge to any writer in the educational field is coping with the rate of change; the shifting goalposts, the moving target. A first draft of this chapter has rapidly been overtaken by the Secretary of State's consultation document on the National Curriculum 5–16. Science, like mathematics and English, is now firmly enshrined in 'the core', the heart of the curriculum. 'Should we teach science to all?' is no longer for debate. Science, like dark Irish stout, is good for you. The National Curriculum is but one shift, albeit a significant one, in the maelstrom of change currently assaulting schools, colleges and local education authorities. Writing against this background with any sense of conviction and permanence of view looks a daunting business. Will the ink be dry before the next major initiative hits press, public and the professionals?

What is established, beyond reasonable doubt, is that 'science for all from 5–16' has acquired political clout and credibility. There is even an emerging consensus about the nature of that science, though practice and conviction at individual teacher and school level remain widely varied. What follows explores some of the motivations, driving forces and rationale behind this promotion of science as a basic entitlement in the educational provision for all young people.

Why Teach Science and Why Teach Science to All?

In the *ASE Science Teachers' Handbook* (Nellist and Nichol (Eds), 1986), Milner in a chapter under just this heading offers the following:

> If we are to justify including science within formal education we need to show:
> 1   that science contributes distinctive skills, concepts and perspectives, i.e. different from those afforded by other areas of experience or forms of knowledge;
> 2   that the acquisition of these distinctly scientific skills, concepts and perspectives is greatly facilitated by structured formal education;
> 3   that it is important for children to acquire the skills, concepts and perspectives of science.

He then goes on to summarize his discussion in Table 1:
It is worth dealing with some of these justifications in a little more detail from three standpoints: student, teacher and the wider society. The overlaps between the separate strands are acknowledged.

Science for the Student

Milner uses the phrase 'to cope more adequately with everyday life in a society permeated by technology', the 'capability' argument. Science

Table 1.

Science for interest (intrinsic justification)	Science for use (instrumental justification)
1. As with any other form of human activity, many people find the distinctive subject matter of science(s), the patterns and relationships which develop and the scientific processes interesting and rewarding. Everyone should have the opportunity to engage in the activity to a sufficient extent to appreciate what it has to offer and to be able to continue with it if they so choose.	2. Both scientific knowledge and science processes enable individuals: (a) to cope more adequately with everyday life in a society permeated by technology, e.g. to make/develop/use/maintain bodies/homes/gardens/devices for basic needs/income/leisure; (b) to make a positive contribution to that society as workers and as citizens having an informed opinion on, for example, matters of environmental importance.

1 and 2 justify the provision of a broad, basic science education for everyone.

3. Those finding particular areas of science especially interesting should be allowed to develop their interests as far as resources allow. Maintaining and developing the activity of science as an area of potential interest (and utility) is of benefit to society also.	4. More advanced and/or specialized studies of science (and/or its applications) for specific purposes are of benefit to individuals, in terms of employment, and to society, which needs scientists, technologists and technicians (whether we subscribe to a future of high technology or of alternative technology).

3 and 4 justify the provision of more advanced or specialized science education for those who want or need it.

educators, and others, rightly feel that young people do need some basic acquaintance with the knowledge and concept base of science in order properly to function as autonomous individuals in today's world. We maintain, too, that the process dimension, i.e. science as a way of working, of looking at the world, offers skills and patterns of thinking which can be used in the solution of everyday problems. This latter rationale is not without its critics. How many of us do solve problems following the classic analytical problem solving cycle? We are it seems as, if not more, likely, to leap to the intuitive, the well aimed kick at the offending part. But, as persuasively argued in *Zen and the Art of Motorcycle Maintenance*, when all else fails the 'scientific method' does have its strengths and ought to be part of the intellectual armoury of the educated individual.

Another side of the capability coin, seen increasingly as important, is the 'science for citizenship' dimension — Milner uses the term 'informed opinion'. There is a real sense in which this aspect of science education has been sadly neglected in years gone by. The scientific and technological have induced mistrust, suspicion and even fear in 'the man on the Clapham omnibus'. This lack of security and confidence is recognized as counterproductive and disabling. On the one hand it exposes the individual and hence society at large to exploitation and manipulation by the politically or commercially motivated. On the other, scientifically ill-founded views may provoke real obstacles to legitimate and beneficial technological development, or contrarily allow, ecologically or otherwise, damaging advances. It is no accident that both the Royal Society and many major industrial concerns see this 'public understanding of science' as a major issue worth intervention and resource.

So for the student, then, there has been over the past few years a shift, sometimes significant, in the balance of their science diet. Textbooks and specific courses do seek increasingly to inject elements of the applied and the technological; 'real world science'; more of science the useful and less 'science the beautiful'. Attempts, too, have been and are made to build in social and economic dimensions. 'Science in Society', 'Science in a Social Context' (SISCON) and 'Science and Technology in Society' (SATIS) are examples of courses, published within the last few years, which seek deliberately to engage the student in more than the acquisition of scientific knowledge and concept.

Needless to say the impact of such new curriculum input is not easy yet to assess in output terms. Schools and teachers have embraced the philosophy to the usual varying degrees but there can be little doubt that the call for 'relevance' is unlikely to go away. Enshrinement in the GCSE criteria (and in sharp assessment terms) for the science subjects will ensure a continuation of the shift in focus and emphasis.

The Teacher's View

Few teachers of science would take issue with Milner's 'justifications', whether intrinsic or instrumental. They may not all regard them as complete but few would make significant deletions. What many of the experienced and long serving would recognize is the shifts in balance noted in the previous paragraphs, i.e. more emphasis on the processes of science, more emphasis on science in the real world context, and less on straight 'knowledge acquisition'. By and large, teachers have accepted and looked to adjust to changes in approach. That there have been 'external' motivations, new schemes, new texts, new examinations, is undeniable (witness, for example, the impact of the Nuffield schemes in the 1960s) but they have, too, recognized the educational force of the arguments. Predominantly content centred science is not an appropriate diet for young people facing today's world. Knowledge dates ever more rapidly; the process case is telling. Equally youngsters expect to see the utility and application of school based work; the potential for enhancing student set and motivation in more relevant science studies has also assisted teacher acceptance of changes in approach and emphasis.

The Wider Perspective

The 'public understanding' issue has already been touched upon, but Milner offers, too, the employment needs of the individual and the needs of society for 'scientists, technologists and technicians'. There is no doubt that both are important drivers in establishing the current primacy of science within the curriculum frame. Parents and students recognize the 'cash in' value of science based qualifications. Governments see the science based industries as the key economic driver and their requirement of skilled and trained manpower as a key component in the scheme of things. It is difficult to overstate this argument in the present climate.

A further consideration, not given explicit mention by Milner and sitting less easily in student, teacher or society perspective, looks to science as a part of common heritage and culture. Access to this heritage ought to be for all. We are, and should be, about defining a 'new classics'. C.P. Snow's 'Two Cultures' has been, and still is, reality — the most trivial research of media pronouncements and output, radio, television or print derived, demonstrates this beyond question. Inaccuracy and misconception in scientific matters abound, terminology is ill-used and coverage in air-time or print terms is limited though, admittedly, growing. Science is a part, and a significant part, of our cultural fabric and an understanding of its imperatives, ways of working and relationship to other areas of knowledge ought properly to be open to all.

In summary then, science has an increasingly secure place in the curriculum of our schools — from 5–16. The Secretary of State decrees it so. But there are two important educational justifications for this privileged and high status position. Education in and through science can be defended and promoted on philosophical and cultural or practical and utilitarian grounds. The shift from knowledge acquisition to broader agendas has been touched upon. This next section looks to deal in somewhat greater detail with the substance of science education as she is and as she might be practised at school level.

What Science Should We Teach?

The National Curriculum Working Party is faced with the unenviable task of advising on 'the knowledge, skills, understanding and aptitudes which pupils should be expected to have acquired at specific ages, taking account of differences in ability ... and on the essential content which should be covered to enable pupils to reach agreed attainment targets'. (DES Press Release, 10 July 1987). We will have the answers, but in the meantime what have we to go on?

ASE, HMI and the Secondary Science Curriculum Review have all made their respective bids into the aims/intentions/content argument, and the degree of consensus is striking. 'For all from 5–16' as noted earlier is beyond debate, as is the 'broad and balanced' notion. All have made authoritative statements about purposes and content. The following are given as samples, both to capture flavour and to give some sense of the consensus and congruence between the different sources. Paragraphs 26 and 27 of *Science Education 5–16: A Statement of Policy* (DES, 1985) run as follows:

> HMI's paper *Science in Primary Schools* (DES, 1982) sets out the following broad criteria for the selection of content:
> (a) the content should, wherever possible, be related to the experiences of the children;
> (b) it should, in accordance with their stages of development, provide them with knowledge and understanding of scientific ideas to help them to understand their own physical and biological environments and to understand themselves;
> (c) it should, where possible, lay the foundations for a progressively deepening knowledge and understanding of scientific concepts and facts that will be useful to them as citizens;
> (d) it should include examples of the application of science to real-life problems, including those of technology.
>
> *Science in Primary Schools* suggests that aspects of science that children should meet in the primary school should include the study of:
> (a) living things and their interaction with the environment;
> (b) materials and their characteristics;
> (c) energy and materials;
> (d) forces and their effects.
>
> The Secretaries of State commend these suggestions on criteria for the selection of content, and on aspects to be covered, as a starting point for the definition by LEAs and schools of the content of science education in primary schools.

ASE in their Policy Statement *Education Through Science* (ASE, 1981) offer the following:

> Education through science should enable the individual by the end of his or her period of compulsory education to have engaged in a study of science which has embodied all the following aims to an appropriate extent.
> (a) The acquisition of a knowledge and understanding of a range

of scientific concepts, generalizations, principles and laws through the systematic study and experience of aspects of the body of knowledge called science.

(b)   The acquisition of a range of cognitive and psycho-motor skills and processes as a result of direct involvement in scientific activities and procedures in the laboratory and the field.

(c)   The utilization of scientific knowledge and processes in the pursuit of further knowledge and deeper understanding, and the development of an ability to function autonomously in an area of science studies to solve practical problems and to communicate that experience to others.

(d)   The attainment of a perspective or way of looking at the world together with some understanding of how it complements and contrasts with other perspectives or ways of organizing knowledge and inquiry.

(e)   The attainment of a basic understanding of the nature of advanced technological societies, the interaction between science and society, and the contribution science makes to our cultural heritage.

(f)   The realization that scientific knowledge and experience is of some value in the process of establishing a sense of personal and social identity.

ASE's view of the world finds strong echoes in the Secondary Science Curriculum Review paper *Science Education 11–16: Proposals for Action and Consultation* (SSCR, 1983):

... to provide, at appropriate stages of a five year programme, adequate opportunities for all students to

(a)   explore the nature of the biological and physical environment through observation, experiment and systematic inquiry;
develop the ability to design and carry out experiments, evaluate evidence and solve problems;
study the key concepts and principles of science that are essential to an understanding of science as a way of looking at the world;
study those aspects of science that are essential to an understanding of oneself, and of one's personal well being;

(b)   use their knowledge of science to design and develop solutions to technological problems, to test and evaluate those solutions and to cost such exercises;
study the key areas of science and technology that relate to the world of work and leisure so that they are better able to participate in a democratic society;
study key concepts that are essential to an understanding of the part science and technology play in a post-industrial and technological society;

279

    (c)   gain some understanding of the historical development and contemporary cultural significance of scientific principles and theories;

           appreciate that technologies are expressions of the desire to understand and control the environment and that technologies change in response to changing social needs;

           appreciate that past scientific explanations were valid in their time and that early technologies are still valid in some cultural contexts;

    (d)   discuss, reflect upon and evaluate their own personal understanding of key scientific concepts, theories and generalizations;

           explore topics or themes which exemplify the limitations of scientific knowledge as an explanation of the human condition.

In broad terms, then, the level of agreement about frameworks for science education between those sources which might properly be regarded as authoritative is high. It is worth noting, too, that the expectations noted earlier about shifting the balance from content acquisition to the development of skills, attitudes, the personal growth of the individual and the setting of science in a wider context are all evident in these statements. None of this is to deny the importance of establishing an appropriate content base for the subject; skills, processes and so on cannot be taught in a content vacuum. Again, lists are plentiful and a useful summary can be found in *ASE Science Teachers' Handbook* (Nellist and Nichol (Eds) 1986). The Secondary Science Curriculum Review, through its publication *Towards the Specification of Minimum Entitlement: Brenda and Friends* (SSCR, 1984), took an interesting, even controversial, line in developing its notions via a series of student biographies, each designed to illustrate the acquisition over time of the concepts/knowledge associated with a particular content area. As recorded earlier, content, particularly in the science and technology domain, does date and date rapidly; tight definitions can then be counterproductive. The phenomenon of the 'steam engine' or 'sabre toothed tiger' curriculum has received frequent critical commentary. Protagonists in the information technology field bewail the irrelevance to real world practice of much that is currently taught. A number of sources look then not just to list content but to establish criteria against which content might be selected. Again the Secondary Science Curriculum Review sampled the field and record their findings in *Better Science: Choosing Content* (Watts and Michell, 1987). The authors settle for their own checklist as follows:

    1   The content included should maximize the possibility of teaching the processes, skills and attitudes important to science, and increase the competence and capability of pupils.

2 It must be able to be taught to, and owned by, all pupils.
3 The content should have some relevance and applicability. It must need to be known and be transferable to a range of contexts during and after school.
4 The content must appeal to both male and female students, and to students of differing cultures.
5 Science content should be consistent with a broad and balanced science curriculum.
6 The necessary teaching strategies and resources must exist to teach it.
7 It must provide a basis for further study.
8 It must take into account local circumstances.

In summary, there is then considerable agreement within what might be thought of as the science education establishment about the framework of the science curriculum; its aims, purposes, contexts and content. That there is such agreement is not surprising. The community of science educators has a tradition of communication and co-operative working and key individuals and influences spread across organizational and constituency boundaries. DES/HMI, LEA Advisers, Department of Education Tutors, ASE and so on do talk. There is a real sense in which the current science curriculum policy as recorded in *Science 5–16: A Statement of Policy* reflects and represents a consensus view drawn from a remarkably broad church. There are, naturally enough, tensions and challenges. This next section seeks to explore some of these issues and how policies and aspirations are making an impact on schools and the wider community.

Science in Primary Schools

If we are in the business of recording curriculum progress, then the penetration of the primary curriculum by a science element can be counted as success. The beginnings were not promising. HMI in their 1979 survey of primary schools *Primary Education in England* (HMI, 1979b) recorded, inter alia, the following:

1 Only a small minority of headteachers recognize the important contribution which science can make to children's intellectual development.
2 Children's interests are being used as starting points for work in science but the potential of such work is seldom exploited.
3 In very few classes are opportunities taken to teach how to make careful observations or to plan and carry out investigations of a scientific nature.
4 Work in observational and experimental science is less well matched to children's capabilities than work in any other curricular area.

5   Teaching of processes and skills such as observing, formulation of hypotheses, experimenting and recording is often superficial.
6   Insufficient attention is paid to ensuring proper coverage of key scientific notions.
7   Few schools have effective programmes for the teaching of science.
8   The degree to which programmes of work in science have been thought out varies considerably from school to school.
9   Science is attempted in a majority of classes but the work is developed seriously in just over 10 per cent.
10 The attention given to science does not vary greatly with the age of the children.

This woeful picture was not painted against a background of previous inertia and inactivity; rather the reverse. Curriculum development activity on a national scale had been high. Nuffield Junior Science, a scheme which, with the benefit of hindsight, was 'before its time', had stimulated real interest but within restricted quarters. The seminal Schools Council project 'Science 5/13' had produced a wealth of publications, rich in ideas and enterprise. In many LEAs individual science advisers and institutes of higher education had supported local developments and in-service work. Yet somehow, the fix, on HMI evidence, had not taken; what was the source of the system's immunity and how might a remedy be sought?

As ever, there was, and is, no single inhibiting factor. But, two were certainly significant: a shortfall in headteacher conviction and commitment and a lack of teacher confidence. This latter is scarcely surprising and echoes back to earlier commentary in this chapter. Science is seen as threatening and difficult. Few teachers in primary school had happy memories of their own education in science and few felt adequately qualified, formally or informally, to deal in this, as they saw it, highly specialist arena.

The years between the publication of HMI's survey have seen a sea-change. The tide has turned and again on authoritative evidence science is making significant inroads into the primary curriculum. It is worth a brief analysis of some of the factors promoting this shift, not least since there may be messages for curriculum progress and development in other fields.

The following, not presented in any hierarchical order, would seem to have been instrumental in bringing about change:

1   science as a core component of the primary curriculum has been formally blessed, even evangelically promoted, by central government through policy statements and other pub-

lications (see *Science in Primary Schools*, a discussion paper produced by the HMI Science Committee, HMSO, 1984, for example);

2   local education authorities have, through their own policy statements, provided an echoing endorsement and encouragement;

3   headteachers, partly at least in response to (1) and (2), have accepted and some actively embraced science as a key curriculum component. (There are now few, if any, headteachers, no matter what real practice is, who would declare openly a 'no science in my school' policy);

4   substantial and well directed in-service programmes have been developed and delivered to support and enable teachers to improve skills knowledge and, above all, to gain security and confidence in the field. The emergence of the school based science co-ordinators, teachers taking on a subject leadership and support role, has been a particularly significant outcome of these INSET activities;

5   the publication locally and nationally of a growing range of books and curriculum materials, some of which are now pupil directed (the teacher resource has been considerable for some years);

6   the deployment under LEA or central funded Education Support Grant (ESG) schemes of advisory teachers, working directly in schools offering both theoretical support in developing school policies and practical expertise at classroom level;

7   the injection of 'other resources', equipment, materials, technical expertise and so on either directly into individual schools or via science centres and curriculum support services;

8   the development of existing or new support networks. ASE, for example, now has some 4000 members in schools 'deemed primary', an advisory teachers' network exists under ASE auspices and many LEAs have local groups meeting regularly, exchanging ideas and preoccupations;

9   the establishment of a national programme of evaluation and dissemination for the ESG Primary Programme ('Initiatives in Primary Science: An Evaluation Project' (IPSE));

10   agreement amongst the active practitioners as to what science in the primary school means and how it might best be delivered;

11   the teaching and time requirements of the above model are a good fit to the organizational structure of the primary school.

The last three of these factors for change are worth some further mention.

The Initiatives in Primary Science: An Evaluation (IPSE) Project, now entering its third and final year, commissioned by the DES, has the task of evaluating the developments and outcomes of the substantial ESG programme designed to promote science in the primary school. That there will be a summative element to its work will be evident; the 'value for money' accountability issue is clearly high on the Department's agenda. Nonetheless, the IPSE team, through their work and interim reports, have contrived a deal of evaluative work with a strong formative element. Key messages about effective practice, notably in the crucial areas of management and organization, have been transmitted to participating LEAs. Newcomers to the scheme are able to learn from the experience of earlier entrants and the team have proved to be an important 'clearing house' for practical and soundly based advice. They have, too, successfully raised the profile of advisory teachers in the field and promoted links across LEA boundaries. The lesson here would seem to be that a centrally funded, and in this case small, team, not charged with development but with evaluation and the dissemination of good practice, can be both sustainer of, and catalyst for, effective change.

In a different sense the commonly held philosophical frame noted at (10) above is also significant. Experienced and committed teachers of science as part of the primary curriculum are, by and large, agreed on what they are about. They have a common language. Science for them is pupil centred and activity based. They see science not for its own sake but as an extension of development or even a mirror of 'good primary practice'. The summary derived by the IPSE team captures the flavour of the shared framework (see Figure 1).

A practical outcome of this consensus of purpose and view is that the science v technology tension referred to later in this chapter is much less of an issue in the primary phase. Primary teachers are not forced into debate and decision about definitions and curriculum territory. On their model science and technology are inextricably linked via activity, process and pupil interest. They are part of a coherent whole. Energy and enterprise can thus be reserved for devising strategies, teaching tactics and curriculum materials consistent with this view. There is little dissipation of effort in boundary defining and territory marking.

The organizational issue noted at (11) is, too, not without significance. The generally open structure of the primary school day and the largely class-teacher based curriculum both lend themselves to topic and project work. Taking on the 'open-ended' investigation is logistically feasible and many teachers in primary schools see individual and small group work as an essential component of their stock in trade. There is, then, a good fit between the requirements of the 'primary science' philosophy and the way in which primary schools deploy both time and staff.

The positive and optimistic frame within which the foregoing is set

Figure 1.

Good/Encouraging Signs of Primary Science Practice (IPSE)

1. Many features of good primary practice are linked to children's science activities.
2. All science involves 'hands on' experience.

Classroom (*children's learning*)	Teacher (*children's experience*)	School (*teacher's experience*)
LEVEL 1 Children enjoying themselves. Children showing curiosity, perseverance and self-discipline. Children able to relate their work to other work, and to everyday experience.	Teacher provides a variety of stimuli and resources for science work. Teacher ensures that equal provision is made for boys and girls, and encourages equal uptake of opportunities by boys and girls.	Headteacher is committed to science as an investigational activity, and makes this commitment and her/his expectations clear to the staff.
LEVEL 2 Children discussing their work with each other and with the teacher, and actively encouraged in this by the teacher.	Teacher encourages discussion and cooperation between children. Teacher accepts that a certain amount of noise, mess, and movement is inevitable in productive science lessons.	Headteacher ensures that suitable resources are provided, and teachers have ready access to these resources and use them.
LEVEL 3 Children undertaking investigational work that is genuine, to the extent that they do not know what the 'answer' will be, even if the teacher does. Where such investigations arise from the children's own interests this would be a further indication of good practice.	Teacher asks questions which draw out connections and lead on to further investigations. Teacher uses a variety of appropriate classroom organizational strategies, depending on the task in hand (e.g. class teaching, group work, work as individuals or in pairs, demonstrations, discussions, workcards, etc.).	Staff hold curriculum development meetings about (or including) science.

285

Figure 1 (cont'd)

LEVEL 4 Children making predictions about the results that they will obtain. Children observing systematically, recording their observations, and looking for patterns. Children drawing conclusions from their observations. Children using appropriate measuring instruments accurately, and choosing a suitable instrument for themselves.	Teacher questions children and discusses their work in a way that helps to relate findings to previous experience in science and in everyday life.	Teacher forecasts or records include work done in science, and show the balance outlined above. Teacher has access to records which show previous work done by children.
LEVEL 5 Children performing and planning experiments in a way that shows understanding of the concept of a 'fair test'. This probably can only be observed properly by talking to the children about what they are doing. Children taking responsibility for devising aspects of investigations themselves, leading on with more experienced children to designing and planning the whole of an experiment.	Teacher encourages children to devise their own investigations and places responsibility for all aspects of experiment design on the children. Teacher questions children in an open-ended way, encouraging them to formulate their own hypotheses, and to devise their own tests for these hypotheses. Teacher promotes and helps refine the idea of 'fair testing' (however it might be referred to) and encourages children to devise experiments with this in mind. Teacher is accepting of, and responsive to, children's own ideas, and does not unswervingly pursue some preconceived plan.	The head facilitates the work of the science coordinator, or, if such a person does not exist, fulfils the role her/himself.

LEVEL 6
Children handling unexpected results by checking, and repeating measurements. *Then*, if results are confirmed, trying to account for them and possibly devising new investigations to confirm their speculations.

Teacher treats unexpected results as a promising source of further investigations, rather than as a 'mistake', and encourages children to do the same.

The head encourages staff to undertake suitable INSET in science, and facilitates this, and there is appropriate uptake of available INSET by staff.

LEVEL 7
Children taking their learning on a stage by looking for further investigations that lead on from their results.

Teacher expectations of children are matched to their age and ability. Teacher ensures a balance over time between physical science and natural science content, and between technological/problem-solving and experimental/exploratory approaches. A further positive indication would be the balance over time between the content areas mentioned in the DES/WO policy document (paragraph 27): living things and their interaction with the environment; materials and their characteristics; energy and materials; forces and their effects.

There is (or is developing) a school policy for science which can aid continuity, and which fulfils the requirements of the DES policy document *Science 5–16* (paragraphs 27–29).

The IPSE team can be contacted
c/o ICI, PO Box 6, Bessemer Road,
Welwyn Garden City, Herts AL7 1HD.

Source: Initiatives in Primary Science: An Evaluation, Project Team (1987) *Primary Science Review* No. 4.

has substance. There are signs of change and growth but critical issues for further development remain. The integration of science within the primary curriculum is in no sense complete. Many teachers and schools remain relatively untouched in terms of their perceptions and practice; insecurities and shortfalls in competence and confidence remain. The formulation and implementation of school policies, appropriately supported and resourced, remains a priority for a large number of schools. There are key questions relating to content and progression which are properly the subject of on-going debate; put simply, which concepts and skills, when and how?

Issues of continuity, too, are important, both within and across phases. Record keeping and assessment and the effective communication of these findings from class to class and school to school are at the heart of such concerns. Bridging the primary/secondary interface represents perhaps the biggest challenge. Ruth Jarman in her paper *Primary Science, Secondary Science: Issues at the Interface* (1984) noted the following:

> Within a single school to encourage the physics teacher to talk to the biology teacher may well be a daunting task. To encourage the science department to communicate with the history department represents an even more daunting exercise. To attempt to cultivate effective liaison between the class teacher in a primary school and the science specialist in a secondary school ten miles down the road is an undertaking so monumental as to appear almost impossible.

Jarman goes on to argue that 'the returns from such an enterprise would need to be considerable to warrant the required major investment of time and energy'. She looks to outcomes in the shape of:

1 The prevention of duplication (the solidly pragmatic).
2 The promotion of continuity.

It is this latter which represents the real challenge. For we are here talking about not continuity in terms of content and process only but in the trickier terrain of teaching styles and strategies. Traditionally the break has been sharp. In extreme terms, from science centred round wide ranging and exciting investigations, often pupil generated at primary level, to laboratory rules and drawing and labelling the Bunsen burner approach in the most sterile of secondary practice. Bridging this gap is not easy — it challenges and threatens. These and related issues are usefully elaborated in *Better Science: Building Primary-Secondary Links* (Barber and Michell, 1987).

For the future then, science in the primary phase, even with National Curriculum interventions, looks set fair for continuing development in both quantity and quality terms. The plant is growing but will need sustained husbandry and steady nourishment if it is to thrive and spread. This is no time either to cut off the light or nutrients or to attempt radical pruning and reshaping.

Science in Secondary Schools

As already recorded, the broad parameters locating science within the framework of the secondary curriculum are clearly established. The right to 'core' status for the subject has been steadily advanced over the years and is now given formal blessing through the stated intentions of the National Curriculum. The Secretary of State sees all pupils, other than those with Statements of special educational needs which specify other-wise, studying science throughout their compulsory schooling and taking a GCSE examination in science or its equivalent. In time allocation terms he projects that between 10 per cent and 15 per cent of total curriculum time is available for science in years 1–3 and between 10 per cent and 20 per cent in years 4 and 5. It is scarcely surprising that this latest prescription follows closely that advocated in *Science 5–16: A Statement of Policy*. There are echoes, too, of the Policy Statement in recommending that in the fourth and fifth years the majority of students, and especially those capable of studying science beyond 16, should take a balanced science course occupying no more than 20 per cent of curricular time, leading to a double GCSE award. And, as they say, therein lies the rub.

The case for broad and balanced science has, as noted earlier, been assiduously advanced by the science education establishment and comment has been on the strength of this consensus. There remains a substantial residue of resistance, notably within the teaching heart of profession, to one central element, the so-called 3 into 2 principle. ASE, SSCR and the DES may be of a mind but there remains, despite persuasion and propaganda, a resistant core. Many teachers in the secondary sector see themselves not as teachers of science but as teachers of biology, chemistry or physics. They are familiar with, and in many cases wedded to, a system which allows young people and especially the most able to continue a study of the three disciplines treated strictly as separate subjects to examination level. In short, a 4th and 5th year curriculum in which, for some, science, in the shape of biology, chemistry and physics, occupied some 30 per cent, not 20 per cent, of curriculum time. The science for all argument may look expansionist to the outsider; to the physics, chemistry or biology specialist it looks like annexation. Arguments in defence of principle and territory can be thrown into the frame. 'Physics, chemistry and biology are discrete and different disciplines with their own distinctive ways of working'. 'Parents do not approve, higher education and employers expect qualifications in the separate subjects', and so on. All these have elements of truth and need riposte and continuing debate. The

Secretary of State recognizes the delicate path he treads but sticks to the Policy Statement last and opines that 'science courses covering selectively and in a co-ordinated way the essential elements of all three sciences are preferable at this stage to study of the sciences as separate subjects'. In short he defends the 3 into 2 principle but does openly promote the integrated science concept preferring the term 'co-ordinated', a nuance of terminology, perhaps lost on the uninitiated, but value laden for many practitioners of science education.

Aside then from the shifts in balance away from content and towards process, towards application and setting science in a variety of contexts, there remains significant work to be done on the basic 3 into 2 principle. There has been progress. A significant and growing number of schools offer balanced science defined in Policy Statement terms. The spread is to date uneven with a distinctly Southern bias. The most striking uptake has often been in those authorities where strong LEA support is evident. Energy, too, is being put, both at national and local level, into communicating the principles, intentions and rationale behind the balanced science proposals to parents, higher education, employers and other legitimate stakeholders in the wider community. The system is recognizing, albeit somewhat belatedly, the need to market its ideas. Policy Statement science at root seeks to offer a better deal to all young people and to promote a better balance within the curriculum as a whole, *even* for the most able. A worthy and altruistic ideal, but it needed, and will continue to need, active and continuing promotion if it is properly to be owned by teachers and the community rather than be only the subject of government edict.

Alongside the broad strategic issues noted above there inevitably runs a series of critical preoccupations, not unique but finding particular focus in the secondary science field. This next section considers a number of these.

Links With Other Subjects

The problematic nature of subject linking and cross-curricular working, particularly in secondary schools, is well recognized and documented despite its theoretical appeal and potential merit. We ought to be about giving students complementary and reinforcing educational experiences whatever the subject label. For science, traditionally and in National Curriculum terms, secondary teachers have been and are being encouraged to look for particular links, notably with mathematics, CDT and home economics. The general case is frequently made, too, for organizational frameworks which fully exploit the contribution which all other subjects can make to the teaching of science and vice versa.

Such exhortations, while finding universal acclaim, are more often pious hopes than practical realities. HMI in their secondary survey days found little evidence of science practices in other curriculum subjects. There have been changes but it is a minority of schools only which have sufficiently well evolved and well fledged whole curriculum policies which effectively promote cross-discipline working.

Accepting these general and fairly gloomy prognostications, there is a real and important Waterloo for science teachers which must be met — the links between science and technology. Technology, under the Government's proposals, is a foundation subject. It is arguably the major growth area in the secondary curriculum. It intersects and overlaps with science in both content and process terms. There are shared interests and aspirations but, equally, potential for territorial disputes. Problems of definition abound but in the words of an experienced practitioner 'like an elephant, you know it when you see it'. Black and Harrison, in their important paper *In Place of Confusion: Technology and Science in the School Curriculum* (1985) explore many of the issues central to the debate. A resolution of the dilemmas and difficulties in practical terms at school level seems an urgent priority for the late eighties and the nineties. Solutions may well challenge conventional organization and timetable frameworks. In the meantime, and in part under the impetus of TVEI and its extension programme, continuing debate and development seem inevitable. Black and Harrison's model for the curriculum is included as Figure 2. It may well provide a useful stimulus to those charged with the planning and delivery of tomorrow's curriculum.

The Work of the Assessment of Performance Unit (APU)

The establishment of the APU some twelve years ago was initially seen as something of a threat by the teaching community. It has turned out to be more challenge than threat and not perhaps in a manner anticipated by earlier antagonists. It has not resulted in assessment-led or teaching-to-the-test developments but it has challenged the efficacy of much that has been regarded as good or certainly conventional practice.

The APU, for the purposes of its testing, defined the categories of science performance as:

1. Use of graphical and symbolic representation
   — reading information from graphs, tables and charts
   — representing information as graphs, tables and charts

2. Use of apparatus and measuring instruments
   — using measuring instruments
   — estimating physical quantities

Figure 2: A model for the curriculum

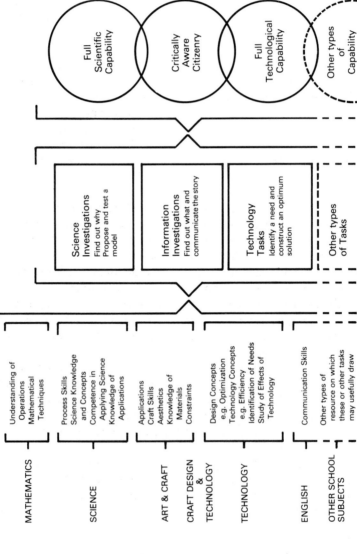

Source: Harrison and Black (1985) 'In Place of Confusion: Technology and Science in The School Curriculum', Nuffield-Chelsea Curriculum Trust and the National Centre for School Technology, Trent Polytechnic.

		— following instructions for practical work
3.	Observation	— making and interpreting observations
4.	Interpretation and application	— I interpreting presented information
		— II applying: Biology concepts Physics concepts Chemistry concepts
5.	Planning of investigations	— planning parts of investigations
		— planning entire investigations
6.	Performance of investigations	— performing entire investigations

This framework, derived in part from an HMI checklist 'defining' school science, and the tests developed within it have provided a powerful insight into the development of young people's skills and their acquisition of scientific concepts. It has provided a rich bank of data for educational researchers and important findings for individual teachers. There is evidence that conventional teaching styles do not deliver for many young people the security of concept and skill acquisition we might predict and to which we might aspire. Personal 'frameworks' and 'views of how the world works' do remain entrenched despite repeated teacher assertions to the contrary and so on.

One important outcome of this evidence has been a timely focus on the issue not just of what, but how, students learn science. The Children's Learning in Science Project (CLISP) represents a tangible and influential development. This project, using APU findings as an analytical base, looks to devise and test alternative approaches to the teaching and learning of science.

Its findings and those of the APU are likely to remain a powerful influence on the day-to-day practice of science education. Penetration of these ideas may yet be limited but there are encouraging signs of assimilation and acceptance.

Science for Students with Special Educational Needs

The provision of an appropriate education for students for whom the conventional diet is not appropriate has long exercised teachers of all subjects. The issue has been given particular sharpness and focus by the publication of the Warnock Report in 1978 which concluded that 'up to one child in five is likely to need special educational provision in the course of his school career'. Warnock went on to point out that 'one in five' did not mean that all such children would be 'handicapped in the traditional sense of the term'. Nonetheless, the Warnock Report has served to sharpen sensibilities and, by its promotion of the concept of integration of the handicapped, increased the challenge — a challenge which is particularly acute for a practically based subject like science.

In their Secondary Survey (*Aspects of Secondary Education in England: A Survey by HM Inspectors of Schools*, HMI, 1979a), HMI record that: 'It was the work of the less able, whatever the type of school, which gave the greatest cause for concern' — a finding largely mirrored in later surveys. The gradual but increasing introduction of other youngsters with different learning disabilities and handicaps is likely only to increase the challenge. But there are hopeful signs. Again in 1979 HMI, again dealing with science for the less able, noted that where teacher expectations were high young people 'showed a good level of practical laboratory skills, the ability to work independently and willingness to speculate when new situations were presented to them'.

In short, many essential prerequisites of effective learning were not closed to them. There are, too, other propitious omens. A growing number of special schools are accepting science as a necessary and legitimate part of their clients' learning entitlement. Expertise is growing and has the potential to spread to the conventional secondary school. Warnock's emphasis on the principle of identifying and providing for individual educational needs can be built upon and science has an important contribution to make. To date, mainline approaches have focused on shifts in content and its organization. The real challenge will be to adjust and adapt the minimum entitlement in science terms to the requirements of the individual. Even within National Curriculum terms the Secretary of State seems to accept the primacy of this principle.

The Science Curriculum and Gender

In *Better Science: For Both Girls and Boys* (1987), Christine Ditchfield asks the question, 'Do school subjects have gender labels?' The diagram at Figure 3, reproduced both here and in her text, demonstrates clearly that they do.

The preference of girls for biologically based subjects rather than the physical sciences has been well recognized for some time. It is well documented and researched. HMI have reported and there have been real efforts to tease out underlying causes for the evident bias in student choices. In simplistic terms, the matter will be resolved by the blanket

Figure 3: Sex Variations in O Level and CSE Entries, 1984
Source: Ditchfield, C. (1987) *Better Science: For Both Girls and Boys*, Heinemann Educational Books/ASE.

Figure 3: Sex Variations in O Level and CSE entries, 1984

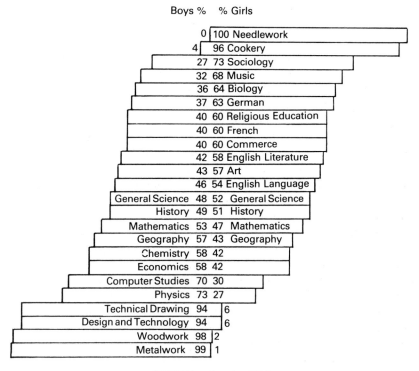

Boys %   % Girls

Boys		Girls
0	100	Needlework
4	96	Cookery
27	73	Sociology
32	68	Music
36	64	Biology
37	63	German
40	60	Religious Education
40	60	French
40	60	Commerce
42	58	English Literature
43	57	Art
46	54	English Language
General Science 48	52	General Science
History 49	51	History
Mathematics 53	47	Mathematics
Geography 57	43	Geography
Chemistry 58	42	
Economics 58	42	
Computer Studies 70	30	
Physics 73	27	
Technical Drawing 94	6	
Design and Technology 94	6	
Woodwork 98	2	
Metalwork 99	1	

GCE 'O' level entries 1984

Source: Ditchfield, C (1987) 'Better Science: For Both Girls and Boys', Heinemann Educational Books/ASE.

imposition of 'science for all'. If choice does not exist then, by definition, all girls will study elements of physical science and all boys the essentials of biology. Such an approach will not, however, solve the problem. The issues are complex — *Better Science: For Both Girls and Boys*, summarizes this complexity.

Simple prescription may ensure compliance during the period of compulsion. It will not generate conviction and involvement; or importantly continuity of science studies or science interest. Figure 4 does, however, point to clear foci for development and attack. Schools' influence on parental and societal attitudes may be marginal — but there can be some influence. The three other influences, not of course independent variables, are open to change. Research does tell us about teacher and

Figure 4.

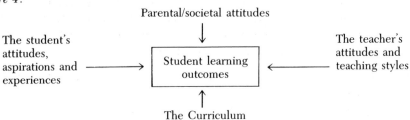

Parental/societal attitudes

The student's attitudes, aspirations and experiences ⟶ Student learning outcomes ⟵ The teacher's attitudes and teaching styles

The Curriculum

student attitudes — even simple awareness of these can be a force for change. The curriculum, at least even in today's climate, in delivery terms is within our control. 'Girl or boy friendly science' may be an uncomfortable concept to many strict scientists schooled in the value free, even person free, model of science. But this is not reality. Science, like any other area of human endeavour, does have values, it does reflect the tone and tenor of the society in which it grows. It is a political and human activity. Science in today's world is seen as a predominantly masculine activity, embracing masculine values and ways of looking at the world. It apparently touches on the humanitarian and the human condition mainly through its biological arm and as such finds some resonance with female perceptions. Compound this view of science with teacher attitudes, albeit unconscious and unintended, which reinforce this perspective and it is scarcely surprising that we have a gender biased uptake of science studies. Political and economic imperatives alluded to earlier, suggest that efforts to redress this bias are morally and pragmatically worth the effort. The issue remains awaiting further treatment. The good news is schools can make a difference. Working at raising awareness and changing practice is worth the effort. Simple prescription, science for all, will not be enough.

Overview

This chapter began by acknowledging the difficulty of writing with security and certainty during a period of intense and rapid change. But will science education match the change? Dr. Richard West, Staff Inspector for Science for ILEA, and one-time Director of the Secondary Science Curriculm Review, recorded in his Presidential Address to the London Region of the Association for Science Education, the following observations:

> I have seen science education adopt innovation after innovation and slowly and carefully adapt them so as to cause no more than a minor ripple in the tranquil sea of accepted good practice.

and again

I have seen major innovations crumble under the weight of existing practice or expectation (the main expectation being that it
won't work or can't work unless ... we have more teachers, more
technicians, more laboratories, more money).

Even allowing for such inertia there are powerful forces which will influence and shape the science curriculum for years to come and for all
young people. In primary schools there are positive signs of growth and
development. Ideas and ways of working which do resonate with the best
of primary practice as we know and understand it look set to expand. At
secondary level balanced science for all is accepted in principle. Translat-
ing the 'cracker motto' into reality remains the issue. The National Curriculum, TVEI and its extension, will provide additional impetus and push.
Initiatives such as the Secondary Science Curriculum Review, the Children's Learning in Science Project and the work of the APU provide
valuable theoretical and practical underpinning. Winning the hearts and
minds of the teaching profession remains a central and rewarding challenge. Much has been achieved through enlightened INSET and careful
and collaborative working between local authorities and their teaching
forces. The Schools Curriculum Development Council in a recent publication on recording achievement noted the following shifts in teaching
methods and learning styles.

The movement from:	to:
— the teacher as information-giver	— the teacher as facilitator of learning
— teacher-controlled learning	— a teacher-learner partnership
— non-participatory learning	— active, experiential learning
— syllabus and course-bound learning	— the negotiated curriculum
— teacher-centred learning	— student-centred learning
— content-bound learning	— skills, concepts, attitudes and content
— time, age and group constraints	— individualized learning
— subject specific	— cross-curricular integration
— teacher-generated assessment	— joint student/staff participation in assessment.

All these shifts sit easily within the broad principles of science for all. The
National Curriculum, whatever its final shape and definition, must build
upon such developments as already exist, utilizing favourable winds and a
promising climate. Hard nosed and reactionary prescription is not the
answer. The extent to which bench marks and age related testing offers
just such an imposition remains to be seen. The Assessment of Performance Unit turned threat into professional challenge. It may be that the
outcomes of the deliberations of the Science Working Group can do the

John Nellist

same. Ingle and Jennings in their text *Science Education in Schools: Which Way Now?* (1981) note that: 'The pamphlet, *Science for All*, published as long ago as 1916, put the case for science education that included biology as well as the physical sciences... In 1918 the committee chaired by J.J. Thomson claimed that the traditional science course of the time was too narrow, out of touch with the many applications of science and so failed to satisfy the natural curiosity of pupils. It recommended that more attention be paid to those aspects of science that bear directly on the objects and experiences of everyday life.'

Some fifty years later, another committee, this time chaired by J.J. Thompson, will seek to advise the Secretary of State on the contribution of science to the overall school curriculum, about the knowledge, skills, understanding and aptitudes which pupils of different abilities should be expected to have attained at 7, 11, 14 and 16, and on a programme of study through 5–16 consistent with these attainment targets.

The task is formidable and there is much to play for.

References

ASSOCIATION FOR SCIENCE EDUCATION (1981) *Education Through Science*, ASE, Hatfield.
ASSOCIATION FOR SCIENCE EDUCATION (1986) *Science and Technology in Society (SATIS)*, ASE, Hatfield.
BARBER, B. and MICHELL, M. (1987) *Better Science: Building Primary/Secondary Links*, Heinemann Educational Books/Association for Science Education.
BLACK, P. and HARRISON, G. (1985) *In Place of Confusion*, Nuffield-Chelsea Trust and the National Centre for School Technology, Trent Polytechnic.
DEPARTMENT OF EDUCATION AND SCIENCE (1985) *Science Education 5–16 A Statement of Policy*, London, HMSO.
DEPARTMENT OF EDUCATION AND SCIENCE (1982) *Science in Primary Schools*, London, HMSO.
DITCHFIELD, C. (1987) *Better Science: For Both Girls and Boys*, Heinemann Educational Books/Association for Science Education.
HER MAJESTY'S INSPECTORATE (1979a) *Aspects of Secondary Education in England*, HMSO.
HER MAJESTY'S INSPECTORATE (1979b) *Primary Education in England*, HMSO.
INGLES, R. and JENNINGS A. (1981) *Science Education in Schools: Which Way Now?* Heinemann Educational Books.
JARMAN, R. (1984) *Primary Science, Secondary Science: Issues at the Interface*, SSCR, London.
NELLIST, J. and NICHOL, B. (Eds) (1986) *ASE Science Teachers' Handbook*, Hutchinson/ASE London.
SECONDARY SCIENCE CURRICULUM REVIEW (1983) *Science Education 11–16; Proposals for Action and Consultation*, SSCR, London.
SECONDARY SCIENCE CURRICULUM REVIEW (1984) *Towards a Specification of Minimum Entitlement: Brenda and Friends*, SSCR, London.
WATTS, M. and MICHELL, M. (1987) *Better Science: Choosing Content*, Heinemann Education Books/Association for Science Education.

Notes on Contributors

Paul Armitage was formerly Lecturer in British History and Social Studies at the University of Paris III and then Senior Lecturer in History at Bulmershe College of H.E., Reading. Since January 1985, he has been Principal Professional Officer for history and the social sciences at the Secondary Examinations Council, London. His current interests include all matters related to the history and social science school curriculum including associated assessment issues.

Patrick Bailey is a Cambridge geographer. He taught in a variety of schools and colleges before taking up his present post as Senior Lecturer in Education and Geography Tutor in the University of Leicester School of Education. His numerous publications include *Teaching Geography* (1974) and books and papers in the three fields in which he has teaching and research interests, geography, geographical education and education management. Since 1953 he has been a Life Member of the Geographical Association. He was founder-editor of its journal for practising teachers, *Teaching Geography*, for ten years before becoming the Association's President for 1985–86. He is now one of the Association's Trustees.

Marilynne J.R. Davies' experience has included working with children at the Primary, Secondary and Tertiary levels, in inner city, urban and rural areas. Her current appointment as Senior Lecturer in Music at the College of Ripon and York St. John involves working with undergraduates on BA and BEd degree courses and with serving teachers on INSET courses. She still maintains her links with primary school children through teaching, conducting workshops, and co-ordinating large scale productions involving students and children.

Anthony Dyson is a freelance art and education consultant and a visiting tutor at the Institute of Education, University of London, where until August 1987 he was full-time Senior Lecturer in the Department of Art and Design. He has recently retired from the Chairmanship of the National Society for Education in the Arts.

He graduated as a specialist teacher of art at the University of Leeds and was trained as an art historian at the Courtauld Institute, University of London, where he gained the PhD for research into the nineteenth century engraving trade.

The history of engraving and the teaching of art history in school have been the main subjects of his many publications.

Elizabeth Foster taught history and humanities for several years in a comprehensive school and tutored adults in history through WEA and OU. She has lectured in education for eight years at the University of Leeds where she is also joint curator of the Museum of the History of Education. Research interests are in municipal and urban history and in the teaching and learning of history in school. Publications include materials for history teaching.

Margaret Jepson has taught in comprehensive schools for fifteen years and is presently Senior Lecturer in Home Economics Education at Liverpool Polytechnic. She is a past President of the National Association of Teachers of Home Economics. Her interests are in assessment, particularly examinations and profiling, curriculum development and in-service training. She is a member of the Secondary Examinations Council 16+ Home Economics Committee considering GCSE syllabi and the 18+ Home Economics Committee considering A/S and 'A' levels. She is a member of the NEA Home Economics Committee and the CGLI Home Economics Committee. She is an author of two textbooks for GCSE Home Economics.

Peter J. Mitchell taught in the East End of London before moving to the City of Portsmouth College of Education, where he became Head of the Department of Religious and Ethical Studies. He is now a University Lecturer at Cambridge University Department of Education, where he has special responsibilities for the teaching of Religious Studies. He also runs courses at various levels on moral education, values in education and moral philosophy and education.

John Nellist is a chemistry graduate from Birmingham University and has taught in grammar and comprehensive schools in Worcestershire and Carlisle. Following a five year period as Science Adviser in Sunderland, he was employed as a General Inspector/Adviser with Cumbria LEA. He has worked with a number of curriculum development projects in science education and was Chairman of the Association for Science Education in 1986. He is currently a member of the National Curriculum Science Working Group.

Brian Page taught in secondary school and is now director of the Language Laboratory, University of Leeds and associate lecturer in the School of Education and the Department of Phonetics/Linguistics. He has been involved in graded objectives schemes since they began and in the creation of new syllabuses and examinations for JMB and subsequently for NEA. He currently holds the chair of the National Coordinating Committee for Graded Objectives in Modern Language Learning and is president of the Joint Council of Language Associations. He is the author of numerous articles and several books.

Jim Parry is a former teacher in schools, colleges and a polytechnic department of education. He is now Lecturer in Philosophy in the Physical Education Department of the University of Leeds and is Course Tutor for the MA in Physical Education. He is currently working on Gramsci's political philosophy and the ideological build-up to the 1988 Olympics.

John Penfold lectures at Brunel University. He is the author of *CDT, Past, Present and Future*, published by Trentham Books.

Robert Protherough is Senior Lecturer in Education, responsible for English in the School of Education at Hull University. He graduated at Oxford University, where he began studies leading to an MLitt research degree. After sixteen years of teaching, the last nine as head of department, he worked in a College of Education before coming to Hull in 1973. He has worked on advanced courses for teachers in Kenya, Canada, Gibraltar and the Caribbean. His PhD was concerned with the ways in which teachers have been presented in English Literature. Dr. Protherough's other main research interests are concerned with aspects of the teaching and learning of English. He is the author of three major books, the co-author of several others, has contributed many articles to journals, chiefly in the field of English curriculum, and was for many years the editor of a major international journal concerned with the teaching of English.

Michael Rayner is Lecturer in Education in the School of Education at Leeds University. After secondary teaching in Huddersfield, he joined the department at Leeds where he teaches philosophy of education and English.

Geoffrey Wain is a senior lecturer in mathematical education in the University of Leeds, School of Education. He was a co-director of the Mathematics Teacher Education Project and is currently directing a project on the use of home-owned microcomputers as a support for mathematics teaching. He was formerly chairman of the Association of University Mathematics Education Teachers and Secretary of the Joint Mathematical Council of the United Kingdom.

Patrick Wiegand taught in primary and secondary schools before taking up his present appointment as lecturer in the School of Education, University of Leeds. His main interests are in the field of Geographical Education at both primary and secondary level. He is especially interested in young children's perceptions of distant people and places. He has written a number of text books for primary and secondary schools and edited several atlases. He is the publications officer of the Geographical Association and has written about various aspects of the teaching and learning of Geography.

Index